Ethics for
Addiction
Professionals

ETHICS FOR ADDICTION PROFESSIONALS
From Principle to Practice

Jennifer D. Berton

WILEY

Library of Congress Cataloging-in-Publication Data:

Berton, Jennifer D.
  Ethics for addiction professionals / Jennifer D. Berton.
    1 online resource.
  Includes bibliographical references and index.
  Description based on print version record and CIP data provided by publisher; resource not viewed.
    ISBN 978-0-470-90719-1 (pbk) – ISBN 978-1-118-41830-7 (ebk) – ISBN 978-1-118-41540-5 (ebk) 1. Alcoholism counselors–Professional ethics–United States. 2. Drug abuse counselors–Professional ethics–United States. I. Title.
  HV5279
  174'.936229186–dc23

                                                                                        2013027939

Printed in the United States of America

SKY10049045_060923

To Peter for providing love, balance, and rarebit.

CONTENTS

The major problem with ethics—hold on, let me climb up on my soapbox—okay, listen, the major problem is that it is not taught (Taleff, 2010). I realize that sounds wrong when you consider how many ethics trainings each clinician will attend throughout his or her career. Ethics trainings are attended more than trainings on any other topic because it is the only specific topic that must be included in the recredentialing process every 2 years, and it has been suggested this requirement should increase (Gallagher, 2010). This means that an individual clinician who has been working in the field for 25 years will attend a minimum of 42 hours of ethics trainings during that time. Despite the significant requirement, ethics education has used more of the "water-cooler technique" of teaching, discussing ethical principles through vignettes *after* they have occurred, as a group of workers meet at the water cooler to discuss important agency issues and gossip. The heavy use of vignettes is only problematic when it is the only resource used; vignettes are quite appropriate and helpful when they are used to illustrate a fact, theory, or principle. But in most ethics education, vignettes are used to discuss appropriate clinical action; the principle is implied with the assumption that the clinician has already mastered it. Addiction professionals are supposed to innately understand the ethical decision (Taleff, 2010). Ethics, it seems, is the one area of clinical practice a new clinician is expected to know *before* becoming a credentialed clinician.

Think about that. Many ethical principles are assumed obvious, as if to be human means you have a general sense of right and wrong behavior. The problem with this thinking is that it isn't true. If you ask any clinician if having sex with a client is ethical, I can't imagine any clinician showing support, yet clinicians have sex with clients every year, and it is among the most violated ethical principle in the helping professions, and the most common complaint against addiction counselors (St. Germaine, 1996). And just as cheating is considered a symptom of a deeper problem in a marriage, having sex with a client is an indication of a deeper problem that started long before the sex: a blurring of boundaries and power. Now if I asked every one of those clinicians who are appalled at the idea of having sex with a client to name a time in their career when they blurred some boundary with a client, every one of those clinicians (if honest) would likely have some story to tell. Thus, even if someone has a good level of personal morals, this does not necessarily indicate that he or she will be an ethical clinician, and so it is not enough to expect that someone interested in becoming a clinician will have a basic sense of ethical behavior. Ethics must be *taught*.

Because many professionals do not have a college degree (Whitter et al., 2006), or obtained a degree in an unrelated field, a large part of the professional population does not get a college education related to ethics and therefore must rely on individual professional trainings to teach basic ethical principles and standards (Gallagher, 2010). If ethical trainings do not teach ethical principles and demonstrate how to build an ethical practice, these clinicians may be out in the workforce, giving direct practice to clients, without having learned the basic ethical tools required of addiction professionals. When we hear of ethical missteps, we may sympathize with the affected clients and blame the clinicians involved, but the clinicians may not have received the education and the support they need to prevent these errors.

Where you are in your career, reader, will not affect the usefulness of the fun we are about to have. If you are a student just entering the profession, let me just say.... *Welcome*! You are the future promise of our work, thus we are all breathing a collective professional sigh of relief that you have made the choice to study our ways. No matter how great existing clinicians are now, the beauty of what we do will fade away if not for you. You will find loads of useful information and resources in this book that will help you understand and develop all of the tools necessary to build the most ethical practice. If you are actively taking an ethics class right now that uses this book, look up right now and beam a smile at your teacher as a thank you for taking your education seriously—Ha, tricked you! You shouldn't be reading this book in class, you should be rapt with attention to whatever great nuggets of knowledge are zooming your way from your teacher. Close this book and listen for now, but come back here after class.

If you are a seasoned professional, you may be thinking, "Oh great, *another* book about ethics. Ethics is *so* exciting, I can't *wait* to dig in" (can you feel the sarcasm?). Well unroll your eyes for a second, and let's think about why that sentiment likely washed over many of you. Ethics historically has been seen as a dry, boring subject. There are two main reasons why it is so perceived. First, many trainings and speakers on the topic have been tedious and unvaried. This is most unfortunate because the topic of ethics contains some of the most emotional material in our clinical practice. It is meant to be living, breathing, dynamic, and engaging. Attendees leaving a training should be in healthy turmoil, not bored into slumber. Trainings need not regurgitate the code of ethics but bring it to life in clinical example (Gallagher, 2010), yet the principles of the code should be included in trainings. In the past, the variety of available ethics trainings typically didn't meet the need for ongoing continuing education requirements, resulting in the majority of clinicians attending the same ethics trainings year after year. This only contributes to the feeling of tediousness, and leads to the second reason ethics trainings are ill-perceived: that clinicians feel the training is unnecessary.

Many clinicians feel they have learned the ethical tools they need and are resentful of the ongoing requirement for additional ethics training. I can't tell you how many times I've heard clinicians sigh with annoyance that they have to go to ethics trainings every 2 years, especially the well-seasoned clinician. "Ugh," they whine, "I've been a clinician forever. I've pretty much seen it all. I would hope by now I know how to act ethically." Perhaps you have had similar thoughts at some point in your career. But if this statement were true, then statistically one would see a decrease in ethical violations by career length, yet my experience with investigating ethical violations showed no indication that ethical violations are more likely to occur in the beginning of one's career. In fact, the research shows those clinicians with less formal education were found to be more sensitive to ethical dilemmas (Gallagher, 2010). Thus, ethics should be taught.

Seasoned clinicians may be less sensitive to ethical dilemmas because they become complacent in their ways. Consider driving a car: New drivers do make errors, but they are also more likely to drive "by the book," since they just learned the book. Seasoned drivers make all sorts of mistakes according to driver's education instruction. (How many of you really put your hands on the wheel at the 10 o'clock and 2 o'clock position all the time?) You don't worry, because you feel your experience makes you a safe driver even if you aren't driving perfectly. Similarly, seasoned clinicians may commit small violations believing them to be innocuous and may feel satisfied that generally they are skilled professionals who do a heap of good in the lives of the clients they serve.

Yet small violations can easily turn into bigger violations, often with a subtle progression that can remain unnoticed by the clinician until it is too late. We try to show our clients that a relapse doesn't just happen; it is the result of a progression of smaller transgressions and rule bending until the relapse has fertile ground. Similarly, if a clinician commits a serious violation, one can look back into the smaller ethical missteps that paved the way for the bigger one. Concurrently, deciding whether a violation is small and harmless is a subjective process. Certainly what may seem innocent to one will appear damaging to another.

A classic example of this would be the use of professional nepotism. If Johnny needs aftercare placement in a sober house, and clinician Mary says, "No problem, Johnny, I know the house director. Let me give him a call and see if I can get you in faster," has she acted ethically? She worked hard to serve her client, using her networking skills to get his needs met. But what of the other equally well-deserving clients who had positions on the waiting list? Who was bumped out of a spot in the house, not because Johnny was in a greater need, but because his counselor happened to know the house director? Mary's actions may have seemed quite harmless to Mary, but would likely appear obnoxious and unprofessional to the counselors who have clients on that waiting list, and unfair to those clients forced to step aside.

The other snag with these small innocuous-seeming violations is they require a rather egocentric perspective in order to appear acceptable. Certainly if one is looking at the individual case, many ethically slippery scenarios would seem like no big deal. But zoom out your perspective and the game changes. What if instead of this one ethical decision with the client in front of you, we are looking at all of your ethical decisions over time in one lump. How will your one decision look in the context of all your decisions? Let's zoom further. Now you are looking through the lens of the profession and you can see that all the decisions clinicians make reflect back on the profession.

If you are only seeing the client in front of you, your perspective is too narrow. And if you are thinking this way, it is likely that other clinicians are as well. And if all the clinicians are walking around making small transgressions then what happens to our profession? But what of the agency, the state, and the profession itself? What may seem like a great action for an individual client can in turn hurt the profession as a whole.

You can see how complex ethical discussions become, and we haven't even scratched the surface! Don't tear your hair out just yet, this is only the beginning ... lots more opportunities for hair pulling in later chapters. For now, the three grounding ideas to take with you are: (1) Wherever you are on your career path, whether a student just starting out fresh, a seasoned practitioner who has been in the field for awhile, or at any point in between, this book was written for you. If you are in other professions we hope you find this book helpful both in your own ethical practice, regardless of discipline, and in your understanding of our profession; (2) No matter how new or seasoned a clinician you are, I guarantee that you violate ethical principles from time to time (because we all do), and here is a reason you need continuous ethical trainings; (3) Ethical principles cannot be assumed, they can and *must* be taught (and often retaught) to every clinician in our profession. If you can entertain these ideas, even skeptically, then read on!

What's This Book About?

Despite the importance of keeping ethics for addiction professionals fresh and bountiful, there is a surprising scarcity of published works devoted specifically to addiction professionals (Geppert & Roberts, 2008; Taleff, 2010). We have been increasing addiction research in recent years, but notably not in the area of ethical standards (Gallagher, 2010). We borrow from great published works on ethics from other helping professions: social work, psychology, marriage and family counseling, even psychiatry (Bass et al., 1996; Corey, Corey,

& Callanan, 2007; Pope & Vasquez, 2010). Yet it has been acknowledged that the addiction field is unique, with its own set of complex ethical issues (Geppert & Roberts, 2008; Taleff, 2010). A consistent, rigorous examination of our own professional ethics is vital to assuring we are giving the best care as a profession (Gallagher, 2010). Why is this not reflected in available material?

There are a few notable offerings for addiction professionals looking for material on ethics. Bissell and Royce (1987) cracked the field open with the first *Ethics for Addiction Professionals*. Published works on addiction ethics then went surprisingly dormant until the past decade. Geppert and Roberts (2008) published *The Book of Ethics: Expert Guidance for Professionals Who Treat Addiction*, a compelling and diverse exploration into the intersection between ethics and a variety of specific clinical settings in the addiction profession. Taleff (2010) published *Advanced Ethics for Addiction Professionals*, which teaches readers how to make sound ethical decisions by merging ethics with critical thinking skills.

Those of you familiar with the Bissell and Royce (1987) book may be scratching your heads wondering why this book has adopted the same title. As discussed, there are few books on ethics for addiction professionals specifically. Those that exist are specialized (Geppert & Roberts, 2008; Taleff, 2010), and since the Bissell and Royce book was published in 1987, those books that give a total overview of ethics are outside of our profession (Corey et al.; Pope & Vasquez, 2010; Reamer, 2001, 2006a, 2006b, 2012). As we work toward strengthening our professional identity, one significant element is to solidify our own ethical practice within this profession. Thus it seemed time to introduce an updated *Ethics for Addiction Professionals*. Over time, as the profession grows and our ethics subsequently adapt, new books, or book editions, will be required to reflect the growth. We should not simply rest on what has been, but instead continue to seek out new material that makes us stronger. As mentioned, ethics is an ever changing field, and our profession must adopt these changes if we are to have a

solid future as a vibrant and vital contribution to the helping professions (Powell & Brodsky, 2004).

Although there are several books and articles specific to addiction ethics, the vast majority of published material is within other helping professions. This book aims to contribute to the field of addiction-specific ethics. Furthermore, the material that has been published often has loads of information but without a clear and concise way of organizing and understanding the information. In fact, some literature includes a table of contents that is so jam-packed with complex sections filled with detailed items it can be overwhelming and confusing to read. This book is organized in a simple way so that readers are able to remember it, and tick off the important categories on one hand.

Much of the published material on ethics does not adequately discuss the Code of Ethics on which our profession is based. Does this surprise you? It should! Many books and articles fail to examine the principles of the code or provide a link between the principles and the theory or topic of discussion. Yet the principles are supposed to be the foundation of our practice, the guidelines that dictate our professional conduct. As such, it should be familiar to all of us, a trusty document that sets us on the right path and aids us in healthy decision making. This book is designed to both highlight the ethical principles in the code, and link them to ethical keys and common pitfalls.

It has been suggested that addiction professionals can sway easily in a debate, without putting care into their decisions, and can make decisions based on a refusal to judge others and a need to be open-minded and inclusive (Taleff, 2010). Teaching how to think critically is a vital part of developing your ethical practice, however there have to be standards set in place so that even if people are thinking logically they have a guide in how to act responsibly. If ethical situations were black and white, teaching how to think would be sufficient in producing the best ethical actions. However, because there are so many gray areas in addiction ethics, and the issues are so complex, addiction professionals can use some concrete teaching about professional parameters of conduct, in addition to thinking critically.

Many books on ethics are designated as either introductory material for the newcomer in our field, or advanced material for the well seasoned. The problem here is that ethical principles don't employ a hierarchical level system. The keys to an ethical practice and the traps we can fall into are not structured within a basic to advanced range. The principles in our Code of Ethics are not categorized with length of time in the profession, nor are they steps that build on each other. Therefore, what you are offered in ethical training material should be applicable wherever you are in your occupational journey. This book is aimed at you, reader, and designed to meet you wherever you are right now. If you are new to the field of addiction treatment, welcome! This book will guide you in developing your ethical practice. If you are a well-seasoned clinician, welcome! This book will guide you to revamp your ethical practice, examine your current practice for ethical snags, and hopefully refresh your ethical thinking so you come out all new and squeaky-clean. If you are in between a newbie and a sage one, this book will guide you in examining, building, and rebuilding aspects of your ethical practice with the goal of helping you become the strongest clinician possible, ethically speaking.

Like Taleff (2010) and Mottley (2012), this book is based on ethics trainings presented in the field. But perhaps this book is most like another ethics book written for the general helping professions, *Issues and Ethics in the Helping Professions* (Corey et al., 2007), which has exams, encourages self-assessment as the first step to building an ethical practice, and discusses the importance of knowing and using your Codes of Ethics. It is a helpful book that should be in the literary repertoire of all addiction professionals, even though they do not include the addiction profession as one of the helping professions in their book.

Specifically, it is our hope that when you set down this book you will have achieved six objectives:

1. You will believe that ethics are alive, interesting, fun, and necessary.
2. You will see that ethics can be taught, regardless of where you are in your practice.
3. You will learn the four best keys to building an ethical practice and how to apply them.
4. You will be able to highlight common pitfalls and will learn how to address them.
5. You will be able to identify the code of ethics and how to apply it to your daily work.
6. You will embrace the profession as an entity into which we must pour our attention and care.

I realize that some of you may be skeptical at this point, doubting whether you have anything new to learn, questioning the claim that we all make ethical errors, or believing that ethics are nuggets of knowledge we innately or intuitively know, and thus questioning the necessity of this book. I get it, I'm not offended by your reaction, and I know I have my work cut out for me, but if you give this book a chance you may be surprised. In fact, I have a sneaking suspicion you may even *enjoy* yourself. Well, come along and see for yourself. Let's begin.

I would like to thank:

Marquita Flemming, Sherry Wasserman, Thomas Caruso, and the rest of the Wiley team, who encouraged me to roam.

David Powell, for all the helpful guidance and support.

Fred Reamer, who ignited the spark and set the bar.

Mac Runyan, for teaching me to wonder and for believing in me before I did.

Peter Manoleas, who taught me the necessary flexibility to have one foot in two different professions without splitting my pants ... or my values.

Bart Grossman, who drilled Flexner into my soul and introduced me to the concept of Ethics and the great F.R.

Kathy Emery, who long ago awakened my critical eye and taught me to define my terms.

Rhonda, Bob T., Warren, Joe, Mark, Aaron, Ruffner, Todd, Peter, Tom, and Laura for meeting me on the path.

Grace, Darrell, Jeanne, Sam, Ahndrea, Tom, Sara, David, and Sue for guiding me in the right direction and showing interest.

All my colleagues, past, present and future, for the teaching, the learning, the growing.

All my clients, past, present, and future, who enrich me in more ways than I can count, and who inspire me with their drive and purpose.

I would especially like to thank my family and friends for cheering me on (you must be exhausted and hoarse), especially to B&S for picking up every last piece of my life without which I would have slipped away long ago. And Sophie and Lily, for reminding me that nothing in life is quite as important or fulfilling as a good belly laugh and a heapin' bowl of mac 'n'; cheese. I love you more than the moon, more than the stars, more than....

Ethics for
Addiction
Professionals

Introduction

1 Chapter

Before we begin our examination of addiction ethics, let's take a moment to define a few terms, a common burden in ethical literature (Geppert & Roberts, 2008; Taleff, 2010). How can we define ethics? Generally, ethics is defined as a set of principles that guide our actions (Barsky, 2010; Corey, Corey, & Callanan, 2007; Geppert & Roberts, 2008; Pope & Vasquez, 2007; Reamer, 2006b; Taleff, 2010).

In a deeper description, Taleff (2010) gives seven criteria for defining ethics: (1) Ethics require other people; (2) Intent makes a difference; (3) Ethics aim to resolve dilemmas; (4) Thinking is necessary for ethics and morality; (5) Ethics ask you to be impartial; (6) Ethics require us to care about the suffering of others; and (7) Ethics judge human behavior (Taleff, 2010). Scott (2000) further defines six ethical situations that are unique to addiction counseling: (1) the lack of communication and continuity between research and clinical practice; (2) the lack of agreement over the necessary professional credentials; (3) the questionable propensity of group work in the addictions field; (4) special issues of confidentiality and privileged communication; (5) boundaries of professional practice in

making treatment decisions; and (6) unusual circumstances of informed consent. We will discuss all of these unique situations throughout the book.

Throughout this book, we will define ethics using the four pillars of ethics borrowed from the medical ethics field (Miller, 2008), constructs that are well utilized in the ethical literature (Castillo & Waldorf, 2008; Corey et al., 2007; Miller, 2008; Taleff, 2010; Venner & Bogenshutz, 2008). As in the book Geppert and Roberts (2008) edited, these pillars will be used throughout each section as a thread that forms the basis of our ethical practice. The four pillars are beneficence, autonomy, nonmaleficence, and justice. Other authors have included additional pillars in their work, such as compassion, truth telling (Castillo & Waldorf, 2008; Geppert & Roberts, 2008; Taleff, 2010), volunteerism (Castillo & Waldorf, 2008, p. 106), privacy, rights, confidentiality (Taleff, 2010), respect for persons (Taleff, 2010; Venner & Bogenshutz, 2008), fidelity, and veracity (National Association for Addiction Professionals [NAADAC], 2011). This book will stick with the four pillars that are consistent in the literature, as the other principles are in some literature but not all, and are concepts that are discussed elsewhere throughout the book.

1

Beneficence refers to actions intended to benefit others: kindness, charity, and goodness. Autonomy is self-directed freedom and independence. Nonmaleficence is the well-known adage: "Do no harm." Justice in this context is defined as the equal and fair treatment across groups or members of the same group. Treatment must uphold existing laws and be fairly given. The four pillars can be interrelated, with each leading into another, as you shall see in the examples we explore. Most of the time, a clinician is tasked with balancing between beneficence and nonmaleficence, which can often be a challenge.

The most successful ethical clinicians ground their clinical practices with these four pillars and tirelessly evaluate their clinical decisions for the best balance between them. The idea is to give treatment interventions that promote justice across the clinical population, that are beneficial to the client, that cause no harm, and that ensure that the client is given the opportunity to understand and contribute to the definitions of the best treatment. Think this is easy? Not so, unfortunately. You must attempt this balance in your practice every day, knowing that sometimes you will succeed and sometimes you will fail. And at times, you can do harm even with very good intentions, violating nonmaleficence without realizing it (White & Kleber, 2008). The following chapters will provide loads of examples revealing how important and difficult this balance is to achieve and maintain.

***

Before we dive in, let's briefly point out the differences between ethics and two similar constructs, law and morality.

Ethics versus the Law: If ethics are a set of parameters that guide our behavior, the law consists of a clear set of predefined rules that are punishable in a court, and defined at the state or federal level (Barsky, 2010; Washington & Demask, 2008). Law is "intentionally definitive" (Nassar-McMillan & Niles, 2011, p. 93). Ethics are not exhaustive, but instead are general guidelines, the least of what

we must do (Nassar-McMillan & Niles, 2011). Just because something is legal, it is not necessarily ethical. For example, there are laws that incarcerate those who use illegal drugs, yet there are those who believe in the disease model of addiction that would see imprisonment as unethical (Washington & Demask, 2008). Clinicians will have to consider both ethics and the law when attempting to determine the best course of action in any given clinical situation.

Ethics versus Morality: Ethics are a set of principles that guide our actions and pilot our professional conduct. Morals, on the other hand, are a person's basic, core feelings of right and wrong (Barsky, 2010; Taleff, 2010). Consider how we differentiate guilt from shame; many conjoin them into one phenomenon, yet they are distinct emotions. Guilt refers to an emotion about a committed action: For example, you may feel guilty about lying to your mom. Shame refers to an emotion about who you feel you are: You may feel shame because you are a liar who lies to his or her own mom. How badly you feel about being a liar depends on the subjective value you assign and internalize. Guilt is about the actions we take; shame is about the core of who we are. It is the same with the differentiation between ethics and morality. Like guilt, ethics are about our actions. Like shame, morality is about our feelings (Taleff, 2010, p. 40). In this way our morality is one guiding force in our ethics. There are other guiding forces: The federal and state governments, our licensing body, and the agencies in which we work are all examples of entities to whom we must answer.

Okay, so moving forward we will understand ethics as a set of principles that guide our professional behavior—built on the pillars of beneficence, autonomy, nonmaleficence, and justice—that are guided by the law, morality, and other influences we will discuss.

How the Book Is Organized

This book is organized in a way that attempts to not only help you organize ethical principles in

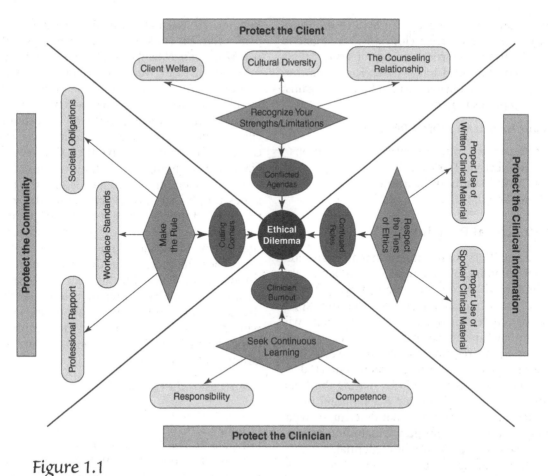

Figure 1.1

How the Book Is Organized

your head, but enable you to quickly and easily refer back to a section when it is needed in the future. The material is grouped into four sections of ethics: those that are aimed at protecting the client, those that protect the clinical information, those that protect the clinician, and those that protect the community. Within each section there is a corresponding Key to an Ethical Practice (Keys), two or three Principles from the Code of Ethics (Principles), and one of the common Pitfalls that cause Ethical Dilemmas (Pitfalls). The Principles are the guides to building each Key, and the Pitfalls are the

traps we risk falling into if we fail to build each Key. Figure 1.1 is a conceptual model to help you get a sense of the material.

The Four Keys to an Ethical Practice

The four Keys highlight the necessary foundation to a healthy ethical practice. Key 1 requires a clinician to complete an in-depth exploration of his or her own strengths and limitations, both personally and professionally. Key 2 requires the clinician to explore the concepts of perfectionism and resistance to education, and how they can lead to unethical behavior. Key 3 requires a clinician to understand and abide by the different entities, or ethical tiers, that influence our decision making. Key 4 requires the clinician to establish a norm of behavior against which exceptions may occur.

The Four Keys to an Ethical Practice

Key 1: Recognize Your Strengths and Limitations
Key 2: Respect the Tiers of Ethics
Key 3: Seek Continuous Learning
Key 4: Make the Rule

The 10 Ethical Principles

The Code of Ethics is a document that all counselors sign on becoming a credentialed member of the field, and to which one must reattest every 2 years as part of the recredentialing process. It is the expectation that credentialed or licensed counselors will adhere to each principle in their clinical practice, and clinicians are required to abide by the principles in order to obtain and maintain their state credential. If a counselor is accused of violating the Code of Ethics, his or her behavior is examined by an appointed Ethics Committee that determines what sanctions, if any, are appropriate, including suspension or revocation of license or credential.

But Houston, we have a problem. There is no universally accepted Code of Ethics in our field. Our national organization, the National Association of Addiction Professionals (NAADAC), has a code that is used in many states, but it is each state-level association that decides the Code by which all credentialed counselors in that state must abide. States vary significantly in their adopted codes.

The principles used in this book are the common elements extracted from the state codes. While many state codes differ in detail, these 10 principles can be found in every code because they are the foundation on which we build our ethical practice. They are the guidelines we turn to when counsel is needed.

After I organized this book into the sections you find here, I came across a book by the great Frederic Reamer, ethicist extraordinaire of the social work profession. His book, *Ethical Standards in Social Work: A Review of the NASW Code of Ethics* (2006), is organized in the same way as this book. Because social workers have one universal code of ethics adopted by all states, Reamer (2006a) was able to do what I could not, organizing the chapters around specific existing principles in their Code. Social workers can open his book and have their Code specifically explained to them, so that they can learn the interplay between the written code and the practical issues they experience every day on the job. Furthermore, if they are caught in an ethical dilemma, they can use the book both to understand the issues surrounding the dilemma and to explore the exact code that pertains to the dilemma. It is what I hoped to achieve with this book, but our lack of a consistent code prevented my success. Perhaps in the future, our profession can adopt one code that will unify and strengthen us. In the meantime, the principles included here are the backbone of what a universal code needs.

The 10 Ethical Principles

Principle 1: Client Welfare
Principle 2: Cultural Diversity
Principle 3: The Counseling Relationship
Principle 4: Proper Use of Written Clinical Material
Principle 5: Proper Use of Spoken Clinical Material
Principle 6: Responsibility
Principle 7: Competency
Principle 8: Workplace Standards
Principle 9: Professional Rapport
Principle 10: Societal Obligations

The Four Pitfalls That Cause Ethical Dilemmas

An ethical dilemma can mean two things, which can occur independently or simultaneously. The first is a situation where the correct action is difficult to discern because at least two courses of action are possible. The second is a situation where the clinician realizes an ethical error has been made and is unsure how to best rectify the situation. Both types of dilemmas are potentially crippling to one's practice and can be agonizing for a clinician. Avoiding dilemmas is a sensible goal, yet even the most vigilant of ethical clinicians will struggle through a dilemma at some point in their careers. Therefore, it is equally important to learn both how to avoid these dilemmas and how to cope with them if they occur.

The first step is to identify common pitfalls that cause these dilemmas. Clinicians are not suddenly hit with ethical dilemmas; they are led into the dilemma through specific traps. There are four common pitfalls that cause ethical dilemmas (referred to from now on as Pitfalls), which violate one of the aforementioned four Keys and correspond to at least one of the 10 ethical Principles. If clinicians can learn to avoid these four Pitfalls, they will maintain a strong ethical practice. However, because it is impossible to perfectly avoid every possible ethical trap, it is also important to recognize each trap and learn the necessary steps to rectify it.

The Four Common Pitfalls

Pitfall 1: Conflicted agendas
Pitfall 2: Confused roles
Pitfall 3: Clinician Burnout
Pitfall 4: Cutting corners

In every pitfall chapter there is a practical application that exposes a "hot topic," a common clinical example of the themes represented in the pitfalls.

In the pitfall of conflicted agendas the hot topic of self-disclosure will be discussed; in confused roles, the scope of practice will be addressed; in Clinician Burnout, faulty supervision will be examined; and in cutting corners, the notion of accepting gifts will be argued.

Questions

In the introduction to each section there are questions for you to answer. It is important that you explore these questions prior to reading the chapters in that section. Remember that a basic premise of this book is that Ethics can and must be taught. These questions are a vital part of that education, because they will get to your primal thoughts before they can be tainted (in a good way) by theories and opinions. And it is your primal thoughts that will most inform ethical missteps in your future; therefore you need to understand what you organically bring to your professional table. The more aware you are of how you think and feel, the better you will be able to maximize your strengths and bolster yourself against limitations, thereby limiting your ethical risk. Please complete the questions! Try to avoid the answer "it depends." Think honestly about how you most typically operate. The more thoroughly you explore your answers to each question, the more ethical your practice will be, the better a clinician you will become, and the more satisfied you will be in your work and in yourself. And isn't that, in the end, the point?

PROTECTING
THE CLIENT

Protecting the Client

Addiction counselors are taught to put the client's needs first. Quite simply, without clients we would have no work, since our work centers on helping individuals reach those specific life goals involved in overcoming addiction and creating and maintaining a healthy lifestyle. The work we do is good work, worthwhile, honorable, rewarding, challenging, and oh-so-necessary, as the discouraging drug-related stories on the 6 o'clock news shows prove. While the majority of our work can often feel like paperwork, politics, or piddling tasks, our most significant work is the direct practice with the client. Thus, ensuring that we create a solid foundation of ethics related to the client is vital to our practice. There are a few snags in the credo of putting clients first that we will discuss later in the book, yet since *most* of the time, counselors should put their clients first, focusing on those ethics that protect the client is a good place to begin.

Ethics that protect the client are based on the four pillars of ethics borrowed from the medical ethics field (Castillo & Waldorf, 2008; Corey, Corey, & Callanan, 2007; Geppert & Roberts, 2008; Miller, 2008; Taleff, 2010; Venner & Bogenshutz, 2008). As discussed in the preface ... wait. Did you skip the preface? Did you merely skim the introduction? Nah, you gotta read those sections because they set us up for the rest of the book. Go back and read them; I'll wait. Okay, so now you know that the four pillars are beneficence, autonomy, nonmaleficence, and justice. Let's see how we can apply them to the protection of the client.

From a client perspective, beneficence indicates a client's right to receive healthy, beneficial care. It is the clinician's responsibility to strive for goodness in all decisions made related to client care. From a client perspective, autonomy refers to a client's ability to make informed decisions about his or her own welfare without being coerced by others. It is the responsibility of the clinician to develop a fertile atmosphere around the client that will encourage his or her freedom.

From a client perspective, nonmaleficence indicates a client's right not to be harmed by the treatment intervention. Addiction is harming enough; treatment is about improving and getting well. It is the counselor's responsibility to refrain from harming the client, both through his or her own treatment and through other treatment he or she recommends to the client. If a treatment intervention is not working, the onus is on the counselor to alter the treatment so that the client is no longer harmed. From a client perspective, justice refers to the client's right to have access to the same treatment, and to be as fairly and evenly treated as another client. It is the counselor's responsibility to give treatment, including access to treatment, sensibly and with fairness.

In your state's code of ethics several principles are aimed at protecting the client. You have a principle that deals with the welfare of the client, and one that demands nondiscriminatory treatment in all your professional behavior. You will also have a principle that addresses the ethical use of the therapeutic relationship between counselor and client. The principle headings may be titled differently, or they may be combined, but the essential points will be in the code.

The key to adhering to these principles is to recognize your own strengths and to understand your limitations. What, you say? How can it be that the key to protecting your clients is to focus on yourself? It may sound wrong, but the best way to help others is to know yourself so well that you protect the relationship from harm caused by your own issues and challenges. If you are aware of your own strengths and limitations, you can effectively address them so that your treatment can be better focused on the client's needs. The better you know yourself, the less likely you are to have personal agendas conflict your practice. If you don't develop this key to your practice you will be in danger of falling into an ethical pitfall that can lead to an ethical dilemma and can affect your ability to protect your client. Specifically, you could be pulled into action by different agendas that clash with your ethical practice. Let's take a closer look.

Part One Questions

1. Why did you get into this profession?
2. Who are you really good at helping? Who are you not good at helping?
3. Who is your professional hero and why? Who is your fallen hero and why?
4. How would you describe the culture in your family growing up? What was valued in your family?

Key: Recognize Your Strengths and Limitations

2
Chapter

It may sound strange to begin our focus on the client with a discussion about you, the clinician. But the first rule in building or reworking your ethical practice is to evaluate aspects of both your personal and your professional self. The strength of your practice lies in the development of your self-awareness and why you make the decisions that you do (Taleff, 2010). To promote client autonomy, clinicians need to learn where their own values have the potential to conflict with the goals of the client (Manuel & Forcehimes, 2008). The better you know yourself, the better your treatment of your clients. How can this be? Because no one can truly separate their personal thoughts, feelings, and experiences from all of their professional work, nor would you want to. While the training can be universal, every clinician is unique. Skilled clinicians use those unique characteristics as assets in their practice, rather than ignoring or attempting to suppress them. Skilled clinicians also learn what aspects of their personal make-up are potential risks to their ethical practice and make the best possible plans to prevent their interference.

Clinicians often use their own life experiences as a guide to understanding and treating clients (Corey, Corey, & Callanan, 2007). Yet clinicians often fail to consider their own values as potentially conflicting with their clinical work (Manuel & Forcehimes, 2008). It is possible this is caused by our tendency to focus on the client more than ourselves, as if these are mutually exclusive. When we are aware of both our strengths and our limitations, we can work to ensure a future where we maximize our strengths and prevent our limitations from allowing us to slip into unethical behavior. Awareness of all the parts of ourselves is the first key to developing an ethical practice. A thorough personal inventory can both enhance the treatment that you give and ensure the prevention of poor treatment, effectively addressing both beneficence and nonmaleficence simultaneously. So let's get out the mirror and get started.

The first requirement is to recognize that one has both strengths and limitations. It often seems easier to name strengths and limitations in others than it is to name them in ourselves; however, in order to be a sound clinician, we must assess both attributes in ourselves, professionally and personally. Which is easier for you, to name your strengths or to list your limitations? We may find it easier to do one or the other, and this may differ if we are examining professional versus personal attributes. Personal limitations may come to the brain more easily; perhaps it feels like bragging when we speak of our personal strengths. This may be reversed when we address professional traits; revealing strengths may feel easier then admitting limitations. Perhaps one feels broadcasting limitations would put one's job in jeopardy, and therefore we become accustomed to emphasizing our positive points and downplaying our challenges. It is helpful to understand how this works for you: which characteristics are easier for you to name, and which are a challenge, as you may need to spend extra time exploring them in order to reach your ethical potential.

Unresolved personal issues of the clinician lead to exploitation of clients (St. Germaine, 1996). Because traits ignored can become ethical pitfalls, spend some time taking a thorough inventory of your personal and professional characteristics, identifying which situations you feel will highlight your strengths and which situations may bring out your limitations. Often a single characteristic could be in both categories at once. For example, if June grew up with an alcoholic mother and felt that no one helped her cope effectively with her mother's illness and its consequences, then June would likely identify "self-perseverance or self-care" as a personal strength and "sensitivity to the needs of a child of an alcoholic" as a professional strength. But she could also write down "possible difficulty empathizing with alcoholic mothers, especially those with daughters" as a possible professional limitation.

This is not meant to predict with certainty that June will have difficulty treating an alcoholic mother; perhaps she will be able to maintain a safe, therapeutic distance. Still it is helpful to know that this is a potential pitfall for June, because once she is aware, she can bring it up with her supervisor at the beginning of her work experience. Then if an alcoholic mother should appear on her caseload, June and her supervisor can regularly check in about June's ability to effectively handle the case

and her own emotional health. You would not advise June never to work with alcoholic mothers, as it is not realistic to do so, and it assumes June will have trouble when perhaps she will not. We can't predict what groups or situations will challenge June; we can only look at any possible risks and plan for them.

We can never remove the possibility of an ethical snag influenced by a personal or professional limitation; they occur sometimes without warning. However, we can increase our odds of preventing them the more we can be aware of ourselves. Later in your career, others may try to point out to you characteristics you are exhibiting that you struggle to see. Knowing that you may struggle will help you recognize the struggle when it occurs, and may help you be less defensive and more allowing of the possible limitation, which will make you a more ethical clinician.

You have already completed the initial questions at the beginning of this chapter, but now that you have been given a bit more explanation, let's dig a little deeper, shall we? Take out a piece of paper and draw a vertical line down the middle. No really, this is helpful. Go get some paper and a pen (see, that was a trick because you should already have a pen and paper so you can adequately answer the section questions. Sneaky, huh?). On the left side, write down your personal strengths, including your supportive characteristics, experiences, and relationships. Under personal strengths you want to list the characteristics that make you, well... you. What are some of your most positive qualities? What are the situations or events that had the most positive influence on you so far? With whom have you had treasured relationships in your life? Then write down your professional strengths, including again your characteristics, experiences, and relationships. Once you have given a thorough inventory of your personal and professional strengths, consider what implications these strengths have for your career. How can you apply each strength at the workplace; what populations or type of treatment services would seem like a good match with each strength? How do you think your personal strengths can be applied to your job?

On the right side of the paper, you want to take the same inventory of your personal and professional limitations, again including applicable characteristics, experiences, and relationships. List the personal limitations you see in yourself; note the challenging experiences and the damaged relationships in your life and the corresponding practical applications. Make a note of any poor supervision in the past. What work implications can be derived from your self-assessment; what suggestions can be made for populations you might consider working with or those that are potentially risky? A sample assessment can be found at clinicalethics blog.com

For example, a clinician who has suffered a parent's death may want to steer clear of running a grief group or counseling someone who also lost his or her parent until that clinician can adequately discuss the potential risk and ensure the ethical care of the client. What of a clinician who stresses out easily? This fact doesn't mean that he or she should refrain from running groups or working with high-stress populations. But knowing how one handles or mishandles stress is the difference between a clinician walking into a potentially risky situation blind and ignorant, and therefore unprepared, and a self-aware clinician walking into a potentially risky situation more confident because the potential risks have been previously identified and strategized with a supervisor or advisor.

Some characteristics, experiences, or relationships can have both beneficial and detrimental implications. Consider a clinician who had to fight to make ends meet and reach his or her dreams. This is a positive experience because it shows perseverance, resourcefulness, and courage. Yet it can also be a limitation because this clinician may have difficulty either helping people in similar situations who do not show the perseverance the clinician showed in life, or helping people who are given the opportunities and financial support in life for which the

clinician had to fight. Again, this is not meant to state the clinician will have difficulty, merely that it is a risk for which to prepare.

Spend some time brooding over your self-assessment chart (great discoveries come from a little brooding). Now let's return to the initial questions in the introduction to Part 1, using your ethical self-awareness chart. The first question, *Why did you get into this profession?* seems simple to answer, as most people have a fairly good idea of how they entered the profession, although often time and reflection can help you develop a deeper answer than you may have first given. The reason for this question may be a bit of a surprise. The reason you got into the profession in the first place is definitely part of your strengths, but it is also part of your limitations. Before I ruffle your feathers too much, read on for my explanation. The reason you got into the profession is the very light that burns in the deepest part of you, the fire that guided you into your career. This is a strong, solid core within you, and therefore it is obviously close to your heart. Whatever it is that guided you into the profession is a huge strength within you, a beacon to which you return when you doubt yourself or your work, when the challenges make you forget why you started this professional journey.

But often those things that make up our strengths are also firmly seated in our limitations and potential risks. Because our reasons are close to our hearts, it is easy to be influenced, even blinded, by them. Have you ever been attracted to a person and slightly bent your rules for him or her when you wouldn't for someone else? Have you ever felt strongly about something, but felt even stronger when a family member was involved? We have our norms, and then we have our exceptions, and those exceptions usually come about because they speak to those things closest to our hearts. The same concept occurs with our career influences. Those influences have acted as beacons to drive us to success. We have been guided by them, we have relied on them, we have been nurtured by and have nurtured them. Thus, we can easily be swayed by them, and each of you will have to watch yourself and use supervision to ensure the risk does not become a reality.

The second question, *Who are you really good at helping?* asks you who you believe you are good at helping, and you can't write everybody or anybody; be specific! This question is easier to answer once you have completed your self-assessment, as often individuals, groups, and situations come into focus as you examine your strengths and limitations. Use your answers to this question as a guide for possible career directions to try. Your initial thoughts may have changed or deepened after completing your self-assessment, so go ahead and add to those answers. Many of you will have a much easier time writing about who you think you can help. If you take all of your supportive characteristics, experiences, and relationships in both personal and professional arenas, what kind of people or situations are suggested by the list? For example, early experiences caring for siblings could suggest an affinity with younger clients, so working in a group setting for adolescents or designing programs for the adolescent population may be a good match.

It is important to realize that this is only a guide and not a guarantee. You may learn that a job that seemed so perfect on paper is less than perfect in reality, and there is no shame in that; in fact it will help you hone in on how and where to put your gifts to work. And as our positive influences can also blind us, so too must we be careful of closing our eyes to any warning signs that come up within the populations we feel we can help. It is possible for us to stay so focused on moving toward the job we think we should be doing that we end up missing other golden opportunities along the way. Keep your eyes open, take risks, surprise yourself. But stay true to who you are.

The other part of this second question, *Who are you not good at helping?* may be harder to answer for most people. It requires putting aside your ego, taking a nice helping of humble pie, and admitting to yourself the simple truth that even the most skilled

and talented clinician cannot help every person. You are not going to be attracted to every person you see in life, nor will you be friends with every person you meet, so why would you expect to be able to personally counsel every client who walks through the door? Perhaps some clinicians confuse discrimination, which we try to avoid, with a difficulty in accessing empathy for certain types of people or situations. This is natural, and does not indicate that you think these people or situations are inferior or judge them in some way, nor does it suggest that you would behave as anything less than professional when working with the people or situations.

It does indicate, however, that there are certain subpopulations that simply don't mesh with you. There is a wide range of possible reasons for this: Perhaps you are not inspired, perhaps you are scared, perhaps you can't separate your personal experiences to effectively treat them, perhaps it brings up too many uncomfortable emotions for you, perhaps you find it too challenging or exhausting. What one clinician may find too exhausting, another clinician may find energizing. Remember, you can *help* anyone that comes through the door, but the help may be first admitting that you are not the best counselor for the individual and then aiding him or her in finding the right match. Often the most ethical and clinically appropriate action is to admit there is another clinician who would be better at helping the individual.

Yet in many cases, awareness of your limitations can result in overcoming those limitations, with good training and guidance. For example, one clinician realized she was afraid of working with convicted felons. She was displeased with this, and made it a goal of supervision to analyze how this fear developed and how to address it so that she could successfully treat clients in this population. The point is to acknowledge your limitations and attempt to grow from them. In some cases, you will be successful; in others the challenge will be too great and you will need to accept that at this time you are not the best choice for the individual or situation.

The third question, *Who is your professional hero and why? Who is your fallen hero and why?* asks you to think about the influential people you have known in your career, whether you are new to the field or a seasoned clinician. We all need inspiration and role models. It helps to have a person in mind whom you respect and whose qualities you would like to emulate. This is someone you can take with you, and when you find yourself smack in the middle of an ethical dilemma, ask yourself what your hero would do, which can be a valuable guide.

We also can receive guidance from the anti-heroes in our lives, those people who were once a positive influence but made poor choices, or were hit with tough circumstances or some other scenario that caused them to "fall from grace." Who did you admire in the past but now feel is someone who chose a path you would not travel? Consider why you respected him or her and how this changed. This is a helpful exploration because we are guided both by who we wish to be and who we wish not to be; it is helpful to be guided both toward healthy conduct and away from damaging actions.

The fourth question, *How would you describe the culture in your family growing up? What was valued in your family?* is asking you to explore your cultural roots. Your first answers may be related to race, ethnicity, or religion, which are all important answers to the question. Go ahead and fill in how you identify in these categories and note any cultural influences from your family. Now let's go deeper. Move beyond the stereotypical cultural categories and explore the specific culture in your family. What did your family members value, what did they find inferior, what did they try to steer you toward and what did they teach you to avoid?

Our families help us begin to develop our personal moral code, beginning by teaching us what we are to value. They teach us these lessons in many different ways, sometimes by showing how we should act and sometimes by showing how we should never act. All of it is education, however, and it is the foundation upon which our ethical practice will grow. Many of us have multiple families, and it would be interesting to answer this question for each family unit that influenced you. You may have a biological family unit and an entirely different unit that raised you. You may have several family units that raised you at different points in your development. If the family unit, or the absence of a family unit, had an influence on you, then include it in this exploration.

Now, armed with our awareness of strengths and limitations, let's look at where this concept connects with the Code of Ethics. The three principles that require the development of this key are Client Welfare, Cultural Diversity, and the Counseling Relationship. All codes address the principles because they are at the heart of what we do—serving the client—and are thus the principles that speak to our ethical demand of protecting the client. If we fail to adhere to these principles, if we bungle the development of our first key, we are at risk of falling into a trap. Specifically, we are in danger of falling into the trap of conflicted agendas. If we struggle with conflicted agendas we will find ourselves quickly stuck in an ethical dilemma, often without a sure pathway out. Let's take a closer look.

Principle: Client Welfare

3
Chapter

The first principle in the ethical code aimed at protecting the client is the principle of Client Welfare. The primary professional responsibility is for the welfare of the client (National Association for Addiction Professionals [NAADAC], 2011). Simply put, this principle mandates that you must protect the integrity and welfare of the client or group of clients whom you are servicing. Our shorthand way of saying this is: "Put the client first." Client Welfare does not mean you will always put the client's request first, as it may not be ethically wise to do so, but it does mean you will do everything in your power to protect clients and ensure their health and safety in all your affairs. It means you will make decisions based on what is the best choice for that client, and not what is the most convenient or easy or efficient course of action. "Zealous client care is demanding, yet crucial, for ethical practice" (Lee, Lim, Yang, & Lee, 2011, p. 256). There can be no corner-cutting when it comes to client welfare; you must go the distance to do right by your clients.

This is a simple concept the importance of which few would argue; however, it is quite easy to get snagged or confused by the concept. Here's our first snag: Who is defining the client's best interest? Who is defining client welfare? Is it the client, is it the agency, is it the clinician? How do you know? There will be times that parties disagree with what is best, your client may be begging you for one response, your agency is expecting another response from you and you believe a different course of action is best. Often we believe we know what is best for the client, based on our experience and training and the relationship we have built with the client. In many situations we are correct, but in other situations our clients have a better idea of what is best for them than we do, or perhaps your supervisor or other staff members have a better idea. Our quandary becomes how to decide what is best for the client. To help us suss it out, we turn to the four Pillars. Can they help or further confuse us?

Beneficence: According to this principle, the concept of goodness is based on the clinician's concern for the well-being of the clients. The clinician will foster respect and sensitivity and will base treatment interventions on those that are most beneficial and that best increase the client's positive life experience (Geppert & Roberts, 2008). The snag here is defining *most beneficial* or *best*. As some of us know from taking our credentialing and licensing exams,

15

deciding on the *best* course of action can be very difficult. Most of us can get those multiple choice answers down to two choices but can then make a good case for either choice. At work, we can fall into the same conundrum. It is often the case that you will be faced with two equally satisfactory actions and will struggle to make a choice of which is best.

It is a primary responsibility of Client Welfare for the clinician to focus on the client's needs, but this does not necessarily mean you side with the client or do what the client is wishing. It means that when in doubt, operate in what you and your advisors feel are the best needs of the client, for that will rarely steer you in the wrong direction. If you are protecting the welfare of the client, then you are likely to be operating in the best interests of the profession as well. You can only do the best you can do. Talk to your advisors, think it through, and make the best choice you can. And know that you will sometimes make mistakes, but as long as you are operating with the best of your ability at the time, you should feel good about the decision you made and learn from your mistakes for next time. The key here is to work with advisors.

Autonomy: The clinician is tasked with promoting freedom and independence in his or her clients, by avoiding goal setting that is not shared by the client and encouraging clients in self-care. A common struggle exists between protecting clients and allowing clients to make their own decisions, remembering that our primary goal is to help clients learn to help themselves. Effective learning often requires mistakes as well as successes. Clinicians often wonder, "Should I step in and prevent their mistake, or should I allow them to learn from their mistakes?" It's a tough call, and usually comes down to the issue of safety, where the clinician will step in if safety is in question. But even safety is not always easy to define! Argh, this quickly gets more convoluted. Yet this does not really help us on our quest. Using autonomy empowers our clients, but what if they are not acting toward their best welfare? I'm thinking nonmaleficence can bail us out.

Nonmaleficence: The most ethical interventions are those that prevent harm for the client. Okay, let's go with that. But wait, even this can become jumbled in certain clinical areas. It can become very challenging to weigh which action will cause more or less harm, and there are many clinical situations in which one can easily make a case for both sides of the ethical argument.

For example, consider the harm reduction model, which promotes beneficence at its core, arguing that reducing harm is better than no treatment at all (Miller, 2008). Thus, giving clean hypodermic needles to a heroin addict may help that addict to abuse heroin, but it diminishes all of the risks of using dirty needles. Similarly, focusing treatment on the cocaine habit that the client identifies as the problem, while ignoring the alcohol use that may also be problematic, may fail to address a potential secondary abuse but allows the client to craft the treatment program they are ready to address. Some treatment is better than no treatment.

The criticism of the harm reduction model is that it fails nonmaleficence because the counselor is willingly allowing or promoting harm to the client. In these examples, the first clinician is aware that providing needles will result in the client using illegal and damaging drugs. The second clinician chooses to ignore another potentially abusive pattern just to keep the client in treatment, even though ignoring the problem gives the client permission to continue the potentially harmful behavior. Where you fall on the harm reduction argument may help inform how you should define the best action for the client. But let's see if the pillar of beneficence can help us better answer our quandary.

Justice: How can the concept of justice help us decipher what is best for the client? Clients have a right to fair treatment, including access to programs on the one hand and equal rules and regulations of practice on the other, based on empirically based treatment practices that are established to be effective in a similar population. Clients have the right to the same treatment as others who are treated by the same clinician, agency, and profession. The addiction counselor agrees to provide equal and effective treatment, including referral, to all individuals regardless of their socioeconomic background and resources, including their ability to pay for services. Clients need equal financial arrangements. For example, clients may not be eligible for all insurances based on criteria, but all clients are eligible for some type of insurance. Justice requires agencies to either accept insurance, offer an alternative payment option, or refer to another agency that can help. You can give a discount to veterans but cannot have special rules for Stanley that you don't apply to Ralph.

For example, Alicia has been attending her required groups as part of Phase I in her local addiction treatment agency. In fact, she has been in Phase I slightly longer than average. Alicia believes she is ready to move into Phase II. She approaches her counseling team, and explains why she feels she is ready to move to Phase II. She gives a compelling argument, and the majority of the team is swayed to comply with her request. Her individual counselor Raquel, however, feels that it would be better to keep her in Phase I for a few more weeks. On paper Alicia looks ready to move, having completed all the criteria. But Raquel senses she is not ready based on the rapport she has built with Alicia. She believes Alicia is trying to convince herself and the staff that she is ready to move based on the motivation stemming from boredom. While the staff sees Alicia as working well with the program, Raquel sees her as getting increasingly impatient and bored with her life as is. And Raquel also worries that Alicia's addictive brain is starting to wear her down, subtly so that Alicia doesn't recognize it. Raquel recommends no change, which infuriates Alicia and causes her to claim angrily that Raquel does not have her interests at heart. However, even though she is disagreeing with Alicia and not giving her what she wants, Raquel is very much working with Alicia's interests at heart, suspecting that her addictive brain will work overtime to get her closer to relapsing and thus that moving her to Phase II

when she is not ready will put Alicia at risk. Raquel has weighed the ethical pillars and feels this is the best course of action to promote client welfare.

The ethical agony that comes with attempting to put the client's needs first and protecting them to the best of our ability can often be found in specific areas where client welfare must be held as the paramount necessity. They are the areas of Loyalty, Referrals, and Collaboration. Additional aspects of client welfare, specifically cultural diversity and counseling relationships, will be discussed later in this section in their own separate chapters.

Loyalty

Clinicians must define for the client, the client's family, other agencies or professionals involved in the case, and the staff at their workplace the exact nature of the relationships involved; the treatment process; the treatment goals; the financial arrangements; and the rules of confidentiality, including information about mandated reporting, the relevant agency, and the clinician's credentials and position in the agency. If the clinician is a student or intern, he or she must inform the client and other parties of the supervising clinician (Manuel & Forcehimes, 2008).

You must put these loyalties in writing and verbally discuss them with clients. This must occur at the beginning of treatment and should be repeated as often as necessary if the information does not seem to have been retained by the client. In the beginning of treatment, many clients will be impaired by recreational drugs, medications, and emotional turmoil, and they may not truly understand or remember aspects of their orientation. It is important to assess whether your client has understood all of the rules and paperwork they were given at the start of treatment. It is helpful to go over the information with clients on the first day, in the first week, and in the first month if it applies to your workplace.

You need to explain your basic loyalty ties and describe any exceptions. This is vital to maintaining integrity as a clinician and respect for the client. It also acts as a form of protection for those we are treating. For example, you may tell your client that your loyalty is to him or her, but that as a member of the clinical team, you have an obligation to complete tasks for the agency or follow agency rules that, if interfering with your client's treatment, will supersede your goals with the client. Can you think of an example?

How about the concept of mandated reporting? The session material between you and your client can remain confidential with several notable exceptions that you must explain to your client. If the client poses a threat to harm his- or herself or another, or is gravely disabled and unable to care for him- or herself, we must report the risk to the appropriate authorities. If there is suspected child or elder abuse, we must also report it to the authorities. These reports trump any loyalty you have formed with the client, and the client must be made immediately aware of these exceptions. States vary on whether addiction counselors are mandated reporters, so check with your supervisor or licensing board to know what is expected of you. Even if not a legally mandated reporter you are ethically obligated to inform your supervisor and inquire into what, if any, additional steps you should take. Document the process for your client's protection, and to protect you, the agency, and the profession.

In addition, consider how your agency works. How is confidential material discussed among staff? If you have staff meetings, are clients discussed using identifiable information? If you have case conferences, are cases discussed using identifiable information? In most agencies, client identity is used when discussing cases among agency staff. When you are discussing treatment goals, progress, and needed interventions with your agency staff, it would not make sense to keep the client's identity veiled, as each case is handled according to the characteristics of each client. In addition, when discussing your clinical performance in supervision, you will surely discuss some of the session material between you and your clients. Some case conferences do not use identifying information

when cases are presented to other staff. Within an agency, this confidentiality is optional, as all staff are expected to uphold the confidentiality laws applicable to the clinical situation. However, when cases are presented outside of the agency, or outside of the clinical team within that agency, then all identifying client information must be withheld. All of this must be explained to each client when they begin treatment with you. You want them in treatment, but you want them to understand that the familiar phrase "What's said in this office stays in this office" is not exactly accurate. You will discuss what is said in your office in certain circumstances; therefore, do not promise clients something you do not intend to deliver. To protect their welfare, they must be made aware by you of what information you will divulge and when. And then you must stick to what you've promised.

Referrals

You can't do everything for everyone—there are limits to what you can do (Bissell & Royce, 1987). There are many reasons we may refer clients to other professionals. Our treatment may be unsuccessful, we may not be a good match for the client, the client may have graduated, or the client may need concurrent services with someone who specializes in another area. Finding the right clinician to treat your client and ensuring the client makes a connection is ethically required no matter what the circumstances that brought on a termination with you. We can't drop clients simply because we gave them the name of someone else with whom to work; we are ethically responsible for clients until it is clear that they are cared for by another clinician or agree that treatment is no longer needed. A successful referral demands that they have attended an appointment with the new clinician and all parties agree to the referred relationship. Terminating a client without a concrete referral can occur too easily, perhaps due to an exhaustive workload of the clinician and a lack of time and patience to ensure appropriate follow through. It is your ethical obligation to ensure your client does not fall through the cracks, particularly if this has been an issue for you in the past.

For example, Dana gives her client, Jack, a referral name and number of an individual therapist in the community who can continue working with Jack after he graduates from his treatment program. Jack promises to call and make an appointment on the day he leaves treatment. Wanting to ensure that Jack gets the care he needs, Dana calls Jack after termination, but he does not return her calls. Dana now has two options for her next course of action. On the one hand, she has completed what she needed to do for the agency requirements. She can document that she gave the referral, tried to call the client, left messages, and closed the case. Her agency would be happy with that; however, Dana feels perhaps there is more she should do. Dana knows that Jack is not engaged with the new therapist, and feels that he is still her responsibility until he can be appropriately connected. Therefore, she does two things. First, she calls the referral and notifies the new clinician that Jack has been terminated, has not been returning phone calls, and gives the clinician Jack's phone number in the hopes that he or she can call Jack and encourage him to make an appointment. Dana can afford this communication because she has a specific consent to release information signed by Jack that details her ability to take this action. Second, she leaves another message for Jack, explaining that his care is still her responsibility and that she will keep calling, and leaving messages, until he makes contact with the new clinician. In this way, Dana ensures her ethical actions and is determined to protect her client's welfare.

What is ethically appropriate when a client refuses our referrals? Let's see how this can play out. Sydney is given a referral after she is deemed less than appropriate for the treatment program in which she is enrolled. She has recently exhibited impaired symptoms that indicate she is not appropriate for groups. Her behavior is not a problem, but her mental capacity is questioned, and it is concluded that she won't get much of anything out of group treatment due to her mental impairment.

She refuses the referral, preferring to stay with the program she knows. It would be easy to just refer her and hope that she uses the program to which you refer her, but if she is clearly stating that she won't attend another treatment program, staff must weigh keeping her in treatment versus discharging her to the community without treatment. In Sydney's case, it may be easier to rule on keeping her in the program because she is not a bother to anyone else in the program; it is simply questioned how much of the current treatment she is able to absorb. Armed with this information, staff may feel the best way with beneficence and nonmaleficence is to keep her as a client.

In another example, Morley has a great attendance record in his treatment program and appears to absorb the lessons taught in individual and group counseling. However, even though he is given specific recommendations about eliminating triggers and building a solid foundation of recovery in his community outside of treatment, Morley makes no progress in this. His counseling team tries to work with him repeatedly on making the necessary changes, but Morley refuses. His treatment team decides to terminate his treatment based on his noncompliant attitude toward following the recommendations he has been given, and refers him to his community, encouraging the use of self-help. Morley says he hates self-help and feels he is being dumped unfairly. His treatment team acknowledges his feelings, reminding him that several attempts were made to make the program work for him and that daily community involvement might be more successful at helping him reach his goals. Morley is given specific community resource information and follow-up calls are made to ensure he has successfully connected with the community.

As you can see, how you should handle a client's refusal is as varied as the clients themselves. Ethically, look to the four pillars as a guide. You want to promote justice, by suggesting and providing access to the same effective referrals to all your clients who are a good match with a specific referral. You want to promote autonomy by collaborating with clients in the referral process whenever possible, and incorporating their opinions about their own care into the referrals you make. You want to promote beneficence by doing right by your clients, making the healthiest, most beneficial referrals possible for each client. Finally, you want to promote nonmaleficence by ensuring that you do no harm to your clients by failing them in the referral process, either by suggesting an inferior or detrimental referral or by neglecting to follow the referral process to a satisfying end.

Collaboration

There are several entities with whom clinicians will need to collaborate during a client's treatment episode, including family, other supports, and professionals. Because addiction is correlated with homelessness, psychiatric issues, and medical conditions, treatment must combine several different areas into one multisystem approach (Whitter et al., 2006). Each collaborative relationship requires that the clinician protect the welfare of clients by ensuring ethical behavior. Generally, the ethical pillars can guide our collaborative efforts. To achieve beneficence, we must seek out the healthiest collaborative persons in order to help foster positive relationships in the client's family and community. To achieve autonomy, we must include our clients in the search for the most beneficial collaborative relationships and allow them the freedom to make choices in their own care. To achieve nonmaleficence, we must consider collaborative relationships that have the potential to harm the client, even if the client is unaware or unwilling to see the potential risks. We must commit to steering the client toward relationships that are healthy and harmless. To achieve justice, we carry forth our tasks with the other pillars with all of the clients that we serve, evenly.

Personal Supports: Personal supports include family members, friends, significant others, employers, and 12-step sponsors, and they should be involved as appropriate to each clinical case. Because the presence of family can be instrumental in recovery efforts, a clinician should make every attempt to engage a supporting person(s) for the client during their treatment, especially if the client is an adolescent (Belitz, 2008; Volkow, 2009; Winters, Botzet, & Fahnhorst, 2011). In one adolescent study, the most significant factor in treatment success was family involvement (Tanner-Smith, Wilson, & Lipsey, 2013). Family involvement can be achieved in two ways: traditional family therapy and psychoeducation. Family can be defined as whoever is a close and healthy support to the client, someone who will provide ongoing, satisfying aid to the client in developing and maintaining his or her recovery program. Your clients' recovery programs will be unique to each client and one client's program may differ from others' programs in significant ways; however, you must ensure that every client has at least one supportive person. Your clients will need as much support as they can get. Clinicians with a rigid routine may have difficulty incorporating alternative definitions of family to include nonfamilial supports, but it is important to do so.

Some families are damaged to a degree that involving them would not be safe or therapeutic for your client, and some clients are not in a place where they are receptive to having family involved. There are times you need to roll with your clients' resistance instead of forcing them to do something they are not ready or willing to do. A good way to get around the family issue is to widen your definition of family beyond the typical family by blood. Who does the client consider "family"? Who will they go to if they need help? It may be a neighbor, or a non-blood relative, or a best friend. Include the best support they have, even if that may not be family, and witness the benefits for your client.

In addition to aiding the client in identifying supporting persons, clinicians should engage the family members in their loved one's treatment program through formal or informal avenues. All involved family members should receive basic education regarding addiction principles, components of developing a recovery program, how to help their loved one in recovery, and where to get their own support (Volkow, 2009). Some agencies provide this psychoeducation through formal groups for family members with loved ones in treatment. Other agencies employ a more informal approach through private family sessions, or at the very least through therapeutic conversations over the phone. Family therapy is less common because it lies outside our scope of practice, so the agency must have appropriately licensed staff to run the therapy group.

Regardless of the manner in which the family is involved, two things are imperative for the clinician to uphold at all times. First, the exact nature of the family involvement must be explained to the client and his or her consent must be given before any family member can be contacted. Second, the clinician must maintain loyalty to his or her primary focus, the client, and not the family. This latter point sounds easy enough on paper but can be quite difficult in practice. We'll discuss it more in the next section.

Professionals: Clinicians assigned as primary counselors must gain consent from the client to communicate with all other providers and professionals working on the treatment team, and other important personnel in the client's recovery plan. Once consent is obtained, communication must be established and maintained regularly throughout the treatment progress. This communication serves to establish collaboration between professionals, to protect the client's rights and ensure that he or she is receiving the best possible care, and to prevent the duplication or abuse of services. Within this collaboration the client's care must be the focus, and the goal is to strive for improvement as needed.

For our clients who are receiving any medication, it is particularly imperative that we employ ongoing collaboration with other health care professionals involved in treating the client (Volkow, 2009). It is not enough to record the names and contact information for other providers, nor is it acceptable to merely create a list of medications the client is taking. Because medications change often in type and dosage, consistent communication with those prescribing the medication is important. You may need to help support your client in taking the medications as prescribed; therefore, you must speak with the prescribing professionals to obtain all the necessary information about the medications to ensure the client successfully adheres to the treatment. You may need to support your client in communicating with their prescribing professional, which is easier if you have already made contact with the professional at the start of treatment.

Collaboration requires conversation, and you must be actively speaking with all providers to ensure the best care of the client. If you are the client's individual counselor and there is no case manager on record, it will be your responsibility to initiate contact with all providers. Do not wait for doctors and other clinicians to call you, as they are likely to be waiting for you as the primary professional on the case. Also remember to list *all* providers, not just those concerned with the client's mental health. Primary care physicians, physical therapists, psychotherapists, probation officers, Department of Children and Families (DCF) caseworkers, lawyers, and any other provider on the case should be listed and contacted.

As an addictions counselor, you are not qualified to diagnose your clients nor to prescribe them medications, but that does not mean you are not qualified to ask questions. And ask you should, especially if you are wondering how other clinicians decided on the diagnoses that your client carries, or if you are confused why he or she is prescribed certain medications. Do not eschew your ethical responsibility to ensure the best care of your client because you are not legally able to diagnose or prescribe. It still remains your responsibility to talk to the professionals who are qualified to perform these duties, giving these professionals your opinions based on your observations, so that your client receives the best, most accurate care.

For example, Reem is a 43-year-old opiate and cocaine abuser with Major Depressive Disorder and Anxiety Disorder not otherwise specified, who recently completed an inpatient dual diagnosis program at another facility. Upon discharge, Reem is given five medications and is referred to Manny's care. Manny notices the referral paperwork lists his diagnosis as depression and gives no rationale for the multiple medications he is on. Manny has a fair amount of knowledge about the classes of medicines, and it seems to him that several are from the same class. He finds it curious that Reem would have so many prescribed. Manny phones the referral source and gathers additional information about his care.

Your conduct with clients, including your loyalty, referral, and collaborative efforts, will dictate how successful you are at applying the principle of client welfare to your ethical practice. The concept of Client Welfare is not black or white, but the muddled gray in between. Let's look at a predicament into which clinicians can easily fall.

VIGNETTE: KEEPING SECRETS

Matthew is a young man in his twenties. Although he has done well in his treatment program, his halfway house is rapidly nearing the limits of its patience with him because of his sudden disruptive manipulating and lying. Matthew may also be jeopardizing his part-time job through similar "using behavior." It appears clear to the treatment team that his recent decompensation is in part caused by the fact that his parents recently moved out of state and his sister has enrolled in a school on the East Coast. Matthew is devastated with the geographical separation and appears to be acting out as a way of sabotaging the move and making his family return to the city in which he resides.

One day, treatment staff are contacted by the parents and are asked to engage in a confidential conversation. During this discussion, the parents reveal that they have not left the city, only moved to a different house nearby. Similarly, the client's sister is actually enrolled at the local university nearby, not a school on the opposite coast. The parents do not wish to tell the client the truth; in fact, they created the lie because they wanted to build distance with the son. They feel it is better for the client to believe they are far away and to learn to adjust while surrounded by staff support. The staff, feeling that the patient should definitely be told such relevant news, communicates this intention with the family. The family reacts with outrage, threatening to drop the patient entirely, to cease all participation in any aspect of his care and placement if the patient is told this information, and to cease all financial support of his treatment. The staff is torn. They recognize that family involvement is crucial to the patient and to his treatment, but wonder if the patient's long-term improvement, and the ethical standards of his treatment, would be better preserved if he understands the truth.

What would you do? How important is telling the truth in the therapeutic relationship? What allegiance, if any, does the therapist have to the client's family? Most importantly, which choice best reflects the welfare of the client: telling the truth or keeping the secret? On the one hand, you could lie to the client but keep him in treatment. On the other hand, you could tell the client and risk losing him in treatment. Which is a better way of ensuring the welfare of the client?

The ethical pillars can help us. The pillar of autonomy would guide us to tell the truth to Matthew, because with the truth he can take a stand for his own care and make informed decisions, even if it means he makes the decision to leave treatment. He will take the reins of his own recovery plan, and that is positive. You made a commitment to Matthew when you began to work with him, and you must be loyal to his interests. You promised honesty, integrity, and to promote client welfare. Individual cases may vary, but if you are looking to establish a norm against which an occasional exception may occur, then consider the integrity you are working to establish in your responsible practice. Lying to your clients, especially by request of a family member, sounds like behavior that questions your integrity and violates beneficence. While keeping the client in treatment is promoting beneficence, coercing him is not the best practice beneficence requires. Coercing Matthew by lying to him also violates autonomy. You and the client collaborate to make the individual treatment goals that are appropriate to each client. You do not want someone outside the agency, in this case a parent, dictating how you run your treatment program, or what goals you should have with your client. You certainly do not want to entertain threats. And lying to the client affects the independence and freedom that autonomy requires. You want to be careful not to seat yourself in the middle of a family drama, which can quickly distract both you and your client from your treatment goals, and can violate nonmaleficence by harming Matthew. You may lose Matthew, the parents may take him out of treatment, but they may not, or the client may find another way to pay to stay in treatment. At the very least, Matthew will leave treatment knowing you were honest with him and did not fall prey to his parents' threats. He will know you cared about him and were a scrupulous clinician who tried not to harm him. And that matters.

Can you see how quickly a seemingly simple concept becomes a muddled mess? Client Welfare involves weighing several variables in each situation in order to determine the best course of action. Because there are options galore in most scenarios, using your supervision to discuss maintaining Client Welfare is imperative to your ethical practice.

There is another aspect of protecting your clients that is part of promoting the welfare of your clients but dense enough to have its own principle. The concept of Cultural Diversity is complex and vital to your ethical practice. When considering client welfare, understanding the role culture plays in the lives of your clients is essential; in fact, it is so vital it deserves its own chapter. Let's take a look.

Principle: Cultural Diversity

4

Chapter

So far you have taken a personal inventory and used its implications to protect your clients and you have explored the concept of client welfare, reviewing how to keep your clients' needs in focus. The welfare of your clients also depends on your ability to respect your clients by understanding and accepting their cultural background. When you don't accept your clients, you are in danger of discriminating against who they are, which violates all four of the ethical pillars. Our world offers a rich diversity that has implications in our profession (Pope & Vasquez, 2007). The addiction population we are treating is becoming more diverse. Even good clinicians can be at a loss in treating clients with other backgrounds. Clinicians must know their own limitations when treating clients (Venner & Bogenschutz, 2008). You can't possibly promote goodness if you are discriminating against some aspect of a client's character, and you will certainly cause harm to your patient with your discrimination.

While clinicians will undoubtedly agree that discriminating against clients is unethical, it occurs regularly in the profession, often by good clinicians just like you, reader. Discrimination can be big and blatant, but it can also be very small and subtle.

If you are not aware of your thoughts and actions, it can even escape your attention. Understanding and accepting the cultural diversity that will make up your client caseload and interprofessional relationships is a necessary task in building an ethical practice. Avoiding discrimination is not the only important aspect of cultural diversity. Understanding a client's cultural influences can give clues to both how his or her addiction developed and what treatment interventions may be suggested in each case. Let's begin by exploring the definition of culture and how it can play a role in your client's addiction and recovery.

Culture refers to a group in which one is a member, that holds rules, values, and norms agreed on and upheld by all members of the shared culture. Traditionally many people view culture as synonymous with ethnicity (Venner & Bogenschutz, 2008), but that is only one type. Culture is so much more. In ethics, we define culture to include age, gender, race, ethnicity, national origin, religion, sexual orientation, disabilities, language, and socioeconomic status (Venner & Bogenschutz, 2008). Most of us have several other cultures to which we belong. The family that raises you provides its own culture, complete with rules, values, and norms. Your age, gender, religion, political affiliation, sexual identity, race, ethnicity, national origin, profession, and workplace are also cultures. Some cultures require an action for membership, such as requiring a credential to be an addictions counselor. Other cultures have no requirements.

Clinicians are taught that clients' culture plays an important role in their identity (Nassar-McMillan & Niles, 2011; Venner & Bogenschutz, 2008), and that it is important to assess culture in the intake interview, namely their ethnicity, religion, and sexual orientation (Corey, Corey, & Callanan, 2007; Pope & Vasquez, 2010). Age and gender are typically obtained from what the client wrote down on the screening form. Because clients will be representing many different cultures, understanding and addressing that diversity is an important part to any clinical practice. Therefore, many cultural diversity courses are offered to clinicians throughout their training. Historically, many classes and books on diversity teach certain culture-specific rules, such as avoiding eye contact with Asian clients as a sign of respect, and clinicians often treat clients based on what was learned in the class or book. We do so feeling confident that we are being culturally competent in our work.

But being culturally competent does not entail taking a workshop on a specific culture and then using that information to automatically treat clients within that culture in a certain way (Nassar-McMillan & Niles, 2011). The problem here is that your clients may not fall under the stereotypes of the culture of which they are a member. What if they are members of two or more distinct cultures and they take bits from each one to make up who they are? How will you know how to treat them if you are only looking at cultural norms? Think about yourself: What cultures are you a part of and what are the stereotypes? Do you fit in perfectly with those stereotypes? You may adhere to some, but I would guess that you don't comply with all stereotypes. Your clients won't either, so don't assume that you know anything about them based on whatever they have written on their intake

documents. Patricia may be a married, heterosexual, African American Christian from the south, but to you she is just Patricia, someone you need to get to know. Any of those labels that Patricia carries are going to mean nothing unless she tells you they mean something to her. Professional education is vital, but you want to use it as background information that informs what questions you will ask your client, not as an excuse not to ask the questions. Close your eyes and say with me, "Tabula Rasa." Your client is a blank slate when you step into that intake assessment, and it is your job to learn everything you can about him or her in order to effectively help him or her. You want to acknowledge each client's independence, uniqueness, and allow each the respect to teach you about themselves, according to the pillar of autonomy. The moral of the story is: Never assume anything about who is sitting in front of you; *ask*.

Cultural competency is "a lifelong process with no endpoint" (Venner & Bogenschutz, 2008, p. 68). You want to connect with all clients regardless of their personal history, according to the pillar of justice. Counselors must recognize that cultural factors exist with each client and influence the counseling process (Nassar-McMillan & Niles, 2011), according to the pillar of beneficence. "The good will of the clinician is not enough for a culturally competent practice.... Clinicians must be aware of general cultural knowledge *and* their own beliefs, biases, and ability to be open-minded" (Venner & Bogenschutz, 2008, p. 68) in order to achieve nonmaleficence.

We live in a world where the concept of being politically correct is in our vernacular, yet our actions don't always reflect our vocal assertions. People will say they don't discriminate against others, and you may be one of them, but when we think of discrimination, we usually think of gross violations of someone's characteristics. We can easily state that not admitting someone into a program because they are a person of color would be hideously inappropriate on every level. But there are more subtle snags that remain undetectable for even seasoned clinicians that must be examined when evaluating your potential risk of cultural discrimination.

Clinicians violate the principle of cultural diversity in one of two ways, by errors of omission and errors of commission (Venner & Bogenschutz, 2008). Errors of omission include not asking the right questions, or assuming that clients' cultures are not involved with their presenting problems or solutions. Errors of commission include prejudice and discrimination (Venner & Bogenschutz, 2008). Let's consider how prejudice and discrimination take place by first examining who typically suffers discrimination and how it can play out in the clinical arena. Characteristics that are often fertile ground for errors of commission are race, ethnicity, national origin, religion, age, gender identity and expression, sexual orientation, disabilities, economic condition, drug(s)/behavior of choice, psychiatric diagnosis, and recovery status of the clinician.

one-half to one-16th degree of blood. Regardless of these rules, an individual client will choose with which country and culture he or she identifies.

It is not the responsibility of the clinician to dictate the appropriate memberships for the clients, or to tell them that their identification is faulty. How a person looks to you may be vastly different than how that person identifies him- or herself. The three questions you *must* ask every client are: (1) With which race and ethnic groups do you most identify? (2) How has your race, ethnicity, and national origin played a role in your experiences (positive and negative)? (3) Do you expect your race, ethnicity, or national origin to have a positive or negative effect on your recovery efforts, or has it already had an effect? Tell me more. Additional questions may emerge from these basic questions.

Race/Ethnicity/National Origin

These three categories are distinct and should not be confused with each other. Race refers to physical characteristics, such as the color of a person's skin, and ethnicity refers to learned behavior, particularly traditions and customs, based on the region in which a person is from. If three people with dark, black skin, are from America, Haiti, and Kenya, they would be members of the same race, yet part of significantly different ethnicities. Similarly, three people with white skin from America, Germany, and Ireland would have the same race but with significantly different ethnic backgrounds.

National origin refers to the nation that clients identify as their home, in which their cultural norms, rules, and traditions were learned and upheld. This is significant because many clients may move into one country, but continue to adhere to the culture of another country. Countries will vary on which generations will be eligible to claim origin; some may welcome people with grandparents born in the country, some may go back further generations. In our own country, different Native American tribes use the term blood quantum to define acceptance into the tribe, which vary from

Spirituality and Religion

The concept of religious identification is similar to race, ethnicity, and national origin. People vary not only in their specific religious membership, if they have one, but also in what they specifically believe. In other words, two Catholics may have very different views. Many people are born into a religion but do not continue their religious membership, or they do to varying degrees. Many people are not members of any organized religion, either because they are agnostic or because they are atheist.

Many people do not subscribe to a formal religion but do have a spiritual connection that serves the same benefits as a formal religion. This spiritual connection can mean many different things to different people. Whether your client identifies as spiritual, religious, or both, clients further vary on the degree to which this identification can aid them in recovery. Some people feel strongly connected and believe this connection can be a great tool in their recovery program; others feel strongly connected but believe this connection to be unhelpful. Asking a client if they are religious is not a sufficient inquiry. You must ask them to describe their spiritual beliefs (Venner & Bogenschutz, 2008).

Specifically, the four basic questions you want to ask every client are: (1) Do you have a sense of spirituality? If so, describe it. (2) Do you belong to any organized religion (if it was not clear from their first answer)? (3) Does your spirituality help you, or do you expect it to help, in your efforts to reach your goals (in the past and in the future)? If so, describe how. (4) Does your lack of spirituality act as a barrier in your efforts to reach your goals (in the past and in the future)? If so, describe how.

Age

Although age can vary between 0 and about 100, you may work at a place that narrows down the age range of your clients and the degree to which you witness age discrimination. People may be treated differently according to where they are on the spectrum of life. Stereotypical examples include treating an adolescent as foolish and immature, or treating a senior citizen as archaic and inflexible. There are many adolescents and older adults who would fit those descriptions, but there are many in these age groups who would not; thus assuming these roles is unfair.

Age can have an impact on how we perceive the world and what our goals might be. Age can determine how people perceive the clients and how the client perceives him or herself. For example, an 18 year old, a 48 year old, and an 80 year old may have different motivations to complete treatment. An 18 year old may want to please his or her parents, a 48 year old may want to keep his job, and an 80 year old may want to die sober. It is also possible that the same motivations can apply to different ages. Assuming the 80-year-old client has the goal to die sober is a subtle way we can make errors of commission.

Three questions to ask every client: (1) Have you ever been treated a specific way based on your age? If so, describe it and how you felt about it. (2) Does your age help you, or do you expect it to help, in your efforts to reach your goals (in the past and in the future)? If so, describe how. (3) Does your age

act as a barrier in your efforts to reach your goals (in the past and in the future)? If so, describe how.

Gender Identity and Expression

Gender is a characteristic that has evolved to include male, female, transgender, or transsexual (or intersex). I assume the options of male and female are obvious to you, reader. "Transgender" refers to a person who was born one gender, but identifies with the other gender. People vary in how they express this identification: some may wear clothes congruent with their perceived gender, or adopt mannerisms, or surgically change their anatomy to better reflect the gender with which they identify. Transsexuals refer to people who are born with characteristics of both genders. Formerly referred to as hermaphrodites, and often referred to as intersex, transsexuals typically choose with which gender they would like to identify, but some clients may have not been able to make a choice, or some may opt not to decide. In some cases, the parents of the child decide at birth which gender the child should adopt, and surgically alter the child to only develop as one gender. Some clients feel their parents chose the wrong gender, and may identify more with the gender that was altered at birth.

Gender is a common influence in both addiction and recovery for some. Others will feel it has no effect. Clinicians must watch their own perceptions of gender to avoid making errors. For example, some clinicians will focus on issues related to children with their female clients only, neglecting the reality that many male clients are also interested in child issues.

A good way to get at the role gender plays in your client's life, as well as a way to keep your own gender biases in check, is to ask the client five questions: (1) With which gender do you most identify? (2) How has gender been addressed in your family growing up and/or now? Were there any stereotypes or gender specific expectations that you felt? What was/is your reaction to those expectations? (3) What role, if any, has gender played in the situation that brought you to my office today? (4) Does your gender help you, or do you expect it to help, in your efforts to reach your goals (in the past and in the future)? If so, describe how. (5) Does your gender act as a barrier in your efforts to reach your goals (in the past and in the future)? If so, describe how.

Sexual Orientation

There are three generally accepted types of orientation: heterosexual, homosexual, and bisexual. "Heterosexual" refers to those who are attracted to members of the opposite gender, "homosexual" refers to those attracted to members of their own gender, and "bisexual" refers to those who are attracted to more than one gender. Your clients may strongly identify or may be questioning, unsure as yet with which sexual orientation to identify. It is important to note that someone can inwardly identify with one orientation, but outwardly act in a different orientation. For example, Jerry could be married to a woman but actually be attracted to other men and would identify as a homosexual. Thus, one cannot assume a person's sexual orientation without directly asking him or her.

A person's orientation, how accepting and comfortable he or she is, and how accepting and supportive the client's family and friends can be vital pieces to understanding a client's addiction development and can be suggestive in how to treat it. Clinicians can create errors of commission based on personal views of sexual orientation, which continues to be a hot topic today in our society. Where you personally fall may clash with your client's views. You will need to put aside your personal opinions. Your job is no place to educate a client on your views.

A good way to get at the role sexual orientation plays in your client's life, as well as a way to keep your own biases in check, is to ask the client four questions: (1) With which sexual orientation do you most identify? (2) What role, if any, has your sexual orientation played in the situation that brought you to my office today? (3) Does your sexual orientation help you, or do you expect it to help, in your efforts to reach your goals (in the past and in the future)? If so, describe how. (4) Does your sexual orientation act as a barrier in your efforts to reach your goals (in the past and in the future)? If so, describe how.

Disabilities

The term "disabilities" is vast and encompasses many people. Types of disabilities range from mild learning disabilities to severe developmental disabilities and everything in between. The ways people discriminate against persons with disabilities is equally varied, from failing to recognize that a disability is present to neglecting to make a program accessible. Learning disabilities are tough because they can easily go unrecognized, or be mistakenly diagnosed as something else, and therefore left untreated. We know more now about these types of disabilities than we used to, but it remains more obscure on the surface than other, more obvious conditions, and therefore discrimination can often come by errors of omission, in the form of neglect or failure to recognize. For example, a client may come to abuse substances because it helps them cope with symptoms of disabilities that are otherwise unrecognized.

Five questions to ask the client: (1) Have you ever been told you have a disability, or do you believe you have a disability? If so, describe your disability. (2) How has your disability been addressed in your family growing up and/or now? With your peers as a child and as an adult? (3) What role, if any, has your disability played in the situation that brought you to my office today? (4) Does your disability help you, or do you expect it to help, in your efforts to reach your goals (in the past and in the future)? If so, describe how. (5) Does your disability act as a barrier in your efforts to reach your goals (in the past and in the future)? If so, describe how.

Economic Condition

Economic condition refers to the status of a person's economy, or his or her wealth and resources. This includes finances, employment status, dwelling, access to nutrition, transportation, and insurance. This may seem an irrelevant form of discrimination, but people are often discriminated against based on their socioeconomic status. Assessing one's economic condition is a bit trickier than assessing the other demographics we have discussed because so many different factors make up the economic condition and to ask may seem impolite or irrelevant. This discomfort can easily lead to errors of omission.

Awareness of socioeconomic differences is an important aspect of working with diversity (Pope & Vasquez, 2007). A good way to ask the client about his or her economic condition is to ask five questions: (1) How would you describe your economic condition growing up, meaning your wealth and resources (finances, employment, dwelling, nutrition, transportation, insurance, childcare)? What was the experience like for you? (2) How would you describe your economic condition now, including how you feel about what you describe? (3) What role, if any, has your economic condition played in the situation that brought you to my office today? (4) Does your economic condition help you, or do you expect it to help, in your efforts to reach your goals (in the past and in the future)? If so, describe how. (5) Does your economic condition act as a barrier in your efforts to reach your goals (in the past and in the future)? If so, describe how. The fourth question is important because it can help clients begin to feel grateful for what they have, a vital part of any recovery program and very effective in fighting the "poor me" attitude that often is a part of addiction. The fifth question is helpful because it will give you a list of barriers you will need to address with your clients to ensure they meet their treatment needs.

Drug and Method of Choice

What? Drug of choice is not a discrimination category, you say? Au contraire! Surprisingly, discriminating against someone's drug of choice is a blunder that even substance abuse counselors make. Drug of choice refers to the specific drug that, if given a choice of all drugs, is the drug a client would choose to use. Some call it a favorite drug, others call it the drug that the client struggles with the most, still others refer to it as the drug that is the hardest to quit. It is usually the drug that your client will identify when they are asked what they are needing treatment to address, although some may hide it and present another drug in its place.

There is a lot of stigma associated with problem drug users (Lloyd, 2012). How we discriminate is quite simple; it works like this: Say you have a cocaine addict walk through your door. What are you going to assume about his cocaine experience? Would you expect that he used cocaine to gain energy? Would you expect stories of feeling ultra-productive, of staying up for hours on end, of neglecting to eat or drink? If you expect these things, you will be correct much of the time, as cocaine is a stimulant that typically gives those outcomes. However, not every cocaine user has that experience. Many cocaine users have a paradoxical experience, cocaine slows or calms them down and focuses them. Let's say you have a heroin addict walk through your door. What are you going to assume about her heroin experience? Would you expect that she uses heroin to numb her pain? Would you expect stories of nodding out or sleeping much of the time, of slowing down and letting the days pass without much productivity? Again, you will be correct much of the time, as heroin is an opiate that typically gives those outcomes. However, not every heroin user has that experience. Many heroin users also have a paradoxical experience; heroin gives them energy and productivity, allowing them to focus on completing necessary tasks. We can also assume experience of drug use, such as heroin use by criminals and cocaine use by the wealthy.

A good way to get at this dynamic in your client's life is to ask the client four questions: (1) Which drug do you identify as your drug of choice? (2) What is your experience when you use the drug: What benefits do you enjoy; what side effects or outcomes annoy you? (3) Does your drug of choice help you, or do you expect it to help, in your efforts to reach your goals (in the past and in the future)? If so, describe how. (4) Does your drug of choice act as a barrier in your efforts to reach your goals (in the past and in the future)? If so, describe how. For example, an alcoholic who has to pass three bars between his train stop and his home.

Diagnosis

A diagnosis is a label that is given to a client by one who is trained and licensed, which indicates the illnesses and chronic conditions that clients have or with which they struggle. Each label denotes a collection of signs and symptoms that make up each illness or condition. All current psychiatric diagnoses, including the addictions, are listed in the *Diagnostic Statistical Manual* (*DSM*).

Historically, addiction diagnoses were teased out of the other psychiatric diagnoses and treated separately (Whitter et al., 2006). Technically, a Substance Abuse Disorder *is* a psychiatric disorder, even though it continues to be treated as a separate condition, and few are diagnosed with only a Substance Disorder these days. Most are labeled dually diagnosed, and treatment efforts are significantly enhanced when addiction counselors include the psychiatric and medical diagnoses and necessary medical treatment in the clients' clinical picture. We cannot treat their medical diagnosis, but we can ensure they have a physician who is able to treat them, and we can discuss their care with that doctor to ensure the best treatment of the client.

Dually diagnosed clients should be an "expectation instead of an exception" (Cline & Minkoff, 2008, p. 55). In reality, most of our clients are triple-diagnosed with an addiction, another psychiatric illness, and a medical disorder (Katzman & Geppert, 2008). They are often not viewed as a priority for care, and are described as misfits to the system, often as if they have "dared to have more than one disorder" (Cline & Minkoff, 2008, p. 57). With programs that are poorly equipped to help the dually diagnosed, this population often suffers poor

outcomes with an increased risk of death (Cline & Minkoff, 2008). Clinicians must anticipate this will be the reality and work hard to accommodate their needs. Stigma against the mentally ill, including discrimination and prejudice is an unfortunate reality for many clients. Clinicians are susceptible to the same errors of commission. We are also at risk of committing errors of omission. One simple way we do this is to assume the diagnoses the client has been given are accurate and supported by the client. Or if not supported by the client we assume they are wrong. Don't assume, ask questions. The first step is assessing the client's diagnoses and the effects they are experiencing. Five questions to ask to assess the effect of diagnosis on your client's life include: (1) What, if any, diagnoses have you been given in your lifetime? With which of those do you agree and disagree? (2) How has your diagnosis(es) been addressed in your family growing up and/or now? What was/is your reaction? (3) What role, if any, has your diagnosis(es) played in the situation that brought you to my office today? (4) Does your diagnosis(es) help you, or do you expect it to help, in your efforts to reach your goals (in the past and in the future)? If so, describe how. (5) Does your diagnosis(es) act as a barrier in your efforts to reach your goals (in the past and in the future)? If so, describe how.

Now that we have a good idea of the different groups that are discriminated against, let's consider how we specifically discriminate in our practices. There are several ways we can discriminate against our clients, some more overt than others, among them access to treatment, judging, forwarding the stereotype, assumptions, language, and humor.

Access to Treatment

Withholding or changing access to treatment services for certain people based on a specific characteristic or membership in a group is an example of professional discrimination. People may not have equal access due to their beliefs (Venner & Bogenschutz, 2008). We have mentioned that the pillar of justice requires us to give equal treatment across a group. This includes the ability to access that treatment. For example, access to treatment is a common way that people with varying economic conditions experience discrimination. People are unable to access needed treatment either due to a lack of funds or a lack of good insurance based on their income level. Access to resources can be another form of discrimination: for example, if a client cannot utilize the resource because of a lack of transportation or a lack of child care.

The second step is to ensure that clients have the best treatment that fits their needs. There is no single best practice for those dually diagnosed; often we try to bend the patient to fit the program, or we bend the program to fit the client (Cline & Minkoff, 2008). The most important aspect of our treatment planning is that we ensure beneficence by treating the dually diagnosed as desirable clients (Cline & Minkoff, 2008).

Judging

Judging someone, or an aspect of someone, because of a characteristic is another example of how we discriminate. People can judge in blatant or subtle ways. We can judge a person based on the psychiatric label with which they arrive. It is acceptable to be frustrated with someone's symptoms—the client most certainly is at times—but it is not ethically fair to judge clients as frustrating because of their illness.

One tactic that can be beneficial and combat discrimination is to encourage clients to separate themselves from the label of their mental health diagnosis. A person is not a diagnosis, a person is a person *with* a diagnosis, meaning that he or she is a person first who happens to also have these extra symptoms that are impairing. Regardless of what is written on paper, you can diagnose him or her in a few seconds, stating:

Instead of focusing on your given diagnosis, let me say truthfully that you have the disorder of [client's name]. You are a cluster of symptoms that are causing you trouble, and the diagnosis is the best label we can come up with that matches

those symptoms. But not everyone has symptoms that are perfectly, concretely in one category. Many have symptoms that fit into more than one category, so I want you to think less about what diagnosis has been assigned to you, and more about the symptoms themselves, as that is what we are going to be focusing on in treatment.

As clinicians, we also need to see each client as Sally with her symptoms, rather than Borderline Sally. If we can separate the two, we have a better chance of treating Sally as Sally, and her symptoms as her symptoms, without mashing them together. It will also help us not have visceral reactions whenever we see a client who has been challenging in the past. If we focus our frustrations on the symptoms and not the person, we should be more amiable when we see him or her, which allows us to give better treatment and to better protect the client.

Forwarding the Stereotype

Forwarding the stereotype occurs when you buy in to an existing stereotype and treat a client as if it is true. For example, there is a hierarchy of drug use that most users adopt as they develop their addiction. It goes something like this: "Well, I may use pot or alcohol, but at least I'm not messing with pills. Serious addicts use those." Until the user begins to use pills; then it is "Well, I may use pills, but at least I don't use meth. Seriously messed up people use meth." But then the user finds meth is not too shabby, so then he or she may say, "Yeah I dabble in meth, but at least it's not snorting cocaine or smoking crack. Those people are wack." And then you hear, "Yeah, stimulants are my thing, but it's not that bad, could be worse. I could be doing heroin. That stuff makes you a serious addict and there is no turning back." And last but not least, most people hold out for IV use, saying "At least I'm not shooting my drugs. Those people are all sorts of messed up."

This same hierarchy can be used by clinicians without realization. We may see pure alcoholics (if we can even find them anymore) as lower maintenance, lower severity, fewer issues, not as hardcore, and more likely to adhere to treatment and succeed in recovery. Those of you who have worked with alcoholics, is any of this true? No, alcoholics have the same pitfalls, challenges, and success rates as any other drug user. Drug addicts lie, steal, cheat, manipulate to get their drugs. Well, wait, so do alcoholics! So do nicotine addicts! Just because the drug itself is legal does not mean the associated behavior is legal or less severe. We certainly don't help by separating out alcohol from the other drugs we treat, as we do in the very title of our credential. Treating clients addicted to heroin as more "hardcore" or sicker than clients addicted to alcohol is forwarding a stereotype.

The best thing to do is challenge it. Sometimes we have to challenge discrimination clients have in themselves. For example, Ashley is the only girl in a family with six children. Having five brothers influenced her life in that she adopted a "tomboy" attitude and avoided "girly" things when she was growing up. Sadly, all of the children developed addictions and other illnesses in young adulthood. Yet while Ashley's parents give their sons unending support in their treatment efforts, viewing their addictions as illnesses they could not control, they judge Ashley for her addiction, viewing it as a moral character flaw. Although they see the need for their sons to obtain treatment, they believe Ashley simply needs to "grow up and snap out of it." As a clinician charged with treating Ashley, challenging the damaging views she has weathered will be vital to her treatment success.

Another example is the attitude toward Alcoholics Anonymous (AA) versus Narcotics Anonymous (NA) meetings. AA is thought to be filled with more serious recovery and NA is seen as filled with more drama. This could be true, depending on what the meetings are like where you live, but this is not always true. Sometimes the opposite is true. As a clinician, you will not only need to educate clients, particularly in the group setting, about this faulty discrimination, you will also need to check yourself to make sure you are not making the same assumptions and teaching a client that more serious recovery can be found in AA meetings and more drama in NA meetings.

Assumptions

When we make assumptions about our clients, we are automatically at risk of making blunders and of discriminating against them even if our intentions are positive. For example, those who are dually diagnosed are often assumed, even by clinicians, to be med seeking (Venner & Bogenschutz, 2008). Clients with a criminal past are assumed to be more severe, tricky, and slippery (Venner & Bogenschutz, 2008). When a client exhibits denial of a problem, we can judge them as noncompliant, forgetting that denial is a fundamental aspect of addiction (Powell & Brodsky, 2004).

A subtle way we can discriminate is by lumping all people together and denying the importance of their differences. For example, Mary is a devout Catholic who believes God is telling her not to use drugs ever again. She also believes He is telling her that all she needs to do is trust in Him and He will remove all her compulsions to use. She is denying any need for formal treatment or self-help, believing instead that attending church services is all she needs to obtain and maintain recovery. Clive is an atheist who bristles at the concept of using religion in the treatment of his addiction. He is staunchly against 12-step programs, the attendance of which is a required component of the treatment program he is attending. Both Mary and Clive are influenced by their religious beliefs and are using their beliefs to inform how they pursue the treatment they need to address their addictions. Can you see how unsuccessful treatment could be in both cases if the clinician did not learn these important client perspectives? If you do not address these viewpoints, and help clients navigate through their restrictions, they will not get the treatment they need. Simply stating the program is not religious, but is spiritual, will not address their needs.

People may use legal and illegal substances as a social lubricant in social settings. This may occur even more often if people are engaging in social situations that access their sexual orientation. Many people use alcohol and drugs simply to make a good time even better. And then many people have no correlation with alcohol, drugs, and their sexual orientation. Remember not to assume the nature of the correlation or that there is a correlation at all. The only way to avoid making erroneous assumptions is to ask your client. Anytime we assume to believe how our clients' addictions work for them, particularly how they intersect with an aspect of their demographics, we are violating the principle of cultural diversity.

We run the risk of missing vital information if we assume and neglect to ask the simple questions: What did the drug do for you? What was your experience like, what did you like and dislike about using? These are the questions that are going to guide your treatment plans because whatever benefits they received from using are going to be the benefits you have to find in other, healthier avenues. If we assume an ecstasy user wants the stereotypical social benefits of the drug, we are going to focus on finding other ways to enhance the client's social life without the drug. But what if we are wrong? What if the client's social life is just fine, but he or she uses the ecstasy to help in a crumbling marriage? Helping a client's social life without assessing the marital distress is going to leave this client with the probability of relapse since we are not giving focus to his or her needs. Ask the questions. You also may get clues about other treatment modalities that are indicated by how they respond to these questions. For example, if you have that cocaine addict who is telling you that cocaine calms him down and allows him to focus and complete tasks, you may want to refer the client to someone who can evaluate him for a type of attention deficit, as there is a correlation suggested in the research between children with ADD or ADHD who later become stimulant addicts (Jaffe et al., 2005). If that is true with your client, you will have to address other ways of coping with those symptoms in order for long-term recovery to be successful.

Language

In addition to making assumptions, the language we use with clients can also reveal judgments based on demographics. The language we use can be subtle and seemingly innocent, but it can also be damaging and unethical. Be careful with the vocabulary you use, the tone of your voice, and the nonverbal language you communicate when asking a client to describe his or her disability. If you clue in the client to your feelings or assumptions you can be quite offensive to your clients, even if unintentionally. Use a neutral tone and ask them to talk a bit about their experiences and how their cultures have affected their life, both enhancing it and challenging it.

For example, Ronald is a competent clinician, and clients seem to benefit from his counseling overall, but he consistently uses language that his co-workers find troubling. Specifically, he speaks with an informal, stereotypically slang speech to clients he perceives have a similar ethnic background to his own. If he walks by a client whom he perceives has a different ethnic background, he calls out "Hello" cheerfully, but if he walks by someone he believes to be of a similar background, he calls out "Wassuuuup!" If he has to admonish a client for breaking a rule, he uses a stern voice with a client of a perceived ethnicity other than his own and a tender voice with a client of a perceived ethnicity similar to his own. If Ronald was asked, he would probably not realize the difference in his language, and would likely believe he treats all of his clients in the same manner. Here's the tricky part. Many may appreciate his style as welcoming and bond-forming, but others may not like it. And what of the other clients who witness this friendly language, noticing it is not how they are treated? Remember the pillars of justice and nonmaleficence.

One of the ways we misuse language seems like a compliment, when really it is a judgment. Here is how it happens: Counselor John comes in to staff meeting and says, "I just met my client Judy. She comes from a wealthy upper-class background. With all her advantages, it is surprising that she ended up a meth addict in this place. Meth knows no boundaries." Now, while this last statement is true, drugs do affect people of all classes, he just judged Judy in the process, stating that because she is wealthy she never should have turned to drugs, as if wealth and advantage should have steered her away from this life. Why would it? Similarly, John is making a judgment if he comes into the meeting and says, "I just met my client Judy. She is from poor crime-infested projects. I can't believe she made it to treatment." Again, this seems like a compliment, but don't you feel the same way about all your clients? It is always a miracle when clients walk through our doors seeking help, no matter what their background. It is not easier to walk into treatment if you are wealthy. It may be easier to access treatment (i.e., pay for it), but walking through those doors for the first time is an extremely hard step no matter who you are.

Another way we discriminate is to joke with people about their characteristics without establishing a rapport that allows for such joking. This is a fast way to laugh *at* someone, not *with* someone, and it makes all the difference. How many times have you sat in a group of clinicians and one says "Oh that Jane is *so* borderline," or "I can't deal with Bipolar Paul today, can someone else talk to him?" Symptoms of various illnesses can be particularly challenging to us, especially on those days when we are not at the top of our game. We need to blow off steam and humor can be a great way to relieve stress. But humor at a client's expense is unethical. The language we use and the attitude we allow toward our clients is of utmost ethical importance.

We discriminate against someone when we fail to accept them, or when we have a visible reaction when learning about him or her. As a clinician, you must train yourself to keep your personal views hidden from view when you are at work with clients. If you know this is an issue for you, do not feel badly. We all have different ways our personal views can

snag us at the workplace. But it is your responsibility to walk into your supervisor's office, sit down, and discuss how to address the issue at the workplace, perhaps role modeling so that you can ensure that your reactions are nondiscriminatory.

How you ask questions of your clients makes a difference. For example, Bob, a client in his seventies, was quite upset about his experience the previous day with the intake coordinator on duty. The counselor, on learning his age, said, "Bob, tell me why you are here for treatment. You are so much closer to the end of your life … why don't you just enjoy it?" Bob took this to mean "Why don't you keep drinking since you have so little time left?" This may scream "offensive" to you, but when the intake coordinator was approached, she was surprised that anyone would be ruffled. She said, "I didn't mean to offend him at all, I was just trying to understand why he was electing to start treatment now. I was trying to be affirming of his circumstances, and not to assume anything about him, but to ask questions instead." Her intentions were quite right, in that we teach clinicians to meet the client where they are, and to ask many questions to understand their specific circumstances. Her mistake was in asking a closed question; a better way to ask the same thing would be: "Tell me why you chose to come to treatment now." And either then or at a different time in the interview, "Do you expect your age to have a positive or negative (or both) impact on your recovery efforts, or has it already? If so, tell me more." This is an open-ended question, and truly allows exploration from the client on all sides of the possible issue, while also allowing him to say that it has no impact at all. It is better because it doesn't assume there is an impact. Let's take a look at some examples.

VIGNETTE: SINGLING OUT

Taylor, a client in her early twenties, was sitting in an early recovery group, which was largely skewed to an older (midlife) crowd. There were two other clients in their twenties in the room, and about 13 clients older than 40 years. Taylor was

(continued)

there for opiate pill use, and the counselor asked whether she had ever used heroin. Taylor replied that she had never touched heroin, nor had any interest in using it. The counselor then rattled off several statistics she had read in a newspaper about the percentage of young adults and teens who were using heroin these days, and implied that there was a good chance she would use it before committing to recovery for the rest of her life. The other adults in the group nodded their heads, one saying, "Yeah, you still got time to hit bottom." The client was so mad she left group, and expressed a desire to leave group treatment altogether. When the clinician was told the client was upset and wanted to leave, her reply was "Yes, she is a young, heated thing, headstrong, hard to educate. I'm not surprised she wants to quit when the heat turns toward her." The clinician saw nothing wrong with her own behavior. When pressed, she stated that she often uses clients in group as examples in what she called "teaching moments."

The clinician is not entirely incorrect: Groups are often filled with teaching moments that come from an interaction with a specific participant. But few people enjoy having statistics spewed at them, especially when loaded with assumptions. It turns out that this particular client, Taylor, felt strongly about not using heroin specifically because her brother had overdosed using it, a fact that the clinician would have known if she had merely *asked* the client why she had no interest in heroin, rather than retorting with the number of youth using the drug as evidence that she would walk the same path. The statistic may be well bolstered in the general public, but that certainly does not prove that the client sitting in front of you will fall into the same fate. Statistics can be used in education, but are better used if you explain the statistic and then ask participants to comment with reactions to the statistic. You are likely to get better results when you allow them a voice. Even if your assumptions prove to be correct, it is better to allow the client to apply the principle, or statistic, to his or her own life.

The other factor in this example is the necessity of scanning your group for the daily demographic before starting in on anything that can single out a few members. If the clinician had realized that the group was skewed toward older adults, one would hope she would have been more sensitive to calling out youth as an issue knowing how it would isolate a few members against the rest. The fact that there was nodding and comments related to age should have given her a clue. She could have covered herself by throwing in a statistic about another age group so that the discussion became more about age in general and not solely teens and young adults, which would have evened the playing field and diversified the topic. If your group has one male and 13 females it would not be a good day to introduce the topic of relating to the opposite gender. If 13 people are talking about men and there is only one man in the room, he is going to feel isolated and perhaps attacked simply by the demographic. You would be better served by waiting until you have a more even gender demographic in the group to bring up that topic.

VIGNETTE: OBSERVING
UNFAIR ASSUMPTIONS

Charlotte attends addiction treatment at an outpatient clinic in a city. She attends AA in a neighboring affluent town, close to where she lives. The meeting has excellent recovery and attendees show a strong commitment to helping each other "work the steps." Lincoln is also in her treatment program and lives in the city, in the poorest section. John, the group counselor, overhears Lincoln asking Charlotte about these AA meetings she talks about, and whether he could attend with her sometime. Because the meetings are outside of the city, and Lincoln cannot afford his own transportation, he is at the mercy of Charlotte and others to give him rides, which unsurprisingly causes him to miss out on many meetings and other opportunities, like employment, outside of the city. John notices Charlotte winces slightly when Lincoln asks her, and hears her tell him, "Oh no, Lincoln, I don't think you would like the meetings. The people are really different there. I'm worried you wouldn't fit in." Discouraged and embarrassed, Lincoln slinks away. Charlotte watches him walk away for a moment, and then turns to another group member and asks if he wants to carpool to the meeting.

John suspects Charlotte is less concerned about Lincoln and more worried about herself and how it would look to members of the meeting if she brought him. John knows that Charlotte and Lincoln come from very different backgrounds and socioeconomic statuses. John is not sure if this is the issue, but it appears suspicious. It would be beneficial to both clients if John can help Charlotte see how she is making assumptions about Lincoln and discriminating against his economic condition. John approaches Charlotte and asks why she is not willing to take Lincoln to the meeting. At first, she tries to give other excuses, but John gently refutes each excuse, telling her he saw the interaction occur and what she said to Lincoln. Charlotte then admits that she does not want to bring him to the meeting, that she feels people will make negative assumptions about her and did not know how to tell him that. With this honesty, John has an opportunity to discuss the idea of treating Lincoln differently because of his background and question whether Charlotte is motivated by her own fears. Charlotte may not change her behavior, as it is entirely her choice to act as she sees fit. The point here is not to change the behavior, but that John makes an attempt, that he does not sit idly by after witnessing discrimination in his clients without attempting to educate them. Many clinicians would turn a blind eye, not wanting to address it, but the ethical action is to work through discomfort in order to honor the principle.

Can you see how you will fail this principle at some point in your practice, and most likely numerous times, often without your awareness? Now that we understand who we are at the risk of discriminating against and how we are at risk of doing it, what can we do in our practice to ensure we act ethically? We want to do all in our power to avoid discriminating against our clients, seeking supervision and counsel every chance we get to ensure our ethical practice. We also must include culture not only in our intake assessment, but in treatment planning as well (Venner & Bogenschutz, 2008). How else can we ensure nondiscrimination? Let's look to the four pillars as a guide.

The pillar of justice suggests that we treat all clients the same. This does not mean that we treat all clients as part of one culture and make assumptions about them based on what we learn of that culture. Hopefully by now it is clear that is not the ethical way to treat your client's cultural background. Instead, you want to treat all cultures, including ones that are personally similar to yours, with the same degree of curiosity and discover the cultural impact within each client. The pillar of autonomy allows for clients to teach us about how culture works for them. Use a neutral tone and ask them to talk a bit about their cultures and how culture impacts them. It will both benefit the clients and decrease our risk of discriminating against them. The pillar of beneficence has us take care to plan, promote, and practice an accepting attitude that keeps the focus on providing good, ethical health services. This focus helps us refrain from cultural discrimination. Finally, the pillar of nonmaleficence helps us avoid directly causing harm. Be mindful of the interactions you have with clients to ensure you are not subtly harming your clients.

While it should be the absolute aim to refrain from discriminating against clients and colleagues based on their characteristics, it is impossible to avoid completely based on the simple fact that we each have scripts in our head that dictate both how we perceive people (which leads to prejudice) and how we react to people (which leads to discrimination). These scripts can come from both personal and professional influences, both of which can lead us down a dark path to an ethical dilemma. Before we examine that, there is one more important principle that guides us to protect the client: Building a healthy relationship is a critical piece of your ethical practice.

Principle: The Counseling Relationship

5

Chapter

The importance of the relationship between the client and the clinician has been studied since Sigmund Freud wrote about the topic (Feller & Cottone, 2012; Safran & Muran, 2000). The therapeutic relationship has been consistently connected to successful treatment outcomes (Feller & Cottone, 2012; Manuel & Forcehimes, 2008; Martin, Garske, & Davis, 2000; Safran & Muran, 2000; Whitter et al., 2006), and the presence of empathy has been noted as a vital component (Feller & Cottone, 2012; Manuel & Forcehimes, 2008). In fact, research has shown the quality of this alliance is a better predictor of treatment success than is the type of treatment intervention (Martin et al., 2000; Wolff & Hayes, 2009). Furthermore, if a successful alliance is developed at the start of treatment, the patient is more likely to view the counseling relationship as therapeutic regardless of the treatment interventions, and will view the relationship as positive at termination, thus suggesting that establishing this rapport in the beginning of treatment is recommended (Martin et al., 2000). Since your ethical practice demands a healthy counseling relationship, a positive therapeutic alliance is both a clinical and an ethical requirement.

The therapeutic relationship or alliance has three distinct components. "Tasks" of therapy are the specific activities that are required of the client in order to benefit from treatment. The "goals" of therapy are the objectives that the treatment contains. The "bond" of therapy refers to the degree to which the client feels valued and understood by the clinicians. These three aspects of the therapeutic alliance influence each other and change over time (Martin et al., 2000; Safran & Muran, 2000). To achieve a healthy therapeutic alliance, the counseling relationship must have an empathetic bond (Feller & Cottone, 2012; Martin et al., 2000; Rogers, 1957; Safran & Muran, 2000), must be surrounded by healthy boundaries (Manuel & Forcehimes, 2008; Martin et al., 2000; Scott, 2000; St. Germaine, 1996), and must address dual relationships.

Empathy

Rogers (1957) believed that a successful therapeutic alliance requires both the client, who is vulnerable, anxious, and in a state of incongruence, and the clinician, who is congruent and integrated in the relationship, to work together in a relationship that effectively communicates unconditional positive regard, empathy, and understanding of the client (Feller & Cottone, 2012).

Unconditional positive regard refers to the therapist's ability to warmly accept every aspect of the client's experience as valid and without condition, giving permission for any feelings the client experiences (Rogers, 1957). Empathy refers to a clinician's ability to feel what the client is experiencing, while maintaining enough distance to prevent confusion of roles (Rogers, 1957). If these conditions are all present, the client will be able to effect the change he or she is seeking; if any one or more of these conditions is not present, the therapeutic change will fail (Rogers, 1957).

Originally a concept steeped in psychoanalytic theory, empathy and the therapeutic relationship have found footing across psychological disciplines (Feller & Cottone, 2012; Manuel & Forcehimes, 2008; Martin et al., 2000). Establishing a positive therapeutic alliance can be challenging, and empathy, while necessary to a successful counseling relationship, can be a confusing construct, difficult to define and to measure (Feller & Cottone, 2012). The four pillars give us a guide. In accordance with justice and autonomy, a clinician must encourage the client's self-sufficiency by building self-esteem and fostering a collaborative relationship, viewing the client and clinician as equals. In accordance with beneficence, a clinician must protect the integrity of the therapeutic alliance and deliver the most beneficial practices with a warm, engaging, genuine attitude. In accordance with nonmaleficence, a clinician must prevent harmful relationship development by anticipating, monitoring, and responding to ethical dilemmas that occur in the relationship (Manuel & Forcehimes, 2008), and by ensuring that the length of care is appropriate.

In addition to empathy, a healthy and effective therapeutic alliance depends on your ability to form and maintain boundaries between you and your client that protect the client (and you, the agency, and the profession).

Boundaries

"Ethical issues related to professional boundaries are the most problematic and challenging" (Reamer, 2001, p. 1). It is vital to a successful clinical relationship that a clinician develop and maintain firmly therapeutic boundaries between him- or herself and the client caseload (Manuel & Forcehimes, 2008; Martin et al., 2000; Scott, 2000; St. Germaine, 1996). Boundaries have been a confusing element of treatment since Freud, who used to regularly dine with patients, accepted gifts from them, and treated his own daughter (Reamer, 2012). Freud is not alone; many of the great thinkers and writers in the helping professions have instructed professionals to develop firm boundaries with those we treat, but actively ignored their own advice (Reamer, 2012). Boundaries are often damaged by substance abuse, and addicted families often weather boundary violations (St. Germaine, 1996); thus it becomes even more critical for clinicians to model effective boundary setting. Boundaries can be small, such as starting sessions on time or establishing how to reach a clinician after hours, or large, such as inappropriate touching (Manuel & Forcehimes, 2008).

Boundaries can be vague and can have mixed messages (Reamer, 2001). Clinicians bear the responsibility of setting appropriate boundaries and actively maintaining them. They are also responsible for communicating these boundaries to their clients (Taleff, 2010). Keep in mind that some of your clients may not have experience with healthy boundaries and you can't assume they will intuitively understand and maintain them. You will have to communicate boundaries with some clients, and you may have to reestablish and reject boundaries more than once. Many times this can be exhausting and frustrating. Boundaries are impaired with substance abuse, and violations are common with alcoholic and drug addicted families.

Experts have made a distinction between two types of boundary breaking: boundary crossing and boundary violations (Manuel & Forcehimes, 2008;

Reamer, 2001, 2012). Boundary crossings are innocuous, a bending rather than breaking (Reamer, 2012). A clinician's self-disclosure is thought to be an example of boundary crossing. Other examples include accepting a student's dinner invitation, hiring a student as a research assistant, or worshipping at the same religious institution (Reamer, 2001). The problem with boundary crossings is that you cannot enter clients' brains, and therefore cannot ensure that what you see as innocuous they do not see as harmful. Boundary violations are exploitative, deceptive, coercive, manipulative, and fraudulent (Reamer, 2012). Potential snags with boundaries include dual relationships, personal gain, transference, and termination. Examples would be having sex with clients, fraudulent billing, or coercing the client to name the clinician in their will (Reamer, 2001). To further confuse the issue, some boundaries appear improper to observers, but are quite acceptable to the client and clinician involved.

While it may seem as if boundary setting should be a reasonable task, it can be quite a challenge for clinicians. Pope and Vasquez (2007) suggest several reasons why clinicians can struggle with the task. First, boundary dilemmas can catch us off guard. When we are surprised, we may not act at our professional best. Second, boundary crossings can tap into our needs and desires, which can lead to unhealthy boundary management. Third, the need for boundary clarity can be taken as a need for inflexibility. Fourth, decisions about boundaries can evoke anxiety and fear. Finally, there is little guidance about boundary crossing in the education and training clinicians receive. If we don't set and maintain firm boundaries we can become confused and conflicted about our conduct with clients, which can result in dual relationships.

Dual Relationships

A dual relationship signifies two different types of relationships between counselor and client, and has been shown to be detrimental to client welfare (Reamer, 2012; St. Germaine, 1996). Dual relationships form when you counsel someone with whom another relationship is already established, or when you create another role with one whom you are already counseling. In addition to harming client welfare, dual relationships are harmful in that they "jeopardize a clinician's judgement" (St. Germaine, 1996, p. 29). Some dual relationships can be avoided, others are inevitable and require ethical coping skills to prevent harm (Reamer, 2012). Dual relationships that exploit the client or affect the counselor's judgment are proscribed as harmful (St. Germaine, 1996). Others are harmless to the therapeutic process (Reamer, 2012). Some dual relationships can be confusing yet have aspects that are reasonable (Reamer, 2001, 2012). The crux of this issue is understanding which types of dual relationships are harmful and learning how to avoid them.

Even if the dual relationship is positive, it can still have an ill effect on the client and his or her recovery. It can divert a client's focus and can lead a client into complacency or avoidance of the other tools the client should be using (Reamer, 2001). Clients may grow so attached that they abandon other vital aspects of their recovery program, such as self-help attendance or social networking, and may subsequently rely too heavily on the dual relationship with the counselor as their main tool. If the relationship does not go well, there is a relapse risk; if the relationship goes well, there is a relapse risk. It is a no-win situation for the client.

Most addiction counselors are aware of dual relationships as unethical, yet most counselors do report encountering clients outside of treatment on a regular basis (St. Germaine, 1996). Counselors can meet clients anywhere in the community, especially in smaller towns with fewer people (Pope & Vasquez, 2007). At times, dual relationships cannot be avoided (Reamer, 2001, 2012). You may find yourself treating a client who is the only mechanic in town, for example. You may begin dating someone you meet in the community, only to later discover he or she is the parent of one of your clients (Reamer, 2001). The stickier situations involve those dual relationships that you may be able to avoid, but with a cost to either you or the client. In these situations, each of the four ethical pillars is called into question. For example, what is your best response to your agency hiring one of your former clients, thrusting you from a counselor-client dynamic to one of colleagues? This dual relationship occurs often in the addiction profession (Gallagher, 2010) and is a common topic in ethical trainings. You could take steps to avoid this dual relationship, by either finding other employment for yourself, or by suggesting to the agency that they do not hire your former client, but you may not have the power to prevent the hire and thus must learn how to manage the dual relationship. Let's consider some common dual relationships that test our boundary formation: intimacy, friendship, treatment of friends and family, and recovery conflicts.

Intimacy: The most widely discussed dual relationship is one in which a counselor engages in a sexual relationship with a client. All mental health professionals prohibit sexual relationships with clients (St. Germaine, 1996). It is the most violated ethical standard of psychologists, the second most frequent claim against licensed professional counselors, a major cause of malpractice, and the most common complaint against addiction counselors. Sex with former clients and other dual relationships are also included in the common ethical complaints against addiction counselors (St. Germaine, 1996).

Engaging in a sexual relationship with a client while in treatment is a very serious ethical misstep (Manuel & Forcehimes, 2008). It can hurt the client by confusing the emotions that are already a mess in early recovery, by impeding their healthy progress in gaining mastery over these emotions; by putting them at risk for eventual rejection, which can be both painful and a major trigger for relapse; and by affecting their ability to trust others, particularly those who seem interested in helping the client. It can also affect one's self-esteem in negative ways, which is often already in low quantities for many clients. Emotional consequences for clients are ambivalence, guilt, emptiness and isolation, sexual

confusion, impaired ability to trust, confused roles and boundaries, emotional liability, suppressed rage, increased suicidal risk, and cognitive dysfunction (Pope & Vasquez, 2007).

The counselor, too, is poorly affected by this action, as he or she runs the risk of job loss; ethical complaints and sanctions, including loss of license/credential; and career termination. If clinicians are in recovery, their own recovery program comes into jeopardy as well, and they are likely to suffer humiliation; isolation; and rejection from friends, family, and colleagues. In addition, this ethical misstep can damage the agency you work for, and the profession in which you are a member. Your misstep can cost all of us, and ding the whole profession in the process.

These behaviors are inappropriate because there is a clear power differential between counselor and client, and clinicians who engage in intimate activity—even that which is consensual—are abusing their power to obtain personal gain. While the client may appear eager, in most cases it would be difficult to turn down a counselor in pursuit without worry of the impending effect on the client and his or her treatment. In other cases the client may pursue the clinician, but in those cases it is the responsibility of the clinician to appropriately (and tenderly) reject these advances and maintain the therapeutic alliance as the primary relationship at all times.

Often the client and clinician are both guilty of crossing the boundary, but our code clearly states that the responsibility to maintain an appropriate relationship lies with the clinician. The clients have no code of ethics to dictate their behavior; it is up to us as professionals to protect the boundaries between counselor and client, even if we wish they could be different. If you are unable to do this, you must excuse yourself from giving the client care and ask your supervisor for help. There is no shame in that; it is better to admit a weakness and ask for help in strengthening it than to try to white knuckle your way through it, which may not be successful.

Training participants always act astonished that anyone would have sex with a client, yet it continues to happen every year across the country. Therefore, the concept of common sense does not apply and it is suspected that those who engage in a sexual relationship with a client feel their situation is an exception to the rule, yet with so many exceptions every year, one can quickly realize that the exceptions become the rule simply by the number of clinicians making the exception. This just can't be! Or perhaps it is better to ask, How *can* this be?

The problems that arise with this part of the principle lie within a definition of terms. First, what exactly does sexual activity entail? Certainly the act of sexual intercourse is off limits, but sexual activities typically include other intimate physical actions, such as kissing and petting. But what of harder-to-define acts of intimacy, such as hugging, or light touching, perhaps on the shoulders or back? What of a lingering look of what we call "bedroom eyes" indicating a seductive expression? Those actions may be harder to prove, but one could easily argue they are no less intimate, and therefore just as unethical. Although some cases may involve a clear attraction from the start of the relationship, many grow into one over time.

Counseling is by nature an intimate activity that requires a close relationship between counselor and client to be most effective in achieving the treatment goals. Because of this necessary close bond, clinical intimacy can be confused with sexual intimacy. Furthermore, although clinicians in other disciplines are taught not to touch and to keep a safe distance (Pope & Vasquez, 2007), touching is a normal part of addiction treatment, especially hugging (Powell & Brodsky, 2004). Clients may have cultural rules regarding touching that influence their reaction and participation (Reamer, 2001). Even if counselors are aware that sex is proscribed, appropriate behavior can be confusing in our liberally intimate environment. This confusion can lead to a blurring of boundaries. All professional Codes of Ethics consider dual relationships unethical but they vary in terms of the conditions under which these relationships can occur. Thus counselors are sometimes confused about the boundaries

and limits of their relationships with clients (St. Germaine, 1996).

Defining sexual activity can be tricky, but defining the term *client* is another conundrum at the heart of the argument (St. Germaine, 1996). When does a client cease being a client, or does a client ever cease being a client? Some say no, a client is always a client no matter how much time has passed. Others say that a client is no longer a client after a prescribed amount of time, usually 1 to 5 years. Currently, NAADAC has the only code that states counselors must not have sex with current or former clients under any circumstances (everyone else says 2 years or doesn't specify time). One of the most damaging issues here is that people don't agree within our field and across the helping professions. Specific professions, and at times individual states, disagree on the definition of a client in terms of length of time, which is confusing. Many ethical codes neglect to define a certain length of time, even if other state organizations are suggesting a specific timeline. This confusion only complicates an already complicated definition, and understandably leads many to shrug and fall back on the trusty ol' answer: "It depends." This is a classic example of the dangers of not setting a rule, and making the exception ("it depends") the new rule. Without a clear guideline the decision is left up to each clinician and the profession weakens as a whole. Dual relationships also intersect with cultural concerns, in that it may be common in certain ethnicities and religious cultures for professionals to also serve as mentors, friends, advisors, and relatives (St. Germaine, 1996).

For example, consider the story of Jerry and June. Jerry was the most respected staff member in the residential facility where he had been the senior counselor for 15 years. Clients loved his easy style; clinicians loved his respectful attitude. He loved his job, and felt great value in helping his clients reach their goals in recovery. He also worked well as a team player, and was happy to both encourage and advise his colleagues whenever he was asked. He was an even, consistent professional with a fabulous sense of humor, a joy to work with for both clients and clinicians. When June was admitted into the program, Jerry acted no differently toward her than he had to any other client. She was assigned to his caseload and they began to work together. At first, there was no indication that an attraction was present, or that he was treating her differently than his other clients.

Then one day he quit his job. The shock was felt for miles. He told his boss that another facility had made a deal he could not turn down, but it felt fishy given Jerry's loyal character. Within a week, rumors started coming to staff that Jerry and June were dating. June anticipated that she would be discharged from the program, and decided to leave. Two weeks later they were living together, and Jerry had ceased all contact with his former colleagues. Jerry's superior reported the rumors to his Ethics Board. The facility staff never quite recovered from their feelings of shock and betrayal, even after it was learned that Jerry and June broke up 8 months later, reportedly due in part to the fact that June relapsed. Was it worth it for Jerry to force his client to leave treatment early, to lose the respect of all his colleagues, to lose a job he valued in which he had worked for more than 15 years, to risk losing his credential, all for a relationship that didn't last? Perhaps Jerry would tell us it was worth it, but it seems like an awful price to pay—embarrassing, shameful, and painful, with a lot of loss.

You can't always choose whom you love, and it can often be inconvenient. But if you are going to be an ethical member of this profession, it is your duty to take every step possible to ensure that you don't end up in Jerry's position. He should have sought help the moment he felt an attraction, *before* he acted on his feelings. To do otherwise risks both the health of the clients you are serving and your own well-being, in addition to making a bad name for the agency and the profession at large. A whole lot of people are begging you to avoid this ethical dilemma and get help if you need it.

The addiction professional should never accept as clients anyone with whom they have engaged in sexual behavior. This is the inverse of the previous discussion, telling us if we have already engaged in a sexual relationship at any point in our past we cannot ethically counsel the person. Unlike the inverse no one seems to argue the timeline here. Codes seem to agree that, once intimate, a counselor can never treat that person.

Let's think about this. If once we engage in a sexual relationship with someone our relationship status is fixed so that counseling is inappropriate, why would the inverse not also be true? Why would it not be true that once we engage in a therapeutic relationship with someone our relationship status is fixed so that a sexual relationship is always inappropriate? It seems the point of this is that once a relationship is defined, once a power differential is established (whether equal as in a sexual relationship or hierarchical as in a therapeutic relationship), it cannot easily be changed and must therefore be respected even after the relationship ends. It does not say you should refrain from counseling someone with whom you are actively engaged in a sexual relationship, it dictates you may not counsel anyone with whom you have *ever* been in a sexual relationship, therefore suggesting that the relationship must be respected even if it has ended. Thus it should also be that a therapeutic relationship should stand the test of time and be regarded as unchanging, suggesting that a sexual relationship with a previous client is never acceptable.

Some ethical codes forward this restriction on sexual activities with anyone who maintains a close relationship with the client, not only family. How can a client trust and collaborate with a counselor who is engaging in a sexual relationship with a client's loved one? The idea is to forbid a relationship when there is a risk of harm or potential exploitation of the client. Wouldn't all sexual relationships with a current or former counselor carry with it a risk of exploitation or potential harm? They may not all harm or exploit, but certainly all are at *risk* of *potentially* causing exploitation or harm.

For example, if a counselor has had a random or short-lived sexual tryst with someone, it is understandable that the counselor may not be concerned about a conflict of interest in treating him or her. If the relationship was not significant, a counselor may feel that it causes no harm. Similarly, if we have a deep or long-term sexual relationship with someone, it is understandable that a counselor may want to work hard to treat someone they care deeply about, and they may not want to trust their care to someone else. Yet this is exactly why we should not be left to make all of our decisions ourselves without guidance, because we may not make the smartest, most ethical choice if we rely on our emotions and experiences. We have trusted sources to guide us, including your Code of Ethics. You want to abide by the rule: Do not treat someone with whom you have had an intimate relationship. If there is an aberrant situation that forces you to make an exception, make sure you are both self-monitoring and using supervision to ensure you maintain an ethical stance.

Friendship: You may think it is easy to refrain from a sexual relationship with a former client, so let's talk about something a bit stickier. How about friendship once your client graduates from treatment? Is it ethical to become friends with a client post-treatment? St. Germaine (1996) found that 36% of the 858 certified counselors surveyed admitted to becoming friends with a client post-treatment. The majority of those counselors (more than 50%) stated it was ethical, ranging from rarely to always, to be friends with a former client (Manuel & Forcehimes, 2008; St. Germaine, 1996).

The ethical concern is that the balance of power formed during the therapeutic relationship may be difficult to change in a friendship, which may cause distress for the client (Manuel & Forcehimes, 2008). It is important to remember that the client may not think the way you do; thus if it feels safe and ethical for you, if you are able to separate the former clinical relationship with a current friendship, you cannot assume that the client is able to do the same. What is clear for you may be confusing to the client, and you can end up violating nonmaleficence and unwittingly creating harm.

Treating friends and family: Nonsexual dual relationships are less clear (St. Germaine, 1996), but can include business and social relationships.

Examples include mechanics, hairdressers, child's school teacher, sister's best friend, son's choir director. You won't always have a choice to avoid working with people with whom you have a nonsexual dual relationship, but it can be awkward.

Another dual relationship example would be counseling family members or friends, employees, supervisees, and students (St. Germaine, 1996). Treating family and friends makes boundary setting impossible and bleeding the personal inevitable. Nevertheless, many clinicians are tempted to help those to whom they are the closest and love the most, probably wishing the best care for their loved ones, and knowing they are technically qualified to give good care. But while there is surely a reader or two out there who can give an exception, the rule for all of us must be to refer family and friends to other practitioners.

For example, Shelly is an alcoholic who is finally ready to get into treatment and start to build a recovery program for herself. She calls the best-known facility for drug treatment and makes an appointment for an intake. When she arrives, she is told that Robin will meet with her in a few minutes. Shelly sits in the waiting room, which is in full view of the administrative office and the staff walking back and forth. She sees her neighbor, Robin, come into the office and inquire if her next appointment is ready. Shelly jumps up to the patient window and asks if Robin Jones is the person she is going to be meeting with, and asks to speak with someone in charge. She lets this supervisor know that she is not comfortable working with Robin, as they are neighbors in the same social circle. After learning the intake process, Shelly decides she can complete the intake with her neighbor but does not wish to work with her individually. Robin learns of this, and comes into the room with Shelly and the supervisor. She greets Shelly warmly, welcoming her to the agency, and assures her that the fact that she is here is something Robin will hold confidential and not reveal outside of the room. She then states that she understands Shelly has agreed to complete the intake, but Robin gently suggests that another clinician might be a better choice. Robin states that coming into treatment is a big deal, and many of the questions on the intake are very personal. She doesn't want any factor to get in the way of Shelly being perfectly comfortable with the process. Shelly feels relieved and grateful, and Robin feels good knowing she made the right ethical choice.

This is one of the reasons why our ethical code suggests we strongly consider possible dual relationships in accepting clients. You have to think beyond the obvious family member, as the awkwardness and discomfort that comes from confusing dual relationships can be experienced even if both parties are not known to you, as in this example. It is better to err on the side of caution here to prevent getting trapped. It is admirable to want to help people you know, respect, and care about, but it may be better to help them by referring them to another great clinician.

Recovery Conflicts: Many counselors are in recovery and thus find themselves in a dual relationship with clients (Doukas & Cullen, 2010; Gallagher, 2010; St. Germaine, 1996). The available research has several suggestions, but no clear description of impact on counselor recovery. One study found that clinicians who were not in recovery were more concerned with the ethics of dual relationships than those clinicians who were in recovery (Hollander, Bauer, Herlihy, & McCollum, 2006). In addtion, it has been suggested that clinicians can violate boundaries by sharing personal details of their own recovery that conflict with the treatment, or by overidentifying with clients (Manuel & Forcehimes, 2008). Sexual contact may be more complicated with addiction counselors because many counselors are in recovery and attending meetings and events where clients will be (St. Germaine, 1996), causing boundary confusion. This leads to professional boundaries being compromised, especially if the counselor relapses (St. Germaine, 1996). Counselors in recovery must keep their recovery separate from that of their clients, or at least are obligated to make the effort (St. Germaine, 1996).

A common dual relationship trap exists for those clinicians in recovery who attend the same self-help meetings that their clients are encouraged to attend (Doukas & Cullen, 2010; Gallagher, 2010; Manuel & Forcehimes, 2008; Powell & Brodsky, 2004; Scott, 2000; St. Germaine, 1996). The very nature of these self-help meetings requires participants to be open and honest about their thoughts, feelings, and experiences. If participants fail to do so, they will not receive the full benefits of the program. But what of the clinicians who attend the same meetings as their clients? How are they supposed to maintain therapeutic boundaries and adhere to their counseling relationship while also opening their personal life to the clients in attendance? If they decide not to speak in self-help meetings, they prevent the clients from learning personal details, but they also have an inferior self-help experience. If they utilize the meetings for personal recovery, they may get the maximum benefit, but they change the power differential between clinician and client and create a dual relationship that has potential problems (Scott, 2000).

Clinicians may be seen as 12-step experts, which can affect their personal time in the program (Doukas & Cullen, 2010). Clinicians can be thrown into the role of rescuer, and may become tangled in a transference and countertransference web (Doukas & Cullen, 2010). Clients may use the personal information against the clinician, they may instill judgment of the effectiveness of counselors with or without addictions, or they may feel responsible to help the clinician, especially if it is learned that the clinician is struggling or has relapsed. If the clinician has relapsed, he or she may be too embarrassed or worried to attend the meetings he or she needs, especially if he or she is concerned that the client will reveal the relapse to the agency, putting the clinician's job in jeopardy (Manuel & Forcehimes, 2008). Clinicians should tell their employers about any relapse, but the point here is that they may avoid the meetings they need because they want to prevent the client from learning of their relapse. It makes for a messy situation. Those clinicians who are also in recovery may have to work harder to set and maintain appropriate boundaries with clients who are aware of the clinician's recovery status.

Certainly in some circumstances, clinicians and clients will be unable to avoid this dual relationship, such as situations in which clinicians live and work in a small community. However, it is the ethical requirement that clinicians attempt to avoid this dual relationship by keeping their own recovery efforts separate from those of their clients. The inverse is also true. Clinicians witness things the client may not wish to be heard or seen. Clients may feel they cannot speak freely, and must avoid meetings. For example, what do you do if you catch a client in a lie? Let's say Tammy has been telling staff at the agency that she has been clean and sober for 2 months; however, you see her at a bus stop drinking a bottle of vodka. Do you tell staff? Do you approach the client? Do you decide to do nothing?

With dual relationships, ethical codes cover the extremes but not the mushy middle that is often what counselors face in the day-to-day (Powell & Brodsky, 2004). Dual relationship literature has focused on exploitative relationships, such as having sex with clients, and not on other, more subtle forms of relationships (Reamer, 2012). The literature has also focused on the consequences to the client, and it is less clear how dual relationships affect the counselor (St. Germaine, 1996). In addition, the literature has failed to help clinicians address what they should do in their practice when such a relationship develops (Reamer, 2012). It would be helpful to know more of the effects and what to do when faced with a dual relationship. What if a counselor wants to end it and is unsuccessful? How does a counselor balance the client's needs with his or her own needs (St. Germaine, 1996)?

Some areas can be particularly sticky regarding the counseling relationship. They include but are not limited to working with minors, personal gain, transference, and termination of the counseling relationship.

Working With Minors or Mentally Incompetent Clients

When you are working with underage clients, all of the same rules for building and maintaining

a collaborative, healthy clinical relationship with adults apply (Belitz, 2008). Clinicians may treat these young clients differently, adopting more of a parental or disciplinary attitude than with adults, but in most cases, it is likely to be more effective to adopt the same collaborative relationship based on autonomy. If they are invested in their own treatment and take an active role in clinical decisions, they will be better able to make healthy decisions once they leave your treatment. You will also build a better rapport, which will allow them to be honest and invested in their treatment.

One caveat to working with minors or mentally incompetent clients is the required communication with their caregivers, regardless of the client's wishes or circumstances (Belitz, 2008). You must inform the guardian about the client's rights, treatment procedures, and the counseling relationship. There is no room for failure on this aspect of the principle either. It is unethical to neglect your responsibility to ensure the capable person in charge is aware of the clinical relationship. The guardian of the minor must understand how the clinical relationship works in order to give consent for the treatment of the minor, and to protect the minor in ongoing treatment efforts. Your counseling relationship in these cases extends to the caregivers.

The age of the client can complicate this issue. If your client is a young child, it is easier to understand that a parent or guardian must be involved, since the child is likely too young to understand the requirements in navigating his or her own care. However, if you work with adolescents, this becomes a bit sticky. The very nature of adolescence is that the teen is no longer a child and not yet an adult; they are in between worlds. This is apparent in the counseling world, as technically they should still have a guardian involved in their treatment, and yet they are capable of understanding ethical principles and at least partially navigating their own care. You may find that your degree of informing a guardian changes as the child grows, from complete notification when they are a child to partial notification when they are an adolescent to absence of notification when they are an adult (Belitz, 2008).

For example, Keely is a 9-year-old client who was referred to you for inhalant abuse. You explain to Keely and her parents that because she is a minor they will be informed of her progress and of any material that is concerning to you, but that you will only tell the parents what is absolutely necessary, keeping your comments as general as possible to protect the details Keely wants to share with you. Chloe is a 17-year-old client who was referred to you for methamphetamine abuse and depression that recently culminated in a suicidal attempt by overdose. Technically, Chloe is 17 years old, and therefore you would want to keep her parents out of most treatment business, except any material that would compromise her safety, in which case you would report to her parents (and perhaps others depending on the level of danger). However, because Chloe has had a recent suicide attempt, you are apt to keep her parents abreast of more detail than if she had not had a recent attempt.

Personal Gain

The clinician should never use the client relationship to promote personal gain or profit of any kind for the clinician or the agency. There is a specific direction to the relationship between counselor and client. The counselor has the power in the relationship, and this will not change. This means that you cannot use your relationships with clients for your own gain even when you can separate the two relationships clearly in your head. Just because you have the ability to do that does not mean your client has the ability to do that. You can't exploit your clients, or take them hostage in your scheming. Because of the power differential, you are always the one who must enforce and reinforce appropriate boundaries between you and your clients, even if you desperately want to break those boundaries for your benefit (Corey, Corey, & Callanan, 2007).

For example, Jackie counsels Maryanne in a residential setting for 8 months. Maryanne is a landscape designer, and a talented one at that.

Jackie just bought a new house and is desperate to have someone work on the exterior of her house, but she has no money to hire a designer for the job. Jackie discusses this problem at some point in the 8 months she has Maryanne as a client, and Maryanne suggests that she design her exterior when she graduates from the program. She is willing to do it for a small fee as a thank you for all the counseling. Jackie, feeling very lucky, agrees to this arrangement. Similarly, Mei, an outpatient clinician, knows nothing about cars and always feels mechanics swindle her because they know she is ignorant. Her client, Mick, is a mechanic. During their sessions, Mei finds small ways to bring up mechanic issues. At first, she attempts to shield her true motive, asking questions as a way of getting to know his background, and later asking if he would give her advice to pass along to "a friend." Eventually, coming up with excuses becomes too difficult and she admits she is seeking information for her own vehicles. Can you detect the personal gain that makes this action unethical? These are all examples of unethical situations in which the counselor abuses his or her power over the client for personal gain. These may be glaring examples, but this abuse can be quite subtle, too.

For example, in a walkathon for charity in which a given agency produces a team each year, participants associated with the agency get to wear special T-shirts, walk together during the event, and attend both a pre- and post-party with other participants from the agency. Each counselor in the agency is expected to advertise this event to his or her clients, as the agency faces yearly pressure for participation numbers. Here is the issue: If a counselor attempts to entice his or her clients into participation, those clients may feel pressure to join the event in order to prevent clinician disappointment. They may not truly wish to be involved in the event, but may feel cajoled by wanting to please their counselor. Yes, the agency and the clinician will benefit from client participation, but the client-counselor relationship will be exploited in the process, and that is a problem.

Transference

Transference refers to the tendency for clients to displace feelings for someone, such as a family member, spouse, or employer, onto the clinician. Originated by Freud, the concept of transference is believed to be an important and useful tool in the counseling relationship (Powell & Brodsky, 2004; Racker, 2002). Clinicians may feel uncomfortable when transference is experienced, and may be inclined to ignore, deny, or downplay the transference, but in doing so a wonderful therapeutic moment is lost.

To work with transference effectively, clinicians must first recognize that transference is occurring, an awareness that comes with good training and experience. They then must decide how to address the transference most effectively, all the while ensuring that their own emotions are not clouding the therapeutic process (Powell & Brodsky, 2004). Clinicians must maintain a safe distance from the clinical process and hold the welfare of the client as the focus (Racker, 2002).

For example, your client Elliot is happy and reasonable during your course of treating him, except when you have to admonish him for breaking a rule of the program. You confront him kindly, but firmly, reminding him of the rules he is expected to uphold. He suddenly becomes enraged, yelling expletives at you and deeply insulting you. He then runs out of the office. This is completely atypical of the behavior you have witnessed during his treatment episode, you suspect you unknowingly triggered some transference in your client. You know Elliot had a challenging childhood, most significantly influenced by a domineering and unstable mother, who was verbally abusive and found fault often in Elliot's actions. You suspect that he has transferred his feelings of his mother onto you. Armed with this idea, you can now help Elliot work through his feelings with his mother, which will help strengthen his recovery. How do you do this? By discussing the case with your supervisor. Do not attempt to address this transference without help, as it is outside your training. There are many great ways to address this transference, just be sure you receive guidance from someone trained to address it.

Termination

The process of ending a relationship with a client is as important as is the counseling process while treatment is progressing. You would think that this would be a desired outcome for clinicians; after all, who wants to work with someone with whom our working relationship has grown stale? But in actuality, many clinicians need to be reminded of this directive, as they prolong clinical relationships long after they should (Taleff, 2010). There are many reasons why this can occur. First, clinicians enjoy working with clients, and do not wish this process to end. Second, some clinicians feel a great sense of purpose in helping clients, and can become dependent on the relationship, finding difficulty in terminating it. Third, clinicians may feel the client did not achieve all of the clinician's goals, even if they achieved all of the client's goals. Fourth, clinicians may fear the outcome for the client if they leave, equating failure of the client with failure of the clinician, and thus wanting to protect themselves from a sense of failure. Fifth, the counselor or the agency may be receiving a considerable fee for working with the client, and may be motivated to continue working with the client for financial reasons. Finally, having a spot open up to a new client means additional work for a clinician, who may be resistant to that work.

How then do you determine when treatment should be closed? The first aspect to consider is the type of treatment the client is receiving. You would not expect a client to be in detox for 6 months, or expect a client to be in residential treatment for 3 to 5 days; different types of individual and group treatment hold different average lengths of time. For example, a standard course of Cognitive Behavioral Therapy (CBT) would be 4 months with follow-up, but standard psychoanalysis holds a minimum of one full year of therapy. In our addiction arena, it would be the difference between early recovery groups, which typically last 4 to 6 weeks, versus

Social Support groups, which can last for years. Depending on the type of treatment you are giving, you may not know how long the client should be attending, and may have to use other clues to determine if the client is ready to end treatment.

If you have been treating the client well during their stay, part of your therapy has been checking in with the client about the frequency of sessions. Most programs have a leveled system, meaning that the first few days or weeks of treatment offer the maximum amount of time, with at least one decrease in attendance frequency as the client progresses. For example, at intake you may prescribe groups 5 days a week and an individual every week for 2 weeks' duration. You may then discuss with the client dropping groups to half days or 3 days a week, and eventually drop individual therapy to every other week. Depending on your program rules, the amount of leeway you have in making these decisions with your client will vary; however, there should be some system in place that eases the client into eventual termination. The reason is simple: It is assumed too shocking for clients to transition from full treatment to no treatment all at once, rendering them at risk for relapse. It is better for clients to slowly lessen the support from the program while they are increasing their supports in their community, making for a smoother transition and less relapse risk.

In private practice you and your client determine levels, and there should be goals to work toward. Thus, an important determination in when to close treatment is the transition progress and the conversations you have with your clients about when they feel ready for discharge, coupled with what you observe about their readiness. If there are other staff within the agency or outside professionals that work directly with your client, a clinical consultation regarding discharge timing is helpful to ascertain whether the other staff feel discharge is appropriate or not. It is also vital to collaborate with family to ensure good timing, if there is a release to allow communication.

It is important to remember that your observation, and that of other staff, is vital to determining readiness, so be sure to include those observations in addition to whatever the client feels is appropriate. Also remember to include your gut, or intuition, in the process, as it rarely leads you astray. For example, your client may be telling you that he or she feels ready to leave treatment, and the other staff members involved in your client's care may agree and see no reason to prevent the client from discharge. Yet you may feel that the client is not quite ready. Perhaps you have specific reasons why you feel this way, something you have observed in your work with the client. Or you may feel something in your gut is telling you that discharging the client now would be a mistake. You can't keep a client in treatment based on your gut—few insurance companies would be willing to pay based on your intuition—however, you may want to postpone discharge for a day or two and suss out what your gut's concerns may be, talking through your feelings in supervision. If no clear concern arises, you will need to discharge the client despite your gut, but at least you tried to listen.

The key to ethical client relationships is to inform the *prospective* client, meaning before they officially become your client, of the rules and boundaries that you intend to firmly maintain. This confession protects you and the client. It is much easier to fall back on a created boundary when you need it than to develop one from scratch in a time of desperate need. The Counseling Relationship is at the heart of what we do in this profession. It is the springboard off which we can do our best work, if it is developed in a healthy manner. One can see how the more work we do to strengthen ourselves as clinicians, the better our counseling relationships will be and the more help we can give. If we do not abide by the first key to our practice, our counseling relationships will suffer, and we will be at risk of sliding into the trap of conflicted agendas. This pitfall can affect our relationships with clients and impair our ability to protect them. Thus, it is vital to adequately examine the pitfall, and learn both how to avoid it and how to cope if our avoiding efforts fail.

Pitfall: Conflicted Agendas

6
Chapter

Let's start with the most obvious and yet one of the slipperiest of ethical dilemmas, one that I promise you are destined to experience, even with the most ethical of practices. Now that I have your attention, let me explain. I may not know you personally, reader, but I am fairly confident that you are human. This means that I know a few important things about you that will be major influences in your practice, even if you are not yet aware. One, you have a set of experiences (including observations) from your past, and two, these experiences have created scripts in your brain of what to expect and how to act or react in a given situation. We all have numerous scripts within us, and they dictate both our emotional response to an event and what action we choose in response. We may unconsciously change our scripts when we meet new people, or experience new encounters that challenge existing scripts, because scripts can be modified as new encounters are experienced. We may also become aware of our scripts and work deliberately to change them, successfully creating new scripts.

Why is this important to your ethical practice? Because these scripts that you have inside yourself come with you everywhere you go, including

the workplace, and they inform both how you perceive people or encounters, and how you react to them. With your clients, these scripts dictate how you view and accept your clients and how you treat them. Scripts influence how we define the four pillars. Scripts inform our agendas, both personal and professional. You just spent time developing an inventory of your strengths and limitations, and it is important to consider how those characteristics can clash, bringing you into an ethical dilemma. It is inevitable that you are going to make mistakes, and your personal agendas are going to creep into your professional behavior, as you can't be a purely objective clinician in all scenarios. Therefore, let's look at some common conflicts and what to do if you find yourself facing such a dilemma. For example, Naomi had a mother who let her choose anything she wanted. She made her own rules, like setting a curfew, and decided her own consequences if she broke a rule. When Naomi became a mother she adopted the same style. In this way the script she developed in childhood has informed how she personally treats those around her.

Now what happens if we are faced with a conflicting agenda that clashes with our script? Let's say

Naomi works at a clinic and adopts the same style with clients, allowing them the freedom to dictate their care. Freedom means autonomy, and autonomy is good, right? So, well done, Naomi? Well, yes and no. Autonomy is a goal, but allowing your clients the space to collaborate in their care doesn't mean they should create their own treatment program while you sit idly by. It is your job to set the structure. Naomi was self-driven, but your clients won't all be that motivated. In this way, personal and professional agendas can clash. Naomi can ignore her personal agenda, ignore her professional agenda, or find a compromise.

Your ability to navigate between your personal and professional agendas is dependent on your flexible nature. How would you describe yourself at work: Do you have routines that are consistent and unvaried regardless of the situation or individual? We will call this a rigid routine. A rigid routine is one where a clinician has basically one course of action or one technique that he or she continuously applies to all clients. Rigid routines are not necessarily inferior or faulty routines, in fact, many situations are improved by adopting the routine, many clients are helped by the chosen treatment technique, and the clinician who adopts a rigid routine can do great work in the field. Rigid routines are beneficial in that a standard of action or care is established and then is rigorously upheld. Standards are healthy; they create a backbone on which our practice rests.

Yet rigid routines can become problematic when they are upheld with fanatical devotion, when they are unyielding to anomalous circumstances or individual differences. If you believe there is one way to treat a client, one mode of therapy that will be successful, one approach to solving a problem, one appropriate response in a given situation, you are at risk of missing other possible courses of action that may be superior to your chosen method. In addition, you discount the individual differences that exist between people and situations. We are not cardboard cutouts or clones of each other; there is a great variety among the clients you counsel and the clinical scenarios you encounter in your daily practice. There are also unforeseen circumstances you

cannot predict that affect your work, and to which you must react. All of these factors demand a degree of flexibility in your regimen in order to best address the variables and to continue to give effective, healthy treatment. If you cannot be flexible in the variety of your work, and instead adopt an unrealistic rigid routine, you are at risk of failing your clients and of developing an unethical practice.

This is especially true of the clinician in recovery because your personal agenda may conflict with your professional agenda. Your personal need to be rigid can conflict with the client's need for innovative trends in treatment. For example, Laura, a counselor in recovery, believes in whatever treatment techniques she feels were significant for her success. "It has worked for me, so it will work for everyone" (St. Germaine, 1996). Perhaps it was involving family in treatment. Perhaps she went to detox, rehab, residential, a halfway house, and a sober house before she lived a clean life independently. Good for her! But that doesn't necessarily mean that her clients have to follow the same path through exhaustive treatment. Sure we believe that the more treatment someone gets, the more likely they will be to remain in recovery, but not every client will be willing or able to take that path. Perhaps you didn't do any of that treatment, and therefore don't believe your clients need to either. Tread lightly here, as many clients will need more formalized treatment to get them on the path you are enjoying. In short, keep your own personal recovery agenda out of your counseling, and you will be a better clinician. Go over all the treatment techniques and options, and match them to each client as best you can.

Favoring a rigid routine is not only about personal recovery; it is about personal beliefs. You may not be in recovery, but you will still hold opinions on how clients should be treated, or what they need to do to recover. A colleague described a clinician she supervised, Charlie, who had spent his career helping veterans through a variety of programs. Having served in the Navy himself, he had always been drawn to helping that specific population in his clinical work. When he came into work one day, he saw that his new client, Joseph, had served in the Army, although there were no dates or type of service listed. During the intake, in addition to the usual questions asked, Charlie briefly asked about his service dates. When later presenting the case to the staff, Charlie framed Joseph's presenting problems about the fact that he was in the military. His anxiety and depression symptoms, in addition to his addiction development, was all explained by the fact that he was in the military during war. However, upon his supervisor's closer examination, it was revealed that Charlie never asked Joseph if *he* thought his military experience was related to the symptoms he was there to treat.

Whatever thoughts you have may be right on for many of your clients, but any time you are thinking "this is *the* way to get clean, or this is the *only* thing that will help" you should use those words as clues that you have adopted a rigid routine, and you will not only neglect to help all of your clients in this way, you will hurt some in the process. And hurting clients is bad, against the core of what we do, right? Similarly, if you persevere on details that you believe are central issues based on your past or your opinions, you are molding the client to follow in your footsteps. Instead of creating copies of you, try giving your clients options, presenting the best researched techniques, and letting them decide in which directions they want to drive their healing.

At times it can be more subtle and confusing. Consider that you are tasked with nurturing autonomy through valuing a collaborative relationship. What are you to do when you and your client disagree on treatment goals, a conundrum that often occurs (Miller, 2008)? At times you will decide that the best way to uphold the welfare of your client is to stick to what you see as the right path and try to coax your client to it. In other situations, you will need to go with what the client is suggesting, even if you do not see it as the best move, because supporting your client's autonomy is more important than advocating your preferred clinical intervention. This approach can prove to be a surprising success, as sometimes your client can sense a better plan than you can (Miller, 2008).

On the other side of the spectrum, we have a lax routine. Just as a rigid routine is too strictly structured, a lax routine is too loosely structured, formless and overly pliant. Clinically, a lax routine is one that modifies with each client and every situation; there is no standard of operation, but rather the rules are created and re-created with each encounter. While this may seem like an advantageous tactic in addiction counseling, a way to "meet each client where they are at," it can be deceptive. If every situation and every client is treated as new, there is no blueprint, no map to guide a counselor into the best clinical and ethical action. This map creates a standard that can be communicated across counselors throughout the entire profession. This communication acts as a strong invisible web connecting clinicians to each other across the globe, strengthening the profession in which we are all members. Each clinician should tap into this web and allow it to guide the backbone of his or her practice. Once the foundation is in place, then a clinician can modify the plan slightly for each client as needed, but the general backbone remains the same across clinical cases.

For example, Tanesha is a counselor in a detox unit. Because she does not work with clients for longer than 5 days at most, she has not devoted a lot of attention to developing a structured routine. She sees her goal as building a rapport with clients to entice them into continued recovery efforts. She is not wrong. Building a rapport and acting as a cheerleader for recovery efforts is a large part of what a detox counselor can do. If she can keep clients engaged, they are likely to continue seeking out treatment, which will improve treatment outcomes. However, she also has an obligation to plant as many recovery tools as she can during the short time she has with the clients. She cannot be as effective if she does not have a structure in place that ensures all receive the basic tools. If Tanesha and her supervisor can identify the most important tools to teach the clients, she will have a blueprint to work with and the clients will benefit.

Your past experiences have a large influence on your agendas. What you encountered in the past dictates the scripts you create, and those scripts inform your practice. It is all too easy, even for careful clinicians, for the past to sneak in and influence your routine. For example, Regina came from a tight-knit, supportive family who promoted honesty and a balance between individuality and group cooperation. Regina respected her parents above all other significant figures in her early life, and knew she was blessed to have been raised in such a stable environment. In her role as supervisor to a group of outpatient clinicians, she tried to emulate her parent's supportive style with her supervisees, both giving and demanding respectful interactions. She was seen as the healthiest and most helpful of supervisors, and retained relationships with many of her supervisees even after they had sought employment elsewhere.

Alternatively, Diana came from a dysfunctional household where each member had a competitive and distrustful attitude toward the other members in the family. Diana's father was raised under a dictator of a father, and he employed the same discipline style with his family. He regarded his children with love, but had a firm hand and believed his opinion was the most important. To settle an argument, he rarely allowed negotiation; he simply stated his opinion and it was followed. Diana was taught not to reason but to follow, and it is this credo that she adopted for her own supervision style. She expected her supervisees to bring questions into their meetings and incorporate the answers she gave them. In this way, Diana was a well-loved supervisor by those clinicians who appreciated a simple "here is what you do" attitude, but those clinicians who wanted a more collaborative relationship were disappointed. It is important to note that in these supervisor examples, both Regina and Diana sought to emulate the style they had been taught, giving further evidence that personal experiences color the way we practice professionally.

Either way, because it is the past you lived, it will feel familiar and … like the right thing to do. At times, that good feeling will correctly produce ethically and clinically appropriate behavior. At other times, it will lead you astray and make you fail to see better options. Your past should suggest, but not demand. Keep your eyes open, talk to trusted sources, check your decision-making process, and always seek alternative routes of behavior. You may decide to adopt your original plan, but if you spend the time ensuring it is the best course of action you will avoid a rigid or lax routine and make a sound decision. You want to be able to stand by your practice with confidence, knowing you have considered the options, rather than simply resting on what has worked in the past. Let's look now at how this conflict can play out in your practice, and what to do if you find yourself in such a dilemma, by examining our first hot topic, self-disclosure.

Practical Application

To Disclose or Not to Disclose …

Because we began this chapter with the obvious and slippery, let's keep that going by immediately launching into one of the biggest, most common, and certainly most controversial questions: whether to disclose a counselor's recovery status to a client or colleague. Before we discuss this question, I want you to think about something: What do you do in your workplace? Do you offer up your recovery status (i.e., whether you are in recovery or not) to clients or colleagues? Do you wait until they ask you and then disclose your status? Do you tell some clients and not others? Do you have a policy never to answer this question, and if so what exactly do you say to the clients and colleagues when they ask? Now think about why you chose your actions. What beliefs do you attach to your actions? Some common answers we hear are: (a) "I tell all my clients when I meet them that I'm in recovery. That way they know where I am coming from, that I've been there, and that I can understand where they are at. Clients seem to really appreciate knowing." (b) "I only tell clients when I think it is important for them to hear it, when it will specifically help their recovery to know it. Otherwise, I don't tell clients."

(c) "I never tell the clients my status. It is none of their business and I tell them that—or I try to avoid the question." (d) "I lie. I think it is easier just to say yes, I am in recovery, than to explain that I am not. The last time I told someone I was not in recovery, they brought it up in every group, challenging everything I said, saying I couldn't know because I hadn't been there. It's too hard, so I just say, yeah I am, and leave it at that."

Perhaps some of these responses feel familiar to you. But which is the most ethically sound response, or is there some other way of responding that provides a more ethical answer? The first thing to do when asking an ethical question is to look at the written Code. If you look at the Code of Ethics (which should be easily accessible at your workplace, right?!) you will notice that it may not specify a rule about disclosure. Nowhere does it give you a crystal clear answer: Yes, tell clients; no, never tell clients. This has always been one of those questions that historically fell to the clinician to decide whether or not to disclose; it was a personal choice of the clinician because it is a personal detail. The emphasis has been on clinician comfort. Perhaps this is what you were taught, or what you currently believe.

More recently, the idea has been to keep the focus on the client, not the clinician. Specifically, that disclosure should only be used for a therapeutic reason (Manuel & Forcehimes, 2008). The idea here is that mass disclosure is inappropriate because it focuses on the clinician rather than the client. We ask clinicians in training to consider who this disclosure serves, themselves or the client. Do you want the client to know you are in recovery so they respect and listen to you? Then this is not a good reason to share the information because it is about you, not them. Or do you feel with a particular client that it would help them to know you have also been there and figured out how to lead a healthier life? Can you think of a situation where this would clinically aid the client? It is an interesting question. Some believe disclosure can help with bonding, trust, and respect (Manuel & Forcehimes, 2008). However,

there is also evidence that with the clinician's self-disclosure the counseling relationship can become more informal, less professional, competitive, and upsetting (Manuel & Forcehimes, 2008).

Now let's think about it in a different way. Instead of thinking about individual circumstances, look at the question from a broader perspective. There are three arguments to suggest never disclosing to clients your recovery status. Read them, ponder them, and see what you think.

1. Why should it matter? Do you believe that clinicians who are not in recovery are not as good at treating clients as counselors in recovery? What is your evidence for this? The truth is that there are many fantastic clinicians who are not in recovery, and there are some lousy clinicians who are in recovery. Just as there are fantastic clinicians who are in recovery and lousy clinicians who are not. It is not your recovery status that makes you a good clinician; it is your skill. And your skill did not come from how many drinks you had, or how often you got high, or how much jail time you served, even though it might feel like it does. Frankly, if you believe this, you are selling yourself short. Your skill comes from all the training the profession requires, all those endless hours of education and practical training you went through to get your credential and continue to go through every recredentialing period. There is also a little innate clinical skill that is inside you—that part of your heart and soul that makes you an empathetic listener, or that allows you to intuit what is at the heart of a client's problem. Some of that cannot be taught and is just a part of who we are as people. These things can be achieved regardless of how tough you've had it, and can also never be achieved even if you have survived the worst addictions. There is also no evidence to suggest counselors in recovery are more ethical clinicians. Counselors in recovery do not differ in their sensitivity to ethical dilemmas from those who are not in recovery (Gallagher, 2010).

Think of it this way: If you have cancer, or diabetes, or HIV, would you only go to a clinician who has cancer, diabetes, or HIV? Would you seek out a heart surgeon based on whether he had ever had a heart attack? If you went into therapy for bipolar disorder, can you imagine saying, "I'm glad I'm in therapy. Sue really knows what I'm going through due to her own bipolar issues. I really love it when she talks about her past experience with symptoms." Of course not, because that shouldn't matter. You go to the clinician who has been trained to help you, with whom you feel comfortable, who you trust can help guide you to health. Addiction clients are the same. Often when they ask your recovery status, they are really asking, "Can you help me? Will you understand me?"

2. The addiction profession is different from other helping professions in this one specific way. We are the only profession in which the personal status of the clinician is a persistent issue in clinical situations. Other professions know this and treat us differently because of it. It likely is one of the reasons we are not seen on the same professional level as other clinical professions. In one state that is fighting for licensure, I was with many colleagues in other fields of psychology, social work, and counseling, who asked: "I know they are really passionate about gaining licensure, but do you really think it wise to give so much power to recovering addicts who help people through their own personal experience?"

They ask this seriously, and with the best intentions, but these statements show the mass ignorance about our profession. No one gets credentialed because they have "been there" or because they once were clients. We are not selling hair tonic, we are a serious profession with rigorous requirements. In fact, our credentialing and recredentialing requirements are often more thorough and challenging than those of other helping professions; we have a specific professional Code of Ethics just as any other helping profession, and we have a mechanism in place to hold our professional members accountable for their clinical actions. Yet we are still seen as this profession of addicts who once struggled and simply preach what worked for them. The false assumptions are that we are all in recovery, and that we get our skill from personal

experience rather than training. There are many ways we can fight against this stigma, and educate the public about our profession. One way is to start thinking less about our personal recovery status and more about the clinical skill we have worked so hard to obtain. This is what is going to make our profession shine! This is what we are fighting for. We are telling each state that we want to be taken seriously because we are more skilled in a specific area of treatment than anyone else, right? So if our skill is what we recognize on the licensure-fighting level, it should also be what we recognize on the daily clinical level.

3. While we are recognizing our specialized skill on a daily clinical level with our clients, let's examine the organization level. At a recent conference of addiction professionals a colleague remarked, "Ah, I love coming into a room of so many addicts in recovery doing good things. My people!" Now, I realize this was intended as a supportive, positive statement, but it is problematic. First, it excludes the number of nonrecovering professionals in that room, which no doubt existed. Second, it characterizes the profession in the same way that others outside our profession characterize us. If we broadcast our recovery status as a group, and lead with that as a qualifying factor in what makes us good counselors, then we can expect others to do the same. We do not like that others call us "that group of recovering addicts who help people through their own experience" but we are as much to blame as anyone for creating that reputation. Every time you disclose your status to clients you are reinforcing the notion that your recovery status is what makes you a good clinician, which teaches those clients to look for the recovery status in other counselors they may see in the future. They may spread the word to other clients that recovery status is something to consider in a good clinician. Every time you see a room of addiction professionals as a room of recovered addicts, you further the erroneous perception. Every time you ask a colleague, "So what's your story? Are you in recovery or what?" you continue the idea that the answer is suggestive of clinical skill and that to respond "No I'm not" will make that

clinician inferior to the rest of the group of professionals. Each time one of our own clinicians stands up in front of us to accept a well-deserved award and spends his or her remarks nostalgically recalling the early days of drinking or drugging, and making no mention of all the education, training, supervision, and professional toil to earn that award, we sell ourselves short. We can do better.

4. Getting back to the clients, there is one other important aspect of this issue to ponder. When an ethically or clinically challenging situation comes up, such as self-disclosure, you should always ask yourself if there is a way for you to therapeutically model something important to the clients. Then you are using the situation to help clients, which is always the goal. Remember that clients are coming to your facility and are being asked to disclose their recovery status in every group and every individual session. Then they go to self-help meetings and are asked to disclose their status every time they raise their hand. It is easy for clients to believe that this is now such a part of their identity that they should be telling everyone they come across. This may fill some clients with pride that they are successfully focusing on the problems in life and attempting to become healthier. This may fill other clients with shame because they feel forever labeled and all failures or shortcomings must be related to this label.

There are places in the client's life where sharing their recovery status could hurt them. Our programs teach honesty, but we should also teach privacy. Clients should be careful to whom they disclose their recovery status beyond who "needs to know." Obviously they should be honest with us, in self-help meetings, with institutions like parole, and with physicians, to name a few. But in other aspects of their lives, particularly personal friendships and places of business, they should be careful. Perhaps you've all heard of clients being fired because an employer discovered they were in recovery (and doing well!), or employers who blamed all successes and failures on the recovery status. There may be people in a client's life who do not need to know that he or she is in recovery, particularly groups of people. Clients should be disclosing their status to

people and places they trust, and this is an important lesson to learn.

We, as clinicians, can help model this behavior by keeping our own recovery status out of the workplace. We should hold in confidence friends, family, and the people who help us. But at work, we all should be careful, too. Telling every client that comes in the door may not be safe for us, and frankly, telling every co-worker may not be smart either. Remember that we want to focus on our skill, and keep our recovery sacred to those with whom we choose to share it. Who knows what clients will do with this information—not only how they will work with you in the workplace, but what they will do with the information outside of the workplace. If you are in recovery, you will always be in recovery, but that is only one part of who you are. You may also be, for example, a parent, a child, a sibling, a sky diver, a knitter, a pet owner, a writer, an artist—you get the idea. You are also a skilled clinician, so be proud of that!

When clients ask about your recovery status, you are given a wonderful opportunity to do some therapeutic good. Instead of redirecting the issue, giving a quick yes or no answer, telling them it is not important, or otherwise dismissing the question, focus on the importance of the issue and the chance to model the importance of privacy. Explain this is your place of business and that you choose to keep your status professionally private, just as they should do when outside the agency. Model for them that the skill of the clinician is more important than the recovery status. Explain that one's recovery status is vital to a sponsor, for example, but that what is important in a clinician is the ability to understand and to help, and reassure them that these are things you are able and willing to do for them. With a response like that, you can support the client, yourself, and the profession all in one statement!

If you do this successfully and refrain from stating your recovery status, be prepared for clients to throw back, "It doesn't matter what you say, I know what your status is anyway. I know you are/are not in recovery. I can just tell." Many clinicians have heard this many times, and have had as many people say they suspect recovery as have refute it. This suggests that clients do not know, perhaps because skill and training is what they detect, not recovery status. And that is the way it should be.

Don't forget, our entire profession is viewed as a merging of the personal with the professional. This profession is unique in the helping professions because of how we are largely viewed, as a group of recovered people wanting to help other people find a similar health path. And we don't help by disclosing our recovery status to every clinician and client we encounter. We can't complain that society doesn't regard us as serious clinicians with a unique and rigorous body of knowledge and expertise, while presenting our personal recovery status as our primary badge of professionalism. It is in this way that our profession is weakened.

So what have we learned so far? We all have both strengths and limitations. The first step is to identify them. The second step is to note any potential ethical risks each strength and limitation may influence. The third step is to take this information to our supervision or to other trusted advisors and make a plan to address each potential risk. You want to tuck your personal beliefs away in your briefcase and keep them from infiltrating how you treat your clients and colleagues. You want to gain an awareness of your personal and professional influences and be prepared to take action in those areas where you are at risk for being the least objective. You want to examine your practice for rigid or lax routines, injecting a bit of flexibility or structure into those areas that are immutable. In short, you want to build your practice on the proverb used in Tai Chi classes: Stand like a mountain, flow like the river. You want a strong foundation but the flexibility to adjust to your surroundings and the needs within them. This will earn you objectivity, even if you allow your gut to co-counsel with you.

Once we do this we can feel confident that we know ourselves well enough to avoid the pitfall of conflicted agendas to the best of our ability. By developing the first key and safeguarding against the first pitfall we can then successfully uphold the ethical principles that direct us to focus on client welfare, to effectively work with cultural diversity, and to build a healthy counseling relationship. You know what this means, don't you? It means that you will have successfully done all in your power to protect the client, and will thus be well on your way to building an ethical practice.

PROTECTING

THE CLINICAL

INFORMATION

Protecting the Clinical Information

The second category of ethics encompasses those that protect clinical information, information related to the client that is used both within and outside of the treatment program. Okay, it doesn't sound as sexy or exciting as the other sections, and I know that as soon as I mention informed consent or HIPAA regulations your eyes are going to start to glaze over and I'm gonna lose some of you. But that's precisely the problem with ethics that protect information. First, even though information enables us to do the parts of our job we love the most, and without clinical material we would not function, it somehow rarely feels that way. Instead we separate the unexciting parts of our job—the endless paperwork, the boring mandated trainings, the frustrating staff meetings—from the exciting part of our job—direct practice with clients and families, supervision of other staff, and clinical collaboration with other professionals.

Yet to treat our clients well, we must protect them, and that includes protecting information about them. Because so much information is given and received at every point of substance abuse counseling, a specific section on the ethical use of the confidential material is warranted. There are three specific legal constructs that apply to the protection of clinical information. The first is *privileged communication*, which restricts information or knowledge by a state statute between a client and specific professionals. This law typically covers lawyers and doctors; whether addiction counselors are included or not will vary by state (Washington & Demask, 2008).

The second is *privacy*, which is the client's right to choose in what circumstances his or her personal information is shared, including when, what, and with whom (Washington & Demask, 2008). We use the term *informed consent* to describe a client's right to privacy. Informed consent is a tool for clinicians, even if it is sometimes seen as an administrative and clinical burden. It allows you and the client to communicate and clarify expectations of the relationship and the treatment process. It is also a tool that can show whether the client understands the clinical approach and what is expected (Pope & Vasquez, 2007). It is a client's right to determine his or her own interests and what direction they should take (Pope & Vasquez, 2007), thus informed consent is an excellent device to achieve client autonomy.

The third is *confidentiality*, which is the clinician's duty to protect a client's information from unapproved sources (Washington & Demask, 2008). This one aspect of our practice is so vital it has its own principle and has been adopted into federal law. Confidentiality is a primary obligation of ours, one of the most important tasks we are faced with on a daily basis. We have a duty to protect the client's rights in all our affairs by not disclosing any confidential information pertaining to our clients. Those in the helping professions must adhere to the rules of privacy set in the Health Insurance Portability and Accountability Act (HIPAA) of 1996, known as Health Information Privacy. HIPAA laws protect identifiable health information, and failure to adhere to the rules set forth in HIPAA is punishable by the government. Even with that level of serious attention, clinicians continue to violate this principle.

The types of people who want information from us, and from whom we want to collect information, are family members, physicians, probation officers, social services, and other professionals and treatment centers (Washington & Demask, 2008), but clients will vary in their cooperation, and may not wish to collaborate. How do we navigate through our administrative responsibilities while still maintaining client welfare? How do we gain access to the information we need to maintain the best practice and at the same time protect a client's right to privacy? Now wait a minute, this just got more interesting. We are really stuck between two ethical pillars, autonomy and beneficence, and arguing which route will be a greater violation of nonmaleficence.

Here is the issue: To promote autonomy we want clients to make their own choices about what information is shared and how it is shared. The very idea of ensuring that a client is well informed before they consent to the use of their information is steeped in the concept of autonomy. It is so vital to human rights that we have created federal and state laws to ensure the client's autonomy is preserved. Surely the best practice is one that promotes autonomy, right? Well, sometimes it is not so simple. Beneficence means you are treating the client's information with the best care that you are able to. What if you know you can treat the client with greater beneficence if you gain more clinical information from a reliable source? What if you do not have consent but you know you could convince the client why it is so imperative to get the information? What if you see the client treated poorly by another, and you know you have information that would promote beneficence and help the client? You ask yourself, which will cause a greater violation of nonmaleficence?

It is the responsibility of the clinician to weigh the client benefits against possible detriments in each applied treatment. It can be agonizing to determine which choice causes less harm to your client. If you are focusing on protecting the clinical material, the pillar of justice can be a helpful tool, too, as you want to be consistent with your use of clinical material across the clinical population. It is not ethically appropriate to mishandle information for one client because you want to gather information, even if your reasons involve helping the client. You must adhere to the protection of the clinical material in all circumstances. Yet some cases require special handling.

To further explore this mandate, we will look at two principles in the Code of Ethics. They are titled many different things in each state Code. All codes have principles related to the proper use of clinical material, such as Confidentiality, Public Statements, Publication Credit, and others. In this book, we combine all of these principles and separate them into two categories, those that are concerned with written material and those that are concerned with spoken material. We will examine how the pillars and the particular legal issues of informed consent and confidentiality play out with the use of written and spoken material. We will also examine the use of technology since the ethical rules surrounding the proper use of information become more complicated as our use of technology increases in the health care system. This convenient technology increases the risk of inappropriate information delivery and the need for more detailed rules that protect all parties involved, particularly for clinicians who operate their own private practices.

The key to upholding the principles involved with the protection of clinical material is to respect the Tiers of Ethics. Ethical tiers are the entities that influence the decisions we make. We have five tiers to which we are held accountable in our ethical practices: federal, state, licensure, agency, and personal. By understanding each tier, and examining how each informs our practice, we can strengthen our daily use of clinical information. If you fail to achieve this key you will be in danger of falling into the pitfall of confused roles. Confusing your roles in your practice can lead you to ethical dilemmas that cause great harm to you, your clients, and the profession at large.

Part Two Questions

1. Consider your ethical and clinical decision making over the past several months or years. Are you influenced most by your agency, your gut, or state mandates?
2. What was the last public statement you made about a specific treatment technique and what were the circumstances (i.e., were you in group, staff meeting, an individual session, or supervision)? Would the profession stand by your statement today?
3. Which of the following best measures your integrity?
   a. How I perform in the midst of a crisis.
   b. How I perform in my daily work.
   c. How I perform with my colleagues.
4. When was the last time you read or referred to your Scope of Practice? What were the circumstances and how did it help you?

Key: Respect the Tiers of Ethics

7
Chapter

There are five tiers of ethics, meaning five levels of ethical responsibility to which clinicians must attend. The five Ethical Tiers are federal, state/county, licensure/credential, agency, and personal. Each tier informs how you treat yourself, your clients, your colleagues, and your profession. There are ethical rules and guidelines at the federal level, such as confidentiality; the state/county level, such as mandated reporting; the licensure/credential level, such as the Scope of Practice; the agency level, such as an employee recovery policy; and the personal level, such as your belief about self-disclosure.

Some have argued there should be a separate county level after state, and I am not opposed to adding it in if you live in an area where the county varies often and significantly enough to separate the sections. Others have argued there should be a level for insurances, to which I respond by begging, "No!" Insurance companies have too much power over our clinical practice as it is, and should not have a say over our ethical practice. Thus, we will work with five Ethical Tiers to which we must attend.

We have several positions we can argue on any given issue (Taleff, 2010). Even if you apply sound

critical reasoning to your ethical dilemmas, you may come up with more than one possible action. Often, ethical dilemmas involve trying to choose the best action between two beneficial actions, or trying to decipher the best entity with which to agree, when both entities have sound ethical arguments. It can be agonizing to choose the best course of action, as when trying to choose between autonomy and beneficence. On the other hand, you may feel there are multiple bad actions to take, each option feeling as uncomfortable as the other. How are you to choose when nothing seems the right thing to do, when violating nonmaleficence seems probable in either choice? One helpful tool in determining the most ethical choice is to analyze the dilemma against each tier of ethical responsibility.

With any given clinical situation, a clinician must identify the appropriate ethical behavior at each level. Because it is a hierarchy, it is helpful to have this conversation with oneself in a hierarchal order, while making sure to address each level. Just because you can answer what to do at the federal level you should not ignore what you would do at the personal level. An ethical clinician is going to understand that we are influenced by each ethical tier and the interplay between them. If you ignore one of the tiers, it can lead to an ethical error. If you disregard the conflict between tiers and underestimate their influence on your decisions, it can also lead to an ethical error. A clinician has to both identify each ethical tier and its influence and determine the best course of action. At times, this is easy to do. But often this can be confusing, and a clinician can feel lost in indecision. Law is often black and white, with a clear boundary of what is a proper and improper response. Ethics is often gray and murky because one tier will clash with another, creating more than one satisfactory and appropriate course of action. You will find yourself drowning, not with the question of what is the appropriate action, but what is the *most* appropriate action.

The federal level is the highest ethical tier and involves any ethical sanctions made by the Federal Government and therefore carried out by all 50 states. An example would be the confidentiality of certain client information in alcohol and drug treatment, titles 42 U.S.C.§§290dd-3 and ee-3 and 42 Code of Federal Regulations, Part 2 (Washington & Demask, 2008). This law protects individuals from the release of any information that identifies them as a drug or alcohol user, created because of the harsh stigma against this population. We as clinicians use this federal law on a daily basis in our practices, committing to memory: "Due to Federal Confidentiality Laws I cannot confirm or deny that the person you speak of is in treatment here." Federal confidentiality laws protect information about clients applying for or receiving services and referral for other treatment. In some criminal cases, a court order is needed to divulge information even if a client has given consent (Scott, 2000).

The state level is often informed by federal mandates, but the individual state can choose how to carry out the mandates and what additional laws are applied. An example would be the concept of mandated reporting. Often people incorrectly assume this to be a federal law, possibly because all 50 states have passed laws about mandated reporting as part of the Federal Child Abuse Prevention and Treatment Act of 1974. Specifically, states vary on the definitions of child abuse and neglect, the circumstances that obligate mandated reports, when the court should take custody of the child, and which forms of maltreatment are punishable by law, thus a counselor must check with his or her state of credential/licensure to learn what is expected (Washington & Demask, 2008).

The Licensing or Credentialing Board refers to those mandates handed down by the organization that provides your license or credential. This ethical tier would include rules against dual relationships with clients, or would dictate who can perform certain professional tasks that make up the Scope of Practice. Information in the licensing tier can also differ by state, further complicating our ethical hierarchy. For example, the amount and what type of recredentialing hours are required every 2 years varies by state board.

The agency tier refers to the rules and ethical standards proclaimed by your agency in their policy and procedure manual or in other employee publications. Agency ethics would include a policy about receiving gifts from clients, or a grievance procedure in case a client wants to file a complaint. It would also include any hierarchical structure that an employee must uphold. For example, at some treatment programs, there is a clinical director and an administrative director. It is the agency policy that the administrative director is there for administration needs only and that a clinician must seek clinical guidance from the clinical director only, and there are serious sanctions if this is not followed. Another program has a policy about taking new clients into the practice, where clinicians are listed in a set order, and new clients are assigned to the next clinician in line. It is unethical to jump the line or deviate from this system, which is in place to ensure that clinicians are assigned clients equally.

Your personal tier of ethics refers to the ethical code you hold within, your morals, which is created by your personality, observations, experiences, and goals. It comes from the mysterious force that educates you on what is right and wrong in any given situation. Last on the totem pole, it may be the tier that informs your actions the most. For example, your personal tier of ethics may inform you that you are uncomfortable accepting gifts, or that you are uncomfortable using your personal car to drive clients to doctor appointments, even when those actions are allowed by your agency. You may feel uncomfortable treating a friend of a relative, even if you have never met that person. You may never feel comfortable befriending a former client even if your licensure level tells you enough time has passed to make it acceptable. It is important that you think about why you believe what you believe, and take a stand (Taleff, 2010). You can learn what the other tiers will tell you to do, but it is just as important to understand what you bring to the ethical table. Instead of deciding on an ethical action because someone—a supervisor, an ethics book, a code of ethics—told you it was the right thing to do, deliberate on why you think it is the right or wrong move. To get to know your personal level of ethics, it can be helpful to consider general ethical quandaries and your views on how to address them (Taleff, 2010).

For example, during your sessions with a client, she continually talks about her neighbor. The neighbor was the only friend your client had, but the two used drugs together, and you are encouraging your client to spend less time with her, or avoid her altogether if she can. Because this is proving to be difficult for your client, she continues to bring in stories about this person and things they do together. The more she does this, the more you hear about the neighbor's life. The neighbor is a methamphetamine-using single mother of four children aged 14 months to 8 years old, without family supports. She continues to use while supposedly caring for her children. As the sessions continue, it sounds as if she is abusing and neglecting her four children, and you are worried for their safety, but you are unsure what to do because this information was told to you confidentially about someone who is *not* your client, whom you have never met. What is the appropriate course

of action here? Do you report the suspected abuse to CPS/DSS/DCF? What are your legal ethical mandates here? What about personal ethics?

Let's examine the tiers. There is no federal tier related to mandated reporting, so that tier cannot help us. At the state level, licensure level, and agency level the same question occurs: Assuming you are a mandated reporter at those levels, should you report someone who is *not* your client? The question is, are you a mandated reporter everywhere you go, or only at the workplace? Legally, it may be unlikely that you will be sued for not reporting a case where the alleged abuser was not known to you, but ethically most people who are mandated reporters may consider this example an ethical obligation to report. What if you live in a state where you are not a mandated reporter at the state, licensure, or agency levels? This is where your gut may come into play. Ask yourself: Would you be able to sleep at night knowing you may be the only one in the position to protect these children if they need protecting, and not taking action to protect them? Remember that making a report does not rip children out of the homes of innocent parents, it merely starts an investigation where the authorities decide whether protection is needed or not. There may be numerous examples of how faulty the system can be, and at times children are taken from innocent parents, but you take that gamble in order to protect a child who may need protection. In this example, your personal tier is steering you.

There can be other tier-related clashing over mandated reporting. Your state may tell you that you are a mandated reporter, but the agency level might dictate that you have to get a supervisor prior to making that report, or the licensed supervisor may be the only one who makes the report. This possibility was recently reported by a clinician who fell into this situation. She wanted to make the report, as it was her duty to do so as mandated at the state tier, but also to satisfy her personal tier. However, her agency told her she could not make the report, that she had to follow the agency protocol and have the proper chain of command make the report. If this happens to you, talk with your supervisor about the possibility of making an additional report if it is a case about which you feel strongly. In many cases, supervisors would be happy to have clinicians take such initiative. Others will not welcome this action for various reasons. If this is you, you may always make an anonymous report to the appropriate authority, or write a detailed progress note in the chart and follow up to make sure the supervisor made the report. In the end, it may not matter who made the report, as long as the report was successfully made.

What becomes quickly interesting about the five tiers of ethics is the frequency with which they clash, and the difficulty of knowing how to resolve things when they do. There will be times we are asked to do something at one level that clashes with another level, and most of us at some point in our careers will have to weigh the risk of losing a job versus losing one's integrity. Your personal tier has a lot of pull in your decision making, as it should. Let's look at some examples of tier clashing and work out what actions are the most ethical.

Recently, a friend told me to watch an episode of a TV show called *Private Practice*, about a group of doctors who share a practice in swanky Los Angeles, that produced a deliciously sticky tier clash. The head of the practice is a fertility expert who helps women get pregnant, often against all odds. This doctor, Naomi, is also strongly pro-life, so her personal tier of ethics informs her that it is wrong to terminate a life once a woman is pregnant. This becomes an issue in the practice when another physician begins performing abortions at the clinic. Naomi is enraged, and tells the doctor it is inappropriate to perform abortions at the clinic, to which the other physician says that it is legal, that doctors are able to perform abortions in the state, and that there is no reason the clinic should not help women in need of the medical procedure. Naomi, even more enraged that she is not supported by the other physicians, approaches the client and tries to convince her to cease her abortion plans. Understandably, when she wins a temporary stay in the proceedings, the patient's physician is outraged that Naomi would approach a patient that is not hers and spout her unsolicited beliefs.

While the show may be overdramatized, this issue is a perfect example of a problematic clashing of tiers. At the state level, abortions are legalized, although states differ on how and when abortions can occur. Naomi's state fully supports abortion, her medical license supports the ethical use of abortion, and the agency in which she works also supports the practice of abortion. All the tiers are in agreement, except her personal tier. She cannot put aside her personal views to perform a professional action, and it clearly causes a great struggle in her. At one point she reveals that she refused to learn how to perform an abortion in medical school, so strong were her personal beliefs against it. So what do we make of Naomi?

On the one hand, clinicians cannot ignore their personal tier of ethics. Acting on something because you are told to act, but feeling in your heart that the action is wrong, can lead to misery in the clinician. Thus, deciding not to perform abortions is an acceptable choice for Naomi. There are other doctors who will, and, while allowed, it is not a procedure that is mandated for all physicians to perform. Where Naomi gets into ethical trouble is by arguing against doctors who have a different personal tier of ethics. She put her own personal views above those of others around her, and it is not ethical to do so. She then violates the patient's right to privacy by discussing her views with a patient who is not hers, and that is a second ethical violation. If you work in an addictions clinic, and you disagree with how a clinician has treated a client, you should not find that client and have a session with him or her, defying the treatment he or she was given by your colleague. Can you imagine that? How would you feel if you learned a colleague had gone behind your back and treated your client? This is a great example of why we have other Ethical Tiers in place beyond the personal tier, and why it is that your practice cannot be solely informed by your personal tier. If we were a profession of personal tiers walking around, it would be very scary indeed.

And yet there are situations where the personal tier of ethics may outweigh a higher tier, as you will see later in this section. You may disagree with a tier that allows you to perform an action that you feel personally is unethical. In some of these cases you may opt for the additional, more stringent ethics your personal tier is needing. Just be sure you don't resolve a tier clash in the other direction. While it is often acceptable to attend to a stricter ethical guideline, it is never okay to choose the more lenient option. For example, if Federal Law dictates you cannot use a client's information in a public speech without their written consent, but personally you know the client would approve, you cannot use the information. Your personal tier does not trump the federal tier.

In preparation for this section, let's not forget to examine the questions asked at the start of the section. The first question, *Are you influenced most by your agency, your gut, or state mandates?* addresses these Ethical Tiers and how you typically use them. It is important to understand what guides the majority of your decision making, so that you can adequately strengthen your ethical practice. It is not appropriate to be guided by only one level the majority of the time. If this is you, you will need to develop an awareness of the other levels to help round out your decision-making process. Contrastingly, maybe you look at all the tiers except your personal tier, denying its importance. This is not advisable either, because your personal tier is a helpful guide for maintaining an ethical practice and ignoring it can lead to job dissatisfaction and a risk of unethical behavior.

The second question, *What was the last public statement you made about a specific treatment technique and what were the circumstances?* asks you to recall your recent statements made in public, particularly those involving treatment techniques. This question gets at a few important aspects of this section. First, we all make public statements, even if we do not consider the statements we make in group or individual sessions or staff meetings as "public." Second, we make claims all the time without necessarily checking our facts or contemplating whether the profession would want us to be making these claims. We make them simply because we believe them, yet we are walking and talking representatives of the profession, and therefore must take our statements seriously. How did you score on this one? If you feel you made an appropriate statement that would be backed, congratulations! If not, don't worry—that is what learning is all about. Read on, and you will gather some good support to help you design your statements more carefully.

The third question, *Which of the following best measures your integrity? (a) How I perform in the midst of a crisis, (b) How I perform in my daily work, or (c) How I perform with my colleagues*, asks you to consider your relationship with integrity. All of these actions can build your integrity, but which do you think is the best measure? Take some time and think about why you chose your answer. Certainly how you perform in the midst of a crisis gives evidence of your courage, your ability to manage stress, your ability to multitask and think under pressure, and your ability to act quickly. The way you work with your colleagues gives evidence of your ability to be a team player, to work well with others, to be considerate, caring, open, engaging, and thoughtful. Finally, how you perform in your daily work can speak volumes about many aspects of your character. This also may be the best measure of your integrity; know why?

It's because of one word it has that the other two options do not, "daily." The best measure of integrity is to observe a person's behavior over time, how he or she consistently performs in a given situation. Thus, how you perform in a crisis may be a great measure of integrity if you experience crises often and consistently. Similarly, what kind of a colleague you are may also be a good measure of integrity if you are being judged over a period of time. How you perform in your daily work gives a consistent picture of your regular behavior.

How you interact with others, how you handle crises, how you treat clients, how you master paperwork, how much people can depend on you in all of your work tasks are all measurements you can decipher when looking at your daily performance. Think about the people in your business life who you would describe as having integrity. What about them makes you describe them this way? Is it that you can depend on them to perform well, to make good decisions, to have a healthy track record of work? Someone with ethical integrity is consistently considering the most ethical course of action in his or her daily work. You won't achieve this perfectly every day of your career, but you want to actively strive for it.

The fourth question, *When was the last time you read or referred to your Scope of Practice? What were the circumstances and how did it help you?* asks you to consider how well you use your Scope of Practice document. If you do not know what a Scope of Practice is, read this whole section please. If you know what it is, but have never actively used it in your work, you are missing out on a tool that can help guide your ethical practice. The Scope gives us helpful boundaries in our practice, and should be a document with which you are familiar and to which you have easy access. If you have used it and it helped, write down a bit about the circumstances, and how the Scope helped. Then share it with your supervisor, maybe even those colleagues on the clinical team. Share the message. We are going to be discussing the scope a lot in this section, so I will save further thoughts until then.

There is perhaps no better example of clashing than when considering how we collect and dispense clinical material. Every tier offers input on what is appropriate and what risks violating nonmaleficence. As a clinician, it can be challenging to wade through the rules and to evaluate all of the various influences that are directing our actions. We can make mistakes without realizing it. Before we know it, we can find ourselves confused about our different roles and to which we should be adhering. This confusion can both be agonizing and can happen without our notice. Many clinicians find themselves in a dilemma, unsure of how to work through their confusion. Others find they didn't realize they were confusing roles until it was too late. Because of this, we need to develop a strong respect for the tiers of ethics and we need to follow the principles that guide us to the most ethical use of clinical material.

Principle: Proper Use of Written Clinical Material

8

Chapter

The addiction profession handles an immense amount of paperwork (Carise, Love, Zur, McLellan, & Kemp, 2009; Whitter et al., 2006) at every level of the 12 core functions that inform our practice, and clinicians often complain of the amount and redundancy of the paperwork demands (Whitter et al., 2006). The ethical principle in your Code of Ethics, which you sign and resign every 2 years, mandates you to uphold the strictest care in storing all clinical information. Each of the five Ethical Tiers has a guideline involving the proper use of written clinical material. The federal tier includes paperwork under the Health Insurance Portability and Accountability Act (HIPAA) of 1996. HIPAA paperwork includes client rights to privacy and informed consent. The state tier includes paperwork related to insurance companies and managed care. The licensure tier includes paperwork related to ethical claims, certification, and recertification. The agency tier has considerable paperwork, including program description and rules, progress notes, treatment plans, discharge summaries, all intake paperwork, and other categories, although some of this paperwork is also guided by other tiers and HIPAA. The personal tier would include paperwork related to supervision, program proposals and grievances, and published articles and books (Carise et al., 2009).

There is also considerable paperwork related to collaboration (Carise et al., 2009). Drug courts, parole, child welfare, social services, referrals, and case conferences all require administrative tasks. In some cases, there will be accreditation paperwork, utilized review, research and outcomes reporting, annual reviews, and other reporting (Carise et al., 2009). Some intake assessments utilize the vast amount of standardized testing, such as the Addiction Severity Index (ASI), the Michigan Alcoholism Screening Test (MAST), and the American Society of Addiction Medicine Patient Placement Criteria (ASAM PPC). Agencies may also employ paperwork that addresses gambling risk, suicidal risk, spirituality, leisure time, nutritional risk, HIV risk, checklists, and quality of life forms (Carise et al., 2009). HIPAA has benefited the field by highlighting the need for client privacy, but has also increased the amount of work clinicians must do in addition to direct practice (Finley & Lenz, 2005).

All of this paperwork contains sensitive information about the clients we serve, and therefore has a healthy dose of ethics surrounding our use of the clinical material. Clients have rights regarding how this information is obtained, used, disseminated, and destroyed. Clinicians must treat the paperwork as if it were the actual client that was being passed around. We work so hard to achieve the healthy welfare of our clients, and most of us are aware that clients can't be tossed around without care. If we thought of paperwork as our actual clients, perhaps we would be more inclined to treat the written clinical material in the same protective manner. Let's get more specific about how this clinical information must be protected.

The clinical world typically understands the importance of documenting that a person was seen for counseling, or attended a training, but we can also flounder on the details of our documentation. While there is little research devoted to the protection of clinical material compared to other ethical areas, there are entire trainings developed on the topic of how to document appropriately, which suggests that a vast mass of us are bungling our ethical responsibilities consistently. Our documentation is the blueprint of all that we do, the proof that we are professional, that we have standards of care, that we know what we are doing. It is also how we justify what we have done for each client throughout their treatment. Ethically, it is vital to show a paper trail of our actions; many clinicians have learned how helpful that trail can become if one's action are called into legal question. The ethical use of written clinical material is dependent on several required characteristics. Written information must have veracity, accuracy, validity/appropriateness, timeliness, and clarity, and must be appropriately signed, credited, consented, and confidential (Corey, Corey, & Callanan, 2007; Finley & Lenz, 2005).

Veracity refers to the truth in what is written in the clinical information. Clinicians must be able to stand by what is written in their paperwork as factual. For example, if a client tells you that he or she has never used cocaine, but you have the police report that verified the drug test administered on arrest showed cocaine in his or her system, you are responsible for including both pieces of information

in the record, the verified police report and the lie the client is telling you.

Accuracy refers to how correctly and precisely the information is documented. A clinician must ensure that all paperwork, instruments, and records used are written with precision. For example, each clinical chart should be thorough in the information recorded. It must match the structure of all clinical charts, and must reflect the treatment, and all other clinical activity, that occurred. If the agency has written its own intake paperwork it must accurately reflect any ethical mandates regarding what material to include. If you are engaged in a phone call related to the client, a detailed record of that phone call must be included in that chart. Omitting it affects the accuracy of that record.

Validity/Appropriateness refers to the appropriateness of using the clinical material with the client in the particular situation. A clinician must make sure that all paperwork used is necessary to the clinical case, and appropriate to the client. For example, you would not give a survey about being a woman in addiction to your male clients, or a questionnaire about marital life to your widow bereavement group. Yet if you worked with convicted clients newly released from prison, developing paperwork to use with the probation and parole department is a priority.

Timeliness refers to the efficiency with which the paperwork is collected and dispensed. A clinician must ensure that he or she is completing paperwork in a timely manner, especially paperwork that is designated for a specific point of treatment, such as intake paperwork, or for a specific purpose, such as a court appearance. For example, it is inappropriate to be completing initial release of information forms when the client is preparing to discharge from your 90-day program.

Clarity refers to the coherence of the written work, both in structure and in penmanship. A clinician must ensure that anyone else involved in the clinical case will be able to pick up your work and easily read it. For example, if you struggle with clear handwriting, you should type your paperwork. Similarly, your clinical charts should follow a structured order that is easy to understand.

Signed refers to the required signatures of each piece of paperwork. A clinician must ensure that all signatures are included, even if those signatures belong to your superiors or other professionals. If the case is on your caseload, you want to be responsible for its completion. If you are signing paperwork as a member of the team, be sure that you know what you are signing. For example, if you are a supervisor who is required to cosign all paperwork for your student intern, then you must read, review, and monitor all that he or she produces. It is not enough to merely sign documents; you must be held accountable for what you are signing.

Credited refers to the mandate to give credit to all authors of the paperwork, including major influences that inspired the work. A clinician must ensure that the appropriate credit is given, especially if the work is to be published in any way. For example, if several people give direct practice to the client during their treatment episode, they each should be credited in the discharge summary that describes the interventions used with the client.

Consented refers to the mandate that a client willingly gives his or her consent to dispense all necessary paperwork. A clinician must ensure that the client is aware of exactly what paperwork is going to be disseminated and to whom it will be sent. For example, if a client's case is going to be used as an education tool for an audience of clinicians outside the agency, that client must be made aware of exactly what information is going to be used, and must agree in writing before the information can be used. The releases must have specific information, as detailed as possible, so that the client is clearly consenting to determined behaviors.

Confidential refers to preventing the release of identifying client information. A clinician must ensure that all clinical information is kept confidential from all sources when specific consent from the clients involved has not been given. For example, when calling a potential referral to check for program appropriateness and availability

no identifying information about the client you might refer is given to the staff. There are a few noted exceptions to this that are discussed in this chapter.

Armed with these characteristics of the paperwork we use, let's look at specific examples of when we work with written clinical material, specifically when paperwork is developed, gathered, stored, dispensed, received, and published.

Developing Written Material

When developing material to use in your clinical practice, you must ensure that the paperwork is prepared within ethical guidelines. Whether you are creating this written material at the agency level or in your private practice, the same ethical guidelines must be upheld.

Veracity: When you develop material, it must be truthful. For example, if you are including statistics in your group handouts, you must ensure that the statistics are factual.

Accuracy: When you develop material, it must be accurate. For example, the agency policy and procedures guide must reflect precisely the procedures that actually take place.

Validity/Appropriateness: When you develop material, it must be appropriate to the purpose you name and the audience you intend. For example, you don't want to develop informed consent documents for underage children and fail to designate a space for guardian consent.

Clarity: All developed materials must be clearly written so that any professional could pick up your work and immediately use it. If your materials are complex, a corresponding training manual should be created.

Signed: All developed materials must be signed by the appropriate personnel when required. You may not backdate signatures or sign an evaluation before it has been made. For example, if you are creating a form letter to be used between your agency and the probation department, you must have it signed by the executives that your agency requires. Typically, agencies have rules regarding approval of all outgoing business correspondence, so be sure to involve them with materials you are creating.

Credited: When developing material, you must credit all those who helped you develop it, and all work, published and unpublished, on which your material is based. For example, the Fresh Start Treatment Program has written its own treatment model, which it manualized for its clients. The manualized program was written by the senior executives of the agency and included original ideas, with one exception. The writers borrowed from a book (Hohman, 2012) that described the lauded Motivational Interviewing Program (Miller & Rollnick, 2002) in part of their program. If they are to use this technique in their program, they must cite the original creators of the program, in this case Miller & Rollnick (2002), and where they, the authors, learned of it, in this case Hohman (2012), so that the reader can also easily seek out the same information on the technique.

Consented: If you are developing material that has specific identifying clinical information related to any client, you must inform the client of your intention to develop the material, inform them of any and all risks of using their information in the material, and have the client sign a statement acknowledging he or she consents to have his or her information used in your material. If you are developing material that involves another organization or another professional, you should also gain their consent when developing the material. For example, if writing a training developed for the agency, you must get the agency's consent.

Confidential: When developing written material, it is unethical to use any identifying information that would expose a client or colleague without their written consent. Even if you have their consent, all efforts must be made to shield their identity unless it is absolutely necessary to disclose it. For example, if you get an idea for a group handout based on your client's personal experience, you must conceal his or her identity when writing the handout.

Gathering Written Material

The clinician should always document materials and techniques used, including those used in his or her therapy or training. We must document all that we do, which means this is the area of paperwork to which you will contribute the most. You will have ample opportunity both to make errors and to fix them. Your paperwork must have:

Veracity: For example, you may not write that you saw a patient when you did not, or made a phone call when you never did. Some clinicians are tempted to write their progress notes before the patients have been seen, in an attempt to increase clinician efficiency. Don't let this be you.

Accuracy: For example, it is not enough to write that a client "attended group." You must write what topics were discussed, what kind of support was given, what tools were recommended, what assignments were given, and when the client is expected to return.

Validity/Appropriateness: The paperwork you gather must be appropriate to the clients of whom you are inquiring. You would not conduct a bipolar assessment test for a client who did not identify with a mood disorder, or obtain a signed consent for an employer when the client is unemployed.

Timeliness: You must gather information with the prescribed timelines for each document you gather. For example, if you are required to write letters to probation every 3 months updating them on the treatment progress of your clients, you must fill these out with your client within those parameters.

Clarity: For example, all information must be typed and clear so that if you go on vacation (which you should! Go plan one right now ...) other clinicians can easily manage your caseload without questions of what has already been done.

Consented: We are not ethically permitted to gather information that has not been expressly stated as acceptable to gather, even if we know that information will be a significant aid in the treatment of your client. Clients' right to privacy comes before their right to the best clinical treatment. You must uphold their right to confidentiality.

To obtain consent, you must write out a consent form for the client to sign. In this form, you must show the nature of the treatment proposed, the known effects of both receiving and not receiving the treatment intervention, if any, and all existing alternatives to the proposed intervention, if any exist (Pope & Vasquez, 2007). A consent must inform the client of his or right to refuse the consent at any time. Informed refusal is as important as informed consent (Pope & Vasquez, 2007). In some cases, a client will face consequences for refusing informed consent, such as those clients who are in the probation system. Clients always have a choice in how they want information about them to be handled, but they need to be informed about all of the known consequences, not only those within your treatment program. It is up to you to inquire with probation what, if any, consequences there will be to your clients, and include that information when developing the consent.

You must also explain all parts of the consent that they are expected to sign. You should go over informed consent regularly during the course of treatment, and not only on the first day with all the other paperwork the client is to sign; it must be recurrent (Pope & Vasquez, 2007). Treatment is often initiated when clients are compromised due to intoxication, medication, or psychological upset, causing the client cognitive dysfunction that renders them unable to make informed decisions (Scott, 2000). Considering following the 1:1:1 rule, which has you repeat essential information to the client at the first session, after the first week of treatment, and after the first month of treatment, depending on the length of the program.

This will ensure the client understands the information and can give an informed consent. You must ensure they are able to understand the consent they are signing (Pope & Vasquez, 2007). One helpful tool to establish their cognitive ability is the Mental Status Exam, which should be a staple of the initial paperwork used during the screening and assessment phases with each incoming client. The MSE is designed to highlight dysfunction that might otherwise be missed. For example, one client I interviewed appeared to be of sound mind, able to coherently answer all of my questions, showing no cause to question his ability to give informed consent, until I got to the questions regarding his perception and thought processes. When I asked him about delusions, inquiring whether he felt he ever received messages from the TV or other device, he enthusiastically responded yes, and proceeded to describe an intricate system of dysfunction I may not have otherwise caught until later in the treatment process.

In another example, I was assessing a woman who had claimed three months of sobriety from all drugs. During the MSE, her behavior appeared unremarkable until I asked her about paranoia. She explained that she believed people were watching her, which is not necessarily alarming. Paranoia can be a side effect of using drugs or it can be an indication of a thought disorder, but it can also be a reality for drug users, as police and other officials may in fact be watching them. When I inquired further with the client, she began to describe a web of connections that made no rational sense. She mapped it on a piece of paper, becoming more agitated as she drew nonsensical connections between people. It soon became clear that either a substance intoxication or another mental disorder was being presented. The standard drug test was collected showing methamphetamine in her system. People with varying degrees of dysfunction may be able to appear of normal capacity, but the right questions can highlight issues that will not only need to be addressed in treatment, but that may render them unable to adequately consent to their care.

In the case of the treatment of children or adolescents, informed consent takes on another dimension. If the client is underage it is the responsibility of the clinician to gain informed consent from the guardian of the client. The guardian must be informed of all material of which you would inform an adult client, so that he or she may make the most informed decisions about the treatment of the minor. This gets a bit trickier for mature minors. Adolescents are given more autonomy, and are allowed to consent to their own treatment in most states (Belitz, 2008), which promotes the ethical pillars.

Confidential: You must uphold your client's right to confidentiality in all information gathering except when required by law. Clinicians are required to notify law enforcement if a client threatens violence of an identified person(s) and the threat is believed to be of a serious nature, known as the Duty to Warn, due to the landmark 1974 case of *Tarasoff v. Board of Regents of the University of California* (Manuel & Forcehimes, 2008). The trick to this is knowing when to report and when to merely document, by assessing the likelihood that the client will carry out the threat. You are encouraged to err on the side of caution and notify law enforcement even if you are unsure of the severity of the threat, as it is your ethical obligation to do so.

However, it is not uncommon for clients to express frustration and anger toward people in their lives, and to vent those feelings in the counseling session. Thus, clinicians will often hear emotions expressed with a desire to retaliate or find a physical outlet for the emotions. You want to create a setting where the client feels comfortable venting regardless of what comes out of their mouth, as sometimes we use harsher words than we intend when expressing negative emotions, and clients may sound more threatening than they intend. Clinicians with a firmly established rapport, especially over a significant amount of time, will be better able to assess statements made by the client as threatening or innocuous venting. Other clinicians will not have a solid relationship to help decide the severity of the threat. Clinicians should also seek counsel in either scenario from supervisors, colleagues, and lawyers to ensure they take the most ethical action (Manuel & Forcehimes, 2008).

Storing Written Material

The appropriate procedure for storing written clinical material is also of great ethical concern.

Confidential: The most significant factor in storing material is Confidentiality. Consider your office: What are the steps you or your superiors have taken to assure the confidentiality of stored records? Are your files locked in a secure setting at all times? This means that records are not only locked away at night when you leave the office, but that while they are being used throughout the day, they are either in a locked setting or under the watchful eye of a staff member. Many clinicians and other staff leave piles of records in their individual and communal office spaces during the day. When they leave to run a group, or attend a meeting, or eat their lunches, the files stay on their desks. If they have office doors that lock, this is not a problem, as long as the clinician or staff member is meticulous about locking their door every time they leave. But in many agencies, doors don't lock or there is an open office setting filled with cubicles without doors. There is nothing to keep another person from glancing at records or taking them away as they pass a cubicle.

At other agencies, doors are supposed to be locked but are not. It may be annoying to carry around a key, but it is far more devastating to be sitting in front of your Ethics Board with your license in jeopardy, having to explain how the law of confidentiality was violated because you were annoyed. Once that record, or any of the papers within it, go into your hands you are in charge of it until you can restore it to the chart/file room. You need to think of that record the same way that a doctor sees a transplant heart. Once someone takes hold of that cooler with ice, they are responsible for it until they can get it to the operating room and the heart into the body of the poor soul waiting for it. That scenario is a tad more dramatic than ours but we need to use the same care.

One of the office areas that is the most fertile ground for ethical violations is the front office, or reception area. This is the busiest part of the office, with staff, clinicians, and clients walking through it all day long. Charts are dropped off and picked up, phone calls are answered every minute, and faxes hum, spitting out paper filled with confidential information. It can be challenging to balance the need for consistent confidentiality with the efficiency that a busy office demands. Yet when met with that predicament, the confidentiality argument must win, every time. All material must be dispensed where it cannot be seen by people who are not authorized to see it.

There are office areas where the client charts of the day are stacked in front of a glass window in perfect sight of anyone speaking with the reception staff. There are fax machines nestled in with the client suggestion box, so that one may peruse the information on faxes while slipping in their suggestion (or pretending to submit one). There are urine collection cups neatly set in a line with labels giving the first name, last name, and birthday of each client. Clients are then asked to enter the room and find the cup with their name, allowing each to peruse the list of client names and birthdays.

A major snag in storing information involves those clinicians who work in the field, and therefore do not have an office or a locked location. These clinicians use their vehicles to meet clients in other locations, such as the client's home. The important outreach work is a valuable part of our profession, but it renders the confidentiality of records a challenge. Many clinicians take the necessary clinical record with them on the road, violating confidentiality in the process. Some clinicians say the records are safely locked in the trunk of their car when not in use. Locking records in the trunk of the car is certainly better than leaving them out in the open on the front seat; however, if the car is stolen, or if some accident befalls the clinician, the records are not secure. It is better to leave the record at the office and bring a notebook for jotting down information to include in progress notes, or blank progress notes without identifying information. If you need to sign paperwork, include only that instead of the whole chart. Put these materials in a locked portable file cabinet. It is still out in the open, but is locked and you have taken what steps you can in the scenario.

If you are in private practice, the same rules apply to storing your records, but it may require a bit more work to ensure you abide by them. You must also store your records in a locked, secure location. If you do not have your own office space, if you are renting, subletting, or sharing a space, you must find another way to secure your records. You can rent storage space, share storage space with other clinicians in your building, or buy a locked file cabinet for the office space. It is unethical to take records to your home, or anywhere else outside of the locked space. If you use electronic records on a computer, laptop, tablet, or other electronic device, you are even more susceptible to ethical error. You must not carry records with you that are not secure.

If using electronic records on a computer in your own office you must ensure they can be securely stored on your computer in a locked office. If you are using a laptop or other portable device that you take with you, confidentiality is harder to maintain. The best-case scenario is securing all written clinical information on a portable USB device (flash or thumb drive), which you then lock up in the office or another secure, locked location you provide. If you are using a device that does not support the use of a small portable storage drive, such as a smart phone, you must password protect your device and change the password often. You must not add a client name to your address book. You need to regularly delete texts, voicemails, and emails from any device. Although it may be efficient and easy to use these portable devices, you should strongly consider a different mode of electronic use, as it is much harder to ensure the safety of the clinical information. If your portable computer device or drive is lost or stolen, you will have violated a federal law and put the welfare of your clients, the future of your practice, and the stability of the profession at risk. The long term storage of files also must include procedures to ensure confidentiality. For example, they must be stored in a locked space in a clear system, so that the records can easily be found.

Dispensing Written Material

How you dispense of the clinical material is of the utmost ethical importance. When that material leaves your hands and travels elsewhere, whatever the mode of travel, there is fertile ground for ethical violations; thus you must do everything in your power to ensure it is protected to the best of your ability. Written material that is often disseminated consists of correspondence, written case consultations, and referral documents, and any other documents that identifies entities you are charged with protecting: clients, client supports, colleagues, and in some cases the agency itself. Here are a few important aspects you need to maintain the ethical dispensation.

Veracity: All clinical material dispensed to the public must be truthful. For example, sending a written referral, you must not omit or change information you think might negatively impact your client's acceptance. If you know that Lou desperately needs sober housing, but that the local sober housing program prohibits prescription medication of any kind, you may not omit the fact that Lou is prescribed antianxiety medication.

Validity: It is extremely important that you send information about the appropriate people to the appropriate people in the appropriate situations. For example, it is unacceptable to refer someone to a program that you know will not be a good fit, simply to have a referral on record in your chart. As another example, it is unacceptable to send client information to your friend who works in a nonsecure part of an agency when protocol demands you send it to a specific intake coordinator.

Clarity: Clinical material to be dispensed must be clearly labeled with accurate information so that it reaches its destination as intended. With all outgoing paperwork, you should have a specific person listed to receive the material, someone you can contact to ensure its safe arrival, and who you can hold accountable if mistakes are made on their end.

Consent: You may only send information for which you have a consent-to-release-information form signed by the client, with explicit understanding that this information will be sent in the manner you are sending it. It is not acceptable to say you are going to send the information in the mail and then email it instead without the client's knowledge. The client must understand the specifics of the agreement and must be notified if there are changes. When corresponding, one should only give information that is absolutely necessary. Because we have federal laws dictating how we should dispense information and there are severe consequences for us if we don't, it is easy to lose the client in our concerns. But the client is who we are ultimately protecting.

Confidentiality: The dispensing of confidential information is just as important and just as easily disobeyed. Again, if you see the paperwork as people, rather than paper, it becomes an easier task to respect the gravity of protecting it. You would not risk the confidentiality of your clients by transporting them places and broadcasting their client status. Thus, you must ensure the clinical information is not available to hands, or eyes, other than your own.

All identifying information pertaining to a client must be dispensed in a clear, confidential format, no matter what the route of transmission. There should be a confidentiality statement attached to all material sent out of your office, such as this example of an email correspondence:

CONFIDENTIALITY NOTICE This electronic mail message and all attachments may contain confidential information belonging to the sender or the intended recipient. This information is intended ONLY for the use of the individual or entity named above. If you are not the intended recipient, you are hereby notified that any disclosure, copying, distribution (electronic or otherwise), forwarding, or taking any action in reliance on the contents of this information is strictly prohibited. If you have received this electronic transmission in error, please immediately notify the sender by telephone, facsimile, or email to arrange for the return of the electronic mail, attachments, or documents.

The same statement may be used for standard snail mail correspondence, faxes, and emails simply by changing the "electronic mail message" to correspond with the method used.

Publishing Written Material

The ethical management of published written material follows similar guidelines to those used with the general dispensation of information we just discussed. Published material has a wider audience, and is material that will be available indefinitely. Thus, errors can be particularly harmful and the clinician must be especially vigilant about following ethical procedures to protect the information. Published material is described by the same rules that have already been discussed. Material must be truthful, precise, appropriate, and published with the strictest confidentiality. If identifiable information is used in any way, it must be thoroughly consented to.

Credit: Clinicians must give credit to all contributors to published material. If your thought came from something you read or heard from another, or even if your thought was inspired by another, you must name the other. You must give credit where credit is due, just as you would want credit given to you for your original ideas. Specifically, you must cite sources on which your ideas are based, include existing joint authors, include other contributors in the footnotes, perhaps those who completed significant clerical work that made your publication possible. You must include both unpublished and published research if it was significant to your work, and you must name an editor and authors if several works are compiled together.

A potential snag in this principle is the definition of a publication. Perhaps the majority of clinicians read this principle and think of journal articles and books, publications that reach a wide audience, but what of smaller publications that might not reach as far? Newsletters, brochures, blogs, and websites are all examples of publications that must uphold the same ethical principles as the more formal types of publications. Now it gets a little more interesting. If you read tons of blogs and websites, as many of you do, you might find that a site that follows these authorship guidelines can be rare. When was the last time you saw authors quoted on a brochure? Space is less of an issue with blogs and websites, so it should be easy to take the space to appropriately credit sources. Newsletters and brochures can be very tricky to make; one needs to stuff a lot of information in a tiny space. Still, we can do better than what is out there.

Using Technology

We have to take a moment and consider again the use of technology in our practices and the effect on confidentiality. Our clinical world is increasingly using and relying on technology to function (Powell & Brodsky, 2004). Voicemail, email, cell phones, texting, electronic records, the Internet, blogs, ebooks, online learning, chat rooms, Facebook, MySpace, LinkedIn, Skype, you name it, we'll find a way to use it. The good news is that aspects of our work get easier and easier with the introduction of technological advances. We enjoy the clinical advantage of having easier access to and for our clients, and it is better for the planet. We are relieved to finally have the administrative advantage of the electronic record; at least our relief has come after the agonizing period of hellish chaos while we changed over to the new electronic record. The electronic record allows us to access clinical material within moments instead of taking hours to hunt down paper records that have a tendency to jump into drawers and other offices when we are looking for them. Conducting sessions online allows access to our clients like never before, with sessions guaranteed even if the client is unable to leave the home (Powell & Brodsky, 2004).

Technology can benefit the counseling process by allowing immediate feedback to all staff, and allowing greater access to material that enhances professional tasks. Specifically, technology can produce: (a) cybercounseling, which consists of sessions from remote locations (Nassar-McMillan & Niles, 2011; Whitter et al., 2006); (b) software that helps us with billing, scheduling, and record keeping (Nassar-McMillan & Niles, 2011); (c) information about diagnosis, testing, treatment, and other references (Nassar-McMillan & Niles, 2011); and (d) online learning (Nassar-McMillan & Niles, 2011; Whitter et al., 2006).

Unfortunately, most computerized systems are reserved for administrative tasks and staff, even though research suggests they can be a whopping benefit to clinical duties (Whitter et al., 2006). While funding technology continues to be a concern for agencies, research shows that recruitment, retention, and work development are all improved by the use of technology, especially with young people who rely on technology in all aspects of their lives (Whitter et al., 2006).

But what effect does this ease of access have on our ability to uphold the confidentiality of our clients? The more technology we use, the less control we have over the information that leaves our hands. This does not indicate that technology works against us; instead it indicates the need for careful attention to the new tools we are using. First, every piece of information pertaining to a client must have a clear confidentiality statement attached, whether it is a formal letter, a fax, an email, or a text. Second, be wary of any form of technology, such as texting or email, that can reveal the identity of your client should the device be stolen. At the very least, you must password protect any device and software that uses clinical information to safeguard against that and inform all clients of the risk as part of the HIPAA privacy form you give clients at the start of treatment.

Third, it is not advised to "friend" clients on social platforms, such as Facebook. It confuses the principle of client relationships, as we've discussed, and isn't healthy boundary setting for your own protection. From a confidentiality perspective, it is ill advised because you could be inadvertently naming clients. If you list your credential and where you work, and your clients reveal their recovery status, people can connect your work with their recovery and assume they are your clients. It simply is information you cannot control. The rules of confidentiality are the same no matter what technology is being used, and the clinician has to be vigilant about ensuring that information is dispensed in a safe manner when using technology.

In addition, technology rules may highlight clashes between the tiers of ethics. For example, Jane both has a private practice and works for an agency. She gives her clients her cell phone number in case they need to reach her, since it is easier to reach her on her cell phone than it is on either office phone. She tells clients to send her a short text if they are running late or if they need to be called for a particular clinical reason. In her private practice, she sends homework and receipts of paid fees to her clients via email. This system works for Jane, and she feels she can better manage both offices and all her client needs using this technology.

However, when her boss at the agency, Shawn, learns of her use of technology, he calls her into his office and tells her she can no longer use her cell phone with clients. Jane balks, explaining the wonderful benefits of using this technology. Shawn agrees, but states that he has no control over information that is traded outside of the agency, and HIPAA laws dictate that the agency manages correspondence in the building. Shawn explains that the agency is liable for the confidentiality, and the agency has no control or knowledge of communication outside of the walls on personal devices. In private practice, it is different because your cell phone may be the only office phone, and because you, the clinician, are in charge of all communication, not an agency. If you work in an agency, check with your supervisor to ensure that you are adhering to ethical mandates.

The moral of the story is that technology is good, but it demands an increase in our ethical vigilance. If you are unsure of how to appropriately use technology in your practice, discuss the idea with your supervisor, trusted advisors, or an Ethics Consultant. Before we take a look at the juicy issues spoken material can give us, let's look at an example or two of how these concepts play out at work.

VIGNETTE: THE DECISION METHOD

Billie struggled with addiction for most of her early life before successfully entering recovery. After being in recovery for a few years, she started training to be a counselor. She successfully became credentialed and had two fulfilling jobs in the profession. She suddenly had inspiration for a different treatment model. Disillusioned by AA, Billie had been more impressed with a cognitive model of treatment. One day, when she was having coffee with a friend, her friend said out loud, "I just wish I could *decide* not to be an alcoholic anymore. That I could *will* myself to not drink, or to not have a problem with it." Billie pondered the possibility. Why couldn't that happen, she wondered? Billie began to develop a new method of treatment in which the client simply decides to no longer have a problem with alcohol. She named it the Decision Method, and based it on the tools of Cognitive Behavioral Therapy she had learned when she was in treatment herself. She began to talk about the Decision Method everywhere she went, and started fleshing out the idea in writing. Her book, *The Decision Method*, was self-published 2 years later, claiming to be the new foolproof technique to treat addiction. Billie claimed that the Decision Method would work for any addict and is the only way to recover. She included a few "scientific" studies in her book that were based on people she interviewed in her community who swore by the technique.

The book was a great success and it made Billie a lot of money and a name for herself in the addiction treatment community. Her name did not make news again until, 3 years later, she was arrested for driving while under the influence of alcohol. While embarrassing, and surely calling to question the success of her treatment technique, her arrest brought about discussions of the ethical nature of her book. The consensus among clinicians is that her book is unethical. Why do you think that was the conclusion? Do you agree?

Consider this: Was the book truthful and honest? Was it presented in a professional and factual way? The book does not have accuracy because it states the method is the only way to recover, which is simply false. Even if the method she is suggesting does in fact work, it is not the only way. The second issue is its credit. Billie does not explain where the idea came from, or more importantly, where her research came from, where the subjects in her "scientific" experiments came from, and where her results came from. The third issue is one of veracity. It is not ethical to claim you are an expert when you have not received substantial training. It is also unethical to write a book based on one single untested idea (unless it is a memoir). Billie may be on to a good idea, but it has to be tested across many groups of people and circumstances before being considered a successful intervention. You must be careful what you put in print and read with a critical eye. What other problems do you detect?

VIGNETTE: WHEN DOES A RELEASE END?

Arlene is in private practice and counseling a 16-year-old young man, Connor, with an opiate addiction. She counsels him into a solid recovery program and is delighted when he continues to maintain his recovery and achieve each of his goals. Throughout his treatment, Arlene meets with Connor's parents and helps the family improve their communication and identify communal family goals, learning to support each other in the process. As the counseling sessions progress, it becomes clear that Connor is ready to decrease his sessions until, during one session, Arlene realizes that he no longer needs her. Since she is aware of the ethical principle that dictates she must terminate when a client no longer needs her, Arlene discusses termination with Connor, and when he is ready, she terminates the therapy and wishes him well. About 3 weeks after termination, Connor's mother contacts Arlene, asking when his next appointment is scheduled, further commenting that she has great concerns about his well-being and would like to update Arlene before she sees him. During his therapy, Arlene had an open release to speak with his parents and it was not unusual for his parents to bring issues to her from time to time, nor was it unusual for a parent to double-check on the session schedule, as they shared one car. If he was still in therapy, Arlene would have verified the session time, listened to her concerns, and then discussed them with Connor in session. Can she still do this, since she has that release?

Raise your hand if you said yes. Okay, put your hands down; you guys are wrong in this case (sorry). Any of you know why? The consent to release information ends on the date specified on the consent, or upon termination, whichever comes first. Connor is no longer her client, and therefore she may not speak to anyone regarding her knowledge of him, even those people with whom she had releases during treatment. She must explain this to the mother, and advise her to go speak with her son directly. It will be awkward, especially if she has forged a therapeutic relationship with the mother as well, but it will be immensely helpful (and ethically appropriate) to spell this out when she begins treatment with a client and with his or her family. That way if she needs to remind them of this when treatment ends, it won't come as a surprise.

The only exception to this is if the client needs you to verify that they were in treatment for some reason, such as a legal case that requires treatment verification. In this case, the client needs to come back and sign a new consent dated with the current posttreatment date. The consent needs to specify that the client is no longer receiving treatment but that you have permission to release specific information that you must write out to the specific person for the specific reason that you name, and then put an immediate termination of consent date, whatever is needed to finish the requested business. Without that, you cannot talk to anyone, even if you want to, even if it is in the best interest of the client to do so. Your confidentiality supersedes any issue of client welfare or good treatment practices. Don't forget that the principle of confidentiality is not only about the one client standing in front of you. Your actions speak to the whole profession, and if you violate confidentiality it puts both your career and the profession at risk.

The use of written clinical material is an unavoidable aspect of our daily work. It is required in every area of our jobs; no wonder we can get overwhelmed by it and resentful of it. While it may seem that the rules are unreasonable or overstated, they are there to protect the client, you and your colleagues, and the profession. Furthermore, following these guidelines may make your job easier. Consider how it will help you adhere to the ethical principles. The more you internalize these rules of the ethical development, gathering, storing, dispensing, and publishing of clinical material, the easier it will become to use the rules across your clinical population and establish a standard of operation, regardless of client differences, that the pillar of justice requires. The care you place in ensuring that all written material is adequately consented to helps you to establish the cooperation of your clients in protecting their own interests that the pillar of autonomy promotes. The control you execute on safeguarding the confidentiality of all written material, including applying the appropriate credit when necessary, demonstrates your attention to the pillar of nonmaleficence by avoiding the harm that will surely come if you fail to take these measures. Finally, adhering to all the elements of protection, veracity, accuracy, validity, timeliness, clarity, credit, consent, and confidentiality confirms your focus on promoting healthy and effective treatment of your clients and profession, in line with the pillar of beneficence. Again, how you care about your clients is reflected in how you handle clinical information that pertains to them.

The crux of this principle is that you need to uphold your professional standards in all written work with honesty and integrity. Although this may seem an easy task, it in fact requires time and rigorous attention to ensure you are satisfying the ethical mandate. This job only becomes more challenging with the ease and inundation of information dispensed through a myriad of portals. Part of respecting the tiers of ethics is acknowledging their expectations of how we handle clinical material. If we develop this key it becomes easier to ensure the proper use of written material. Before we explore what happens if we are unsuccessful in our efforts, let's look at the proper use of spoken clinical material.

Principle: Proper Use of Spoken Clinical Material

9

Chapter

In addition to protecting clinical information in writing, clinicians must also be mindful of the clinical information that is spoken. In your code of ethics there is a principle devoted to public statements; it may even have that title. It may be that clinicians scan through this principle, feeling it only pertains to press statements behind a microphone, and therefore not to them. In fact, any clinical material that you broadcast, no matter the size of the audience, must be ethically protected. True, this principle pertains to those of us who spend some time up on a soapbox speaking to groups of people, but it also pertains to those of us who make statements to our client groups, or colleagues at a staff meeting, or client families. You may not be as famous as the leader of a movement, and you may not have as wide an audience as a conference speaker, but as a member of this profession, every statement you make is reflected back to those groups of which you are a member or employee. This means what you say to your clients, your colleagues, and your students is also included in the clinical material you need to protect. This changes things, doesn't it? Read on....

In case this is not clear, this means that just because few are there to hear it, you are not free to broadcast your opinions without ensuring their veracity, accuracy, validity, consent, and confidentiality, and crediting them as solely your opinion. We must ensure that we do not forward our own agenda through our public statements. We also must be careful to avoid forwarding our own judgments or discriminations about other people in our public statements. We must ensure that our spoken material is truthful, accurate, clear, timely, confidential, and consented to by all parties involved.

Although we must ensure the proper use of spoken clinical material in all that we do there are a few areas that come up particularly often. These areas—counseling, teaching and training, and communication and consultation—deserve special attention.

Counseling

The material we use in our individual and group counseling must fall under the same guidelines as other material we use on a daily basis. Clients and other professionals come to you as an expert, as someone who can help them achieve a goal. With that responsibility comes an obligation to be mindful about what you are saying out loud.

Veracity: As clinicians, we should not lie to our clients. To promote autonomy, we cannot prevent them from knowing the truth about situations that concern them. For example, it is unacceptable to tell your client that attending her brother's wedding will not be triggering if she follows your counseling advice.

Accuracy: As clinicians we must acknowledge that information on the principles and treatment of addiction is limited, meaning that we must understand and admit to others that information may progress beyond what you are teaching today. We learn something new every day, they say, so be prepared for changes in the information you are presenting and do not tout it as factual beyond the possibility of modification. This statement also takes into account that there are aspects of addiction we may never understand, and it is important to state this, particularly when asked direct questions for which there are no current answers. In short, don't make something up; respect that there are questions you will not be able to answer.

Can you see how this would apply to everyone, and not just trainers and elected officials? How often are you asked a question in group and shudder to have to say those three little words: "I don't know." Perhaps we think this makes us appear a weak clinician, that somehow we should know all the answers and be able to give them verbatim at any moment. That's just silly; no one can do that. It is perfectly acceptable—in fact, it is your ethical obligation—to tell the questioner that you do not know the best answer, but that you are willing to look into it. At times an answer will be available with the right research, and at times there is no available answer yet. This also means that you must acknowledge that the information and advice you are giving to clients is subject to change, especially if you have been in the field for some time. Here is an obvious example. In the "olden" days,

addiction was thought of as a moral impairment, and treatment consisted of punishment, typically involving straight-jackets or other restraints, and seclusion from life until the subject could "snap out of it" (Beam, 2001; Grob, 1994; Torrey & Miller, 2001; Whitaker, 2002). Today, we would see such treatment as barbaric, but counselors of that day believed it was the answer. More recently, we utilized the corporeal model, where clinicians would confront clients, cut them down with harsh words, and then (technically) build them back up to a stable person who did not want to use. There may be places where these techniques are still used, and a specific subpopulation may respond well to this treatment, but most experts today would argue that the confrontational model risks doing more harm than good, and it has largely fallen out of fashion (Whitter et al., 2006).

A current example of this would be the encouragement and use of AA and other 12-step based programs. In the not-too-distant past, the 12-step model was seen as the only available self-help technique, and treatment programs adopted it so successfully that in many places it has become a requirement in the program (Whitter et al., 2006). However, just as there is no one treatment technique that works for every single client, there is no one self-help program that works for every single client. The majority are likely to gain some benefit from attending 12-step meetings and immersing themselves in the 12-step program, as there is no question that the principles of the program are helpful. Yet not everyone responds well to the 12-step program, for a variety of reasons. Other self-help programs have been created, such as Rational Recovery (Trimpey, 1996), and while certainly not as accessible, they offer an alternative to 12-step-based programs. Some clients create their own self-help program, without any specific formal entity. They take all the best components and create the same outcome using different avenues. It may not be as streamlined as a formal program, but it may work wonders for your client. If you personally are a hardcore 12-step promoter, you are going to have to acknowledge that new information may have been produced that is potentially helpful to your clientele. It is your ethical responsibility to present all the information, in this case in the form of self-help options, to your clients.

Confidentiality: The counselor should reveal confidential information to authorities only when there is a clear and imminent danger to the client or to other persons. The conditions under which we can reveal information are specific: if there is a danger of our client engaging in self-harm or suicide, if there is a danger of our client harming another person, if there is a risk of child or elderly endangerment or abuse, if a client is incapable of caring for him or herself (Pope & Vasquez, 2007; Washington & Demask, 2008). Easy, right? Well, not really.

Clinicians can get snagged by the definition of danger, either by underestimating or overestimating what they observe. It is much worse to underestimate danger. If you fail to read the danger signs your client gives you, or if you explain them away as baseless when they should be investigated, you can land yourself in hot water indeed, even finding yourself facing a suspension or revocation of your license/credential. Not to mention that people can die if you ignore the signs. There are not always signs that your client is in trouble, and you can only act on what information comes your way. It is when you do not act on information that you get into trouble.

It can be challenging to read behavior and verbal messages; clients are consumed with swirls of emotions they are learning to manage. At times they may express angry threats they do not intend to carry out, or cries for help that are not warranted. You may suspect that there is not a great risk presenting itself. In those cases, discuss it with your supervisor or other superior and check your decision making with them. If they disagree, or if you have any gnawing feeling (remember, that is your gut talking!), it is wise to make a report. You must act according to your state's procedures. If you overestimate danger and act accordingly, you may anger certain people involved but you will always be able to stand your ground with "I acted with the best information that I had at the time, and thought it better to be safe than sorry." You need to document your heart out, explaining what you observed and why you made your choice of action.

How you deal with your concerns matters a great deal. You don't want to overreact or get so freaked out by your own liability that you abandon client welfare. For example, a client once told me about the following experience with a previous counselor. The client was struggling, and his depression symptoms had recently increased, which kicked up his anxiety symptoms and caused him to relapse … which caused his depression symptoms to increase further. You can detect the pattern. During one session, the client was expressing his despair and said, "More and more I'm thinking it would be easier if I just wasn't around. I just can't fight anymore." According to the client, the counselor's eyes grew wider and he asked, "Are you thinking of committing suicide?" The client acknowledged that he had been thinking about it. The counselor then said, "Would you excuse me for a minute, I'll be right back" and left the room. The client heard a click on the door, and suddenly his counselor's voice came through a hidden speaker telling the client that he had called the police and locked the client into the office for safety until the police could arrive. The client was incredulous, because he did not feel he was at that level of risk; he had no history of suicidal behavior. Most importantly, he felt the counselor overreacted, and did not spend any time assessing how much risk was present. There were no words of comfort or understanding, and the client spent years mistrusting counseling as a result.

On the other hand, you must be prepared that taking the appropriate ethical step will not always be supported by your clients. Many clients will fault you for interfering, for overreacting, or for betraying their trust. They may leave treatment because of your actions, and you may never see them again. I have had clients screaming expletives at me in the background while speaking on the telephone with the police I had called to report my clinical concern and to request a safety assessment. Although certainly unpleasant, it is better to have an alive and angry client than one who is no longer around to express emotions. Always remember that divulging confidential information for the sake of reporting a risky situation is your right and your ethical duty, just as keeping your client's information confidential in nonrisky situations is also your ethical duty.

Teaching/Training

The material we use in teaching and trainings must follow the same guidelines. It is imperative that your trainings have veracity, meaning that when you present yourself as an expert on a topic or clinical scenario you give truthful information, and clarity and timeliness, in addition to the following requirements.

Accuracy: Accurate information means you have studied what you are saying and know that it is up-to-date, fact-based, and error-free. I'm sure you can all name trainings you have attended that cannot hold claim to this definition of accuracy, despite what the presenter may have stated. Fair information means that the information must be unbiased, legitimate, and honest. It is difficult to be passionate enough about a topic to develop and present trainings on it without becoming biased.

Group leaders tend to stick to the information they have been giving in past groups; it is pragmatic to do so when one has a limited time to spend on group preparation. But how do you know you are presenting the most accurate and fair information if you are not actively engaging in the research available to ensure there is no better information to present? This principle is essentially stating that it is the obligation of all counselors and trainers to maintain their own education on the topics they are aiming to teach, whether individually, through group counseling, or through a workshop or training. You cannot simply rest on your laurels and present the same material time and again.

For example, Mohammed is a trainer of a workshop that explores using spirituality in addiction treatment. Since Mohammed had an early career as a theology student, he brings a vast knowledge of spirituality to his trainings. However, Mohammed also recognizes that his early career can make him biased. He comments on his background and bias potential at the start of each training he gives. He discusses how he came to understand the information he presents to the group, and encourages the audience members at every training to do their own research on the topic, giving additional authors to read. This is the ethical way to present information to a group.

Validity: When teaching or training, you must craft and deliver appropriate trainings that fit with the setting and population you are treating, utilizing information that is valid. For example, a trainer, let's call him Chad, presented about 20 minutes of good material, and about 5 hours and 40 minutes of *really* personal information. Participants learned about his recent near-death experience and the steps he needed to take to keep his body alive. They learned about the effect of this experience on his marriage and his self-esteem, and how his work suffered until he could pull it back into shape. He also spent a great deal of time advertising his publications he had available for sale, and discussing how amazing it was that people loved him so much. It was grandiose and it was shocking. Sadly, this presenter had many good things to teach, if he could have stuck to the material. It was also concerning that the company, a reputable one, continued to hire him. So do not be a Chad; stick to the professional material.

Perhaps a good way to think about this principle is by remembering the notion that what comes out of your mouth matters. You do not own your mouth alone, it now belongs to a collective voice, that of the agency in which you work, the licensing body that gave you your credential, the organizations with which you are affiliated, and the profession of which you are a member. All of those entities are relying on your adherence to these ethical principles.

Credit: Trainers must reveal to the audience the necessary training and qualifications required to properly perform the skills and techniques in their trainings. Really? Huh. This is a great idea, but I'm certain this is not always done. We train on fantastic topics with capable trainers, but their trainings do not always include a component of how to become qualified in the topic of the training. Consider the last training you attended; did the trainer tell you how you can train on the topic? If so, great! But if not, I would not be surprised. Even if you are attending a training on Cognitive Behavioral Therapy (CBT), you may learn a lot about what CBT is and how it can be a wonderful intervention with different populations of clients suffering from different diagnoses. But does the trainer tell you, here is where to go to get specific CBT training; to become an expert on CBT take classes here; or read these books? This is not to say that you have to provide the training, just that you need to provide the information on how to become qualified in the topic. Any trainer who is presenting the information on a topic, such as CBT, should know how to become qualified in the area, as they are purported to be an expert on the topic. If you are a trainer and cannot provide this information on your topic, go now and do your homework before your next training.

If you don't have time to do this, provide a handout to trainees, or list a website that gives all the ethically necessary information. It can be that easy to abide by the principle. Why is it so important for us to do this? First, it ensures the credibility of the trainers and shows they have done their own homework in producing the training materials. Second, it makes it easy for the trainees to further develop their skills and expertise. Third, a profession must have clear, communicable techniques in order to be considered a valid profession. We will discuss this more in the next section. This principle ensures that will be the case. Thus, this small portion of the principle satisfies both the clinician and the profession.

Consent: When using client material in trainings, you must obtain the client's consent. You must ensure that you have explained yourself well to your client in representing how the interviews or recordings will take place, giving detailed information so that the client may make an informed choice. If he or she elects not to participate, you must comply with his or her wishes, even if it hurts your clinical or academic agenda. At times, you will want to avoid client participation to protect the client, regardless of whether the client agrees with you.

For example, Marcus is a client of Helen's who is graduating from the treatment program in one week. He has 4 months of recovery and has created a solid recovery framework with good sober supports. Once every 6 weeks, Helen's weekly family education group meets to hear a panel of clients in recovery and family members who graduated from the group speak about their experiences. When Marcus was a client in the program and attended that particular group, he told Helen with excitement that he looked forward to the day he could be a panelist. At the time, Helen responded with encouragement, feeling Marcus would be an excellent candidate for the panel.

However, while he is in Phase II of the treatment program, a new client enters into Phase I of the program, a client known to Marcus. It is Marcus's employer, and neither knows the other has an addiction. Helen thinks it would be potentially damaging to Marcus if he appears as a panelist in a group that includes his employer as a client. She does not want Marcus to be fired or treated differently because of his addiction or recovery status. However, she cannot explain this problem to Marcus without abusing the confidentiality of the employer client. What should she do?

Typically, ethical vignettes describe a scenario between a client and a nonclient, and the counselor must choose between them. These vignettes can be tricky, but the answer usually lies with the client, with whom you must maintain loyalty. But here, both subjects are clients, which means Helen must be equally loyal, so how can it be solved? You shout out your ideas, and then I'll tell you mine. Okay, so hopefully by this point in the book you are fairly certain it will be suggested that Helen seeks out guidance from a supervisor and/or a trusted advisor.

This is a cloudy scenario, so she should not go about solving it alone without some support. Next, consider her responsibility. Is she obligated to protect both clients equally? On one hand, she should uphold the confidentiality of both people to the best of her ability. On the other hand, the employer is her active client who must attend the group and Marcus will be a graduate who is attending the group by choice. He's the one to work with for this reason. Helen should say nothing to the employer at any time. She should prohibit Marcus from speaking at the event, but she will need to find a reason that does not destroy the confidentiality of the employer.

At a recent training in which this example was evaluated, it was suggested that Helen tell Marcus that there was someone in the group that he knew without naming the person. This way she is not lying to Marcus, but is also not divulging the confidentiality of the employer. Good? Do you see a potential problem with that? In this case, if Helen tells Marcus that there is someone in the group he knows, she will have said too much. Helen has no way of knowing what Marcus will do with this information. Perhaps he will be unable to contain his curiosity and will hide outside the agency, waiting to see who arrives for group. At the very least, he is likely to flip through the Rolodex in his brain trying to suss out the identity of the client he knows. For all Helen knows it may not take much effort. Perhaps there are few people he knows who could possibly have an addiction; perhaps it will be easy for him to identify his employer based on the little she told him. You just do not want to mess with confidentiality.

Instead, it is better to manipulate the scenario to uphold the confidentiality, but with as little lying as possible. Helen could simply tell Marcus that she cannot use him as a panelist this time around, but is looking forward to using him in the following scheduled panel in 6 weeks' time. She could even bolster this by telling Marcus it will be better to wait anyway as he will have 6 more weeks of recovery time to discuss with the group. Focus on the positive; downplay the fact that he cannot be on the upcoming panel; do not give specific reasons that will be lies. If he pointedly asks her why, Helen can say, "There are a few reasons I can't go into, but rest assured there is no problem with you. We just need to do it next time. Let's get back together in a few weeks to plan the next panel." While it may feel manipulative, it is the best option to protect everyone involved.

We use clinical information from session notes or recorded interviews all the time in our trainings, case presentations, or other public conversations. You absolutely may not use client information without the expressed written permission of the client, which must include a detailed description of how the client information will be used, and then you may not, under any circumstances, divert from the stated description. For example, Bea is presenting a case in front of the clinical staff at the mother organization that hosts the agency where she works. She obtains permission from her client to present the case, and assures him that the information she will reveal will be limited to the statements he made in sessions that Bea indicated in the consent. He agrees, but during Bea's case presentation, several questions are posed by the audience that require her to reveal more than the statements her client made in sessions. They want to know more about his demographic information as a possible key to why he made the statements in sessions, so they ask about his background. Bea is trapped, knowing that the information they are asking is important to their understanding of her case.

Let's make it more interesting and say that the people asking are Bea's superiors whom she is anxious to impress in the hopes of gaining a sought-after promotion. Now Bea is torn between knowing that answering their questions is outside the boundaries of her consensual agreement and feeling that answering the questions will put her in a better light for her superiors. She may try to convince herself that it is okay to tell her supervisors, that they will know to keep the information confidential, but she would be ethically incorrect. Her agreement with the client is more important that any other aspect of this scenario, and she must keep to what she designed with the client. If someone asks her a question outside of the boundaries she set, she should state the truth, letting everyone know of the agreement she made with the client and that she will have to check with him before revealing any other information. Bea will be honoring her duty to protect her client, and the hope is that her supervisors will be more excited about her maintaining the ethical obligations than they would be by whatever answers she could have provided. They should give her the promotion based on her ethical prowess! Yet, even if Bea's actions are not well received by her supervisors at the meeting she can feel good knowing she did not violate nonmaleficence.

Confidentiality: The counselor should disguise the identity of the client when using material in classroom teaching. You should never divulge information about a client in a teaching arena. Not only should you not divulge it, you also must make a reasonable effort to disguise the client. Change information that is obvious, such as the client's name, and not obvious, such as his or her gender (if gender is not essential to the issue). We can make errors and say too much without realizing it.

Let's say Isobel is presenting a case from one of your groups. Isobel says, "I have a client I'll choose to call Hans. Hans attended my trauma group...." This statement would be fine, until you realize that the trauma group is small, only five participants. Right away you have narrowed the possible client choices down to five people. Then you realize that the group is made up of four women and one man. Guess who Hans is? Just changing the name does not necessarily disguise the client enough, especially if there is a chance her audience has some knowledge of the setting or people. In the fourth section in this book, I give an example from my own clinical past that gave the detail of an aftercare group. If in my career there was only one job that had an aftercare group, I would have given readers direct information about where this incident occurred. I also state that the client in the scenario had been in treatment for several years. If there were not many clients whom I had treated for several years, I would have betrayed

that client's confidence by giving those two details. Because every outpatient and residential setting in my career has included an aftercare group, I felt safe in reporting that detail. Since I have various clients on my caseloads that I have seen for several years, I felt confident that the client's identity would be hidden.

What should you do if you make a mistake? Let's say you have a very specific clinical example to share with a group you are training. You take every precaution on paper to write out your case example in neutral language that reveals nothing about the client's identity. But when you get up in front of everyone, and swallow a bit of butterflies in your stomach, you become a little distracted and accidentally name the client. To make matters worse, as soon as you name the client you realize your mistake and quickly blurt out the cover name you had planned, which only serves to show that the first name you called out is in fact the client name. Now you have a room full of people who know which client you are discussing, and you have a consent to release information signed by your client that you just violated. What do you do now? First, if there is any way to recover, do it. For example, I once used the correct name of a client, John, then immediately blurted out the prepared stage name, William, in a terrible attempt at recovery. I quickly stopped my talk, and said, "*Man*! I was just talking to my friend John this morning and that is the second time my brain has used his name where it didn't belong. I've got John on the brain! I apologize. So about William...." I did not poll people afterward, but I think it worked. If you are skilled at ad libbing convincingly, then you may want to improvise. If this will not work, don't try to fix the error, just finish your training, taking great care to prevent another error.

Whether you ad lib or not, your next move is to go to your supervisor, or whomever is in charge, and admit the error. You want someone else to know of your error for two reasons. First, so that you can gain support and brainstorm what you should do next. Second, so that in case there is fallout from the client, colleagues, or other professionals, the important officials are already aware of the situation and can anticipate the appropriate reaction. One question you want to be sure to address in your supervisory meeting is whether your client should be told of your blunder. You think about it, and we will come up with a plan.

What are your reasons for telling the client the truth? Honesty is a valued virtue, and it is hard to argue that lying to a client keeps their welfare at the forefront, as we discussed in the vignette when the parents wanted the counselor to lie to Matthew about where they were living. You expect that your clients will be honest with you, even when they make a mistake that works against their recovery, such as relapsing. It's a good idea to model what you expect and afford them the same respect you want to receive. Also, in the event that there will be fallout from saying the client's name out loud, your client deserves to be warned. The likelihood of fallout will depend on the audience in your talk.

What are your reasons for not telling the client of your error? Perhaps you suspect it will damage the client and you worry that to tell him will result in one of the following outcomes: (a) the client will be pained, (b) the client will leave treatment, (c) the client will be upset with you, (d) the client will relapse, or (e) the client will retaliate. All of these are possible, but does the risk outweigh the choice of truthfulness?

Perhaps the best bet is to err on the side of safety, and to inform the client of what occurred in case there are additional protective measures they want to take. While mistakes happen, you owe the client a sincere apology. You may want your supervisor to be present for this conversation to support both you and the client, and the agency, come to think of it. Even if the client is unconcerned with your error, you will have shown him or her that you take their confidentiality seriously and do not take your mistake lightly.

Communication

We spend much of our professional time communicating about the clients we serve, either through letters and phone calls, case consultations, or referrals. We must attend to the areas of veracity, accuracy, validity, timeliness, and clarity that have already been discussed. In addition there is a particular interest in ensuring that all communication is consented and confidential.

Consented: In phone conversations, you must do everything in your power to ensure that the person on the other end of the line is the one named on the informed consent. You must stick to the information that is specified on the consent to release information, and refrain from revealing any other information, even when directly asked for it by the recipient of your phone conversation. There is a common clinical error that clinicians often make, particularly over the phone. It goes something like this: A friend or family member calls you, wanting to tell you some important clinical information about your client, but your client has not signed a release for this person, therefore you can't even say whether you know this client, nor whether he or she is a client of your agency or practice. Yet you are anxious to hear whatever information they have, knowing it may help you treat your client. Perhaps you have been stuck with this particular client, feeling that there is a vital piece of information you are missing. You know you cannot give the caller information, so you say the words: "Due to Federal Confidentiality I cannot confirm or deny whether the person you are calling about is a patient here. However, if you want to talk I can listen to what you have to say."

Have you said this, or something like it? Have you heard others say it? It is generally seen as an acceptable corner-cutting strategy, but it is problematic. Sure, you said the correct words; you did not identify that you knew the client. The problem is that you acknowledged that you know the person by insinuation. Would you say the same words if someone called about a client who was not on your caseload? Some person you had never heard of? Of course not. Who has time to sit on the phone and listen to a story of a client who is not yours? You don't even have time to sit on the phone and listen to a story of a client who *is* yours! By telling the caller you are willing to sit and listen to what they have to say you are insinuating you know the client.

Remember this is not about you, even if you can spin it that more information means better treatment, and thus it is a matter of client welfare. The truth is, you are wanting the information for yourself, forgetting that there may be a specific reason that your client has not signed a release for the person calling. Perhaps the client does not want you to speak to the caller, and that is his or her right. Even if you are fairly certain that the client would not mind you speaking to the caller, you still cannot violate the principle. Sorry Charlie, you are going to have to gather information solely from the sources you have authorization to speak with, and no one else.

Confidentiality: Phone calls where any private information is to be discussed must occur where they cannot be heard. That means that if you answer a phone in the larger reception area, or anywhere in hearing range of clients or other unauthorized persons, you may not reveal any identifying information. You have to close the glass window (if you have one) or move yourself to a safer place before continuing your conversation. It helps to have a healthy awareness of your own voice. Are you quiet as a mouse or robust as a lion, even in your normal speaking voice? If you tend to have a loud voice you must be extra careful about your volume when speaking about confidential information. It won't always be welcome and may slow down your day to make the appropriate accommodations, but it is vital to your ethical practice to abide by these restrictions. I have observed clinicians answering phone calls about one client while in a session or meeting with another client sitting right in front of them. I have heard many clinicians joking in the break room, which happens to be next to the group room with paper-thin walls in between, cringing at the clinical information passed about with no realization that it can all be easily heard. What have you witnessed?

What is your clinical setting like? Do clinicians congregate and gossip about clients? Do they have private case consultations when they want to ask for advice? How do you typically operate? Gossip is ill advised, but clinicians are also human. At times, they may need comic relief when facing a stressful clinical situation, or may need to share their wonder at a clinical example they just encountered. In these cases, all identifying information must be held strictly confidential, even among peers, as there is no therapeutic need to divulge information. There must be a treatment-related reason to dole out identifying information, which should only be used in case consultation. Case consultation is appropriate in private settings at the workplace. Outside of the workplace or in public areas of the workplace precaution should be made to protect the identifying information of the client.

For example, if Holly is struggling between wanting to be honest with loved ones about her HIV status, and feeling triggered to use every time she thinks about revealing her status, Henry, her counselor, may want advice on how to direct her. In discussing the case with a colleague, Henry would obviously need to point out that the client is HIV positive, as that is at the crux of the issue. However, there would be no reason to indicate that the client is female, unless her gender has some bearing on the treatment issue or advice.

There is a caveat to confidentiality for those of you who conduct group counseling. While you, the clinician, are mandated to protect the rights of the clients you treat, the group members are not similarly mandated (Mottley, 2012; Scott, 2000). You ask them to keep all identity and other clinical information confidential, and should have them sign a confidentiality statement. This would be generated from the agency tier, and you will want to enforce this confidentiality to the best of your clinical ability. Yet your confidentiality mandates come from the federal tier, with grave consequences if ignored. Thus, group members can report information communicated in the group to others, even authorities, without legal repercussion, and can even testify in court (Scott, 2000).

Let's throw in a few vignettes for good measure before moving on. Nah, forget vignettes, let's have a quiz. Take out your pencils.

Quiz

A very talented and able public speaker—we'll name her Dr. B.—gives a workshop on relapse prevention. After discussing the concept of triggers according to Dr. B., she tells her audience that the way to cope with triggers and to develop a stable sober lifestyle is through the attendance of AA/NA and "working" the 12 steps. She tells the crowd, "This is the way to recover. I know, I did it." J. D., a clinician and attendee of her training, approaches Dr. B. after her workshop and tells her that he found her training unethical. Why?

Think about it and jot down an answer. [The *Jeopardy!* theme is playing....] Okay, what did you come up with? Hopefully, you spotted several mistakes. First, what principle did the doctor violate? Shout it out with me: "Proper Use of Spoken Material!" Nice job. Now, what specifically went awry in that principle?

- *Validity*: Dr. B. spouted concepts according to her, and did not appear to cite any other sources, or name other experts, or reveal other areas to obtain research or topic-specific information. You cannot present your theory of life; your opinions, observations, and experiences must be rooted in existing science; even if they are a diversion from existing theory, the existing theory must be presented before your amendments can be revealed.

- *Accuracy*: Second, you cannot say *the* way to address a problem is through a given treatment technique. As we've discussed, there is not one single technique that works for every possible person who suffers from addiction. You can say "The best tool I've seen...." or "The most favorable tool in the research or among clients I've treated is...." or even "One of the best is...." In short, a statement that leaves the possibility for alternatives is a must. Remember in Part I we discussed the dilemma of adopting a rigid style. Here we are again, discussing the same concept in a different principle. Rigid public statements are a sure way to earn yourself an unethical stamp. You can present your knowledge with clients or groups with enthusiasm and conviction; just understand that you need to be accurate, fair, and appropriate in all that you present.

- *Credited*: Dr. B. does not explain how to train in self-help groups, specifically 12-step programs, so that trainees can learn more about the specific techniques she is touting as the best tool.

What other problems can you find in this scenario? I gave you three, but there are more. Write them down and go discuss with a supervisor or trusted advisor or your teacher.

Okay, I feel badly about not giving you vignettes and forcing a quiz on you instead, so here are a few examples.

VIGNETTE: HIDDEN TRUTHS

Leo explains to his client Whitney that she should sign a release for her parents for the purposes of inviting them to the family group. Whitney signs a consent to release information for her parents, with the specific information to be released listed as "information pertaining to the Family Education Group" and the reason for release of information listed as "to invite and encourage participation in the Family Education Group." The release is listed as open for one year unless the client is terminated from the program before that date. Whitney agrees to this release and signs it. Leo then sits in his office and phones Whitney's family. He starts out by introducing himself and explaining his role as Whitney's counselor. He then tells the family about the group and encourages them to attend. He should stop the conversation right there, but he has questions he wants to ask, questions that he feels would help steer him in the right direction of therapy for Whitney. So he begins to discuss her past with the parents, trying to gather helpful information. Leo shares a bit about what Whitney has stated, checking her statements against the parents' impressions. In this way, Leo actually divulges quite a bit of information about Whitney, assuming that as her parents, they already know the details.

When she learns of this, Whitney is incensed and distraught, but too emotional to discuss her feelings with Leo. She says nothing, but begins to retreat inside herself, developing physical ailments that keep her away from counseling appointments, until she fades away out of treatment. In supervision, Leo discusses the case, portraying Whitney as a serious addict who "clearly wasn't done using" and who he guesses has relapsed and is back to her old ways. It never occurs to Leo that his own behavior might have been the reason she left treatment. He takes no ownership whatsoever, instead blaming Whitney and her disease for taking her out of treatment. Leo has entirely missed the point.

There may be significant reasons Whitney does not want her parents to have information. In this case, Whitney's father has a long history of sexually abusing her, abuse that he has never admitted to and she has never revealed. She continues to be haunted by her past, and her only solace is in staying as far away as possible from her father, keeping any personal detail away from his ears. She continues to see him with her mother, but ensures that he doesn't know anything personal about her that he can use to manipulate her. In part she does not want him to manipulate her, and in part she does not want to give him what he wants: information. If she withholds that information, she has something he cannot get, and that feels good to her.

Leo has just broken that boundary and has given the father information about Whitney that he didn't have before. Leo has broken through the invisible line that kept the father at arm's length, and kept Whitney feeling safe. In short, he just violated nonmaleficence by doing a whole lot of harm to his client, all of which could have easily been avoided if he had engaged in an honest discussion about the consent form and had followed its directions. You won't always know why your clients refuse to sign consents, or wish them to be written in a specific way, but you have to abide by their wishes and not decide that you know more than the client. Their actions may be far more deliberate than you realize.

VIGNETTE: WHY HELLO!

It is Saturday night, and Zahra's family is taking her and her spouse to a nice dinner out on the town. They go to her favorite local joint, and while waiting for a table she hears a familiar voice. She turns and there is her client out on a date of his own. Her eyes lock with his as her family turns to see who she is looking at. What should she say?

(continued)

Some of you may believe that she should not say anything, not acknowledge the client at all, and simply turn back around to focus on her family or the menu, or whatever distracting material she can find. Some of you may believe that she should say hello to the client, and introduce the client to her family using his first name only and not divulging how she knows him. Others will say she should wait until the client speaks first, and then follow his lead.

Many clinicians will be in this situation several times, and will try each of the choices mentioned and encounter problems with all of them. If Zahra says nothing and turns back around, she may feel awkward, thinking that everyone could see the recognition. And since her family knows what she does for a living, she may have inadvertently announced that the man was a client. Plus, her client may experience rejection and be hurt by this reaction. If Zahra says hello but does not introduce the client, another awkward hush may fall over the crowd and the client and clinician may squirm with discomfort. If she says hello and introduces the client by name, she may feel like she is pushing the boundaries of confidentiality, as perhaps he did not want his name used.

Waiting to see what the client will do can create a host of reactions. Either the client looks desperate, not knowing how to handle the situation either, and the awkward silence grows, or the client describes Zahra in a way that makes the date suspicious and Zahra uncomfortable. It can be the stickiest situation, and it does not take more than a second to feel trapped.

Prevention may prove the most useful tool in this scenario. You and your client should decide in early sessions how you would want to address this inevitable scene, and discuss with each client who walks in your office door exactly how the two of you would handle this situation. Do not wait until you are in the scene to make a decision; it will be too hard and awkward, and you will not have an idea of how your client wants it to be handled. Different clients may have different wishes for how they would want an encounter to be handled; therefore, a specific discussion is recommended. Make a written note of whatever you decide, which will cover you if the client later changes his or her mind and takes issue with how you handled the encounter. Your urgency in this will also depend on where you live. If you live in a big city where meeting clients is possible but not likely, you will want to address it, but perhaps with less urgency than if you live in a small community and see clients all the time.

You can see how complicated the issue of confidentiality can be, and we only discussed a few examples. It is an ever-growing topic that demands our constant vigilance. If we fail to address these principles and if we do not develop respect for the tiers of ethics we are in danger of sliding into the pitfall of confused roles, which can be agonizing. Ready to squirm in some tough predicaments? It will be fun.

Pitfall: Confused Roles

10
Chapter

In the first pitfall, we discussed what occurs when we face conflicted agendas in our practice. In this second pitfall, we will examine what occurs when our roles become confused. As addiction counselors, we have many hats that we must wear in our daily work. We give direct practice to people who have become addicted to substances; we give education and support to their family members; we collaborate with other professionals servicing each of our clients; we give support to and receive support from our colleagues, especially those who work on our clinical team; we comply with administrative duties mandated by all the tiers of ethics; we cooperate with tasks given to us by our supervisors, directors, and others who advise our work; and we attempt to be decent to ourselves and follow our guts in making the best choices. These roles are constant, relentless in demands, impatient, unyielding, and exhausting. How are we to ensure we satisfy all of the requirements within each role, and what are we to do if those requirements clash? How do we choose between two (or more) roles that are equally appropriate?

Can you think of some examples from your own career where you felt unsure about which role should steer your conduct, or which aspect within a specific role was the superior route to take? It probably occurs more than we realize, given the vast amount of nuances to the roles we take on. Some of us have learned to keep our roles as simple as possible, making it easier to define and maintain an ethical course of action. But even those clinicians will run into the pitfall of confused roles on occasion. No matter how simple and defined you make your practice, the nature of the profession is that you will become confused at some point. For example, consider when we have more than one set of rights to protect, such as the case of a pregnant woman who is using. Do you protect her rights, and continue to treat her without mandated reporting, or do you protect the rights of the fetus, and report the woman for child endangerment (Castillo & Waldorf, 2008)?

Let's look at how that happens and then think up ways to address it, starting with an exploration of the many hats we wear in our roles with our clients, with our colleagues and other professions, and with our profession. Once we establish all our roles within those categories, we can examine what happens when the categories clash.

Roles With Our Clients

There are many ways to confuse our roles with clients. We are supports, teachers, cheerleaders, boundary-setters, challengers, and more. We are all of these things; sometimes it is clear which role is best in a given situation, and other times more than one role can be applied and it can be hard to choose. The following are some common themes that can be confusing in our roles with clients.

Guiding Versus Gushing

We sometimes confuse when to guide our clients and when to gush, talk, or cheerlead. Clinicians vary on how often they speak and how much they allow for client input. When do you soak them with comments based on your opinions and expertise, and when do you gently guide them to where they express a desire to be? How do you know when you went too far, when your guiding becomes gushing?

For example, Leslie has been treating a 14-year-old adolescent girl for the past 8 months, and has formed a solid therapeutic bond with her. Initially, she did not trust Leslie, who worked hard over the months to establish a supportive and trusting rapport. She started to open up to Leslie, who began to see marked changes in her lifestyle, as the client began to recover from her drug use. However, something was clearly still preventing her from a solid recovery, and Leslie continues to worry about her relapse risk. After 8 months of working with her, in one weekly session, she discloses to Leslie that she was molested by her stepfather, with whom she still lives, when she was 7 years old. The abuse only happened two times, she claims, and has not occurred since then. She demands that Leslie tell no one, and Leslie is concerned that if she does tell someone, her client will leave treatment and not return. What are Leslie's ethical obligations here? What is her responsibility to the client?

Oh man, do we have to discuss this one? This is so hard. The first step is to separate her legal and ethical responsibilities. Each state not only defines who is legally mandated to report abuse, and

may not hold substance abuse counselors as mandated reporters, but also defines the statute of limitations on reporting abuse (Washington & Demask, 2008). Some states define a specific timeline, such as 3 or 7 years, after which the abuse is no longer reportable. Other states have no set statute of limitations on child abuse, and abuse that occurred years earlier is still reportable by law. So Leslie should go to her state statutes and learn whether she is legally a mandated reporter and what, if any, statute of limitations exist. If she is legally mandated to report this abuse, she will need to discuss with her supervisor the most therapeutic way to approach the client and discuss why she needs to report it.

There are few situations where it would be clinically wise to make the report without discussing it with the client, even though she is legally entitled to do so. The client still lives there, so making a report will directly affect her, perhaps her safety. Leslie also wants her to continue in treatment, which she may not wish to do, but she is less likely to want anything to do with Leslie if Leslie goes behind her back and reports something without warning her. Leslie can role play with her supervisor and trusted advisors to determine how to address it tenderly with her client. In the end, the client may remain disgruntled and leave treatment, but at least she will have acted in her client's best interest legally, and sometimes that is the best you can do. If she is legally obligated, Leslie must make the report regardless of how her client reacts.

Leslie may feel an ethical obligation to report the abuse to someone. On the one hand, it appears that the abuse is acting as a barrier to her client's ongoing recovery and quality of life, even if the stepfather has not abused her in 7 years. This suggests an ethical responsibility to help the client remove these barriers and gain the healthy ground she needs. On the other hand, reporting the abuse could cause great clinical harm to the client. Not only is she at risk of leaving treatment, which would obviously have negative effects on her, but she may also feel that counselors are not trustworthy. This could have negative effects on her therapeutic future, the need for which is guaranteed if she does not complete treatment now. She may also be unsafe at home if action is taken. Leslie will need to assess the chances that the stepfather will retaliate in an attempt to ensure the client's safety before taking any action. The client's safety has to be Leslie's primary concern throughout all that she does. Do you see how this decision quickly becomes agonizing? It is not always easy to determine the best clinical course of action for your client.

On the other hand, it is possible that the client does want Leslie to help her, otherwise she would not have revealed the abuse to her in the first place. The client may not be aware of it, so Leslie does not challenge her, but somewhere inside the client, perhaps she knows she needs help and is trusting Leslie to help her. If Leslie does nothing, she is inadvertently teaching her client that asking for help does nothing, and that is one lesson that is against our professional goal. This question would be easier to answer if the abuse was current, but remember that this case is further complicated by the fact that the abuse is no longer occurring and has not for 7 years. If we hold on to the notion that our primary obligation is to help the client help themselves, then the best approach may be to help the client come to her own healthy decision. The first therapeutic task is to gain her awareness that this is a problem, that she does have loads of feelings related to the abuse that have not been addressed, and that the abuse is continuing to have an ill effect on her life.

Once the client is aware, Leslie can help her determine a course of action. This is the difference between guiding and gushing. As a clinician, you can gush about what you think is important, or a healthy goal or decision to make, or what you see as the problem, but change may be more beneficial and effective if clients have ownership of their own care and ideas come from within. Thus, it is better to guide a client by asking questions and making subtle nudges in this case. There are many answers here, and the best answer is the one that both Leslie and the client feels is best, which may take time to assess.

If Leslie does this, think of how she will have helped the client. She will have shown her that counselors can be trusted, that they are going to neither ignore you nor go behind your back. Leslie will have shown her client that no problem is beyond her ability to improve; some just take a bit of creativity and time to figure out. She will have shown her client that she can face her fears and bad experiences and find a way through them, rather than carry them around forever. She will have shown her client that she can figure all this out, and have instilled in her the hope that she can help herself in the future. Leslie will have helped her client learn how to stand up for her needs, by confronting her stepfather, or by revealing the abuse to someone else who can support her. She will have accomplished all of this through guiding her client's autonomy rather than gushing her own agenda. That's a good day's work.

Teaching Versus Preaching

We can confuse teaching for preaching, as it can be difficult to assess the difference in certain subtle situations. How do we maintain a teaching role, promoting client learning in our groups and sessions, without sounding preachy and opinionated as if what we teach is the only way to act?

Let's say you are treating Rhonda, a polysubstance addict whose only source of income is governmental assistance, who is homeless living in a shelter, and who tells you she cannot get to meetings, social events, volunteer work, or a grocery store because of her financial situation. Yet Rhonda smokes cigarettes, about a pack a day, and chooses to use her small income to buy them. You are incensed by this, and admonish your client for choosing to buy cigarettes instead of the resources she desperately needs.

After listening to the audiotape of this session, your supervisor tells you she is concerned by your behavior. She asks you if you addressed smoking with all of your clients, using the same argument that they should not be spending the money on it.

She especially wants to know if you used the same tone as you did with this client. You explore your behavior and realize that although you have suggested to other clients that their nicotine addiction should be addressed, you have never admonished them for choosing to smoke. You have included the financial burden as a reason to quit cigarette smoking, but you have never judged other clients for choosing to spend money on cigarettes. You only had this reaction to your client who was experiencing a severely low economic condition.

You admit this to your supervisor, who gently reminds you that poverty is not a cure for addiction and nicotine addiction affects the poor and the rich equally. Just because someone cannot afford to pay for their drug, including nicotine, does not mean they won't find a way to pay for it. Many addicts must steal in order to keep their addiction going, so it should be no surprise that other addicts would use their welfare checks to fund their addiction instead of paying for their basic needs. You can see how you changed from teacher to preacher. The more ethical approach would be to help guide your client into a discussion of the total impact of their cigarette addiction, including the financial repercussions. You can teach the knowledge and give the resources without the attitude and judgment that comes with preaching.

Providing Versus Pressuring

We can also become confused in balancing when we provide information and support, hopefully guiding the client to the healthiest decision, and when we pressure our clients to do the right thing. We cannot make our clients act in any particular way, but we can apply enough pressure with certain clients that will strongly encourage one decision that is in line with our beliefs. For example, how would you handle a client who you know drove a car during a relapse? Do you simply treat him or her, providing support in their renewed effort, or would you lean on them to report to the police (Taleff, 2010)?

For example, Heart Hospital is an inpatient and outpatient facility for treating addictions. Carter is the clinical director of the outpatient program and his job involves overseeing the clinical health of both clients and clinicians. Several clinicians have opted to open private practices outside of their agency work. Since it is the regular practice to refer clients to private therapists in the community when clients graduate from the outpatient program, clinicians feel that their clients in the agency should be referred to their private practice. While acknowledging there would be benefits to continuing therapy with a clinician with which the client has already built a rapport, Carter tells his staff he feels this would be unethical and decrees that clients cannot be referred to the private practices of Heart Hospital clinicians. Any ideas why?

Although Carter can see there is a great benefit to his clinicians if clients are referred to their private practices, and he would like to help them grow their practices, Carter is concerned for the agency clients. He worries that if they urge clients to access the private practices of the employees the clients will feel pressured to continue with counselors in their private practices. He worries that if both the counselors and the agency staff encourage this, the clients will not feel comfortable refusing the referral. Because there is an established direction of power in the relationship between counselor and client, he does not want the clients to feel that they have to accept the referral. Is there a way around this? Can you think of a way to address Carter's concerns while still allowing referrals between agency and private practice?

There may be more than one way to address this in a positive and healthy manner. Carter's roles are as follows: With the agency, he must address the concept of competition and ensure its healthy future; with clinicians he wants to support them in their professional endeavors, especially knowing that if he finds a way to support them without abandoning agency demands, he is likely to keep them as employees, which benefits the agency; and with the client, he feels responsible for ensuring he or she is not being pressured to accept these clinicians' referrals. Carter decides to address the situation in the following way. Just as he employs intake clinicians whose responsibility is to meet with each incoming client and outline their treatment plan, Carter uses the same clinicians to serve as aftercare clinicians. Typically, the assigned therapist would have the last session and close out the case, making any necessary referrals.

As discussed, Carter worried that clinicians who suggested clients continue to see them in their private practices would unethically persuade them to join their practice. So if this interview is conducted by a more neutral employee, clients will not have to face the potential clinician when accepting or rejecting his or her service. Aftercare clinicians are tasked with giving the exiting client many options for aftercare placement, *one* of which is the clinician they worked with during their treatment at the agency. Certainly the individual counselor who has built a rapport during the client treatment episode will want to discuss aftercare before terminating the counseling relationship. However, after sessions cease, the aftercare clinician meets with the client, as in an exit interview, and presents the aftercare options objectively. This way the client can feel good about the option of care, the clinician can feel good about the option of referrals, and the agency can feel good about the option of serving the client, the employees, and the agency all at the same time.

Stretching Versus Supporting

We can also become confused about when to help stretch our clients, challenging them to see things or act in a different way, and when we should stand by them, supporting the choices that they make. For example, we are taught that clients should be treated with respect and that their cultural beliefs should be honored, right? But what do we do when it would be of great therapeutic value if the beliefs were to change, such as with a client who believes that alcoholism is a moral weakness or a possession of spirits, and therefore doesn't need our treatment (Venner & Bogenschutz, 2008)? How can we respect our clients' beliefs when we can see a better way? Is our role to respect them or is our role to try to challenge them?

For example, Ernie runs his group with military precision. During the check-in portion of the group, he allows 2 minutes or less for each client to check in. He has created a list of topics that he feels are essential to building a solid recovery plan, and he brings a topic to each group. He has a defined order to the topics and satisfies each one before going to the next on the list. He spends 30 minutes on check-in and 2.5 hours on the topic, not including breaks. He believes in the 12-step self-help programs and brings in at least one slogan to every group. When clients have questions, he answers by leading the client back to a slogan, step, or principle of the 12-step program. He believes his main role is connecting the clients to the 12-step programs.

Debbie runs her group like a glorified coffee klatch, where the 3-hour program consists of each group member checking in and supporting others. Debbie does not bring topics to groups and doesn't spend much time teaching principles to the group members. Instead, she bonds with the group members, which convinces them to come back for more treatment each day. She gives them room to explore the topics they wish to explore, and spends a lot of time building rapport by discussing matters outside of recovery-specific material. Debbie believes her main role is to listen to her clients and make treatment a fun place.

Jill runs her group with a flexible framework. She conducts a brief check-in with her clients, and then either launches into the topic she brought to share or brings up a topic based on one of the client's check-ins. She always brings material to discuss, and often has an accompanying handout or worksheet. This material comes from a list of topics she has created that includes all the topics necessary for building a solid recovery foundation. She does employ a good sense of flexibility though, so that if an important topic is raised during the check-in portion of the group, she will replace her planned topic with the important topic that was raised. At times she manages to touch on both the prepared and spontaneous topics in the same group. She is engaging but focused, and adept at pulling the focus of the group back to the topic at hand if they get off-topic. Jill believes her main role is to create a program that teaches the basic principles of recovery while allowing for individual differences in creating each client's foundation, and to teach the totality of building a program so that clients may learn how to do that for themselves.

Let's examine this vignette for therapist qualities. Say you are a floater, responsible for covering groups when Ernie, Debbie, and Jill are on vacations. Your supervisor asks you to rate how each group functions when you act as a substitute counselor. (1) How do they welcome you? (2) What is their attitude toward you as the counselor? (3) How do they react to topics and tasks? (4) Are they adaptable to change? (5) How do they feel when they leave? When you are working with Ernie's group, you notice that clients welcome you in to the group and act relieved that another clinician is there. The clients complain about Ernie's style, and tell you stories about clients walking out of group in anger because Ernie would not listen to their alternative views to self-help. Many clients feel the slogans are not a sufficient answer to some of the more complex questions that get asked in group. For those who attend 12-step groups, the feeling about Ernie's style is favorable. Those who do not agree with 12-step programs describe Ernie as set in his ways and trying to brainwash his clients. When you leave group, you feel wiped out from having to work to refocus clients from complaining to getting back on task.

When you are working with Debbie's group, you notice the clients are not very welcoming, eyeing you with suspicion for most of the group time. The clients do not complain about Debbie's style, in fact they do not want to talk about her at all, but when they do mention Debbie it is clearly with admiration. The clients are oddly silent while you are there, and you have to work hard to pull material from them for group discussion. They have a hard time staying on task and focusing on the topics you bring to the group. When asked to share topics of their own they do not contribute. They do make jokes with each other, and give feedback to each other, but fall silent when redirected or asked a general recovery question. When you leave group, you feel wiped out from trying to engage the clients.

When you are working with Jill's group, you notice the clients welcome you into the group and immediately focus on the material you have prepared. The clients appear to want to work on the topic instead of chatting about Jill or other topics. When they do comment on Jill it is with admiration of her style. They give good feedback to each other and help refocus each other back to the topic at hand when needed. The group is happy to discuss any topic and do a good job of relating the topic to their own recovery. At the end of group, the clients have positive things to say about you and the day's discussion. When you leave group, you feel energized and inspired to relay details of the good group discussion with other colleagues.

What you have witnessed is an interesting portrayal of a range of counseling styles. Ernie clearly has a rigid routine. Some of his clients will like this style, and some will not like this style. Your experience is that most did not like this style, you felt exhausted and frustrated after the group, and you worry that the clients will not get all of the tools needed to build their recovery program. Debbie clearly has a lax routine. Although the majority of her clients seemed happy with Debbie's style, you question its effectiveness in building recovery programs. Clients may like Debbie and find her groups fun, but it is not clear to you that treatment is occurring and that the clients couldn't get the same benefit from sitting with friends at an actual coffee shop. The insular attitude and mistrust of anyone else coming in is also concerning to you because it suggests that the clients are more interested in the counselor and group members than they are with their own recovery goals. They seem to be there for each other, not necessarily for their own health.

Jill clearly has neither a rigid nor a lax routine. She is firm yet flexible, and it shows in the client attitude you witness. The clients enjoy coming, as Debbie's clients do, but they come to work regardless of which counselor is running the group.

They are the clients you feel the most confident will build a long-lasting recovery program, which is the overarching goal for each client involved. Plus, as a clinician you felt the best after running Jill's group, which you believe is an indication of how successfully the group is run. If you had to bet on a clinician's success, you would bet on Jill. Because her style is flexible and her material varies, her groups are energizing rather than exhausting, and she is less likely to experience clincian burnout than the other two clinicians. Ernie and Debbie do not stretch their clients. Although their styles differ, both take more of a passive supporting role than a stretching one. Jill is all about stretching her clients to discover new heights of health. If you had to bet on the success of a set of clients, you would bet on Jill's clients. They are working with Jill in a collaborative style, which affords them some responsibility in directing their own recovery, yet also ensures they have all of the tools needed to succeed. They experience a positive treatment experience, unlike Ernie's clients, but also gain the education they need, unlike Debbie's clients. They will leave the treatment program with a good prognosis for continued recovery.

Roles With Our Colleagues and Other Professions

We can become confused in our roles with the people who work around us. We have different roles at work; we may be line staff, senior staff, administrative staff, supervisors, program directors, mentors, or colleagues, and sometimes more than one of these roles are held by one clinician. Furthermore, we can struggle with deciphering whether we are acting as the staff of a program or as a client's counselor, because those are two different roles. These roles can become complicated as we move jobs around our agencies: Our colleagues become our supervisees; our interns become our directors. With each of these changes, new conduct is expected of us, and it can be a challenge to keep our roles straight.

Some of us have further confusion in other professions of which we are members, either helping professions such as social work, or other professions, such as attorneys at law. It quickly becomes a challenge for the practitioner to determine which "hat" they are wearing and when, particularly when the guidelines of conduct within each profession conflict. For example, if Quentin is both a credentialed addictions counselor and a licensed clinical social worker, he will have some deviations in ethical codes that may become confusing with the agency tier of influence. He is a licensed social worker (LCSW), so he is able to diagnose any client who arrives at the agency for an intake assessment; however, his hired role in the agency is as a line staff addictions clinician. All of his colleagues on his level on the personnel hierarchy are credentialed addictions counselors but do not have an LCSW. Supervisors above them are licensed social workers, but while Quentin shares their license, he does not share their position on the personnel hierarchy. Therefore, Quentin's supervisor tells him that he must refrain from diagnosing clients, and must perform the same duties, with the same restrictions, as his fellow line staff colleagues. This is a challenge for Quentin, who feels his training and job requirements clash. It is not enough to understand your training and credential/license parameters; you must evaluate how these interact with your professional workplace.

Roles With Our Profession

Who doesn't love that moment in *A Few Good Men* when Tom Cruise badgers Wolfgang Bodison into snarling out the Marine honor code: "Unit, Corps, God, Country"? Our profession employs a similar motto: Client, Clinician, Agency, Profession. Numerous trainings promote the idea that the client must always come first. We act in the best interest of the client first, put our needs second, unless we are in danger of Clinician Burnout, in which case we rush to put our own needs first until the burnout scare passes, and then we are typically expected to resume putting the client first. We usually complain about the agency level, focusing more on how the actions of the agency affect the clinicians and the clients we serve, rather than examining how our actions and the behavior of our clients affect the agency. And the profession? That is too big and faceless an entity to worry about. It's like telling a teenager not to smoke cigarettes because 20 years from now they may get cancer; the consequences are simply too big and distant to matter much to them in the here and now.

Well, I submit to you that the opposite order is a more ethical motto to employ: Profession, Agency, Clinician, Client. I realize there will be a rousing chorus of shocked voices at the notion of putting the client (gasp!) *last*, but allow me to defend my position. The profession is the primary entity that dictates the existence of the others, and is therefore the most important. If we do not attend to the needs of the profession, the needs of the agency, clinician, and client won't matter, as there will not be an organizing body to structure those needs. Historically, the promoted opinion has been if we attend to the needs of the client we *are* attending to the needs of the profession, because happy clients make a happy profession. It is not that this is false; it is just a problematic way of thinking. If we are attending to the needs of the client as our primary concern, it is easier to choose the appropriate actions solely based on the needs of individuals, which can lead to ethical violations. It is better to ask, "What is the best course of action for the profession as a whole?" Typically, when considering the needs of the profession, the best ethical choice *is* one that benefits the client, even if the individual client would also have benefited from an alternative course of action.

Let's consider an example already used throughout the book: self-disclosure. It has already been argued that preventing self-disclosure actually strengthens our profession by allowing our members to depend on their skill and education, rather than on personal experience. In addition, if we focus on the prohibition of self-disclosure to protect the profession from critics who see it as a glorified

self-help profession, we in turn protect clinicians from hiding their qualifications and skills, and give clients treatment based on rigorous expertise. Everyone wins.

Now if you are putting the client as your first focus, you may make a different decision that is not as good for the profession as a whole. You might decide that your client, Yoko, really needs to hear that you, her clinician, also had an addiction problem and are now enjoying the benefits of recovery. You may feel this was the right move for Yoko, but what you may not realize is that while your intention was to teach her that she is not alone and that she can succeed as you have, you instead may have taught Yoko that the reason why she feels you can help her is due to your recovery status. She may then decide that only counselors who are in recovery can help, and she may spread this opinion to her friends in the community, and she may influence a fair few to similar opinions. This is how one action that would seem to be helpful to an individual can, in fact, hurt the profession. The more people who believe the only helpful counselors are those in recovery, the more our reputation as a profession of recovered addicts is solidified.

While the concept of putting the profession first may seem foreign to you, it shouldn't. You already have plenty of examples of actions you have taken for the greater good, even at the sacrifice of the individual good. Don't think so? I'll give you some examples. Let's say you are a group leader of a relapse prevention group and a member of your group begins to describe a trauma that he experienced which led to his substance abuse. Individually, this member would gain significant benefits from sharing this trauma, from opening up and trusting others with his experiences, and from connecting his experiences with his subsequent abuse. You have been trying to encourage this sharing in your individual sessions with the client, and are therefore delighted when he finally begins to share with the group. If we focus on the individual, this would be clinically appropriate and encouraged. However, while running group you are no longer wearing the hat of the individual clinician, you are wearing the hat of the group clinician, and that changes things a bit. While sharing details of a traumatic experience may be therapeutic to the individual group member, it may be significantly detrimental to other members in the group. Perhaps there are others in the group who experienced trauma but who are not yet ready to discuss or share their experiences, and perhaps those members feel trapped when sitting in a room and listening to others share trauma experiences; perhaps it even influences symptoms of posttraumatic stress disorder (PTSD).

Well-trained and experienced group counselors will tell you that in running a group the client becomes *the group* and not the individual group members. The group needs become the focus, as if the group takes on an identity itself (Jacobs, Masson, & Harvill, 2009; Yalom & Leszcz, 2005). This means group counselors have the double objective of keeping individual group members safe and of keeping the group itself safe, which can be difficult indeed. If the group has its own identity needing protection and care, then a clinician's actions may change. If our focus is on the individual, we wish our group member to self-disclose; if our focus is on the group, we may wish our group member not to divulge details. Especially because you are not running a trauma-specific group, you have to be careful of how individual sharing will affect the group as a whole. As a clinician, you should explain to the group members, upon entering the group, that sharing of certain experiences may be triggering for other group members, and that the member may be asked to refrain from sharing details of a sensitive topic in the group setting (but encourage them to spill all the details in an individual session or experience-specific group). This does not mean they can't share at all, but rather to keep their sharing detail-free regarding the trigger information. Since talking about any drug use can be triggering to group members in any addiction-related group, this is a concept that should already be part of your group orientation with every group member. You may also need to redirect an individual member, or refocus the group itself during the course of group therapy if you observe that members are becoming triggered. Look for nonverbal signs in your group members and the energy shift of the group as a whole. This is an example of putting the greater good (that of the group) as a focus over the individual good (that of the client).

Here is another example. Let's say you work in a residential setting and one of the residents relapses. You work with this resident in individual counseling and you are aware that relapsing is often part of her history, but that she usually takes several years after a relapse to enter back into recovery. This time, the resident acted differently, coming to staff immediately after relapsing and showing insight into how the relapse occurred and what parts of her recovery program needed to be strengthened. The resident begged not to be discharged, which is the agency policy on resident relapse. As her clinician, you know that discharging her will put her ongoing recovery at great risk, that she will likely return to the same environmental triggers that have influenced her use in the past. You know that keeping her in the program will support her recovery efforts, and if the focus was solely on the resident, the obvious choice would be to keep her in the program. What's the problem with that?

The problem is that while your focus as an individual clinician is on the individual, your focus as an employee of the residential setting should be on the residence, or the program it contains. The program itself becomes your client, so to speak, and it may have needs that conflict with an individual member's needs. In this example, the reason most residential settings have a no-tolerance policy toward relapse is to protect the residential program as a whole, and all the participants as a group. If you allow a relapse and continued participation of that relapser, you send the message to the group that relapsing is accepted and tolerated. If you broadcast that view, what is to prevent the other members of the group from relapsing and breaking rules of the house? If you allow one relapsing client to remain in the house, how will that impact the other members of the house? Can you imagine they would be triggered knowing someone in the house is using, or has recently used, and perhaps tempted to do the same? The goal of a residential setting is to provide a safe place where drugs are not allowed, and the consequences of using act as a motivator for continued recovery efforts. If residents want the safe environment and the program support, they have to do their part in keeping that residence safe for all its members, by not using and following the established rules. Therefore, while it may benefit one resident to turn a blind eye to the relapse rule, you could be harming many more residents in the process. It may hurt your clinical heart to do so, but focusing on the best needs of the residence is the most ethical choice and the choice with the most clinical benefit to the whole.

As you can see from these examples, it is quite easy to have more than one role in a given clinical situation. Do you focus on the client in front of you, or the group around you? Do you make the best choice for the client, or do you make the best choice for the agency, or the profession at large? It is easy to become confused about your different roles and which is the most ethical one to prioritize. This role confusion can be very subtle and twisted. Now that we have mishmashed our roles effectively, what can we do about it? How can we alleviate our role confusion?

1. We prioritize our roles in a list. Some roles may carry more weight than others, and so we must give them a higher ranking on our list. This can guide us into choosing which role to prioritize in a given situation. 2. We ask ourselves if there is any role that will address two issues at once, thereby giving it more importance than other roles. 3. We can compare the consequences of prioritizing our different roles by asking ourselves "Would you rather be in this role or the other role, do this action or the other action, make this choice or the other choice?" Comparing which outcomes cause more harm can be a helpful guide in choosing a role to

follow. 4. We can seek supervision to help us make sense of our different roles, and choose the best path. 5. We can check our Scope of Practice and hope that it will guide us in which roles and actions best serve our ethical practice.

The purpose of a Scope of Practice is to outline the requirements and roles within a specific credential or license. It establishes a standard of training and required experience for the clinician and gives a set of guidelines on behavior appropriate to the credential or license. In addition, a Scope of Practice acts to safeguard the public from unprofessional service by unauthorized people and noncertified clinicians. You should have at the ready a copy of the Scope of Practice associated with your credential or license. If you do not, close this book and call your credentialing board or your membership board and ask for a copy. In some wonderful cases it might be easily available on the state board's website, as it should be for all of us. A sample Scope is also available at clinicalethicsblog.com. The Scope of Practice includes these components:

Purpose
Requirements
Role of the credentialed or licensed clinician
Setting for the delivery of services
Definitions

The requirements within a Scope of Practice include a list of competencies, a thorough description of the required hours of education and supervision, and a determination of the recredentialing criteria and timeline. Of note, the requirements state the professional will abide by the corresponding Code of Ethics. The roles within a Scope of Practice include a detailed description of each task that is expected of the credentialed or licensed professional. It is, in fact, the most specific section of the Scope; the specificity that clinicians often wish for from the Code of Ethics. All addiction clinicians must be adept in the Twelve Core Functions of what we do, and therefore our Scope is based on these functions.

They are screening, intake, orientation, assessment, treatment planning, counseling, case management, crisis intervention, client education, referral, report and record keeping, and consultation with other professionals in regard to client treatment/services (Whitter et al., 2006). The Scope also includes a section delineating appropriate settings in which the services may occur. The Scope ends with a definition of what type of clinicians to whom the Scope refers and which clinicians and/or conditions to whom the Scope does not refer (i.e., other members of the helping professions).

The Scope differentiates our role as counselor from the other possible roles, namely sponsor, linker, colleague, friend, supervisor, and general support person. For example, let's consider the latter role question of support versus counseling. There are several reasons you must separate support from therapy in your practice. First, there is only so much counseling you can give, and most of us are pulling our hair out trying to get in all the therapy for the clients we already have in the hours we have to administer it. If you try to take on the treatment of family members and others not on your formal caseload, you will be doing a disservice to yourself, and will find yourself in Clinician Burnout faster than you can say "crispy." Second, you run the risk of disservicing your client. If you add on clients to your already bursting caseload, your treatment of your clients will suffer, plain and simple. There is only so much of wonderful you to go around, so if you split yourself more, each client is getting a smaller bit of you, which is not very fair to them.

Finally, you want to separate support from therapy concerning the family member. While you may be able to separate support from counseling, the family member may not, and you do not want to begin giving help you know you can't sustain. It can be damaging to the family member to start venting and getting help without the chance to continue in the therapy they may need. It's not responsible practice, and you need to be careful of not creating more damage for the family. If we ignore our Scope of Practice, or fail to abide by its parameters, we are at risk of sliding down the slippery slope of a scopeless practice, our next pitfall to learn how to avoid.

Practical Application

A "Scopeless" Practice

The problem with the Scope of Practice is that you will feel you are capable, trained even, to work slightly outside of it. Not much, just an inch, to help someone you *know* you are capable of helping. And are we not in the business of helping people? It is difficult to tell someone that you can't help them because it is outside of your Scope of Practice to do so, especially if a client is sitting in front of you weeping with despair, or a boss is requiring you to act. Most of us would ignore the Scope and help the person. But again, what may seem like an innocuous infraction quickly becomes an epidemic when everyone is making these small missteps. While the person in front of you will be grateful for your help, the profession will soften because of it.

You wouldn't go to a psychiatrist to set a dislocated elbow, even though psychiatrists attend medical school and likely learn early in their academic career how to reset a dislocation. Similarly, you should not go to a social worker for your addiction problem, even though they generally learned about addictions in their basic education, unless they can prove additional competency. You also don't want to go to an addictions counselor for help with your mood disorder, even if he or she has taken several courses on working with bipolar clients. That training is designed to help them understand your needs, not to treat your needs. That is the difference between education and training. You can be educated on many topics, but your Scope of Practice delineates what training you need to perform the duties in your credential or title.

As discussed, the Scope of Practice is an instructive document we can use to navigate through the many roles we regularly employ. When asked about the use of the Scope of Practice, here are several common responses:

1. What is a Scope of Practice?
2. I did not realize that was the purpose of the Scope of Practice.
3. I am sure the Scope says that I can....
4. I realize this is outside of my Scope of Practice, but it should not be.
5. I am just going to help this one person I know I can help. Then I will promise to work within my Scope parameters.

Have you discovered yourself saying any of these responses, or heard them from others? Any one of them may seem acceptable, but each is problematic at a closer glance.

What is a Scope of Practice? Sigh. Unless you are brand new to the profession, working toward getting your credential, you should know the answer to this question. If you do not, you want to read Part Three because your competency may be in question and you may need some additional training.

I did not realize that was the purpose of the Scope of Practice and *I am sure the Scope says that I can....* both show a clinician that is aware of the existence of the Scope, but is uninformed of its contents. If this is you, go grab your Scope and study it so that you will not be caught adrift again.

I realize this is outside of my Scope of Practice, but it should not be is a bit of a bolder claim, and perhaps a deeper problem. An ignorant clinician has an understandable reason, even if unethical, for acting outside of his or her Scope. But a clinician who is aware of the Scope parameters and deliberately crosses them is a clinician whose personal and professional agendas are in turmoil. A clinician may take this stance out of a sense of justice, an attempt at advocacy, or sheer laziness. Whatever the reason, though, deliberately acting against your code is not the best way of pursuing your interests. Although it may air your concern, it also renders you faulty in your clinical practice, and that can land you in a heap of trouble. If you disagree with your Scope, it is better to discuss with your supervisor, and seek out elected members of your state membership and credentialing organizations. You may want to get involved at this level in order to effect the best change.

I am just going to help this one person I know I can help. The most common violation of the Scope of Practice is helping a specific person or a specific situation that is beyond the designated roles within the credential because you believe you can be helpful. Treating family members is a common snag that we discussed in Part One. Family therapy lies outside our Scope of Practice, and we must refer family members to other professionals if we assess the need. It may be difficult to feel we are not directly helping people in need, but referring them is the most ethical way to help.

For another example, a credentialed addictions counselor may have taken 12 hours of training on working with Borderline Personality Disorder, knowing that many of his or her clients would be dually diagnosed with addiction and Borderline PD. However, the credentialed addictions counselor's Scope of Practice does not allow him or her to treat Borderline PD. It is acceptable to understand the symptoms of Borderline PD in order to recognize it, but that clinician must refer the Borderline PD client to another clinician who has a Scope of Practice that includes the treatment of Borderline PD (Manuel & Forcehimes, 2008). In trainings, often two questions are posed with this example. First, "But if we discuss the Borderline symptoms in the context of addiction, wouldn't that be right?" Technically, yes; if you were only discussing how symptoms were affected by the client's addiction, or how the addiction is affected by the Borderline symptoms, it could be argued to be within the Scope. But although that may pass ethically, it certainly does not clinically. It would not be appropriate to bring up the interaction between Borderline PD and addiction, and then just leave it at that. You would want to address the Borderline as you would the addiction, by putting specific goals on the client's treatment plan. You must because you know that those dually diagnosed will not succeed if only one diagnosis is treated.

Second, "I get that I can't treat the Borderline, but I usually just don't mention it at all, because I'm trying to build a rapport with this client. If I talk about what I can't do, I'm afraid I will lose them and then I'm not helping at all. Is it okay to bring it up later?" But how many clinicians actually bring it up later? Will your client feel swindled if you knew this all along and waited to tell him or her? Wouldn't you? You do not want to be dishonest, as it may be even worse for that rapport you are intent on building. And you may lose your client later after they have been working toward recovery as a result of your deception, which will be worse as they are leaving you with negative feelings that can certainly be triggers to relapse. The simple way around this is to introduce your parameters at the beginning of the interview, before the client has a chance to reveal what you can't treat. For example, you would start out by saying,

Hello Jasmine, I'm Sydney and I'm glad you made it in today. What we are going to do for the next hour or so is to go over everything that makes you Jasmine, and highlight the things you wish were different. Then we can make a plan for how to treat each of those things so that you can reach your goals. Some of those goals we will be able to address here together, and some will be better addressed by someone else outside of this office, and maybe outside of this agency. But I can promise you that I will help you find the best person to reach each of your goals.

If you begin every initial session this way, the client should feel supported. You are instilling loads of hope into the very first session, you are acknowledging that it is the client's goals that you will be addressing, and you are setting the client up to understand you may not be able to help with everything. Later if something comes up outside your Scope of Practice, you can listen to the issue the client brings up, and then tell him or her that it is a good example of something you do not address here, but that you know someone great who can address it and will help the client get connected

with that person. If the client questions why you cannot help with a non-Scope-approved area, you simply explain that your education and training has been focused on addiction, because that is such a complex area and you really wanted to build an expertise in one area rather than knowing a little about many areas. Always remember that the more confident (confident, not cocky) you are in yourself, the more confident clients will be in you. Don't forget that you will be teaching them that it is acceptable to admit your limitations to others, a powerful lesson they can apply to their own lives without shame.

This need to state your Scope will be particularly necessary for two distinct groups of clinicians that bear special mention. First, if you are an addiction counselor working in private practice, it will be particularly important for you to outline your Scope parameters to clients, as clients will not necessarily understand the distinction between you and a social worker in private practice who can treat all diagnoses, including addiction. The best-case scenario would be to have your office in a building where other types of therapists also work and you can work together as a team addressing each client need. If you do not have that set-up, find therapists who are willing to work with you on client cases; then you will have your referrals ready to go before you meet your clients.

The second group of clinicians who need to be careful are those who have moved to being a Licensed Alcohol and Drug Addiction Counselor (LADC) from a Credentialed Alcohol and Drug Addiction Counselor (CADC), or whatever your state's initials may be. States vary widely in this area: Some states have the LADC in place and it is the most common level of credential/license; some states have the LADC but the CADC remains the most common level; other states do not have the LADC at all. In some states, the Scope of Practice for the LADC is not the same as the CADC; therefore it is important to know the differences and be able to communicate them with clients and other clinicians who may not know the definitions.

At least one state membership organization has decided to introduce the LADC level to their career path even though the state does not offer state-approved licensure to addiction counselors. They argue that introducing the nongovernmental LADC now will allow clinicians to prepare for the time when state licensure is available. While this may seem sound, it leaves a lot of room for ethical confusion. Clients, practitioners, and the general public are not likely to understand the distinction. Since a LADC is generally recognized as a clinician with a state-sanctioned licensure, using the same letters to denote something different is confusing because it implies that you have something you do not have. Therefore, if you live in a state that uses the LADC in a nongovernmental licensure, be sure you understand the difference and that you use it with people who also understand what it is, educating those who do not.

There is also confusion with other professional Scopes for those double-dippers who have more than one credential or license in different disciplines. A social worker or marriage and family therapist has a vastly different Scope of Practice compared with addiction counselors. Many clinicians have credentials or licenses in more than one helping profession.

No matter what your credential or licensure, we are all at risk of sliding out of our Scope. It is extremely easy to do because we are typically gifted individuals who have been trained on a variety of topics to ensure we give our clients the best care. But that training can give us a false sense of ownership over material that is outside of our Scope. This means that what we know how to do is not necessarily what we are allowed to do. Yes, you will struggle with this. So what do you do *when* this happens to you?

1. Admit your foible, that you slid or were starting to slide outside your Scope. You need to admit this freely, without berating yourself, knowing that it happens to all clinicians. The quicker you can identify your slippage, the quicker it can be addressed.

2. Go to your supervisor and ask for help. Explain where you are struggling and why you think you are finding it a challenge before coming up with possible ways to address it. Different situations may call for different actions, so discuss it with your trusted sources and come up with more than one game plan, in case the first falls flat.

3. If you have violated your Scope before, you will need to learn your warning signs so that you can reverse the pattern of unethical behavior you are setting.

If you can address the slip and settle back into the boundaries of your Scope of Practice, you will maintain your ethical practice, particularly if you use the experience to identify warning signs for the future. Sometimes you don't have time to check with a supervisor.

For example, what if your client, Jackson, has just been admitted under dramatic circumstances, after being found comatose from an overdose of heroin, and part of your tasks during assessment is to notify a family member that your client is there, in an attempt to gain pertinent identifying information about the client that you may lack. Jackson did sign a release form on admittance allowing you to speak with his mother. While you are on the phone with the client's mother, the mother breaks down and starts crying about her son's addiction, how it has affected the family, how scared she is for her son. You want to listen, knowing you can help her, but you are not sure how much time you should spend with her. You suspect a Scope of Practice issue but she is on the phone and you do not have the luxury of waiting for your next supervision session. What do you do?

You know what you need before you can answer this question ethically? Yup, the Scope of Practice. Go ahead and get yours, I'll wait. I'm sure you have it at the ready for these times when it is called into question. No, you say? You don't have your Code of Ethics and Scope of Practice in a defined space in your office? Does the agency have them clearly placed? If you answered no to both of these questions, you and your agency have some decorating to do, but let's finish the chapter first. So you grab your Scope; now what?

- Familiarize yourself with the Scope before you need it. Know the sections for quick reference; get to know or rehearse the content.
- Scan a relevant section. For example, you may see in the *Role* section that the Scope clearly states you should assist clients with alcohol/drug abuse or dependence and support their family members and others to attain and maintain abstinence as appropriate. Clearly, you are entitled to provide support to family members, such as Jackson's mother. In fact, you are likely entitled to give "quality professional counseling" to clients and their family members. Therefore, your first conclusion is that you can sit on the phone with Jackson's mother, listen to her woes, and aid her to the best of your clinical ability. But wait! There are other aspects to consider.

If you read the Scope all the way through, it is clear that you can provide assistance and support to the family member. You may also give quality counseling, but the Scope may specify that the counseling be limited to psycho-education. This means you can educate family members on addiction and recovery principles, including defense mechanisms as denoted in the Scope. But the other aspects of counseling—treatment planning, self-awareness processing, relapse-prevention plans, facilitating problem solving, establishing life skills, understanding family roles and the involvement of the family in the addiction process, and all of the 12 core functions—are reserved for work with the client. So while you can support family members and teach them important principles that will aid the client in his or her recovery endeavors, and hopefully aid the family member into his or her own recovery process as well, you must maintain your focus on your true client, the addicted person, as your primary concern. I like to think of it as the difference between support and therapy. You may support anyone surrounding the addicted client, but you reserve counseling for the addicted client only.

- Say "hold, please" and ask a supervisor. If it is possible to speak with a supervisory staff member while the family member waits, do it. You can get an answer to your concern right away and be able to act effectively and ethically on the spot. If you cannot access such a staff member right away, you may have to tell the client or family member that you need to get back to them.
- When in doubt…wait. For example, perhaps Jackson does not want you to talk to his mother at length. You know nothing of their relationship yet, and you haven't had an opportunity to discuss with Jackson, your client, how he wishes to involve your mother. Perhaps he will feel you are siding with her by talking with her, or ganging up on him, or any other emotion, some of which can cause a backward slide in therapy. Remember, your consent to release information should be written to include only the task at hand: notifying her that he is a client and obtaining identifying information if necessary. Your primary concern is your client Jackson, so you will want to have a discussion with him and write a detailed consent before discussing details with his mother.
- Be proactive and give an introductory preventative statement. Okay, so what *can* you say that will stay within the parameters of the Scope of Practice and will effectively protect you, your client, and your family member? In a case like the Jackson example, the best you can do is to describe the kind of information you are seeking and what help you are able to give before the mother has a chance to launch into her life story. She does not mean to force you outside your Scope; she most likely knows nothing about your Scope. You can help her by guiding her to the type of information you are seeking. For example, you will want to say something like this:

Hi, Mrs. Brown, this is Jennifer Berton calling from This Agency, and I've been authorized to call you and verify that your son, Jackson, was admitted into our program this morning. I'm a bit limited in what I can discuss with you today, but we may have a chance later to talk in more detail if needed. For now, I wanted to notify you that Jackson is with us, and verify with you that he lives on 37 Hope Lane, is that correct? Great, thank you. In this program, we have a family education group that meets once a week. If Jackson agrees, would you be interested in attending that group to support Jackson and learn more about what he is learning here? Great! We know that addiction affects not only the person using drugs, but everyone around that person as well. I'm sure you have all sorts of feelings related to Jackson. I just wanted to let you know that while Jackson is my first priority as my client, I would be happy to assist you in finding resources to help you as well. Do you have any questions about the program or resources for you?

If Mrs. Brown has general questions about the program, you should answer them. If she talks about her needs, you can refer her to a person or an agency related to the needs she is expressing. If there is something important about Jackson that she wants you to know, you can listen (because you do have that initial consent), but you should not discuss Jackson with her. You can simply thank her for the information. If she tries to steer you back to therapy for her, it is easier to remind her that you need to keep this conversation narrowly focused because you already stated that at the beginning of the call. In general, if you don't state your boundaries at the beginning of interviews, it becomes difficult, at times impossible, to redirect the person with whom you are speaking. Plus, the person usually feels rejected or dismissed when you try to set a boundary later in the conversation, and that can do significant damage to your rapport and to the person's general feelings of self.

- Regardless of which strategy you choose, address later in supervision, and document, document, document everything.

Sliding out of your Scope of Practice is all too easy. Thus far, we discussed slipping with good intentions—wanting to help those around us in need. There are many other reasons why clinicians would slide. There may be a financial benefit to taking on a role outside of your Scope. There may be

someone you wish to impress, expanding your skill set to make you look more appealing or impressive. There have even been cases of clinicians going in the opposite direction, stating they were not allowed to do certain undesirable tasks that were in fact listed in their Scope. Whatever the reason, if you find yourself sliding out of your Scope, whether on purpose or by accident, it is your ethical responsibility to snap back into the boundaries of your Scope, notifying your supervisor of your slip in order to decide the best course of action for you and your clients. Although sliding outside of your Scope occurs often, and may typically seem rather harmless, it can be quite damaging for all involved and should be taken seriously.

Supervision can help you see you are sliding even when it escapes your notice. For example, Agnes is a group counselor who runs an outpatient program; specifically, she carries a caseload of individual clients and runs several groups. One group she runs is a family education group, in which clients and at least one family member attend. Agnes enjoys educating families on substance abuse principles and aiding families in the healing process necessary after addiction has devastated all that was once good. Last month, she welcomed the Justice family, who attended with their son, Mack, a client Agnes also sees individually. Mrs. Justice is proud of her son's dedication to his recovery, and admits there is much she does not know about addiction. She welcomes the chance to be involved in the group and engages Agnes in many discussions.

As time passes, Agnes notices that Mrs. Justice hangs around her after group, and the volume of questions she asks Agnes is increasing each week. She is also starting to include comments with her questions, typically comments about herself. Agnes finds these comments interesting, as they are small insights into what Mack's family life is all about and his mother's comments may provide clues to his addiction that would offer implications in his treatment plan. Thus, Agnes encourages these interactions with Mrs. Justice, which helps to increase them, until it is the weekly norm for Agnes to spend at least 20 minutes after group, and often longer, conversing with Mrs. Justice alone. During these conversations, Mack and his father typically are on the other side of the room, chatting and waiting. The material in the conversations begins with questions and comments concerning Mack, but then begins to change to a more subjective stance, as Mrs. Justice begins to divulge her feelings and experiences, highlighting issues and challenges that she faces. Agnes listens, exhibiting empathetic behavior, gives several suggestions, including resources, and works to instill hope in Mrs. Justice.

In supervision this week, Agnes is discussing Mack's case. After listening to an audiotape of the last session between them, Agnes' supervisor comments that Mack appears to exhibit lower energy than in past sessions, and questions whether Agnes has noticed that he seems different. Agnes agrees that Mack has seemed sad and relatively withdrawn in the last few sessions. Agnes goes on to say, "I'm not too surprised, however. He has done this before. He can be really difficult and suck the happiness out of all around him." Taken aback, the supervisor says, "Wait, all I suggested was that his energy was low. How did you come to 'sucking the happiness from everyone'? Did he tell you that he does this?" When Agnes admits that he did not tell her this, the supervisor appropriately asks who told her this opinion, and she reveals Mack's mother told her this. "It's been really hard on her. She just wishes that he appreciated all she has done for him." The supervisor stops Agnes from continuing the conversation, and tells her that she has fallen into an ethical trap and has acted unethically. Agnes can't see it, can you?

The supervisor explains that Agnes has subtly gained Mrs. Justice as a client, and reveals how this process has occurred, describing how Agnes shifted from seeing his mother as a source of helpful information to seeing his mother as an active part of his treatment, one whom Agnes is meant to educate. Agnes then began supplementing education for sympathy and suggestions, and before long, therapy. The supervisor then points out that the original focus on Mack has been lost, which seems to have had an effect on him. While we don't know what Mack thinks or feels, we do know that he is exhibiting an observable energy change, which may indicate a shift in mood for him. Instead of being concerned with her client, Agnes views this behavior through the eyes of his mother, who is not her client. The supervisor advises Agnes to take a step back, strategize the best way to cease therapy with the mother, and return to her work as Mack's counselor.

The Scope is there to guide us when we are at risk of confusing our many roles, but to benefit from the tool we must actively use it. The other ways to avoid role confusion are to respect the tiers of ethics and regularly consider the various influences in our daily practice. If we can do that, we cannot only prevent role mashing, we can use the tiers of ethics as a guide to the proper use of clinical material, written and spoken, and ensure that materials are protected, all of which strengthens this ethical practice you are building.

ARE WE A PROFESSION?

Trainings, meetings, self-help groups, rehearsals, and sporting events all offer a break during the course of their activity, a chance to stretch your body and give your brain a break from the path it has been on. It's halftime, so let's do the same here, and take a coffee break. Your brain has been working hard, digesting all the material and perhaps noticing some ideas popping up or questions coming to the surface. This is all good stuff, but let's take a step back and consider the larger implications of what we have learned so far, and add another layer to what we have been discussing.

Thus far, we've been throwing around the term *profession* when describing ourselves. Is this an accurate description? Are we a profession or are we something else? Discuss that or think about it for a few seconds and jot down an answer on mental paper. What does your intellect tell you? What does your experience tell you? What does your gut tell you? All important voices to consider. Now let's see how your thoughts match up with what we can examine. Some of you already feel very strongly one way or another on this topic. That's cool, you can bring your emotions and opinions with you on this coffee break! Just keep an open mind to the possibility of being challenged in your views. Let's have some fun.

The field of addiction counseling is currently in the midst of a professional identity crisis. Often seen as "chronically precarious" (Vilardaga et al., 2011), the field of addictions is struggling to be accepted as a qualified profession (Whitter et al., 2006), as other professions have in the past. In the existing literature that combines all of the helping professions or human services, addiction counseling is not included in the list of professions (Barsky, 2010; Corey, Corey, & Callanan, 2007; Reamer, 2001, 2012). Two of the most significant reasons for this are the beliefs that (1) addiction counselors do not bring skills that other helping professions do not already have, and (2) the field is made up of recovered addicts working to help others into recovery, glorified sponsors if you will, and not a rigorous profession of clinicians with a unique set of skills trained to the highest standard.

The first view—that we do not bring skills that do not otherwise exist in other helping professions—is misguided. There are indeed many other professions that also treat addictions, such as social workers, physicians, nurses, and psychologists, but that do not bring the specific level of competency addiction counselors can offer; in fact there are no competency standards for other professionals who practice in the addiction field (Whitter et al., 2006). Wolff and Hayes (2009) reported a study in which 74% of 1,200 psychologists reported no formal education or training in addiction, yet 91% reported working with addiction clients. Similarly, schools of social work provide little education on addictions and only 2% of social workers count addiction treatment as their primary role (Whitley, 2010).

Any helping profession can grow addiction specialists but it requires an interest and willingness on the part of the clinician; it is not required as part of the helping profession. It is possible to have a nurse, for example, who is also trained in addictions and able to use both set of skills as well as an addictions counselor. But that would require the nurse to self-motivate and take optional courses in addiction treatment and elect to work in the field of addictions before becoming an equal expert.

Let's use social workers as another example. In the standardized curriculum for a master's level social work program, there is not one single substance abuse course required, although at least one is usually offered in the 2-year program. Yet the majority of field placements offered in the social work program have the possibility of treating clients with substance abuse problems. Therefore, the view that any helping profession can offer the same level of services is simply false. One elective does not equal the years of education and training that is required before obtaining an addictions counseling credential or license. It is vigorous and specialized.

The second view is that our field is made up of a bunch of recovering addicts, who are more like AA sponsors or paraprofessionals than authentic professionals. While this view is not entirely accurate, it is understandable why many people believe it. In the 1940s, due to a shortage of professional counselors, recovered addicts were encouraged into the role (Doukas & Cullen, 2010), and many counselors in recovery use their past experience as a credential (Doukas & Cullen, 2011). It is suspected that no other human service profession has the prevalence of members who were once clients within the system, and that a "common characteristic within the culture of the profession is that many counselors have a history of dependency and are currently working as a recovering professional" (Gallagher, 2010, p. 186). But where are the studies looking at the numbers of recovering people in other professions? It is not big news that addicted people are drawn to the field, but people act as if that is the only contribution and this is not true. A heart surgeon may be drawn to the medical field because his or her brother died of heart disease. But we don't question that surgeon's ability to operate because we know his or her experience does not dictate how good a surgeon he or she will be; his or her training and professional experience does. Why is it not the same philosophy with addiction professionals?

The truth is that our "hopeful" profession is filled with both people who are personally in recovery from addictions and people who are not. This is true in every profession. In other professions, a person's recovery status is not what makes the person successful at his or her job. Similarly, a person's recovery status is not what makes him or her an effective or ineffective clinician. However, many clinicians within our field will need as much convincing of that fact as people do outside our profession. This has been and will again be discussed at length in later chapters, so read on, especially if you are fired up by the idea that your recovery status is *not* what makes you a good clinician. The perception that the field is full of clinicians trained solely by their personal experience is a notion that is hurting us, a notion that is preventing us from being treated as the unique and necessary profession that we truly can be.

Despite the view that we are paraprofessionals using our personal experience as our skill set, there is an existing set of skills that are based on theoretical knowledge developed from evidence-based practice and scientific experiments. Our field has grown significantly in the past several decades, as scientific discoveries explained the biological, genetic, and psychological components of addiction, and how addiction is played out in the biological, psychological, social, and spiritual arenas. This new knowledge has not only helped to develop an understanding of the mechanics of addiction, it has informed our practice by implying appropriate treatment modalities that are most effective in addressing the myriad deficiencies addictions create.

In addition to a skill set, there is an extensive period of education to obtain a credential and/or license. In fact, it can take years for counselors to satisfy all of the requirements to obtain the initial credentialing level. Historically, training for addictions treatment tended to resemble an apprentice model, which emphasizes experience over formal education, in which knowledge and skills are taught through supervision (Substance Abuse and Mental Health Services Administration [SAMHSA], 2005; Whitley, 2010; Whitter et al., 2006), but this is changing (Whitley, 2010). With the rise of evidence-based practices in the literature and its application in the workforce, the demand for more formal types of education is increasing, and states are beginning to require both formal education and supervision in credentialing and licensure standards (SAMHSA, 2005). The demand for this type of education can be demonstrated in the rise of addiction studies programs in academic institutions across the nation, even though these institutions rely on a variety of standards instead of one set of national competencies (Whitter et al., 2006). It was reported 10 years ago that 442 colleges and universities across the country offer addictions studies programs, with 18% at the graduate level, 13% at the undergraduate level, and 69% at the associate level (Taleff,

2010). These numbers are expected to continue to rise (SAMHSA, 2005; Whitter et al., 2006).

Accompanying this education is required institutional training with supervisory hours included. When the National Institute on Alcohol Abuse and Alcoholism (NIAAA) began to certify alcohol and drug counselors in the 1970s, they were reluctant to establish formal education requirements, thus education and supervision requirements vary significantly by state (Whitley, 2010). The profession created and codified standards of substance abuse treatment in 1981, with the National Certification Reciprocity Consortium (NCRC) and published federal guidelines for practice, and the Addiction Counseling Competencies, in 1998 (Whitley, 2010). Ongoing additional training is a requirement, the proof of which must be submitted every 2 years. The required amount of credentialing and recredentialing hours trumps those requirements of some professions thought to be more sophisticated and rigorous, such as social workers. There is also a testing of competence, with multiple levels of expertise offered at the state level. This testing involves both oral and written formats, although some states have made efforts to abolish the oral section of the exam, as other helping professions have achieved. All states offer credentialing, and some states offer licensure. Several states have fought for licensure but have yet to obtain it, their bills defeated at the state level thus far.

If we examine the significant characteristics of a profession gathered from several sources (Brown, 1992; Jackson, 2010; Larson, 1978) and summarized in Wikipedia, we can analyze how our "field" measures up. As discussed, we have the skill set, education, and training. Work autonomy is also present in our field, as each clinician has control over his or her work and has control over his or her knowledge. We are also self-regulated, meaning we are separate from the government and ruled by respected, experienced, senior members of our field. Public service is apparent and we can confidently expect remuneration for our services because our treatment improves public health.

Altruism is directly specified in the Code of Ethics, with the specific mandate that clinicians devote a portion of their career to volunteer efforts with the population we serve.

Characteristics of a Profession

Skill-based on theoretical knowledge	Professional association
Extensive period of education	Testing of competence
Institutional training	Licensed practitioners
Work autonomy	Self-regulation
Code of professional conduct or ethic	Public service and altruism

This leaves a professional association and a code of professional conduct and ethics as the last two requirements of a profession. Technically, we have both. There are both state-level associations and a national and international membership association, with the majority of states adopting a dual membership for its credentialed and licensed inhabitants. We do employ a Code of Ethics in every state, which provides specific behavioral guidelines and mandates of conduct, on which this book is based.

So there you have it, we must be a profession given that we have adopted each of the 10 characteristics that make a profession. And yet, we are still considered more of a field than a profession. We have mentioned some of the views of our field, which may be one important explanation, yet there are also two other areas of significant concern that act as barriers to the acceptance of our field as an authentic profession, and our profession will likely remain a *field* until the fractures can be repaired. The first is a lack of national standards, and the second is a lack of professional confidence.

National Standards

Our profession has been affected by a lack of national occupation standards (Whitter et al., 2006)

a need that is just now being recognized (Whitley, 2010). First, although there is a National Membership Association (NAADAC), there is no national standard in any part of our profession. Our profession is dependent on each state, and each state has significantly different definitions and procedures. The four main differences between states are: (1) name of the profession; (2) credential versus licensure; (3) association membership; and (4) Code of Ethics.

What's in a Name?

Perhaps the most confusing and concerning fracture in our field is our variety of names. Depending on where you live, you could be a substance abuse counselor, an addictions counselor, an alcohol and drug addictions counselor, or other combinations. It is no wonder we are a fractured profession when we can't even define what it is we do or who exactly we are helping. The most common name is the "alcohol and drug addictions counselor," which is seriously flawed. First, why does alcohol continue to be separated out from all other drugs? Is somehow the addiction to alcohol different from the addiction to other drugs? Hopefully, you answered no, as it is not.

Originally there was a professional belief that the processes of both addiction and recovery were different for alcoholics. More recently it was believed that since alcohol is legal, it should be separated from other drugs. But what of cigarettes, prescription drugs, gambling, sex? They are all legal and among the addictions we treat. In the 1960s and 1970s, treatment programs for alcohol and drug dependence were separated because they were believed to be unrelated disorders (Whitley, 2010). Separating alcohol suggests that it is different in some way, which can be most damaging to our clients. If we promote separatism, we can wound the unity that influences healing. It was a common belief that addiction to drugs was stronger than addiction to alcohol, and that drug addiction led to more violent and criminal behaviors. This term was likely influenced by the separation of AA from other groups. When AA was created, the focus was on alcoholism, which was a big enough battle to bring into the limelight, and other drugs were less common then. In the beginning, it may have been sensible to separate alcohol, but we know now that the development and treatment of alcohol addiction and addiction to other drugs does not differ significantly. Even though our profession has finally realized these disorders are related and has combined treatment efforts into inclusive substance abuse treatment programs (Whitley, 2010), our name continues to reflect the original division. Even our national organization, NAADAC, recently changed its name to the National Association of Addiction Professionals to reflect the growth in the profession, but it oddly did not change its initials, thus the division remains (Whitley, 2010). In addition, we have so many different government-sponsored groups with a spoon in the pot, it can be dizzying to grasp who represents what part of the profession.

"Substance abuse counselor" includes alcohol with all the other drugs, but is flawed because it also only addresses one addiction, and fails to include the behavioral addictions, such as sex or gambling. Think about what that means: It means that if we call ourselves substance abuse counselors, or alcohol and drug abuse counselors, we are limiting our scope of practice to only those addicted to substances, and ethically cannot treat people with gambling, sex, Internet addictions, or those who are codependent. How many of you with a CADC, LADC, CASAC, CSACA also treat behavioral addictions in your agencies or practices?

Several states offer a specific gambling addiction certification, but why? If the components of behavioral addictions, even down to a genetic link, are similar to those of substance addictions, and if they can be treated with the same tools, why are they separated? If we counselors treat all types of addictions, why is that not reflected in our name?

If we compare ourselves to other established helping professions, we see they have a clear identity, for example, MD, social worker, nurse, and then have more specific specialties under that identity, for example, school social worker or psychiatric social worker. A pediatrician, cardiologist, and psychiatrist differ in their specialties but they all have an MD and went through the same initial training and examination to obtain that standard. Social workers create a basic practitioner who will then specialize in a specific field of practice. There is first schooling to obtain a degree, followed by work experience in the field to obtain a credential or licensure (Whitley, 2010). These helping professions have a baseline within their profession that carries one easily identifiable name that defines what they do. We do not have that. Even our membership and credentialing organizations do not carry the same names in each state, as a simple scan of the International Certification & Reciprocity Consortium (IC&RC) website demonstrates. Our field would be strengthened if we were all addictions counselors with the option of specializing in certain areas or with specific populations.

What's in a License?

In addition to the confusion over our name, we also have varying state-specific rules regarding credentialing and licensure (Whitter et al., 2006). Despite all the efforts made to strengthen our education and training requirements, we still do not have a national standard of training and performance (Whitley, 2010). Some states have only credentialed counselors; some states offer both credentialed and licensed counselors. Some states offer two types of credentialed counselors, separated by length of time in the profession (e.g., CADC-I and CADC-II). At least one state offers a nongovernment-sanctioned licensure, which only furthers the confusion. The state level then competes with two separate national credentials through NAADAC and IC&RC. With additional testing and money required, one could have a CADC, MAC, and ICAC, yet there doesn't seem to be a clear benefit or distinction between them.

Many states offer additional credentials, such as gambling, clinical supervisor, criminal justice, dual diagnosis, or prevention specialist certifications. Furthermore, there is a lack of agreement on who works in the field. Some agencies hire a master's level clinician with no addictions background; others hire counselors without a bachelor's degree. Some states require nothing, and some require a master's and license (St. Germaine, 1996).

Establishing national core competencies and a national career path will decrease the variation in clinical practice; the quality of care will be improved and the profession will become more credible (Whitter et al., 2006, p. 27). If we rename ourselves "addictions counselors," the gambling certification will become a specialization, one of many important specializations for specific populations within our profession. Additional training and examination are required to obtain these credentials. However, not all states have adopted these specializations, which weakens their importance and their value. It also means that if a clinician moves from a state that has a Credentialed Prevention Specialist license (which incidentally is a Credentialed Prevention Professional license in some states) to one that does not, he or she is not recognized as a specialized provider, and all that training and testing means nothing.

The profession needs national titles for our credentials and licenses (Whitter et al., 2006). The strongest course of action would be to have one universal license for addictions counselors in every state, and then have these specialized certifications for specific skill sets, such as criminal justice, adolescent treatment, clinical supervisor, and prevention specialist, in all states (Whitter et al., 2006). States should be allowed to vary their credentials to meet the needs within the state, but it seems that there are several that would be needed in all states. Not only would this aid reciprocity between states, but it would promote a nationwide standard that would

strengthen our profession and the perception of it. Additional career paths could become available as the field relies more on recovery support services (Whitter et al., 2006), such as the relatively new field of recovery coaching (White, 2006). By developing career paths with clearly defined competencies, the profession will show its commitment to maintaining professional standards for all individuals in the treatment and recovery workforce (Whitter et al., 2006). This need has been recognized, and in 2005, NAADAC and IC&RC attempted to merge for one national credential (Whitter et al., 2006), but it failed, with no formal explanation or plan to continue the effort.

What's in a Membership?

Another aspect of those helping professions is their organization. When you get an MD, or RN, or LCSW, you become a member of a national organization, such as the American Psychiatric Association (APA), or the National Association of Social Workers (NASW), which organizes all the members who hold the same title. For addictions counselors, there is not one national organization that represents *all* members of the profession. Both IC&RC and NAADAC comes close, but while any professional may join NAADAC, not all 50 states are affiliated with NAADAC. There are states that have opted to break off partnership with NAADAC over political and procedural disputes. In addition, some states have more than one state-level organization and members can choose which they want to join. The associations differ throughout their policy and procedures and often do not work together, further widening the profession's fracture. Therefore, while each state has a "self-organized brotherhood" of members that is required in a profession, there is not a cohesive brotherhood in our nation as in other helping professions. Our field would be strengthened by adopting one national organization that can represent the profession with state organizations that can handle business at the state level.

What's in a Code?

The Code of Ethics is the recognized backbone of a profession, the guidelines by which all members must adhere (Reamer, 2006a), and is the document that shows evidence of the profession's growth over time (Gallagher, 2010). There is no other document that holds more importance than this Code, yet our field has not agreed on one Code. The other helping professions each have one Code of Ethics, and each state has adopted it (Reamer, 2006b). We instead have a fractured system that varies among states.

NAADAC has one Code of Ethics that has changed over the years. Its most popular Code was adopted by the majority of the states, the majority of which continue to utilize it today. However, NAADAC changed its Code in 2004, adopting in its place an inferior Code. NAADAC put this Code on its annual agenda in 2010 and rewrote it, making many significant and positive changes (National Association for Addiction Professionals [NAADAC], 2011). This superior Code could be used by all 50 states as a way to unite us in one uniform profession, yet many states have not adopted the Code, either using an older code or one the state wrote for itself.

Further examination of the state Codes is even more confusing. Most states declare on their websites that they adopt the NAADAC Code of Ethics, however, the vast majority of these states list the Code used prior to the previous Code, not the current NAADAC Code. The fact that states do not seem aware that the Code they are promoting as NAADAC's is not the current NAADAC Code does not reflect a cohesive profession. Many states have written their own Codes, some close to the original NAADAC Code that many states utilize, but several altered their Codes significantly. A few states adopted formal legal language in their Codes, a far departure from the loosely informal Code NAADAC previously had on its website.

States also vary significantly in their professional websites, if one exists. Some states do not have websites, or at least have websites that can easily be found. Many websites give little information, or are difficult to navigate, and most websites do not list the Code of Ethics anywhere on the website for easy accessibility. There are a few standouts with websites that give all pertinent information in a coherent design that is user-friendly and easy to navigate, with a clear direct link to the state's Code of Ethics. This should be the model for each state to adopt, especially given the need for descriptive information due to the vast differences among states in the standards discussed. The profession needs to adopt uniform ethical principles in a national code of ethics (Whitter et al., 2006) and adopt clear websites at the very least with uniform basic information.

Self-Confidence

If you recall, there are two widespread problems preventing us from being a solid profession. The first is the lack of a national set of standards. The second is that we suffer, as a group, from a general lack of confidence. On the one hand, we know that what we do is important, but we also are not sure exactly where we fit in. We have all these established professions around us looking down on us, and like anyone suffering from constant criticism, we start to believe it. Some of us hide behind aspects of ourselves, such as personal recovery statuses, as the reason they are good at what they do. As we have discussed, it is important to realize that keeping our recovery status at the forefront of our individual gifts doesn't help. If we don't stand up and believe in our hearts the fact that we are a group trained with skills that others do not have and that we should be afforded the appropriate respect, we will never be a sound profession. Who will believe in us if we do not believe in ourselves?

Practitioners in the helping professions treat substance abuse using their own learned models of theory and practice (Powell & Brodsky, 2004), borrowing from many helping professions without a systematic procedure of our own (Powell & Brodsky, 2004). Yet what we do is specialized and vital to the health of a substantially large part of the population, and should be its own discipline (Powell & Brodsky, 2004; SAMHSA, 2005; Whitter et al., 2006). Whitter et al. (2006) reported a study from Columbia University in which it was reported that 94% of primary care physicians and 40% of pediatricians, when presented with a person with a substance use disorder, failed to diagnose the problem properly. If similar studies were available for other health professionals (e.g., nurses, psychologists, pharmacists, social workers, dentists), the results would likely be similar (Whitter et al., 2006). Because there are many other professionals who treat the addicted population, we must form a solid and *loud* identity to firm up our place in the treatment of addicts.

The aging of program managers further compounds the need to develop a new generation of leaders. Most directors are retiring and the turnover rate is high, reportedly as high as 53% in 2002 (McLellan, Carise, & Kleber, 2003). Preparing a new generation of leaders is critical to any profession's survival, yet most addiction organizations have not established training programs for these positions or coordinated a plan to prevent future leadership gaps (McLellan et al., 2003; Whitter et al., 2006). This does not demonstrate a confident industry.

Are We a Profession?

So where does this leave us? At the state level, we achieve the characteristics of a profession by definition, and yet nationally, we have serious flaws that fracture us from each other and weaken our whole. We exist in that "in between"—not quite a profession yet, but much more than a field. We are close to becoming as solid a profession as the other established helping professions, but we need a bit of identity strengthening. Individual states have all the necessary ingredients of a profession. Because the profession is clearly strong on the individual state level, all we need to do is to apply these state-level components to a national level. If we can adopt the same exhaustive professionalism that states have utilized, imagine how strong a national profession we will have. We will be as strong, and then perhaps as respected, as the other helping professions that have historically been superior to ours. We already have what we need; we just need to work together and make some agreements.

It is possible for the addictions counselors of the nation to unite in the fight to strengthen our field into a powerful profession. We are not the first group to take on this goal. Social workers were criticized for lacking the qualities that make a profession (Flexner, 1915), which forced them to strengthen the field into the profession it is today. There is no reason addiction counselors cannot achieve the same success. We are a relatively new field (Whitley, 2010), but we do need a consistent identity, both in our name and in our organization; we need a streamlined licensing process, and we need to solidify our Code of Ethics. We also need to gain in confidence what we have in skill, and make an effort to educate those who perceive us incorrectly both within and outside of our field. While it is vital that we come together to develop a national standard, by solidifying our name, our mother organization, our licensing process, and our Code of Ethics, we also must address the views about our profession. The fact that many states have experienced a struggle to obtain licensure is revealing, and we don't help by how we view ourselves and how we express those views. We need to empower ourselves and then we need to educate those around us, showing them the skills we possess, the importance of our work, the precision of our standards, and the eligibility of our profession. With this work we will earn our place as a solid and undeniable profession. "The growing acceptance of a national standard of practice will provide the addiction counseling profession with an important element for further professionalization" (Whitley, 2010, p. 356).

You may be wondering, reader, what this all means to you. How can you make a difference?

How can you strengthen our big near-profession? Turns out it is simple: You can help by strengthening your own ethical practice to the best of your ability. You can start by reading this book, thoughtfully answering the questions, talking to your supervisors and colleagues, and working hard to strengthen your practice. If all of our members were to do just that, our profession would be the strongest it has ever been, because a profession is only as strong as the members it holds. Start there, and let's see where it gets us. At the very least, you can sleep at night knowing you are doing your part to better your practice and strengthen the entire profession. And that is a very good feeling indeed.

PROTECTING
THE CLINICIAN

Ethics That Protect the Clinician

Ah, finally, we get to turn the focus on us, the clinicians who make up this profession. Thus far we have learned about ethics that protect the clients we serve and the clinical information we use. It is also vital that we learn to protect ourselves, both from ourselves and others. We are taught that the client's welfare comes first, which implies that we put our own welfare second, at least. Yet if we are not healthy, our work suffers, and if our work suffers then our clients suffer. We cannot adequately protect our clients and clinical information if we cannot protect ourselves. When we discuss counselor protection, we are usually concerned with preventing clinician burnout, an admirable goal, but counselor protection is so much more.

Counselors need to be protected from unethical situations involving clients, colleagues, and the profession at large. Our own safety, satisfaction, emotional well-being, and professional value should be daily concerns. Just as our profession relies on our clients, as without them we would have no profession, it also depends on the clinicians, as without us nothing much would happen. We are the movers and the shakers, and as such need to be healthy and respected. We need to protect ourselves against clinician burnout, a complex phenomenon that is a surefire path to ethical dilemmas, but we also need to tend to our happiness in client relationships and to our ability to do our job. In this way, building healthy practices becomes not only about the clients we serve with the practice, but about us as well. Thus, the more responsible and competent you are, the more you will be protected.

Let us begin by examining the four ethical pillars. From a counselor perspective, beneficence indicates a clinician's right to a healthy working environment and a strong professional identity. It is the clinician's responsibility to do his or her part in creating and maintaining this atmosphere. From a counselor perspective, autonomy refers to a clinician's ability to make informed decisions related to his or her work without coercion from others. It is the responsibility of the agency to develop a fertile atmosphere around the clinicians that will encourage their autonomy, but it may be necessary for the clinicians to fight for their own autonomy, or gather supportive advisors around them who will encourage autonomy. From a clinician's perspective, nonmaleficence indicates a clinician's right not to be harmed by his or her poor practices. It is the counselor's responsibility to refrain from harmful treatment of his or her own making. From a counselor perspective, justice refers to the clinician's right to have access to employment, and to be fairly and evenly treated as any another professional. It is the counselor's responsibility to treat others the way he or she would like to be treated, with courtesy, respect, fairness, and kindness.

In your state's Code of Ethics two principles are aimed at protecting the counselor. The principle of responsibility guides the clinician into developing a practice based on objectivity, integrity, and standards. The more responsible the practice, the greater the clinician is protected. The second principle is competence, and it follows a similar pattern. The more competent the clinician, the better he or she is protected. Both of these principles also safeguard the profession and the clients it serves. The more responsible and competent our clinicians, the better treatment of the clients, and the stronger the profession will be.

The key to adhering to these principles is to seek continuous learning. While perfection is not a requirement, taking steps to continue your growth is vital to your ethical practice. If you feel you have learned enough to effectively do your job, you are wrong. Knowledge does not end. The profession is growing and it is your honor and burden to grow with it. If you fail to develop this key to your practice you will be in danger of falling into the unpleasant trap of clinician burnout. If you continue to do the same thing, and fail to grow or stretch and challenge yourself in new ways, you become distressed. With enough constant exposure, that distress becomes burnout. When in a state of burnout, you are more likely to commit ethical infractions, and you can quickly land both feet in a thick ethical dilemma with an impaired ability to effectively handle it. And that's no good for anyone.

Part Three Questions

1. Name the three areas of training in which you feel the most competent (e.g., ethics, diversity, forensics, women in recovery, diversity, dual diagnosis). Now name the three areas in which you feel the least competent.
2. Have you ever been described by a colleague, supervisor, or teacher? If so, what words were used to describe you? Do you agree with his or her assessment, and why or why not?
3. Consider the last time you felt clinician burnout (maybe it's now!). What did you do to alleviate your distress? Did it work? Why or why not?
4. Think back to your best supervision (I hope you have had one!); what made it successful? Think back to your worst supervision; what made it fail?

Key: Seek Continuous Learning

Perfection is not a requirement, but continuous learning must be sought. "Progress not perfection" is a slogan we often use with our clients in an attempt to support them when they make mistakes and to encourage them in pursuing recovery efforts without giving up and relapsing. It is about acknowledging that you can't be perfect, that you will make mistakes, and that you can learn from them and adjust your recovery efforts, which should enhance the quality of your recovery. Clinicians may also benefit from similar reminders that no clinician is ethically perfect or knows what to do in every situation (Corey, Corey, & Callanan, 2007; Reamer, 2001, 2006b; Taleff, 2010). Often admitting that you do not know what to do in a clinical situation *is* the most ethical thing you can do, particularly if you follow it up with the action of asking for help from a trusted advisor.

However, for some clinicians, saying the words "I don't know" appears to be quite difficult. Perhaps it is due to the balance of power in the clinical relationship that some clinicians feel it is their job to know, to advise, to answer, and that to show uncertainty gives a negative, weak, ignorant portrayal of the clinician. Perhaps some clinicians do not want

to disappoint the client by failing to help them with an answer, or perhaps some clinicians worry about how they will be perceived by colleagues or superiors on the job. Similarly, some clinicians may feel they need to be competent in front of other professionals, especially those they are supervising or who rest under their position on the agency hierarchy.

Whatever the reason, clinicians often choke when in a situation they know not how to handle, and instead of stating they don't have the answer but will find it, or admitting to themselves that they are in a situation they need help to decipher, they reach for a response or reaction, often a damaging or unethical one. Don't let this be you. You will mess up, you will be at loss for an answer, you will have moments of chaos and confusion, as all clinicians experience at different points in their career. Your ethical responsibility is to admit all of this and ask for help, knowing that it will make you a stronger clinician, not a weaker one.

However, as important as it is to acknowledge that one is not perfect in all clinical and ethical matters, it is equally important to stress that the goal is to strive toward perfection. All clinicians should be working toward that goal, even knowing they will never actually achieve it. This may sound obvious to you, but many clinicians feel they have been in the field long enough to rest on their laurels. They diminish their active learning and feel they are as close to perfection as they are going to come; essentially they cease growing. If you are reading this and realizing that you may be one of these people, don't panic! Awareness is the first key to change, and there is always time to do something about it. Sign up for a training; go find inspiration in a book, or a colleague; design a challenge for yourself and keep in the game. Acknowledging that you are not perfect but maintaining continuous learning and growth as a constant goal is the second key to an ethical practice.

One of the best ways to foster learning is to take a diverse set of trainings that pinpoint different areas. You want to seek knowledge you are lacking or seek to strengthen areas that are weaker than others. Don't simply take trainings on topics that interest you; take trainings on topics that do not interest you. You may be surprised and learn a new set of skills you didn't even realize you wanted! Perhaps you will take a training that inspires you to further your own research in the area—whether this inspiration comes from a successful or unsuccessful training. Good progress often comes from trainings you didn't enjoy, because it can cause you to seek out better information through self-research, another training, or ongoing discussions with peers and advisors. Developing self-awareness of your competency is a great tool to guide you in deciphering what you need.

The questions at the start of this section are a good place to start. The first question, *Name the three areas of training in which you feel the most competent.... Now name the three areas in which you feel the least competent*, acts as a guide to areas you may need to strengthen by asking you to analyze your competency. Depending on how aware you are, this may vary in degree of difficulty to complete. If you can answer the question lickety-split, go ahead, but then take some time to do research and see if your answer changes. If you try to answer and you come up with bupkes, the same research can help you.

The easiest way to research answers to this question is to peruse some websites of online learning that list available topics, or pull out the flyers you may get in the mail advertising trainings across the nation. If you read through a list and notice a topic you have never heard of before, take that as a clue that it is likely an area you could strengthen. Similarly, if you see topics that are familiar because you have filled multiple training hours in the area, you may want to consider it as an area of competency.

It may be easier for people to list areas in which they do not feel competent than to list areas where they do feel competent. Some people may entertain a general lack of self-confidence in their professional prowess, perhaps undeserved. Some may feel it is professional bragging to name areas of competency. Others may feel that claiming competency negates the need for continuous growth. Continuous growth is certainly imperative for all clinicians, yet it is acceptable to claim competency in certain subjects you have studied well, as long as you do not cease learning. Part of what makes people competent is their continual updating of knowledge, which is often a full-time job with the loads of new information continually developed.

If you are struggling with naming areas where you don't feel as competent, maybe this will help swirl the creative juices in your brain: If the Wizard of Oz exists, and you met him and were granted one wish to strengthen one aspect of your clinical skills, what would you ask the Wizard to strengthen or grant in your professional skills? Your answer will guide you to an area of needed training and/or supervision. Appropriate answers can be either specific or general; for example, you may seek strength in learning to say no to client or agency demands outside of your job description. You could seek assertiveness training, or seek aid from your supervision. Alternatively, you may seek strength in working with personality disorders and subsequently look for trainings on treating this specific population.

Courage is required to answer this question. Courage, because once we admit the answer we will effectively be setting a goal for ourselves. If the trait or skill we are looking for is something we wish the Wizard could instantly deliver, then one or more of the following three is likely to be true: (1) that the skill is important to our practice; (2) that it typically takes a long time to develop; and (3) that it is very difficult to master, otherwise we would not be asking for magical interventions. Because it is unlikely that we will come across the Wizard any time soon, it can be assumed that we will need courage to tackle the skill development.

Whatever you name is also cause for great excitement, as it is exactly where you should be directing some of your professional energy. It may even be a goal you had not previously realized was in you. Whatever it is can be a new direction for you, inspiration can really pump some new life into your practice, which some of you may have needed for some time. Now that you have the goal, go off and research how to make it happen. Be sure to share it with your supervisor or other trusted advisor. Sharing it with another makes it more real and may further motivate you to work toward achieving the goal.

The second question, *Have you ever been described by a colleague, supervisor, or teacher? If so, what words were used to describe you? Do you agree with his or her assessment, and why or why not?* asks you to explore how you work with others according to their view. Have you been described favorably? Are you embarrassed and angered by how you have been described? Was it a just description or do you feel misunderstood?

How would you describe your ability to work with others? What kind of colleague are you? Do you lean on others for support or do you tend to keep to yourself? Do you find yourself jealous of others? Do you find you are competitive or do you enjoy encouraging your colleagues? Do you prefer to work alone? There are no right or wrong answers here, even if it seems so. The necessity to work as a team player is usually the company line in most jobs you seek, but here in the comfort of wherever you are reading this book, you should feel safe to answer this question truthfully.

Just because we are in the business of helping people does not necessarily mean we organically work well with others. Some of you will find it easy to work with other people and will deliberately focus on being a positive collaborator and supporter. Some of you will find it a challenge in some areas and easy in others, and some of you will find all of this area challenging. How you interact with people at work is an important part of your ethical makeup, and one with which you should be familiar. Maybe you exhibit typical behavior in most situations, but have a few scenarios that would influence you to act differently. Perhaps you exhibit consistent behavior across situations, keeping true to authentic you. As you can guess, awareness of how you interact with people can suggest both strengths and challenges in your ethical practice, and can highlight areas you need to address.

Now how does your assessment compare to received feedback from others about your work personality? Was the feedback congruent with your self-image or were there deviations? Your professional behavior can be assessed by others, particularly supervisors, because they are supposed to be in the business of closely observing your professional decorum. If they are doing their job correctly, you will have a series of written evaluations that describe your observed interprofessional behavior, dependent on how long you have worked at your current location. Sadly, many of you are not fortunate to have appropriate supervision, and may not have written evaluations at your disposal, which we will address later in this section.

Other assessments can be gathered by colleagues, therapists, client evaluations, and all other supports, including spouses and family members. While these people may not directly observe you at your place of business, they often have useful information in hearing you discuss work over a period of time. None of these nonsupervisory informants can solely give you a picture of your observed conduct, but information taken from more than one source will give you a helpful picture of how you are generally seen by others. What do you do with this information? Ask yourself, (a) Are you proud of how you have been described? (b) If not, can you change? (c) If so, how do you change? It may be the case that what you think you are giving others is not exactly what they are receiving. It is important to consider what personality we are communicating to ensure that it is what we want people to receive. In this section we will talk about the dangers of failing to assess this aspect of your practice, and how to address it.

The third question, *Consider the last time you felt Clinician Burnout (maybe it's now!). What did you do to alleviate your distress? Did it work? Why or why not?* asks you to consider your burnout experiences, at least the most recent one. Every clinician is at risk for Clinician Burnout, which is the feeling of being chronically distressed, overwhelmed, exhausted, frustrated, and unhappy at work. Some may be more susceptible, either because of an unsatisfying job or ongoing personal stress that bleeds into the workplace. Some personality styles may tend to wander toward stress, creating it around them, yet even the healthiest among us has experienced Clinician Burnout at some point in our careers; therefore you should have an answer to this question. If you are brand spankin' new to the field, then imagine how you suspect Clinician Burnout would occur in you. Prevention is possible with good self-awareness, so be proud that you will be ahead of the game if you take the time to predict your stress to the best of your ability.

If you have experienced Clinician Burnout, consider where you believe it began; what were notable influences (people, situations, thoughts, feelings) that led you on the path? Typically, stress grows into Clinician Burnout over time—days or week or even months—so be mindful of tracking your mental health and professional performance back a bit from the time you were aware that Clinician Burnout was occurring. How did you know you were in Clinician Burnout? What were your first signs? This will be radically important, as those same signs may be your guides to act in the future prevention of Clinician Burnout.

Next, what did you do about this Clinician Burnout when it occurred? Did you hide in your office until it went away or did you actively try to squelch it, and if so, what tactics did you try? Of those tactics, which were successful, which were a failure, and which were somewhere in between? Remember, your history can inform your future decision making, so make sure you acknowledge every action you have tried. Use this list to make a plan of things that worked and should be repeated, and those that failed and maybe should be avoided. Take the time to plan this now before you are in a position of desperately needing it. It will be harder to create when you are under pressure. Clinician Burnout occurs even with ethically aware clinicians, but clinicians who painstakingly analyze their own competency levels, firming up weaker areas, rehearsing proficient areas, and exploring patterns that lead to the risk of Clinician Burnout, will experience burnout much less often. Your practice will not be perfectly unblemished, but the goal is to build as strong a practice as is possible to achieve.

The fourth question, *Think back to your best supervision (I hope you have had one!); what made it successful? Think back to your worst supervision; what made it fail* is obviously aimed at exploring your experience with supervision. Unless you are new to the profession, chances are you have had more than one supervisory experience. If you are a seasoned clinician you have had many supervisors over your years in the profession. Many of us have had a glimpse of good supervision, even if briefly. And sadly, many—perhaps most—of us have experienced poor supervision in our careers. Although good supervision can lift us up to the full height of our potential, poor supervision can prevent us from ever reaching it. We will go over what makes supervision successful, where it can often fail, and how to get the best supervision to meet your needs.

Now that we have given you permission to *not* be perfect, but have demanded that you never cease your efforts to *grow*, let us examine how this idea plays out in the Code of Ethics, with the principles of responsibility and competency, and look at how easy it can be to fall into the trap of Clinician Burnout if we neglect our continuous learning.

Principle: Responsibility

12
Chapter

Addiction counselors must strive for excellence in all their professional affairs. We are going to define professional excellence with three components: objectivity, integrity, and standards. Right about now you may be wondering, reader, what all this has to do with protecting the clinician when it sounds an awful lot like we're talking about how to treat the clients. We are talking about how clients should be treated, but that is only part of a responsible practice. We are concerned with our objectivity, integrity, and standards in *all* of our professional affairs, not limited to those that involve our clients. How we treat clients, colleagues, documentation, the community, and especially ourselves is all an integral part of a responsible practice. We have obligations to our clients, ourselves, other professionals, and our community (Bissell & Royce, 1987). If we do not develop and ensure the consistent success of a responsible practice we risk damaging our professional satisfaction and integrity. Our damaged practice then puts us at risk of professional embarrassment, shame, ridicule, investigation, sanction, and Clinician Burnout (not necessarily in that order). Therefore, focusing on adopting a responsible practice is one important step in ethically protecting ourselves. Let's look at these three components that your ethical practice requires.

Objectivity

It is often difficult to obtain objectivity in all your affairs; after all, you are human and collecting subjective experiences every day. How well one separates work objectivity from personal subjectivity is one mark of an ethical clinician. You will not be able to eliminate your subjectivity, nor should you completely. Your subjectivity can be immensely helpful to you in sensing what a client needs when you imagine what your needs would be in your client's shoes. This can lead to ideas that can be used in the treatment. Your subjective perspective can inform your practice and guide your actions; it is the unique stamp on your work that separates you from other clinicians. Your intuition, or your gut, is part of your subjective experience. We don't speak of a clinician's intuition often, as it is not something we can measure, yet it can be a helpful guide.

If you aren't sure what I'm talking about, have you ever been sitting in front of a client and heard yourself asking a question or making a suggestion but had no idea why you were asking it or where it was coming from? Or have you ever been running a group and had a topic planned, but gotten a sense that what you should present was another topic? You don't know why, but you just feel that the second topic is more of what the clients need to hear that day. This is your intuition, ladies and gentlemen, and you should listen to it when you can. The problem with your intuition is that it is entirely subjective, and you must balance it with the objectivity that is needed to be an ethical clinician.

This becomes easier when you have well-developed objectivity. Objectivity means you separate your needs from the needs, wants, and opinions of others and look at the situation in front of you as if you are not affected by it. Someone who is objective can see the big picture beyond one subjective experience and can judge the state of affairs without bias or influence. Because the client cannot be objective regarding his or her own care, it is the clinician's responsibility to keep emotions from clouding over the tasks at hand.

To be objective, clinicians must fight against the tendency to be a partial owner in a client's recovery. For example, clients who resist the tenets of the classic disease model are labeled as being in *denial*, yet research indicates not all alcoholics are forever dependent, they can develop it as a reaction to stage in life problems (St. Germaine, 1996). The tendency to reduce all client resistance to denial obscures the possibility that the problem may lie in the treatment model, not the client. Counselors are supposed to help clients discover their own paths to recovery and thus should possess the flexibility to guide clients in different directions. Screening clients to assess their appropriateness or inappropriateness for group therapy is paramount. In many treatment centers, individuals are automatically put into groups with little or no screening. Judges often mandate that people attend AA/NA. Insurance companies mandate participations and treatment centers often make AA attendance mandatory and sometimes require attendance to continue treatment at the facility. But mandating treatment and defining nonconformity as denial often increases resistance and fails to explore alternative therapies that may be more fitting. Counselors must do their best to serve their clients, recognizing that services may not be providing the intended purpose. If the client is not benefiting from these services, it is the counselor's responsibility to stop treatment and, when necessary, refer the client for more appropriate treatment if it is available (St. Germaine, 1996).

Integrity

The concept of integrity is even harder to define, and thus harder to master. What makes integrity? Consistent traits of honesty, probity, rectitude, honor, principles, morals, righteousness, virtue, decency, fairness, scrupulousness, sincerity, truthfulness, and trustworthiness are requirements for integrity. Are you all of these things in the majority of your professional affairs? If you are, I bow down to you, for you are worthy. If you are not all of these things, fear not, for we are all in a growing process. For example, a clinician must recognize the limitations of his or her counselor's competencies and not offer services or use techniques outside of these professional competencies.

The best way to start your growth is to identify a role model who defines integrity for you. I bet you know someone who holds these characteristics, even if it is not you. These people are usually easy to spot because they feel stable to be around; they are the people from whom you find yourself asking for advice no matter what their actual role; they are steady, even, and consistent in their professional affairs. Clients adore them because they are fair; clinicians revere them because they are stable, decent, and easy to work with. They are usually unflappable in objective decision making, thinking through every angle before deciding on a course of action; rarely do they jump to action without thought. Find people you know who possess these qualities, and then attempt to channel them in your own affairs. In a given scenario, ask yourself what would my integrity model do in this situation? You won't be exactly like them, nor should you be, but it will allow you to practice building your own integrity. As with many things, the more you practice it, the more it will likely become part of you. Before you know it, people will be asking you for advice, and that is one great feeling.

Another way to think of integrity is to ask yourself, "If someone could see me right now with what I am doing and the decision I am making, would they be proud of me? Would I be proud of myself?" Someone with integrity would be able to answer yes. If you can't answer yes, consider that a red flag to change your behavior. It is not enough to ask this once. Integrity depends on consistent goodness, not simply one good decision. You have to show that this is your pattern, that you can be trusted to make good decisions, that you are consistently fair in your treatment of others. This will give you integrity.

Standards

A responsible practitioner includes the highest standards in the services he or she provides. "Well, of course I do" you might respond, but do you really? If we maintain high standards we are consistently delivering quality services to our clients, developing excellent rapport with all clients and professionals, and promoting a caliber of business affairs that will make our profession proud. We won't all achieve these standards in every moment of our career, but a responsible practice demands that you try.

In our profession, we have legal, ethical, and moral standards, and your Code of Ethics will include them all. You must identify and adhere to these standards in order to claim a responsible practice. Legal standards are those standards punishable by law. For example, you may not claim to have credentials or licenses you do not have. Legal standards may change and it is imperative that you investigate and keep abreast of your legal obligations by asking your supervisor, and reading membership newsletters and journals. Ethical standards are listed in your Code of Ethics for your convenience. Although not necessarily punishable by law, it is expected by your state credentialing board that you will uphold these standards in all of

your professional affairs. Failure to do so will bear consequences including sanctions that the board determines. For example, you may not use group counseling to teach any agenda of your own that is not evidence-based or agency-approved. Moral standards are those standards that exist within your value system. Moral standards guide your personal definition of right and wrong conduct. For example, you should not coerce your colleague into picking up additional shifts so that you can sleep in, while telling her that you have to visit your aunt in the hospital. While not necessarily punishable by law or sanctioned by your state board, moral missteps may affect your self-worth and will affect your integrity with others.

In addiction, clinicians must uphold the familiar pillars of ethics: beneficence, autonomy, non-maleficence, and justice. Maintaining the highest standards in everything you do means never cutting corners. Most of us cut corners every day: Some we cut consciously, and others we cut without realization. Some cuts we make for our own reasons; others are forced on us by higher forces. There are many ways to cut corners, and you may not be able to avoid all of them; however, there is no question we can improve our standards by keeping those corners sharp. We will explore common examples of cutting corners in the last section of this book, as it is a common pitfall we clinicians face.

Let's examine a few specific standards that we must uphold in our practices. Your Code of Ethics will mention the many standards in several areas. For clarity, we will group them into our roles of professional member, practitioner, teacher, and supervisor. Our interprofessional standards are discussed in Part Four. Each of these groups has several guidelines that we are responsible for following in our daily work.

Professional Member Role

Falsifying qualifications: The addiction counselor cannot claim or imply professional qualifications or affiliations he or she does not possess. There are some clinicians who outright lie about their qualifications, stating they have had training or experience they have not had, or affiliations, falsely claiming to be connected with businesses or people. Be careful what you say or write everywhere, including your signature. You must present accurate information about your qualifications and your affiliations at all times.

For example, when speaking at a conference, Pam bumps into an old colleague, Martin, who runs a treatment facility. Earlier in the month, she had received an email from an acquaintance, Alexia, whose email signature included an affiliation with Martin's facility. While jovially catching up with Martin, Pam mentions how nice it is that Alexia is now on the board of the facility. Martin immediately corrects her, revealing that Alexia is not on the board. He leaves in a huff to investigate, and Pam is left feeling she has just let a large cat out of a small bag. Written and electronic affiliations are just as important as verbal ones, so take care in the printed associations with your name.

Here is another example you may have encountered. As we discussed in Part Two, most of us wear many hats indicating more than one role. This duality can be seen at annual conferences where we adopt the role of student. Yet many of us cannot completely abandon our other roles, even if we would really enjoy it, thus we must also wear our work hats, or at least keep them in our pockets in the form of a cell phone or pager. It is often the case that these clinicians will be called away from their workshops for some work-related concern. At times, they return to the workshop, but at times they do not. How many of these professionals, called away from a workshop, submit that workshop as a completed training in their recertification package? How many of you reading this have been guilty of saying you were trained in a topic when you know the information did not get into your brain, either because you were physically called away on other business, or you were simply unfocused during the presentation? Are you honest

when this occurs? Do you admit that you were not trained enough on the topic to ethically claim you deserve the hours? When first thinking about falsifying information, it is easy to condemn guilty counselors, viewing their behavior as shocking. But it is easy to blur the lines, especially when considering how difficult it is to maintain one's credential with all the other tasks we must complete.

Affiliation misuse: Clinicians should not use their affiliations with professional organizations and associations to pursue goals that are inconsistent with the stated purposes of the organizations. This relates to the ethical tier of the licensure/credential level. The organization that credentials you and the membership organization (if different) are organizations that depend on your ethical behavior and willingness to protect the mission of the organization. Organizations cannot thrive without the consistent professional behavior of its members. Specifically, you can't be throwing around your membership or credential without taking care of what you are saying, ensuring that it would be approved by the mission, objectives, and beliefs of the organization.

For another example, let's say you are interviewed by a local news agency, who agreed to interview you because of your affiliation with the organization. You sold yourself that way, stating they should interview you because you are connected with them. In the interview, your connection with your membership organization is established, and then you are asked your opinion on a local treatment program. In response, you state your belief that treatment programs do not work and that addicts can only recover in private practice individual counseling. You then advertise your private practice, inviting viewers to obtain counseling with you. This would be using your affiliation for your own gain, and expressly against the organization's purpose.

Do you consider the purposes of your association before acknowledging your connection with the association? Do you believe your elected and appointed leaders do? To ensure that you do not violate this principle, you must first become aware of the stated purposes of the association in which you are a member. It is not enough to assume you know what these are; you must read them in writing. Think that's easy? Well, it may not be, depending on in which state you live and in which organization you are a member. Some organizations have stellar websites that clearly list the purposes of the organization, or send their members informative packets with missions statements included. If you are a member, and your membership package does not adequately express the stated purposes and the website does not provide illumination, it is your ethical responsibility to call the organization's leaders and inquire, and while you are at it, suggest they revamp their website.

Misleading services: The alcoholism and drug abuse counselor should not associate with or permit the counselor's name to be used in connection with any services or products in a way that is incorrect or misleading. The clinician must adhere to information that has been scientifically verified, and cannot make unsubstantiated claims about the services they are giving (National Association for Addiction Professionals [NAADAC], 2011). You must not accept as factual information that has not been proven, even if you personally believe it to be true. In those cases, it is your responsibility to research the topic to gain the most educated stance.

This may seem reasonable, obvious even, but there are many ways for well-intentioned clinicians to get snagged on this principle. This means anything associated with your name must be truthful and clear. Let's look at each of those elements. To be truthful means to be accurate, factual, and timely. This can be difficult because it requires you to constantly update your information and acknowledge the constant change and growth in our field. Due to our friend the World Wide Web, your name can be permanently associated with all sorts of information that may no longer be considered correct or truthful. To be clear, and not misleading, any information associated with your name must be well written and evident in stated purpose and content. For many of us, our name is affiliated with all sorts

of projects, agencies, and organizations that may fall short of presenting clear information, especially on websites. Websites can be confusing and misleading, as can newspaper articles and other media, particularly as it becomes easier to self-publish materials without rigorous editing standards.

Can you account for every piece of material that is associated with your name? Are you even aware of what is out there with your name attached in some way? Go ahead and Google yourself as an experiment. You may learn a thing or two about that name you carry. The opportunity for your name to be used increases the more you put your name out there in publications, leadership positions, or other forms of notoriety. This principle is asking you to be aware and to do everything in your power to prevent your name from being used with incorrect or misleading information. Many people will not be able to perfect this standard, as the information out there is too great, but you can start with the information that *you* put out there, ensuring that to what you knowingly attach your name is current, truthful, and clear. Also if you see that your name is attached to something that does not follow these guidelines, ask that it be improved or your name removed. That may just motivate a person or organization that needs to step up its reporting skills, which helps the profession as a whole.

For example, how many of you use social media platforms such as Facebook, MySpace, online dating sites, and others? How much information about you and your work is listed there? If you list your membership, credential, or licensure, you are attaching the profession to whatever you post on these sites. They are affiliated with you for all to see. Now have I got your attention? Yes, this is a bit more concerning when you think of it this way. Most of us do not realize what we put out there because we think of our information as private information that we can dispense as we see fit. But when you have letters after your name, and when you identify your membership in organizations, your world is no longer completely as independent as you think. You are part of a group now, and whatever you do and say reflects back to the organization.

Publication responsibility: As discussed in Part Two, clinicians who are associated with published products must ensure the materials are presented in a factual way. The material within these publications must be truthful, and the manner in which it is being sold must be truthful, two components that are equally important. The example that comes to mind is James Frey (2003), who wrote a memoir about addiction that was publicly lauded by Oprah, which was then revealed as partially erroneous and misleading. The public was outraged that elements of his memoir were falsely created for dramatic effect. Once that truth was exposed, the book lost its integrity, as did Mr. Frey.

It is equally important that the material is sold in an honest way. Part of the criticism regarding the Frey book was that the publisher should have been fact-checking the work, as that is typically part of the service they provide. If the publisher had advance knowledge that there were misleading or factually questionable moments in the book and these remained in the publication, the publisher should also be liable. If you are in charge of selling or promoting a work you had better know what you are selling and ensure to the best of your ability that the material is professional and that you present it in such a manner.

Self-care: We thoroughly explore the concept of self-care in the next two chapters, but it has been listed as an ethical standard in this section of the Code of Ethics (NAADAC, 2011), and thus bears mention here. Self-care indicates that you will take care of your mental and physical health so that it does not impact your work in the profession. Emotions that ruin our moral decision making are anger, disgust, contempt, guilt, shame, embarrassment, pride, gratitude, elevation, sympathy, compassion, and empathy (Taleff, 2010). This is a normal process, and not necessarily harmful to the work we do. Yet it is an emotional type of work, and requires a healthy person to manage it. We all have moments of needing to take a step back,

reevaluate our health, and take steps to care for ourselves. There is no shame in that. The problem is only when we fail to recognize the need, or recognize it but fail to take the necessary steps to regain our health. This lands us in the pitfall of Clinician Burnout.

It is an ethical expectation that you will take steps to seek help and guidance if your professional performance becomes impaired or is at serious risk of impairment. NAADAC (2011) directly states that those clinicians in recovery are required to maintain a support system that will keep them healthy and will protect their work. All clinicians are also expected to obtain protective insurance policies that safeguard the clinician and the agency. This is particularly vital for those clinicians in private practice who don't have the benefit of an agency umbrella.

Practitioner Role

In addition to objectivity and integrity, there are standards that the practitioner must develop and maintain, which have been discussed throughout the book. For example, it is imperative that you safeguard your client's care. It is part of your responsibility to plan for the scenario of your inability to care for your caseload. In the event of your incapacitation or death, your client's care must be protected. Pope and Vasquez (2010) refer to this safety plan as a professional "will" (p. 67). You must designate who will be responsible for the ongoing treatment or referral of your clients, the maintenance or closure of your office, the management of your schedule, the notification of your condition, other communication, maintenance and storing of your records, your liability insurance, and any billing concerns (Pope & Vasquez, 2010).

Countertransference: We discussed the concept of transference in Part One, exploring how a client might displace feelings about someone in his or her life onto you, the clinician. We discussed it as a normal process in the therapeutic relationship, and one that can be used as a tool to help the client reach his or her goals. Countertransference is the same process, but in the other direction. It occurs when we, the clinicians, displace feelings about someone in our lives onto the client (Bass et al., 1996; Corey, Corey, & Callanan, 2007; Nassar-McMillan & Niles, 2011; Reamer, 2001, 2012). It, too, may be a normal part of the counseling process (Powell & Brodsky, 2004); however, it is not a tool that can be used to help the client. Instead it is a tool that can suggest to the clinician that he or she needs to take steps to become more objective, and to address a few issues in supervision. If the countertransference is significant, and indicative of a more serious problem, it is likely that the clinician will need to seek therapy to help address it, as it will require more specific care than supervision can address alone. A helpful tool of supervision is to separate the reasonable countertransference from the problematic countertransference (Powell & Brodsky, 2004).

Countertransference can be quite scary for a clinician, and many feel "sick" when realizing they have fallen victim to its snare. But just as transference can be a useful clinical tool for use with your clients, countertransference can be a vital tool to understanding yourself and what you need to strengthen in your ethical practice. There is no shame in it; you did not choose to think of your client in this way. The shame only comes from not asking for help when you know you need it. Actually, there is no shame in this, only responsibility that you need to take seriously. Unrecognized it can become a bigger problem and can lead to boundary crossing and other unethical behavior. If you recognize it early and get help to address it, you will avoid potential misery for everyone involved, including the profession.

Countertransference is often unrealized until it is observed by someone else, so it is important that you listen to others when they ask you or point out behavior they see. If you begin questioning your feelings, or if someone brings concerning behavior to your attention, don't laugh it off or storm off in a huff; bring it all to your supervisor or therapist. If it turns out not to be countertransference, then

you will be happy you checked it out. If it turns out to be, then you will have nipped it in the bud early and given yourself a chance to attend to what you needed to address. It is a win-win situation.

Consider the examples of the clinician, Jacob. From a young age, Jacob knew he wanted to help others. He knew it because he had helped his younger sister through several rough patches with boyfriends as she was growing up, and she often told him that he should make a career out of his ability to lend support and nonjudging love, not to mention his ability to stay calm in a crisis. Eventually, Jacob found his way into the detox unit of his local hospital, and found the work invigorating and felt he was good at the job. He did struggle, however, when a certain type of person was admitted under his care. Specific physical characteristics coupled with a combative, hostile attitude were the features that immediately produced a reaction in Jacob, one best described as a mixture of adrenaline, anger, and fear. Jacob could recognize that these characteristics reminded him of his sister's boyfriends from the past, the ones from whom she had needed rescuing. Do you think Jacob will be able to give fair treatment to these men who remind him of the past? What should he do in this situation?

When Jacob became a counselor, he accepted the responsibility of being an objective clinician, and what that would personally and professionally entail. It is his responsibility to give fair treatment to all his clients, regardless of any issues from his own past that potentially color his relationships. If it is a challenge to treat his clients with integrity, it is a challenge he must accept and rigorously carry out. If he struggles to do this, it is his responsibility to get help from his trusted advisors, so that his objective to give healthy, fair treatment is not lost, and his standards of practice remain intact.

It is important to note that it is never acceptable to discuss your countertransference with clients. This reverses the power differential upon which the relationship is built, and can put the client in an awkward position with no appropriate course of action, and perhaps little support to aid them in knowing how to handle the situation. It is your responsibility to get the help you need to address your countertransference, and that support must come from a trusted, healthy, appropriate advisor. Due to the taboo of countertransference, clinicians may deny the presence of countertransference, which may prevent them from seeking the help they need (Wolff & Hayes, 2009). Supervisors should be well-trained in recognizing countertransference and in reducing anxiety, helping the clinician to develop insight and conceptualizing skills (Wolff & Hayes, 2009).

Termination: The primary role of a counselor is to help others get the knowledge and skills necessary for treating addiction. In other words, the point of a clinician is to become pointless; you want to teach your clients what they need so you are not needed. If your ego is anywhere in your practice, it will argue this point, and many clinicians carry on with clients far too long based on their own need to feel needed. You may feel good at the end of the day, but you are doing a grave disservice to your clients. If they become dependent on you, you will have taught them that they cannot help themselves, that they need your guidance and approval before making a decision or taking action. Are you going to be the parent, spouse, friend, and clinician to this person for the rest of his or her life? Because that is what you are setting up, and I don't know anyone who can make that lifelong commitment. More to the point, they shouldn't have to, as your clients already have everything they need to carry on their own life; they just need to be shown that they can do it. You teach, or coach, clients into their own self-help ... and then you set them free. That is what great therapy is all about, and there is nothing more rewarding than watching a client spread his or her wings and take flight. If you coddle your clients, you will miss that.

Does a certain ethical pillar come to mind? Autonomy perhaps? The idea that the point of counseling is to become pointless is steeped in autonomy. The trick to a responsible practice is to balance the need for your clients to take the reins of their own

recovery with the need for your clients to gain education and skill. You don't want to push them into independence before they are ready and you don't want to hover over them long after they need it. You will probably find that your success varies; at times you will balance this well in your first attempt. Other times you will need to pull clients back under your wing or loosen your grasp on them faster. If you are constantly monitoring your role as teacher and making the necessary adjustments with each client you will be employing a responsible practice.

For example, Joy is a well-respected, seasoned clinician working at an outpatient clinic, running groups and carrying a caseload for individual counseling. Clients adore her counseling style, and clinicians respect her fair style and dignity in all her work. Her colleague, Daphne, has always admired her and strived to emulate her professionalism. After several years of revering Joy, Daphne is troubled to observe some questionable behavior. Joy has a client, Buck, who is seeing her individually for counseling of his addiction and PTSD diagnoses. Joy has been working with Buck for 3 years, the longest time on her caseload. The agency typically works with clients for less than 1 year, so Buck's treatment is clearly an aberration. In fact, Daphne has struggled to keep several of her own clients in treatment, but has been told by the agency administration that she needs to discharge them because insurance will no longer pay. Daphne watches in frustration as Buck is allowed to stay without any change to his treatment, yet her own clients are passed through the system faster than is clinically indicated.

As time goes by, and Buck continues to receive treatment, Daphne grows suspicious of Joy's motives in keeping him on her caseload. She confronts Joy, who gives her weak clinical reasoning to keep him in treatment. Ultimately, Daphne feels she must report Joy to their supervisor. Daphne is unsure why Joy would keep a client beyond what it clinically indicated, but she suspects countertransference is at play. It is not her job to guess what reasons Joy has for her behavior, as she is her colleague and not her boss. Daphne's responsibility is to report the activity to her supervisor and let that person investigate and address any issues uncovered.

Teacher Role

Similarly, there are objectivity, integrity, and standards requirements of the teacher role. Although we are all in a teacher role with our clients, teaching the tools needed to establish and maintain recovery, some professionals hold more formal teaching roles. If you are in a position to teach others, there are standards you are expected to uphold.

As discussed in Part Two, you will need to ensure the information you are presenting is accurate, timely, clear, fair, and relevant. You must represent your affiliations ethically. For example, this year I was scheduled to give a training on diagnosis to a group of social workers. Just before my training, a new edition of the *Diagnostic and Statistical Manual of Mental Disorders* (DSM) was released. I could have given my training as written, explaining that the new manual had just been released. But that would have been unethical. The new manual incorporated many changes that affected my training material, making some of what I had written obsolete. It made for a few late nights while I learned the new manual well enough to present the changes in the training. Despite that annoyance it was the ethical move. Otherwise, I would have knowingly given erroneous and irrelevant information to the group. It's a good example of the need to uphold the ethical standards even if it is fairly easy to convince others you have not acted unethically, even if no one will never know of your infraction. You will know and that should be enough.

Supervisor Role

Clinical supervision is recognized as a necessary contributing factor to successful professional development in crafting an effective ethical practice (Bogo, Paterson, Tufford, & King, 2011a; Powell & Brodsky, 2004; Whitley, 2010). It has been linked with improved staff competence and job satisfaction, organization commitment, retention, job performance, and clinician well-being, and is protective against Clinician Burnout, in addition to ensuring the best client outcomes (Bogo et al., 2011a; Whitley, 2010). Positive clinical supervision provides general administrative and emotional support, a healthy interaction that promotes positive interprofessional skills, task assistance, and case consultation, and can also aid us in establishing a professional identity (Bogo et al., 2011a). While your agency or place of employment should supply you with decent supervision, it is your responsibility to ensure that you have it. Thus, if you are in private practice, or if the supervision given to you is insufficient, you must take steps to find your own or improve what has been offered. This is discussed in great detail later in this section.

There are also standards for those in our profession who are actively supervising other clinicians. If you are the supervisor you agree to aid in their professional development by providing accurate and current information, by giving timely evaluations, and by giving constructive consultation (Powell & Brodsky, 2004). How many supervisors effectively fulfill all three of these requirements consistently? First, supervisors must provide timely and truthful information. This means if you are a supervisor you have an additional responsibility to keep up-to-date with new information, and to know it well enough to present it to those you supervise. I can hear the snorts of readers who are currently supervisors. "Yeah, right. With what time?" you retort, and I don't blame you. It's hard enough balancing clinical, administrative, and supervisory time into a normal work week; journal and book reading just don't make it in.

Yet it is part of being a supervisor, and part of what you agreed to do. Thus, finding creative ways to sneak in research time will become an important task. Reading abstracts instead of full articles is a great way of keeping up-to-date without becoming bogged down in hours of reading time. Then if an article is particularly captivating or relevant, you can read it in full. Some journals come right to your email box at no cost or a small cost to you. You can scan headlines, skipping what you don't need and focusing on the rest. You can also read websites or blogs of clinicians who are reading the full research and are summarizing its key points on their pages. Just be sure to find the full article if it is research you are planning on teaching, as the blog writer may have misinterpreted facts. You would not want to spread faulty information around. You can keep a small portion of your individual or group supervision time to discuss what clinicians have read in the literature, an awesome way to increase the amount of knowledge without taking the time to read it all.

Supervisors must also give timely evaluations, and these evaluations need not only to be timely, but to be thoughtful, instructive, and constructive (Powell & Brodsky, 2004). Here is a good example of where supervisors may tend to cut corners, either by neglecting to have evaluations, or by skimming through them quickly and without detail, or by revealing only one half of what an evaluation is supposed to be, such as writing only praise or only criticism. Evaluations should be written, with clear questions that allow the supervisor to evaluate the whole clinician, not just empty space for the clinician to write whatever comes to mind. Evaluations should occur in regular intervals that the agency or supervisor defines in advance. Quarterly evaluations are common; at least two a year should be

standard. To write a complete evaluation, a supervisor must adequately observe the clinician (Powell & Brodsky, 2004). Many supervisors can write their evaluation based on what they observe in the supervisory hours they complete with the clinician, but that won't give a complete picture. Clinicians must be observed through direct observation, audio or videotaping. We will discuss this more in the chapter on supervision.

Finally, a supervisor must give constructive consultation (Powell & Brodsky, 2004). Supervisors must not only point out what the client needs to work on, but make suggestions on improving those areas. At the same time, the supervisor must highlight what strengths the clinician brings to his or her work, and encourage the clinician to continue building on those strengths. Constructive means useful, productive, positive, encouraging, practical, and valuable. Negative comments are less helpful if you omit suggestions for improvement. Your evaluation is an important document, not only because it will be the blueprint for that clinician's future work, but because it exists in that clinician's file forever and reflects back on both your clinician and you (Powell & Brodsky, 2004). Take the time to write a thorough evaluation; it will help your clinician improve and will reveal you to be the excellent supervisor you are.

Okay, now that we have examined all the parts of this principle, let's look at how it plays out in the clinical world with a few vignettes. Are you excited? Good, me too.

VIGNETTE: CAN FOCUS HARM?

Margaret is a 25-year-old female client who has been in treatment for 3 months. She approaches Peter, the supervisor of staff, and reports that her male counselor, Geoff, has been acting in a way that makes her question his motives, and she is not sure what to do. From the beginning of their sessions together, Margaret feels much of the content of the therapy focused on her feelings about sex or sexual issues. Geoff seems to find ways to talk about this during every session, even though Margaret does not believe sexual issues are relevant to her recovery. If he is not asking her about sex, he is talking about attraction. Once he even used his own extramarital affair as an example to make a point during the session.

Peter thanks the client for coming to him, and acknowledges it took courage. Next, he assesses what actions, if any, Margaret has taken. Has she asked Geoff to talk about other things, has she explained her discomfort to him, has she attempted any redirection of the conversation? Peter is not necessarily suggesting she needs to do these things, he just needs to obtain all the information. Once he has determined any strategies she has used, he asks her if she is comfortable talking about the issue with Geoff. The client may be uncomfortable approaching the counselor, but if she is willing, direct communication can be therapeutic for both parties. Peter will want to be there for this conversation, should it take place, as a neutral support for both sides. It is smart to have a witness for conversations like these, so it can be safe and avoid a he-said, she-said argument that can't be solved. If she is unwilling to address the issue directly with the counselor, or if Peter assesses that it would be unsafe or not recommended to do so, the other option is for Peter to approach Geoff privately.

Let's say Peter does approach the clinician, who says, "I just treated her the same as everyone else by assessing a possible sex addiction, sexual dysfunction, or other sexual issues. I do it with everyone." This would be one example where taped sessions would be very helpful, as Peter would be able to see what the clinician does with the majority of clients, and whether he does act differently with Margaret. Assuming Peter doesn't have such observation handy, what would be his next move? Perhaps he would explore with Geoff possible reasons that Margaret would feel this way. Ask Geoff to examine his own behavior and look for any clues to what could have been misunderstood, or look for clues in the client's presentation and history that may suggest a sensitivity to this area.

In addition to protecting Margaret, Peter's responsibility as the supervisor is to facilitate further development of the clinician. He is charged with helping Geoff evaluate whether his conduct with Margaret has been ethical, whether there is a bleeding of personal and professional agendas, and what the next move should be. Peter will want to help Margaret and Geoff work through this issue rather than just make a quick ruling to discipline Geoff or drop it. His best course of action is to make a plan with Geoff to address the issue with the individual client. This plan will vary depending on the situation; there is no one clear way to address it. Whatever plan they set in place, Peter should jot it down, and follow up in later supervisions, and include the experience in his next evaluation. This analysis would be much smoother if Peter has diligently observed the client's behavior using written, audio, or video means. He will want to be sure that future sessions are taped between Margaret and Geoff to ensure ethical treatment is utilized. Peter will also want to have another meeting with Margaret alone to ensure her satisfaction with the way he addressed the situation and her happiness in continuing treatment.

When presenting this vignette at trainings, two questions are often posed. First, in what sense can it be argued that the client had a moral responsibility in this

(continued)

issue, since she felt this was wrong from the very start but didn't say anything until now? How would you answer that? Yes, it can be argued that Margaret should have come forward when she began to feel uncomfortable, but remember that the power differential in counseling dictates that the clinician is supposed to be strong and healthy for the client, who is seeking treatment because she is not healthy in some areas of her life. Because of this power differential, it may be difficult for a client to criticize a clinician. We are responsible for giving clients the best care, so the duty to evaluate and make necessary changes falls on us.

Second, would the vignette example be different if the genders were reversed? This is a great question that hits on gender discrimination. What do you think? Do you think there is a double standard, meaning that you would see the case differently if the counselor were a woman and the client were a man? Men have the reputation of being more seductively predatory, but women can be just as inappropriate as men. Gender should make no difference here, whether it was one man and one woman, two men, or two women involved. The two issues involved are (1) that the client was uncomfortable with the sexual content of the discussion and (2) that the client was uncomfortable with the continuous questioning on that topic. Don't forget that you want to assess why the clinician was bringing this topic up in every session, if the client's claim is accurate. Clinicians should not be so rigid in what they bring to sessions that they are bringing the same topics in every session. Rehearsal of important concepts is a valuable tool in treatment, but constant repetition leads to a rigid routine, which we know can be problematic.

VIGNETTE: COUNTERTRANSFERENCE

When you were 5 years old, your parents died in a car crash and your mother's best friend, Irene, raised you. Irene was a lovely, nurturing woman, and you enjoyed a happy, loving childhood in Irene's care. Irene's description includes dark black hair set in a poofy style, a soft medium-dark skin tone, crooked white teeth, a very low soothing voice that always sounded like a cello to you, and an ability to wear a smile on her face in almost any situation. Five years ago, Irene died peacefully in her sleep, and although you are happy that Irene did not suffer, you miss your surrogate mother very much.

You are a counselor at a residential program for substance abusers. Upon coming into work one day, you hear a slightly familiar voice down the hall in the residents' common room. You greet the staff on duty, who tells you of a new resident, Gigi. She gives you the usual quick background information and leaves for the day. You would typically go to the office and read the initial chart on the new resident before meeting her, but something compels you to walk down and introduce yourself to Gigi first. When you enter the room and see Gigi sitting on the couch with her fellow residents, you feel instantly warm. Gigi looks at you, smiling, and you introduce yourself, holding out your hand. Gigi takes it, and you note the smooth quality in Gigi's dark skin and the depth of Gigi's voice when she says "hello," her crooked teeth shining through her smile. You instantly feel soothed and comfy, as you walk back to the office to complete your paperwork for the day.

As Gigi continues her participation in the program, you support her as you do all of the residents in the program, but you feel a special closeness in your bond with her. While in treatment, Gigi often receives a little more attention from you than other counselors, including the one who is assigned to her as her primary counselor. You do small things, such as granting Gigi small requests before granting the requests of other residents, or letting her stay on the phone with her family a little bit past curfew when you are supposed to be telling residents to get to their rooms. But the most significant difference occurs during clinical staff meetings, whenever Gigi's case is discussed. If staff has critical things to say about Gigi's progress, you immediately defend Gigi and become quite intense in your defense of her. Yet when staff begins to discuss Gigi's discharge, you begin producing reasons for Gigi to stay. It is not that what you say about Gigi in these meetings is false or inappropriate; in fact you are thorough and empathetic. But you are noticeably advocating with more care and attention than you do with other clients.

What are your thoughts on your ethical behavior? Can you see how a specific relationship from your past could influence your professional behavior? If you develop a good radar, your specialized treatment of Gigi will not escape your notice. Once aware, seek help in supervision or with a trusted advisor. Remember there is no shame in seeking help, only in avoiding the help you need.

VIGNETTE: A FRIEND IN NEED

David and Johnny met as undergraduate students, both majoring in addiction counseling. After getting credentials and becoming members of their state organization, David and Johnny both established themselves in the field by working for similar agencies. David then moved on, opening a successful private practice office. Johnny struggled a bit to develop the same success, and wanted to open his own private practice, but needed referrals. He was approached by a new agency opening up, and was asked to be a spokesperson for the agency because he had become somewhat well known in the community. Johnny consulted, giving a few quotes for their written advertising materials, but ultimately decided not to be involved. He pulled out of the deal once he learned that the agency did not believe that addiction was a disease, and planned instead to treat addiction as a social disease, seeing clients as morally corrupt. Johnny disagreed with this approach, and therefore removed himself. But his quote appeared on the brochure after he quit.

(continued)

He called the agency to complain and was told it cost too much money to have the brochure remade. Johnny, feeling hopeless, did nothing. Across town, David was fully planning on using Johnny for referrals, figuring they could help each other out as their careers grew. But David happened upon the brochure and was turned off by what was written there. Surprised to see Johnny's endorsement, David figured he had grown in a different direction since school, and decided against using him for referrals. He didn't want to work with someone who would affiliate with the organization. He never told Johnny this, who never knew that he had a chance for numerous referrals but did not get them because of his affiliation with the flawed organization.

Can you see how an affiliation can have repercussions of which you are not aware? You cannot possibly account for everyone's reaction to information about you; therefore, a better plan is to do your best to control the information about you. Surely you can't have control over every single piece of information, but we each must strive to do just that. Don't be relaxed about your affiliations. They matter. They matter to you, and they matter to the profession.

Establishing and maintaining a responsible practice is a complex process with many factors that demand our attention. It can be tiring in the constant vigilance it requires, particularly for those of us with more than one role. Yet we must continue to strive for objectivity, integrity, and standards in our work. One helpful task that helps us with our responsibility is to focus on building our competency. The more competent we are, the greater our chances of objectivity, integrity, and standards. Let's take a look.

Principle: Competency

13
Chapter

To be a good ethical clinician we have to be competent in what we do. This straightforward ethical principle is at the heart of protecting ourselves because the more competent we are, the less likely we are to make ethical errors and keep our practice unsanctioned. In addition to the benefits to the client and the clinician, competency also has great advantages for the profession. Our profession's maturity is evidenced in our training, our knowledge, our evidence-based practices, and our multidisciplinary approach (Gallagher, 2010).

Addiction is a changing phenomenon, and our understanding of its process has morphed significantly from our views in the 1940s when it was believed to be a moral disease based on a lack of willpower (Doukas & Cullen, 2010). For example, drug use patterns have been changing, with injection rates surpassing other methods; prescription pain reliever abuse and elder adult use is on the rise; and admission rates show alcohol decreasing and marijuana increasing (Whitter et al., 2006). Co-occurring disorders have become an expectation not an exception (Cline & Minkoff, 2008): It has been reported that 60% of drug users seeking treatment were found to have an independent mood disorder (Whitter et al., 2006). If we don't adopt our practices to reflect the change in the drug, method, and population that is abusing it, we will be left trying to effectively treat a population that is not there, and miss the needs of the clients who are presented to us. Big fail. Counselors need to be competent in all of these issues (Whitley, 2010).

What does it mean to be competent at your job? How do we measure competency? How do you build a competent practice? Perhaps you are thinking that training has something to do with your competence. Turns out, you are right! But competency is about more than your training. It is also about applied theory, therapist qualities, respecting your limitations, ongoing supervision, and maintaining healthy self-care. Competency is a complex process that requires rigorous attention, but the benefits of that focus are experienced by the client, the clinician, and the profession. Let's examine how to achieve this principle.

Training

First, you must be careful not to fall into the training trap. Competency is not necessarily the same as training for recertification. Your certification and recertification requirements are limited to trainings that offer continued education hours (CEH) by an approved education provider. Luckily, there are many providers in our country, but while sticking to approved trainings will satisfy your CEH requirements, it will not necessarily satisfy your competency gaps. I get it: You don't have much money to spend on training, and your time is already squeezed by all that you do in your personal and professional life. You become pragmatic in obtaining training, looking for the cheapest workshops, or the ones that fit into your schedule without you taking time off (or workshops that demand you take paid time off), or the ones that are offered at a convenient place, or the ones that offer online education, or the ones that allow you to "double-dip" (satisfying more than one requirement or more than one credential or licensure requirement). That may be what you feel you need to do to get those required hours in on time, but it does not necessarily make you a competent clinician, and it certainly doesn't make you an ethical one.

Competency comes from ongoing training on a full range of topics that make up our profession, and the topics are ever changing to reflect the growth in theory and practice. The knowledge that made you competent 20 years ago may now be outdated and replaced with newer advancements. The competent clinician keeps an eye out for new information, seeking it out by engaging in conversations with colleagues; reading journal articles, newsletters, and magazines; and conducting random Internet searches, sleuthing out websites on different topics. You may find a wealth of information outside of approved trainings that strengthens your practice. Sometimes you can find an interesting idea and fail to find trainings on the topic. There are training companies that may be able to develop the training upon your request, or you may

be interested enough to conduct thorough research on the topic and develop a training session yourself. Some of the best trainings out there likely came from a trainer's frustration in not finding the topic elsewhere. Adequate training is the first requirement of a competent clinician.

Applied Theory

"The gap between what we know and what we practice is sizable" (Whitter et al., 2006, p. 14), which suggests that clients are either not getting training on the existing techniques that are most likely to produce the best outcomes, or they are obtaining them but not using them with clients. The addiction profession is challenged to disseminate evidence-based practices into routine clinical settings (McGovern, Fox, Xie, & Drake, 2004). Clinicians are more motivated to adopt some evidence-based practices, such as 12-step facilitation and motivational interviewing, than others such as pharmacotherapy (McGovern et al., 2004).

Historically, addiction counseling has relied more on faith than science or empirical findings (St. Germaine, 1996). In the past quarter century, research shifted to chemical addiction as a brain disease triggered by frequent use of drugs that change the biochemistry and anatomy of neurons, but the integration of theory and research into clinical practice for either chemical or behavioral addictions has been slow (St. Germaine, 1996). Practitioners tend to cling rigidly to their favorite theory, most often without a full understanding of all its concepts and implications, and other theories may be unwittingly disregarded (St. Germaine, 1996). Practitioners may not understand research reports, have limited access to research, and be unaware that literature exists. Counselors need to improve professional practices, services, and research. They must adopt a lifelong learning in seeking relevant research related to addictions counseling (St. Germaine, 1996).

We live in a world with a constant swirl of information circling, coming from a variety of sources, some valid and some ... not so valid. You should avoid believing in a theory or principle, and certainly a treatment technique, because you heard or read about it from one source. Part of research is examining information for both validity and reliability, and this becomes increasingly important as the Internet exhausts us with available information. Develop and use your critical eye to read everything with a healthy measure of skepticism, and look for corroborating sources. Competent trainers and books will cite additional sources that back up their claims when possible. Try out what you learn with your clients. If techniques are not immediately available, try to modify them, discuss them with your supervisor, and take additional training. But if a theory or technique continues to fail or is inferior to other options, do not continue to use it because it has been touted as the next best thing. Some fads are short-lived, and for good reason. Stick with evidence-based practices, those that have been tested and are reliably valuable.

For example, Pedro is a group counselor at both an inpatient hospital and an attached outpatient clinic. He runs a relapse prevention group in both settings, and he uses the same basic technique in both groups. He believes that clients should create the needed topics in the group, so he waits until a client brings something up to discuss. Once the conversation begins, he may add information and will redirect the group back to the topic at hand, but he won't instigate topics. Other clinicians, and likely some clients, view Pedro as lazy, but in fact he is quite purposeful with his technique. He strongly believes that it is an important aspect of recovery to recognize your needs and ask for the help you need, rather than sit through a group topic that may not refer to your needs. Pedro has been working in the field for more than 25 years and has never diverted from this technique, which he uses as proof that the technique is a good one with staying power. However, you have a bit of inside information as one of the individual clinicians who work with members of Pedro's group. Over the years you have heard many clients laud his style, saying they got a lot of help from the group and crediting it with contributing

significantly to their recovery successes. On the other hand, you have received an equal amount of complaints from clients who feel they got nothing helpful from the group and found it boring and Pedro ineffective. What is the problem with Pedro's technique? You think about it for a second or two, and then we will discuss.

So what did you come up with? Perhaps you are thinking that it is the role of a clinician to teach clients how to help themselves, to coach them in building such a strong recovery foundation that the clinician is no longer needed. Was that your thought? Well then yay! You should allow for groups that encourage the client to create the topic, or even to have a portion of each group devoted to client topics, but you must also relay the basic tools that clients will need for their recovery. You can tell a kid, "There is a bike, go ride it. Let me know if you have questions." But that kid is destined to have more success if you give them a few basics about how to sit, steer, and balance before they try it on their own. Similarly, clients will benefit from you giving them some guidance rather than leaving their treatment up to them before learning what it is they need.

Perhaps that was not your answer. Instead, you thought that Pedro's method is unethical because it is too rigid. He has used the same method for every client group in 25 years no matter where they are in recovery, and this is the very definition of a rigid routine. Plus, he uses the same group technique for both inpatient and outpatient clients. Inpatient clients are in very early recovery, and will likely need even more coaching and educating on needed tools to establish recovery than outpatient clients who presumably have successfully begun to build a recovery program. Many of the same principles would be discussed in both groups, but it is odd to have the two groups identical since their needs vary. If this was your answer, yay for you! This is also correct. You need to know where your clients are in their recovery and adjust your style accordingly. If you adopt a rigid routine for all of your clients you most definitely will help some who fit with that style, but you will lose others who don't. Effectively connecting your training with your practice is the second requirement of a competent clinician.

Supervision

While training and its application to the clinical practice are essential to competency, they alone do not ensure a competent practice over time (White & Kleber, 2008; Whitter et al., 2006). Often, clinicians will learn a new skill, practice it with their clients, but then return to the old familiar way of doing business, because they become either discouraged, bored, or lazy. At other times, clinicians can harm clients by believing in fad treatments without adequately understanding the applications, limitations, or context of the intervention (White & Kleber, 2008). The best way to guarantee that new essential components of competency are sustained is through intensive supervision (Whitter et al., 2006). The addiction profession is "rapidly recognizing" the need and importance of clinical supervision (Whitley, 2010). Effective supervision will aid a clinician in proper diagnosis, in applying the most appropriate interventions, in analyzing client progress, and in troubleshooting when needed (Bogo, Paterson, Tufford, & King, 2011a; Powell & Brodsky, 2004).

Supervision should adapt to the specific needs at different stages of a person's career (Bogo et al., 2011a). Students and interns will have specific supervisory needs related to entering the field and developing a competency base. Newly credentialed clinicians will have supervisory needs related to establishing a sound clinical and ethical practice, and setting goals for increasing competency. Seasoned clinicians will have specific supervisory needs related to maintaining a fresh passion for the work, and continuing to keep that competency base growing.

Your competency can benefit from support and monitoring. Clinicians' perception of competency and job satisfaction is positively affected by a supportive interprofessional team, and leaders who effectively balance the tension between expectations of employee performance and providing needed support (Bogo, Paterson, Tufford, & King, 2011b). A major goal of supervision is to encourage growth by reinforcing positive qualities and working on limitations (Powell & Brodsky, 2004). Supervision is a good place to talk about countertransference issues, struggles at work, and processing the way we practice, all of which focuses less on the client and more on what makes us competent clinicians (Bogo et al., 2011a). It follows that the better the supervision, the more competent the clinician will perceive themselves to be (Bogo et al., 2011b). "Counselors with a more favorable view of their supervisors report more job satisfaction, organizational commitment, perceived organizational support, and less perceived role overload and burnout" (Bogo et al., 2011a, p. 126).

Studies show that clinicians want regular supervision, even though workload demands make it a challenge (Bogo et al., 2011a). The quality of the supervisor matters to addiction clinicians. Supervision is safe if trust is present. Supervision should be a reciprocal process built on respect, with the clinician validated and accepted and both strengths and challenges in their practices explored (Bogo et al., 2011a; Powell & Brodsky, 2004). Clinicians recognize the value of learning new skills to use with clients, and using supervision to develop their professional identity, in addition to the value of analyzing their practices for potential problems (Bogo et al., 2011a; Powell & Brodsky, 2004).

There are no state or national requirements of addiction professionals receiving supervision from other addiction counselors (Whitley, 2010). In fact, supervision is often offered by a professional from another discipline outside of the addiction profession (Bogo et al., 2011a), typically licensed social workers (Whitley, 2010), because social workers are drawn to the field by managed care reimbursement requirements of graduate education and in some cases licensure (Whitley, 2010). This can work as long as the supervisor has relevant clinical knowledge (Bogo et al., 2011a; Whitley, 2010). Yet clinicians will need to discuss new trends specific to the addiction profession, stressors relevant to the addiction profession, and other issues (Bogo et al., 2011a; Whitley, 2010). If they cannot get this with a provided supervisor, it is essential that the clinician and supervisor ensure that the clinician is getting this profession-based support elsewhere.

Because clinical supervisors are critical in sustaining and developing staff competencies there should be a focus on their professional development efforts (Whitter et al., 2006). Supervisors need ongoing training to build the competencies and maintain the skill required to be successful supervisors in this climate of scientific advancement (Powell & Brodsky, 2004; Whitter et al., 2006). Yet individuals are often promoted to supervisory positions without management training or proper orientation and support. Competency-based training must acknowledge supervisors' varying skill levels. Further, training for clinical supervisors must be based on a set of core competencies (Whitter et al., 2006). Healthy and appropriate supervision, both giving and receiving it, is the third requirement for a competent clinician.

Therapist Qualities

If you recall from Part One, we are aware that therapist qualities are better indicators of good outcomes than treatment intervention type, and in Part Two, we suggested different aspects of our roles that make us effective, yet little research has focused on what those positive therapist qualities are (Wolff & Hayes, 2009). The main focus in the literature has been whether the clinician is in recovery or not (Gallagher, 2010; Wolff & Hayes, 2009), as we discussed in our first pitfall chapter. The crux of the argument is whether a counselor in recovery is at an advantage or disadvantage.

Although no studies have been conducted to link recovery status specifically with therapeutic alliance or positive outcomes (Whitter et al., 2006), stakeholders in our profession continue to promote the idea that personal experience of recovery is a valuable asset to the field, and that clients may prefer a counselor in recovery (Whitter et al., 2006). But is this true? Is it possible that we promote the idea because we believe in it ourselves? When we disclose to clients, they may internalize that as part of what makes us good clinicians, and we may promote the idea that what is good about us is our personal history. But if we were to give a blind taste test to our clients, taking several clinicians with varying personal experiences in addiction and asking clients to rate them on several measures, would recovery status impact how the clients were rated? While this has not been researched, perhaps we can draw evidence from other helping professions. For example, if your marriage was in trouble, and you went to a social worker that specialized in couples therapy, you probably would not say: "Judy is a fantastic marital therapist. I learned so much from her and she really understood me based on her own marital trouble." If you were seeking therapy, would you say: "My psychologist is so helpful. Learning about his daily struggle with bipolar has really helped me"? Would your search for a medical doctor be based on his or her past experience, such as "I chose my primary care physician because he has diabetes and a past sexual addiction, just like me! I wanted someone who had walked in my shoes to help me."

Most likely you think these all sound ridiculous, so why is it okay to judge a clinician's personal life in our field? You wouldn't say to your client: "So your goal is to become a musician. Hmm, too bad. I'm tone deaf so I can't help you with that. But Paul over there plays guitar on Thursday nights, so let's transfer your care over to him so he can help you reach those goals." Of course not. You should not even discuss your own musical history. You would say, "Ooo, tell me more." What kind of musician; what does music do for you? How can we chop up that goal into smaller goals you can start working on now? You don't need to be a musician to help your client identify goals. So why would you need to be in recovery to help your client build their own recovery program? They should not be examining your life and thinking, "I want to emulate that." That is a sponsor's role.

Some research suggests there are significant differences between recovering and nonrecovering clinicians in therapist qualities (Doukas & Cullen, 2010; Wolff & Hayes, 2009); other studies found no effect (Doukas & Cullen, 2010). Some argue that a counselor in recovery is better able to empathize with clients, identify potential problems in building a recovery program, expose denial and resistance, and instill hope in clients than their non-recovery counterparts (Wolff & Hayes, 2009), and to offer street credibility (Doukas & Cullen, 2010).

Others argue that a counselor in recovery is more susceptible to poor boundaries, overidentifies with clients more often, fails to maintain personal recovery (Wolff & Hayes, 2009), and may be inflexible and resistant (Doukas & Cullen, 2010). They may stop addressing their own recovery needs and drown themselves in the needs of their clients as a way to maintain their own sobriety, which is rarely sufficient (Gallagher, 2010). Failure to meet recovery needs is the primary relapse factor that leads to burnout if clinicians in recovery fail to seek supervision. A lack of detachment and overcommitment are other contributing factors (Doukas & Cullen, 2010). Recovering clinicians adhere to a disease process, exhibit less flexibility in treatment planning, hold less favorable views on professional training, and are more rigid thinkers than nonrecovering therapists (Wolff & Hayes, 2009). It has also been suggested that counselors in recovery are inflexible, are overcommitted, use a limited frame of reference that can lead to overdiagnosis (Doukas & Cullen, 2011), and don't believe in trainings because they believe they already have the important tools from their personal experiences (Doukas & Cullen, 2011; Gallagher, 2010; Whitley, 2010; Wolff & Hayes, 2009).

Clinicians in recovery must be aware of their sensitivities to profession-induced triggers, as they may see people they used with or sold to (Doukas & Cullen, 2011). The majority of addiction professionals are attracted to the field by personal or family experiences, and many addiction counselors began their education in the AA program, which promotes sharing honestly with another (Whitley, 2010). In the 1970s, counselors were recruited when they were still in treatment and many lacked sufficient training and supervision to handle the job (Whitley, 2010), although many built solid professions. This can help with stigma against dependence, but it can also create subjective attitudes toward clients. Counselors in recovery may have lower self-esteem about their past, their lack of education, and their older age compared to counselors not in recovery, as suggested (Doukas & Cullen, 2011). Atoning for one's past by entering a career or measuring one's personal success through a client's treatment experience can destroy the client–counselor relationship. Agencies need screening to ensure that counselors in recovery are also healthy before taking on direct practice (Doukas & Cullen, 2010).

Despite the general opinion that personal recovery experience is either an asset or a detriment to successful addiction counseling, the research has not found a significant effect (Wolff & Hayes, 2009). To what then can we attribute successful therapist qualities? It has been suggested that if recovery status is not a significant factor, perhaps the overall mental health of the therapist is a better indicator of successful treatment (Wolff & Hayes, 2009). If clinicians are experiencing Clinician Burnout, or are struggling with emotional health issues, they may be less able to be successfully empathetic with clients, they may not work as deeply, or they may fail to serve as positive role models (Wolff & Hayes, 2009, p. 53). Addiction clients can be hostile and provocative, avoidant, and helpless and defensive, which can cause a whole host of emotions for clinicians, such as anger, defensiveness, inadequacy, and a desire to withdraw (Wolff & Hayes, 2009). The better the clinician's mental health, the better they will be able to handle the emotional challenges of the work.

Perhaps a good therapist contains something more basic. At the end of the day, maybe what we do most of all is instill a sense of hope, loan it out if the client can't muster it, or beam it outward when the client falls back into doubt. No matter what technique we use, or who the client is, if hope is not alive nothing will work. We know this, so we work extra hard on finding hope in the direst of situations, encouraging clients to keep trying and believing that change is possible. It may be the most important thing you do, as in many cases your office is the only place they are going to gain hope, until they can learn to generate it on their own, or increase their hope stations in others. If you feel hopeless, your clients can begin to feel like a lost cause and treatment may be likely to fail. Therapist qualities are the fourth requirement of a competent clinician. Additional research is needed to adequately explore this concept to test what therapist qualities are measured most effective in producing positive client outcomes.

Self-Care

Did you know that it is your ethical obligation to take care of yourself, meaning that if you don't you are committing an ethical violation? Now, you're smart, so I assume you realize that taking care of yourself is the kind thing to do for your health; you may even acknowledge that it is the clinically appropriate thing to do in order to best serve your clients and your practice as a whole. But perhaps few people look at clinician self-care as an ethical issue, yet it turns out to be. Remember in the beginning of the book when I promised you that you had violated an ethical principle at some point? Well, if I had not convinced you yet then, I would bargain that I have now. No clinician is perfect in maintaining self-care, but some of us are particularly lacking in this area. In fact, most of us at some point fall into one of three categories: self-care avoider, self-care procrastinator, or self-care botcher.

If you have heard yourself say, "No, no, I'm fine. I can handle whatever comes my way," you are at risk of being a self-care avoider. You ignore your needs, brush off your red flags, and keep your focus firmly planted on the client or other needs (e.g., supervisor, agency, employer, volunteer work). Perhaps you think the most important part of your job is to help other people, even to your own detriment. Why would you think this way? Because it is professionally driven into you that client needs comes first. You may not be purposely ignoring your needs as a form of punishment; you may have an odd sense of confidence and unrealistic self-value that makes you feel you are immune to professional self-damage. You may feel that you can weather whatever comes your way, which sounds like you are cemented with a strong self-image. In fact, you may feel that asking for help undermines that strength, so you keep trudging along, avoiding your body's pleas. But this may actually make you weaker, not stronger. The strongest clinician is the one who can be in a state of constant self-evaluation, recognize the body's cues when it is overstressed, and know exactly where to go and what to do to prevent burnout. If this is not you, you have some work to do! Don't worry, the next chapter is all about Clinician Burnout.... Wait! Don't skip ahead just yet, I have more to say in *this* chapter.

If you have heard yourself say, "I know I need to take a break, and I totally will...just after I finish these tasks on my desk. I just need to get my work done, and *then* I will de-stress and care for myself," you are at risk of being a self-care procrastinator. You do not ignore your needs, you are perfectly aware of them, you just put them off until it is more convenient for you to address them. Perhaps you feel confident that your needs can abide by a schedule that you fix in place, that you can muscle through for now without consequences. Perhaps you don't recognize a pattern, feeling that you are putting off your self-care just this one time and then you will get back on the self-care wagon. Yes sure, it is possible to hold off on attending to your needs because you have something particularly taxing going on, such as planning a big event, or preparing for a review by the Joint Commission (TJC). We all have times when we just have to keep our eye on the task, knowing that stress will automatically lift when the event ends.

Don't feel badly if you have been through this at some point; it is unavoidable. But many of us exist stringing one event to another event, so that our self-care is consistently left out in the cold. Take a moment and look back over the past year, or the past 5 years, and evaluate your patterns of stress and self-care. If you have had moments of holding off on self-care while you focus on work, then you are not a true self-care procrastinator. But if you can see the majority of the time, you are postponing addressing your own needs, then welcome to the self-care procrastinator club. You are at a significant burnout risk, and if you do burn out it will likely feel sudden and surprising, but in fact it will have been growing for some time without your attention.

If you have heard yourself say, "I keep trying to take care of my needs and it doesn't work. I'm just as busy and stressed as I was before. I might as well stop taking the time to focus on myself and just keep to my tasks," then you are at risk of being a self-care botcher. You have great intentions, but you miss the mark on connecting your needs to the specific help you give yourself. You lend support in all the wrong places. Either you are incorrectly evaluating the areas you need to address, or you are utilizing the wrong mechanism to fix it. Stress at the workplace is a complicated arena, and it is easier than you think to misattribute stress in one area for another. It is equally easy to patch it up with the wrong salve.

A potential reason that it is difficult to suss out the exact problem area is that we may displace our stress from one thing onto another, often safer, thing. We can be so good at this, we do not see it. You know how you can have a very stressful day at work, come home, and snap at your unsuspecting innocent spouse? So, too, can we be stressed about one aspect of our work, such as our funding being cut, and take it out elsewhere, perhaps on the clinician we are supervising. If you are a self-care botcher, you need to work on strengthening your self-analysis skills. It is a perfect thing to bring to supervision, or whomever your trusted advisors may be, to gain a better perspective, talking out what could be out of joint in your professional world. Proper self-care is the fifth requirement for a competent clinician. Let's examine some examples of these concepts to see how they may play out in the clinical scene.

VIGNETTE: KNOW THYSELF

Salima is a counselor at an outpatient agency and is responsible for running daily group and individual therapy. Recently, her father died. She was very close with him, and the death was unexpected. Salima took 5 days off from work to plan the funeral and attend to her mental health. Her first day back, she noticed that her clients were particularly needy, constantly asking her for help. Her second day back she couldn't stand her co-workers continually gossiping and blabbering about unimportant things. On the third day, the administrative staff forgot to pull her charts and when she approached the boss to complain, her boss told her it would be addressed tomorrow. Salima reacted by screaming out loud in front of staff and clients, expressing her frustration with staff, feeling that they were being unreasonably incompetent. Unethical? Is Salima a self-care avoider, a self-care procrastinator, or a self-care botcher? What could Salima have done differently?

How many of you think she is a self-care botcher? Okay, put your hands down. You are correct—Salima is a classic example of a self-care botcher. She recognized that with the sad loss of her father, she would need a bit of self-care, so she took 5 days off. This is good self-care, right? Well, yes and no. It is a good start, although many people suffering a loss will need more than 5 days off from work. More importantly, what is she doing in those 5 days? First, those 5 days were not completely "off," as she was planning the funeral during that time. Second, the vignette does not mention any therapy, or even talking with a trusted colleague or friend. Simply removing yourself from the workplace does not alleviate the stress and emotion associated with a loss. Salima will need lots of support. Third, what measures did she take to ensure she was ready to return? Did she discuss it with her supervisor, therapist, colleagues, family members? Did she make a good plan for her return, including contingencies if unplanned events or feelings occurred?

Even if Salima did all of these things well, when she returned to work she had immediate clues that something was amiss. Her first clue was that she felt her clients were particularly needy. Clients are always needy; the very nature of a client is to be in need of help, so this should not be a surprise to Salima. But if she feels they are more needy than usual, it is her first clue that the problem may be with her ability to handle the neediness. It may be that the clients are more needy, as can occur after a clinician takes time off. But it is also possible that the clients have not changed in their neediness; it is Salima who has changed her ability to hear it. If this happens to you, you want to ask yourself: Are these clients needier than usual or am I less able to help them right now? If you are not sure, speak with colleagues and definitely head right to your supervisor's office. We get a bigger clue on her second day back, when she is annoyed at her co-workers for discussing unimportant things. Since it is unlikely that all of her co-workers suddenly changed their behavior into a more annoying display, Salima should suspect that the problem is likely in her low frustration tolerance, common during acute grief. If everyone else seems to be fine with the way the conversation is going, it is a clue that something may be out of whack for Salima. This is a good time to reassess what she needs to help her recover. Clearly, on the third day her frustration bubbles over and she reacts inappropriately. This could have been prevented if she had paid attention to clues she gave herself on the first 2 days. You have got to give yourself a break when life intervenes with your work. You are only human after all.

VIGNETTE: SUPERMAN!

Richard is a star employee, an agency favorite. He always arrives for work on time, is the first to volunteer for overtime or extra work when it is needed, is always available to consult on a case, and is quick to lend support to anyone who needs it. Clients adore him, saying they feel he is "present," "understanding," and

(continued)

really takes time with each client to assess and address their needs. Richard also volunteers at a local community center, where he teaches the illiterate to read, and tutors some children on English lessons. He sings in his church choir, and is devoted to his partner and their two children. Richard appears to be content in his professional and personal worlds. His only complaint is back and neck pain that will not let up no matter what he tries. It has been getting increasingly worse, and is starting to affect his good mood. Just yesterday, he was miffed that his supervisor did not attend their scheduled meeting, which was important to him because he had several timely questions he needed answered about a current task. "Oh well," Richard thinks, "I'll just have to wing it. Perhaps it's okay that she forgot the meeting anyway, because my back is killing me and it would have been hard to sit for an hour. Best to keep on plugging." Which is Richard: self-care avoider, a self-care procrastinator, or a self-care botcher? What do you think he needs?

Richard is a nice example of a self-care avoider (did you get it right?). Everyone loves him because he never says no and continues to work beyond reasonable limits. Be careful if you are a Richard, as those around you will be happy to keep piling work on top of your load. Don't expect anyone else to realize you are overtaxed; as long as you agree, people will continue to add to the heap. Learning how to say no will be difficult, but imperative for the self-care avoider. It can also be tricky to recognize when you have enough (or too much) on your plate. In Richard's case, he has a helpful clue. That's right, his body is betraying his avoidance. His back and neck pain, which seems to worsen when stress increases, is a solid clue that he is avoiding self-care. Richard provides a good example of how the mind-body connection exists and can be helpful in recognizing what we need. He has become so adept at avoiding his own needs, his body may be attempting to awaken him so that he is forced to care for himself. For that is Richard's future: If he doesn't take care of himself, it is likely his back will continue to deteriorate until he will be forced to get medical care that will require him to be absent from work altogether.

VIGNETTE: TOMORROW IS ANOTHER DAY

Padma is a clinical director at an outpatient program, which employees 25 clinicians and staff, and treats about 150 clients a day in group and individual counseling. She is also one of the agency's favorite speakers, and is often sent to trainings to represent the agency and discuss its ongoing research endeavors. Padma knows she has a lot on her plate, and often laments to her friends that she wishes her work life could be a bit less dramatic and needy. When her friends suggest that she take action to make it easier, such as delegating more work, or cutting back on the number of trainings she conducts in a year, she smiles and says, "You know what, I will. Those are good ideas. As soon as I get through the next month of trainings I will definitely make some changes." Her friends roll their eyes, as they have heard this song and dance before. What is Padma: a self-care avoider, a self-care procrastinator, or a self-care botcher?

Yes, Padma is a self-care procrastinator. She is aware that her friends are correct, and that she needs to simplify her work life, yet she wants to wait until it is a good time, which may not be likely to happen. There may never be a perfect time in your work life to make a change in your stress level. The best time, the only time, is now. Obviously, if there is a big event you are working on, it's okay to wait until it is over. You may not have a choice in that. But while you are enjoying your moment of down time after the event passes, make the changes, before you ramp up to the next event. Remember that you may have to retrain your brain to understand that this is not a form of weakness, which your work brain may tell you; it is a sign of strength for you to set limits for yourself. Also, self-care procrastinators are susceptible to the same physical and mental health consequences if they don't care for their health. If you don't slow down, your body may figure out a way to make you slow down.

The crux of the principle of Competency is much more complex than simply being trained to do what you are doing at your workplace. It involves your ongoing education, your specific training, adhering to the boundaries of your credential, and seeking help for yourself when you need it. It involves putting your training into a beneficent practice with your clients. It involves building on a foundation of therapist qualities and treatment techniques that support the pillars. It involves obtaining and giving healthy and effective supervision. If you build a responsible practice within the confines of your competency, you will establish a solid set of ethics that protect yourself and your career. If you are not successful in building an ethical practice that protects your interests you are in danger of developing Clinician Burnout. As you will see, this is a serious pitfall. Let's check it out.

Pitfall: Clinician Burnout

14

Chapter

A h, good old Clinician Burnout. The very fact that we have a term for this condition speaks volumes to how often it occurs. There are a host of problems that come with Clinician Burnout: it feels uncomfortable for the clinician (to put it mildly); it usually affects every aspect of that clinician's world, potentially leading to poor clinical decisions, many possible ethical dilemmas (Lim, Kim, Kim, Yang, & Lee, 2010), and the violation of all ethical pillars (Reamer, 2001). Burnout has been correlated with both personal and professional outcomes. Personal outcomes include poor mental health including depression, poor physical ailments (Lee, Lim, Yang, & Lee, 2011; Lim et al., 2010; Morse, Salyers, Rollins, Monroe-De Vita, & Pfahler, 2012), sleep disturbances (Lim et al., 2010), and negative effects with family and friends (Lim et al., 2010). Professional outcomes include poor job performance (Lee et al., 2011; Lim et al., 2010), absenteeism (Lee et al., 2011; Lim et al., 2010; Morse et al., 2012), decreased commitment to the organization (Morse et al., 2012), and high job turnover (Knudsen, Ducharme, & Roman, 2008; Lee et al., 2011; Lim et al., 2010; Morse et al., 2012). Burnout affects clients (Lim et al., 2010) because it can cause negative clinician attitudes toward clients, which likely increases patient dissatisfaction (Morse et al., 2012). Burnout affects the profession (Leykin, Cucciare, & Weingardt, 2011; Lim et al., 2010) because high rates of absences, turnover, and distressed attitudes cause an increase in time and cost to recruit and train new staff (Knudsen et al., 2008; Morse et al., 2012).

In short, it is bad news. It feels bad, but it is not necessarily bad news if it is used well. Just like a relapse is a sign that something needs to be adjusted in one's recovery plan, Clinician Burnout is a great way to let clinicians know something is out of whack in their own plan. As is the case with many relapses, clinical burnout can be a long process (Corey, Corey, & Callanan, 2007). If you can recognize Clinician Burnout early, and adjust where you need to, it can become a very helpful tool in your arsenal of self-care. Before we can discuss how to do this, we need to carefully examine exactly what Clinician Burnout is about, as it can be a misunderstood phenomenon.

To examine the principles of Clinician Burnout, let's look at the most common causes. The three most commonly named causes of burnout are *emotional exhaustion*, when physical and emotional resources have been depleted; *depersonalization*, when a cynical attitude and lack of empathy develops toward clients; and a *decrease in personal accomplishments*, when contributions don't feel meaningful, and clinicians feel incompetent (Corey et al., 2007; Lee et al., 2011; Leykin et al., 2011; Lim et al., 2010; Vilardaga et al., 2011). These three causes have been well studied in the literature. We have a few more significant causes to round out the discussion, both within the clinicians and within the organization. This list illustrates the top causes.

Six Common Causes of Clinician Burnout

1. Weariness
2. Bleeding the personal
3. Slipping on SDEPS
4. Passion deficiency
5. Underchallenged versus exploitation
6. Poor supervision

Weariness

Thought to be the most significant contribution to Clinician Burnout (Knudsen et al., 2008), this has been called other names, such as emotional exhaustion, compassion fatigue, and emotion building, which all describe the overwhelmed feelings clinicians can develop when caring for others and managing the pressures of the job. Compassion fatigue is certainly part of this weariness, as caring for others can be exhausting, can be thankless, and can even feel hopeless at times. We can "become deeply affected by a client's pain" (Corey et al., 2007, p. 58). Our risk of weariness is not limited to our compassion; there are other emotions that can build and become overwhelming. We may become frustrated at our clients when they are obstreperous, contrary, or suicidal (Corey et al., 2007); we may feel guilty about our frustrations toward the people toward whom we are supposed to feel undying compassion. We may feel responsible for clients' failures or struggles (Corey et al., 2007).

Addiction counselors work under difficult conditions, with funds being continuously cut, restrictions on our services a reality, certification and licensure standards changing on us, and just when we feel competent, the population we serve developing new specialized conditions that require additional training (Vilardaga et al., 2011). We don't get paid very much; we watch our colleagues come and go often; we feel driven to migrate to the best working conditions, even if it means we have to switch jobs more than we would like (Vilardaga et al., 2011). Just thinking about it all is exhausting; no wonder a lot of us are walking around feeling professionally pooped.

Addiction counselors can be in danger of compulsive work, especially as a replacement for addiction for clinicians in recovery (Doukas & Cullen, 2010). It may be difficult to create healthy boundaries around our tasks when clients are in need of help, but this can result in too much work and may lead to a resentment toward our clients. Both risks of disliking our clients and being attracted to them can lead to fatigue (Corey et al., 2007). We may become weary from thinking about work too much, or "taking work home," being unable to compartmentalize our work worries (Corey et al., 2007), or we may be so adept at compartmentalizing we suppress our emotions to the point of creating exhaustion. Finally, it can be tiring to endure a client's anger toward the clinician, whether legitimate, unreasonable, or through transference. This exhaustion can lead to poor health and decrease in job performance (Knudsen et al., 2008).

Weariness has led to negative consequences for the profession (Knudsen et al., 2008). It can spread to other employees (Knudsen et al., 2008), and it can also develop from our interprofessional relationships. We can also feel the same frustration, guilt, obsession, and lack of compassion for our colleagues that we do for our clients. In addition, conflicts with our colleagues can significantly add to our weariness (Corey et al., 2007). We can become weary from tolerating poor or unethical behavior from our colleagues and fellow staff. We can become frustrated in our role as teachers and supervisors, particularly when collaborating with combative and recalcitrant workers. These emotions can occur simultaneously with the emotions surrounding client care, further overwhelming the clinician into a state of weary exhaustion. There is a paradoxical effect in that client welfare is a source of personal accomplishment but also is draining (Lee et al., 2011), which can be a burnout trap.

Bleeding the Personal

Working with clients can open up personal themes in the clinician (Corey et al., 2007). These personal themes can lead us down a path of countertransference. When the client's pain connects with our old or current pain, we can set ourselves up for a burnout risk (Corey et al., 2007). We can confuse dislike of clients or being attracted to clients with other relationships we have known (Corey et al., 2007). Clinicians can become overinvolved with their clients and the treatment (Lee et al., 2011).

Even if countertransference does not develop, we can be at risk of burnout simply by bringing our personal issues into the workplace. We constantly advise clinicians to keep work at work, and to not bring work to home, meaning that we need a break from thinking about work, and certainly a break from doing the work. If all we do is work-related, we burn out because we are too imbalanced; we never get a break from dealing with work stress.

What if we flip it around and take the same advice about bringing home to work? Keep your personal world away from the workplace, leave home at home, or you will be at the same risk of burning out. Many clinicians spend a great deal of time talking about themselves with their co-workers and learning about them as well. Walk into any break room of an agency and you are likely to see the conversation turn quickly personal. Moreover, co-workers who don't share aspects of their personal life may be called all sorts of names, none of them pretty, such as *cold* or *snooty*. Harsh words for someone who may just be trying to set a boundary for themselves and may be trying to keep the personal from bleeding into the workplace.

It is understandable that people want to feel like they know their co-workers; they want them to be real and want to learn where they are coming from. It's human nature to be social creatures, so it is no surprise that this socialization occurs. But in many circumstances bringing personal issues into the workplace may lead to burnout, simply because you are never getting a break from the pressures, problems, even positive traits, of home. And once people know of them, they are likely to ask you how it is going. Bleeding your personal issues can lead to a constant barrage of questions and comments leaving the issues firmly placed in your here and now. Soon you can't get away from it, and that is when you can start to crumble, whether you realize it or not.

Bleeding the personal can mean anything personal. It could be about an argument you are having with your spouse, or the dread you are feeling with an in-law's impending visit, or the test material you are studying, really anything that comes from outside of your work life. Certainly your recovery status, if you have one, should be included here. If you are disclosing at work, then it travels with you everywhere you go. You may become Bob-in-Recovery, never just Bob. Any comments you make, suggestions you offer, or advice you lend may be colored by the personal facts people know about you. "Of course Bob would suggest that, he's in recovery." Even if the people around you see your recovery status as a positive aspect, it may be an aspect of yourself that is always there. Perhaps they may only see your positive traits or your successes as a product of your recovery status, and not because you worked hard to make them happen. Here are two examples.

Leroy was a client of mine, a bright, talented, young man who was forced to make a career turn when he was found using drugs at the workplace. He was working on what new career path to choose, and was beginning to take various academic courses to guide him. While in school, he needed a job in order to pay his bills, so she got a job at a local facility for substance abusers, after meeting their year-in-recovery guideline. Leroy spent his days admitting addicts into detox and rehab, and would attend AA and NA meetings faithfully at the end of his workday. He formed many friends through the anonymous programs, and over time encouraged many of his friends to apply for jobs at the same agency where he worked. He also recommended the organization to his brother, who took a job there and who met and married a co-worker at the same agency. During his therapy with me, it became immediately clear that Leroy had bled his personal into his workplace to such an extent that there was no longer any clear division between work and home. He saw the same people socially, at 12-step meetings, and at work, because they all worked in the same department. His own fiancée started working there as well, on a different shift. What seemed fun to him at first soon became suffocating. He couldn't escape his personal world—it was constantly brought to him. His co-workers knew everything about him, and he knew everything about them. To make matters worse, Leroy was quickly promoted to supervisor, making him the superior of his friends and sister-in-law.

Over time this became, as you may suspect, disastrous for Leroy. At work he would try and supervise his subordinates, but because they were his friends, they did not afford him the same respect as they would a colleague they didn't see socially. They would constantly approach him wanting to gossip and continue conversations that had begun outside of work. If he mentioned an issue at a morning NA meeting, it would come back to him during the workday, either by worker-friends constantly checking in with him, or even with worker-friends saying, "Don't listen to him today. He's just getting annoyed with us because he has XYZ going on in his life right now. He talked about it at the meeting last night." This would happen when Leroy would attempt to do his job and point out work areas that needed improving. Leroy could not escape his personal life, and he quickly lost perspective. It became clear that Leroy needed to change his work environment. He needed to set boundaries with his friends and stop discussing his personal life at work. Ultimately, the only way for him to be happy was to change his place of employment, a tough decision

considering how many years of hard work he had placed in the agency.

On the other hand, there is Declan. He is a truly great clinician, but what sets him apart from others is his uncanny ability to bond with co-workers without sharing personal details from his life. Everyone loves him; he is typically upbeat, although he will commiserate with the rest of the staff when some grave injustice is passed down from the executive levels above; he listens in when groups of co-workers are gabbing during breaks; he laughs at jokes, presents jokes to the group, talks about all sorts of things with people, yet somehow nothing too personal. It is unclear if he is in recovery or not; he never mentions it. If he ever has strife with his wife, or pressure from other family, or personal struggles he must weather, or even great triumphs he has accomplished, he simply does not share any of it at work, setting a firm boundary for himself.

Yet, he would never be labeled *cold* or a *snob* because he is still able to build a rapport with his co-workers. He does this by talking about nonwork things that are not overtly personal. For example, he may discuss the plot of a TV show he had watched the night before, or laugh about a headline he caught in the morning paper. He also will dutifully listen to others who produce personal information, but he never divulges that information in any circumstance. If you reveal something about yourself, and he happens to hear it, he will never mention it. He is masterful at showing the best of both worlds, keeping the personal protected while bonding with others. Go off and try it—be a Declan!

Slipping on SDEPS

In exploring competency, we discussed the notion of faulty self-care, specifically the three categories: self-care avoider, self-care procrastinator, and self-care botcher. Remember that self-care avoiders are great at helping everyone else, but avoid taking care of their own needs, denying that they have needs in the first place. These "workaholics" typically ignore their own needs until it is too late and clinician burnout has developed. Self-care procrastinators are aware that they have self-care needs but chronically muscle through stressful events, postponing their own self-care. Self-care botchers are aware they have self-care needs and take steps to address them, but unfortunately the steps they take are not the right steps or not enough to fulfill their self-care needs. If you are in any of these categories, you must take steps to better attend to your self-care.

What does that mean exactly, *self-care*? If you are going to make a better stab at caring for yourself, it helps to understand what is involved with caring for yourself well. I call it the SDEPS of personal care, which consists of Sleep, Diet, Exercise, Pleasure, and Support. How well you rate on the scale depends on how much attention you are paying to these five areas. It is similar to the 12-step slogan HALT (Hungry, Angry, Lonely, Tired) that we teach our clients to address.

Sleep: Good sleep hygiene is imperative to general health and can directly affect your stress levels at the workplace. Lack of sleep not only affects us physically, it affects us mentally, as we are much more likely to be irritable with too little sleep. We can be forgetful, too, and make mistakes we would not make under good sleep conditions. Sleep is often affected by too much going on in the brain, especially too much worry. Because the majority of our daily hours are spent at work, it is likely that some, if not most, of that worry is spent on work-related things. How successful are you at keeping work at work? Do you find you are thinking about a tough case after hours? Are you worried about a meeting you have the next day, or are you in such despair about the nature of our faulty system that it keeps you up at night? If you answered yes to any of these questions, welcome to the club of normalcy. People will tell you that you shouldn't carry work home with you, but we have all done it at some point. It's unavoidable. The trick is you want to keep it on the side of infrequent in order to maintain optimal stress health. If it is happening frequently go directly to your supervisor or therapist and ask for help.

If infrequent, your task is to find a way to push it out of your mind so that you can sleep. Count sheep; listen to music or white noise; focus on your happy place; purposely think about something, but have it be something pleasurable that makes you drowsy. Perhaps you are having a hard time sleeping for other reasons, such as too few hours in the day for your workload, or a sporadic schedule that has you sleeping at different times of day and night (a killer for good sleep hygiene), or children in the house who wake up in the middle of the night needing something from you. Whatever the barrier may be, it will be up to you to figure out a work-around so that sleep may come regularly. Talk to your doctor before using over-the-counter sleep aids. What may seem like a good fix in the present can lead to a whole pile of problems in the future. If you can't easily see what barriers are interfering with your sleep, consult your primary physician and other doctors to assess possible contributing factors. There may be another physical or mental issue involved.

Diet: Good diet and nutrition is also a vital part of optimal stress health. Not enough food, too much food, an imbalance of nutrients, too much sugar, or too many carbohydrates are all factors in nutritional health. If we eat poorly, or out of balance, our energy will be too high, too low, or too labile. We will be irritable, giddy, sleepy, or will experience mood swings that are no fun for anyone around us. One way to ensure good nutritional health is to bring your own food to work. It requires time to prepare, but you will be glad you made the time. Make sure you are balancing your overall day with the food groups and the best possible nutritional value in what you are eating. This will help you avoid the work lunches, which often cause you to eat greater amounts of rich content foods that are inferior for your health. Engaging the aid of a nutritionist can be helpful in analyzing your diet and learning both foods to avoid and food that can decrease stress and increase energy. In addition, there are many accessible documentaries on nutrition that can easily educate and inspire you to improve your diet.

Three helpful nutritional tools to try if nutrition is an issue for you (1) write down every single thing that you eat each day; (2) drink loads of water every day; (3) moderate or eliminate sugar, caffeine, and processed foods. If you focus on these three things, your diet is sure to improve and, with it, your health and stress level.

Exercise: Good exercise may be our best tool to a healthy lifestyle, because if we are exercising well, it is likely to have a positive effect on our nutrition and our sleep. It also has beneficial effects on our short- and long-term physical and emotional health, including our mood. In addition, it is perhaps the most prominent tool we have for reducing stress, because it provides an outlet for the stress to exit and an opportunity for us to rebalance our emotions. While being an effective tool in our arsenal, it is also one of the toughest to use, not because the tool itself is hard, but because it takes time, motivation, and energy to use the tool. This is where you get snagged, yes? The best advice is to kick yourself in the butt and *just do it*, to borrow from Nike. You may have to use every ounce of willpower you've got to push through the motivation lapse and get your body moving, but once you do it will likely become easier every day. Just like your lack of exercise can snowball into daily inertia, so, too, can your victorious day of exercise snowball into a new regime.

You may need to trick yourself at first, park in the farthest spot in the parking lot of your local megastore, and walk as quickly as you can to the store and back to your car after shopping. Create a shopping list that forces you to circle the store several times before checking out. Visit the windows of every shop in your nearest mall, the bigger the better. Take your kid, or borrow a friend's kid, to the park and play tag. Run your dog, or walk twice around the block instead of once. Dump your laundry on the floor and squat to pick up one piece at a time. Just for fun, drop it all again and repeat. Take the stairs instead of the elevator. Pace around the house while talking on the phone instead of sitting in a chair. You get the idea. There are loads of ways to infuse your daily routine with exercise that are much easier to implement than finding the time and mental energy to head over the gym for a few hours. You'll get there, but if you are starting from nothing, you've got to start small and build on your successes. Consider how many minutes it took you to read this section on exercise. If you were actually reading the section while walking on a treadmill, say, think of how much healthier you would be!

Pleasure: Good pleasure is one of those things that people can take to the extreme, either too much or too little. Our jobs are all about helping people who focus on pleasure too much and take it a bit too far. Some clinicians tend to go the other direction in their own lives and seek too little pleasure. How much fun are you having in your life really? How often do you play? When was the last time you had an honest-to-goodness belly laugh? What was the last thing you did to embrace the ridiculous? What makes your heart skip a beat or feel all warm and gooey? Who or what can change your mood around, even if you are feeling stormy or gloomy? Pleasure is something that we can skimp on, because there are too few hours in the day, and let's face it, no one ever paid rent with pleasure, legally speaking anyway. And pleasure does not get the school lunches made, or the aging parent comfortable, and so on. Yet you will not be able to do all of those things consistently if you don't take time to enjoy your life around you.

You have heard that life is short, often very, very short, so ... how do you want to spend it? Do you want to be a robot and go from work to home and back again, with no variation? In the beginning of a silly movie called *Joe vs. the Volcano*, Tom Hanks plays a man who is dressed like every other man, swept up in a dull march to work. Every face expressionless, every movement timed, the depressing group punches the clock, completes their tasks, and marches home to the same tune. The one piece of sunny life, a yellow flower, is stepped on, unnoticed, by the group of workers, but Tom notices the flower as his world begins to change, and it is the start of his transformation out of the doldrums. You don't want to miss your flower; go out there and find it.

On the other side of the spectrum, we can implant too much pleasure into our lives. If we are focused too much on pleasure, we can miss other important things, such as the people around us. Addiction can develop from an overabundance of pleasure. The trick is to maintain a good balance, ensuring enough pleasure to make life fulfilling but not so much to lose oneself in it. This balance will tip in both directions at different times in life, but with awareness it is possible to maintain a good equilibrium.

If you begin to need pleasure to function, it is no longer pleasurable. If whatever brings you joy becomes a chore, it is no longer pleasurable. If Lee loves to garden and becomes involved with a local Garden Club, the expectation is that this will be a positive change in her life. But if Lee is strong-armed into serving on the board of directors against her better judgment, or if she ignores her warning gut and becomes overinvolved in the club, this pleasure can quickly dissolve into pressure.

Support: Good support is vital to anyone's happiness, but it is particularly ideal for those of us who have made a career out of giving support. At times it seems that those who give support take less support than average, yet those who give support need more support than average. Thus we find ourselves in the position of needing support, but not getting enough of it, either because we have not set ourselves up with good support, or because the support we have is faulty in some way. I'm sure you have had clients who put all their support eggs in the sponsor's basket. They work hard to get a self-help sponsor—not an easy task, mind you—and then they rely completely on that person to provide all of their social and emotional support. And then what happens? At some point the client needs support, calls on his or her sponsor, and (gasp!) the sponsor is unavailable. The client, having executed the appropriate plan, watches the plan fail and feels he or she has no other choice but to use. Sound familiar? So in this case, you would help the client understand

that relying solely on one person is dangerous indeed, because that sponsor is human and will have other obligations apart from his or her sponsorship. Your client will want to diversify his or her support group, so that if one person is unavailable, several other choices are possible.

It is the same with clinicians (that means you). If you are relying solely on your supervisor, or your favorite colleague, or your spouse, there will be a time, probably many times, when that person is unavailable and you are left adrift without the support you need. You are also in danger of burning out that one support, as most people will become tired of being the only support; even our most treasured supports have a limit. Spread the love around; find more than one kind of support. Not only will you be covered, but you will get the benefit of a diverse pool of advice. You may opt to approach specific people for specific support, matching your needs with a supporter's gifts.

For example, if you are dealing with a domineering supervisor who always treats you as if you have committed a grave clinical error, you might go to your friend Sharon to talk about it, knowing that a few years back, Sharon had the same kind of supervisor. You ask her how she dealt with it and get some ideas of what to do or what not to do. Sharon may be a better choice than someone who has never encountered that particular problem. On the other hand, if you are struggling with a co-worker who you find competitive and at times mean, you could go to your friend Joe, who always has your back, and who shows you all the reasons why you are justified in your feelings. You would feel validated by Joe, but he may not present a good solution to the problem. Sometimes you just want to be validated, so in those times Joe is your man.

Alternatively, you could go to your friend Miguel, who is masterful at presenting the other side of the argument. He would be able to make suggestions based on the co-worker's point of view, stretching your perspective to allow in other reasons for the co-worker's behavior. These alternative explanations can help you realize that (shocker!)

it is not all about you, and there may be another reason the co-worker is treating you this way. With those alternative reasons in hand, several possible courses of action present themselves, and you can approach the co-worker in a supportive, rather than antagonistic, way to address the issue. Sometimes you need a Joe, but many times you need a Miguel, someone who will support you by arguing against you, playing devil's advocate, if you will.

The trick with support is to gather lots of sources, who have different roles with you. We sell ourselves short when we limit our work-related support needs to work-related people. Some of the most useful advice for work-related issues can come from people outside of our profession. These people are helpful in two ways: (1) They have nothing to lose or gain by stating it as they see it. They are outside of the profession, and therefore have an objective view on the problem. Often it is helpful to see the issue from outside of your little work world; it helps to put things into a better, more grounded, perspective. (2) These people know you in a very different way. Outside of work, we are all different people, and our friends and family have a wider, longer-term perspective on us. That can help because they can connect this work issue with other similar issues we've had in the past, suggesting both the reason for the issue (maybe it *is* all about us) and how to fix the pattern.

Are you thinking of possible supports as you read this? Well, don't slack off; you should be making a mental list right now! The more the merrier, but leave room for surprises. You can't predict what anyone is going to say, so be prepared for someone you have listed in one category to jump to another category. Also, no matter who is on your list, here are two, perhaps odd, suggestions. Everyone should have kids and dogs on their list, unless children or canines drive you to a place of madness, in which case they will not be very supportive. The reason you want kids on your support list is because kids are basically one big Id walking around, all about play and pleasure and "the now." That can be fantastically grounding as you are worrying about all the ills of your life. Take your stress and go get your kid, or borrow one (legally) from a friend, and go play. Do whatever the kid wants to do and see what happens to your stress. Get in touch with your inner goof; unleash it. As adults, we don't play nearly enough, and we suffer for it. Similarly, a dog is typically one big goofball. Go find one and run around outside. I defy you to play these games and maintain your stress level. I don't think it's possible. Sure, it will not solve the problems you are facing, but it can give you a mighty respite that your mind and body desperately need.

Passion Deficiency

Play along with me for a second: Close your eyes and drum up what you were thinking about when you started in this field. Get a nice picture of the person you were (or are), why you chose this field, what you thought you could contribute, what you wanted to accomplish. This was your passion and it drove your perspective of the field and your abilities. This may require you to think far into the past or may be how you feel today if you are a new student or worker. Whatever your specific thoughts and feelings may be or have been, and they vary significantly, I will take a wild guess and state that those thoughts were positive. Perhaps you believed you could make a difference; perhaps you focused on the good people you believe deserve a shot at a happy life, and your interest in helping them get there. Perhaps you saw great value or worth in this type of work and wanted to be part of something involving transformation.

Regardless of the specifics, your thoughts were likely positive. Few people think about entering a field consumed with negative thoughts about oneself and the profession. I doubt you were thinking, "Okay, well, the relapse rate is very high, and most of my clients probably won't reach their goals, I'll probably spend most of my time frustrated about the system and helpless to do anything to change it, and I expect to have supervisors that don't support me and directors who don't know me, and of course

I will get paid well under what I am worth and what I need to keep my family afloat." It is unlikely anyone who entertained these thoughts would choose to enter the profession, believing in such a grim outcome.

Typically, we start out excited and eager to make a difference. If you work very hard, and perhaps enjoy a bit of luck, you keep this passion through the majority of your career. But often the great light that consumes you in the beginning of your career begins to fade the longer you are in the profession, and in some cases blows out all together. This light can fade due to life circumstances that affect your perspective at work, such as the death of a loved one, loss of a house, or financial devastation—events that can change your perspective on life in general and make you question your work, your purpose, and your very existence. It can be difficult to hold on to your passion at work when the rest of your world is in doubt, and many people can't help but bleed their home difficulties into the workplace. Suddenly, aspects of your job and the people you work with that were mere annoyances become large obstacles that don't move and start to wear you down.

In some circumstances, you may find your pressures at work grow larger than the pressures outside of work; at times the events that have changed in your life are so hurtful that it feels easier or safer to focus the frustration, the desperation, the rage, or whatever else you are feeling onto work-related activities or people. Just as we can displace our feelings onto another person to whom it is "safer" to vent those feelings, so, too, can we displace our feelings from one area of our life to another. Therefore, often when we are a mess at home, our work suffers.

This is not the only way our work passion can suffer. Our inner light can also fade from pressures that originate at the workplace. The truth about our work is that it is equally rewarding and frustrating. It is an amazing honor to witness the positive transformation of a client, yet it can be equally discouraging to see clients weather setbacks, or leave our

care altogether. Some clients die; others fade away without your knowledge of where they are or how they are. The statistics on successes in our field are not rosy, and it can truly dampen your spirit if you focus on the grim. If this is you, take heart in our tactics. We get around this by building a healthier perspective of what we do. We focus on the one; we focus on the good. We try to ignore the rest.

Also, you may benefit from engaging a broader perspective. It helps to think of yourself as a gardener. Your job is to plant seeds in every individual you aim to help. In some cases, you are able to water the seed and see it sprout. In those best cases, you will see the changes occur in the client as they form their own foundation for long-lasting healing. But in many cases, your clients will leave your care before you can see those changes take place. You can either be discouraged by this, or hopeful that you have given the client the tools they need, so that when they are ready, or the right circumstances present themselves, they will make the necessary life changes to allow those tools to work for them.

There will be rewarding moments when clients from your past resurface and say something to the effect of, "Well, I remembered what you said back when I was here," or "I finally got what you were saying all those years ago...." These statements prove that you planted seeds that were later there when the client was ready or able to nurture them. This is how we get around the feeling that our work is doomed to fail. In fact, if you stretch your definition of success beyond the treatment experience at your office, and look at a bigger picture of client life, I would wager that our success rate is rather good. If we use the gardening theory of counseling, I suspect the majority of our clients are successfully treated.

Okay, great, you say, I plant seeds. But what if my professional despair is coming not from individual clients, but from the system itself? Even if we are able to muster hope for the clients and ignore the statistics, many of us get snagged on larger immovable barriers at many levels. Perhaps you are getting snagged within your agency, with agency policy that you believe conflicts with your work. Perhaps you are affected by the constant change in political climate that greatly affects who we can help and how we can help them, particularly by changing what funding we are entitled to access. It doesn't take long to feel like the garden you were working to create is the garden you are asked to cut down, your hoe replaced with a scythe.

Clinicians may experience insufficient resources to perform their jobs, which will affect their job performance and their attitude about the work (Lee et al., 2011; Morse et al., 2012). Clinicians may become disillusioned after their clients have been repeatedly denied needed services (Morse et al., 2012). Frustrations of dealing with systemic issues, coupled with time pressures and the feeling of working harder to make money, dampen the passion. All of this may make clinicians doubt the profession and their interest in staying in it (Corey et al., 2007), and may affect their effort, attentiveness, collaboration, and ability to be empathetic (Morse et al., 2012). True, the goals may be too high; the clinician may be a perfectionist or have unrealistic expectations (Lim et al., 2010), but the result is a tragic dimming of the excitement that once fueled that clinician's practice.

Underchallenged Versus Exploitation

Clinician Burnout is often used synonymously with stress, but they are not the same. Most stress management techniques are aimed at preventing or removing stress (Corey et al., 2007). Stress is not always negative; in fact, what we call stress is more appropriately named distress, which is negative, uncomfortable, and generally something to be avoided or removed. In contrast, stress can be positive, motivating, and a vital force that informs our actions. Stress can stimulate thinking, motivate change, promote risk taking, influence self-preservation, enhance personal growth, generate new ideas, maintain interest, boost mood, amplify self-esteem, create opportunities, raise energy, increase productivity, and bolster a balanced

lifestyle. Stress can be a vital catalyst to needed change. Therefore, instead of removing stress many people may benefit from increasing it. Stress can build up swift and strong, but it can lie untapped, too. Although stress can be positive, distress is a negative consequence of overuse. Distress indicates professional dysfunction that can lead to burnout, which is chronic and long-term (Lee et al., 2011).

Stress is often discussed in black-and-white terms—either you have it or you don't—but let's think of it as more of a continuum that spreads from low (insufficient) to high (excessive). In any given situation, or at any moment in time, your stress level will fall somewhere on this scale. The ideal is to be in the optimal range as much as possible. This is the level where we are most efficient, where we perform at our best. Operating at a low stress level indicates that you are not being challenged enough; operating at a high stress level means you are being overchallenged. If you are operating at a high level on the scale for too long, stress can become distress. But distress also comes from operating at a low level for too long.

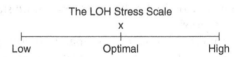

The LOH Stress Scale

Low   Optimal   High

Consider the calf muscle. If you don't exercise a muscle it will atrophy and become unusable. If you overexercise a muscle, it becomes strained and unusable. But if you can exercise a muscle without overdoing it, your muscle is at its happiest: taut and strong, at its optimal health. It is the same with stress level. Too little stress and one may experience low energy, lethargy, sadness, and fatigue. Too much stress and one may experience anxiety, the feeling of being overwhelmed, and fatigue. Optimal stress is stress that is manageable and motivating, and when at this level, one may experience exhilaration. It is this level of stress that you should always be shooting for.

The same process can be seen with stress at the workplace. Low stress would be experienced in a job that is unchallenging or uninspiring. You need to have passion and purpose. High stress would be experienced in a job that was unrealistically challenging and consuming, often thankless. Optimal stress would be experienced in a job that was challenging, inspiring, and encouraging, where you felt capable, appreciated, and supported. You have passion and purpose and a sense of importance in the field or agency. You have that amazing feeling at the end of the workday, as you walk or drive home and you realize: "I love my job. And I'm good at it!" Even if your job is very hectic, and you have moments of high stress, you have an overall balance, and that generally gives you a satisfactory sigh at the end of the day.

What we learn from the LOH scale is that our goal is not to remove stress but to balance it so that we are operating at our optimal level. But how do you know your optimal level; how can it be recognized? Your optimal level of stress is recognizable by how you feel when working at your job. If you feel invigorated, inspired, confident, alive, at the top of your game, then you have achieved your optimal level.

Feelings of exploitation come from unfair pressures and unrealistic expectations. When funding decreases and responsibilities increase, Clinician Burnout will be evident (Morse et al., 2012). We are inundated with paperwork, which leads to job dissatisfaction and increases our risk of Clinician Burnout (Carise, Love, Zur, McLellan & Kemp, 2009; Whitter et al., 2006). The pressure to accept too many clients creates caseloads too high, which can lead to exploitation (Corey at al., 2007; Morse et al., 2012). The pressure from a large responsibility, especially if you are not a part of the decision-making process, may be a factor (Corey et al., 2007; Knudsen et al., 2008). Feeling isolated from other professionals and not feeling gratitude are also factors (Corey et al., 2007). Feeling out of control of the system and the quality of client services and not feeling secure in a professional identity can be factors (Lee et al., 2011). Performing your job well without being adequately compensated can also be a factor (Knudsen et al., 2008; Lee et al., 2011).

Clinician burnout does not occur suddenly. Much like a relapse, there are always signs that you are headed for trouble. If you don't learn to recognize those signs they can pass you by without notice, and you can find yourself surprised and in pain, wondering how it got so bad. Distress in the workplace is common and costly, mostly due to work productivity losses (Baer, 2010). This is worsened when staff return to work before they are ready to do so and due to the small percentage of clinicians who receive professional help (Baer, 2010). Thus, we as a profession need to take all possible steps to adequately address Clinician Burnout.

Now that we understand Clinician Burnout, we can take steps to prevent it. But if we miss the signs or we fail to prevent it, how then do we cope? There are formal and informal interventions to aid burnout management. Formal interventions to reduce Clinician Burnout have been suggested at both the individual and organizational levels (Baer, 2010; Leykin et al., 2011; Lim et al., 2010; Morse et al., 2012). Most burnout prevention programs for other helping professions have focused on individual and not organizational interventions (Morse et al., 2012).

Formal individual interventions focus on "enhancing coping skills and resources" (Baer, 2010). Individual interventions have included meditation and mindfulness, cognitive-behavioral therapy (CBT) (Baer, 2010; Morse et al., 2012; Vilardaga et al., 2011), and muscle relaxation (Baer, 2010). There is a suggestion that distress at the workplace involves cognitive distortions that are the foundation of CBT, and therefore may not be the best fit (Baer, 2010). Another intervention is acceptance and commitment therapy (ACT), which has been linked with more favorable attitudes toward clients, increased acceptance of new evidence-based practices (Baer, 2010), and lower rates of Clinician Burnout in substance abuse counselors (Baer, 2010; Hayes et al., 2004).

Organization interventions are few (Morse et al., 2012), yet significant (Leykin et al., 2011;

Morse et al., 2012), and typically focus on reducing work-related stressors at the source (Baer, 2010). Structured management has been correlated with increased weariness and high staff turnover (Leykin et al., 2011). Therefore, flexible training models and increased staff autonomy is recommended (Leykin et al., 2011). Other organizational interventions include a supportive environment (Leykin et al., 2011), which requires trained supervisors (Morse et al., 2012), decreasing workloads while promoting self-care (Morse et al., 2012), more staff autonomy, and increased staff cohesiveness (Leykin et al., 2011).

There is a need for combined interventions (Morse et al., 2012). It has been shown that age is correlated with burnout; the younger the clinician, the greater the risk of burnout (Lim et al., 2010). Thus, students and new professionals must understand that the profession is more than the rewards of helping others; it is also a risky profession that requires care and consideration (Corey et al., 2007). Gender and education have also been studied, with an implication that males are at a greater risk of burnout, as are those with higher education (Lim et al., 2010). The latter is an interesting finding that the authors believe is due to a greater feeling of being underchallenged due to higher education experiences and, thus, greater expectations (Lim et al., 2010). Furthermore, those clinicians working in private practice were found to have lower burnout risk than those who work in agencies (Lim et al., 2010). Perhaps this is due to an increase in pressure coming from the agency, an increase in paperwork and policies to follow. Creating a supportive environment is a relatively simple change with the potential of a huge impact (Leykin et al., 2011). Better support leads to an enhanced sense of accomplishment even if exhaustion and depersonalization are present (Lee et al., 2011).

Informally, there are two steps we can take to strengthen our ethical practices and alleviate established burnout, which also reduces future burnout risk. For each common cause of burnout, there are actions we can take. Let's take a look.

Borrow Hope

If you feel weary, the best thing to do is exactly what your clients are attempting with you: You've got to fill up your hope bucket with someone's help. You want to go to where hope is most alive, which typically involves a person or situation against all odds, that makes a monumental change through sheer tenacity of hope when all else is lost. Luckily, you can find these circumstances through a variety of avenues. If you know of someone who is fighting through misery successfully, hang out with him or her. It won't take long for their hope to show itself and you can bask in its glow until your hope bucket begins to fill. This is often where volunteer work can prove helpful. Go hang with people in a slightly different world than your office, and see how your passion can be rekindled. If you don't have access to someone like this, fear not, the media of the world is at your fingertips. There are stories of hope all around us. Look for memoirs, which usually portray some misery conquered, or magazine articles depicting similar stories of victory. Even gossip rags, like *People* magazine, have a weekly column, "Heroes Among Us," that often can inspire hope in us. The Internet can certainly lend you a hand; just search for stories of hope, or inspirational stories. Look for these stories now, when you *do not* need them; fill up a file of them so that when you do need them they are at your fingertips with no effort needed.

There are ways to rediscover lost passion in our careers. We can talk to colleagues who are not in the midst of the burnout trap, allowing their passion to infect us simply by being around these colleagues and asking them about what drives them. We can also borrow hope from supervisors, therapists, and other trusted advisors. These sage figures may have ideas about why your passion diminished and how to foster its return.

Burnout comes from being boxed in, and you've got to find a way to get out of the box. You can get out of the box by working on reconnecting with that passion that got you here, that early perspective that allowed in the hope that you wrote about in the

Part One initial questions, or you can get out of the box by borrowing the hope of others and working a new perspective with the world you live in now. It may take some creativity. Okay, it may take a lot of creativity, but you can do it. After all, isn't that exactly what you teach your clients?

Optimize Stress

The best way to achieve and maintain the optimal stress zone is to recognize one's personal optimal stress level and to recognize one's professional optimal stress level. Recognizing one's personal optimal stress level means knowing what level of stress you need to function at your best. Each of us has a different level of stress where we operate in the most efficient, most optimal manner. Explore how you function best, for example—are you good at accomplishing a short list of tasks in a large amount of time, or are you better at accomplishing a long list of tasks in a small amount of time? Think about how you operate at work. What kind of days are you most efficient, most productive? What kinds of activities are you doing? How many people are around you? What is the stress level of the environment? Do you need a lot of time to complete few tasks, or are you more successful if you have many tasks and only a little time to complete them?

You may also want to consider how other people describe you. Ask those who know you well at the workplace to describe how they see you function under stress, including what they believe is your optimal stress level. What words are used to describe you? But be careful of attributing meaning to those labels without considering alternative meaning. For example, the label *procrastinator* denotes a lazy person who purposely waits until the last moment to complete a task. Alternatively, your optimal stress level may be tipped toward the high stress end of the spectrum, indicating that if you do not have enough stress you will create it by procrastinating on tasks, collecting them until you have your optimal level with which you best function so that

the tasks can be completed. Perhaps you are seen as unengaged, but there is a chance that what looks like unengaged is in fact an optimal level of stress that leans toward the low stress end of the spectrum. The trick is to know the level of stress you require to help you function optimally, and then organize your daily activities around that level.

Now consider how this translates into the professional arena. If you are the type of person who operates better under a good amount of stress, one who needs many tasks and few hours to complete successfully, then you are likely to need the same level of activity at work. You are likely drawn to high-energy positions, where there are few moments to rest, with many tasks to fit into your work day. Someone in this category may enjoy a job where they are managing staff and clients, developing new programs in addition to the ones they are running, managing several different program sites at the same time, actively working on several different committees, or some combination of all these tasks. He or she may also like positions that exist in high stress locations, such as hospitals. If this is you, it is important that you have enough on your plate to maximize your efficiency. If you don't, you will become easily bored and will not complete tasks. You will become distressed and eventually experience Clinician Burnout, so pile on those tasks appropriately. You may need a supervisor's help in organizing your schedule effectively.

On the other end of the spectrum, if you are the type of person who operates best under low levels of stress, one who needs many hours and few tasks to complete successfully, then you are likely to require the same level of activity at work. You will function best when you can focus on one or two tasks, and do them well, before attending to other tasks. Someone in this category can enjoy all of the same tasks, but will function better with less on his or her plate at one time. He or she may also like positions that exist in lower stress locations, such as a small residential program. This does not imply that residential treatment is not stressful for the staff; it can be immensely stressful. The direct practice is likely to be equally stressful no matter where you work, but the surrounding atmosphere can differ in the level of activity it demands. Because it is smaller with fewer residential clients it may be less chaotic than a big hospital setting. If this is you, it is important that you don't overload yourself. You may have many interests, and a wish to help others, which can quickly land you with many tasks and a rising stress level. If you put too much on your plate, you will stop functioning well and will eventually experience Clinician Burnout. Take a step back, reassess, and omit or postpone what does not need to happen today. You may need a supervisor's help in organizing your schedule effectively.

In addition to understanding your own optimal stress level, good stress management involves recognizing a specific situation for its stress potential. For example, if one part of your job—running a family group—is consistently producing high stress, you want to make sure other parts of your workday produce lower stress so the day is balanced. Our reality in addiction counseling is that most days are quite stressful—and there is little we can do about it; it is the nature of helping professions. We therefore do not often have the luxury of planning our workday to swim in the optimal stress zone. Thus, it is imperative that we keep our overall life well balanced.

While impossible to manage an optimal stress level at all times, the goal is to strive for an overall optimal stress level. Every clinician needs to seek a balance between low and high stress with a significant amount of optimal stress. Mindfulness, a value-based approach, and the power of positive thinking can be helpful tools. Keeping a fresh and positive view on the work can be useful. For example, while we all wish that addiction counselors were better compensated for their hard work, studies do show that with higher salaries comes an increased level of exhaustion and depersonalization, likely because of greater organization demands on higher salaried staff (Vilardaga et al., 2011). We should be careful what we wish for; it is also a helpful lesson that while the grass may seem greener in someone else's yard, there are elements we cannot

see from our own yard. Attending to these concepts will help you live an optimal-stressed life in your job and outside of work, in everything you do.

Supervision

Good support is vital to optimal stress health, as we have discussed, and supervision is one avenue of support. Supervision is a vital component of any clinical practice (Knudsen et al., 2008; Powell & Brodsky, 2004), yet it is often an aspect that is missed or tossed aside (Powell & Brodsky, 2004). To put it clearly, you cannot reach your potential as an effective and ethical clinician without good supervision; it is that important. You probably already know this from your own experiences. In Part One, when you were completing your personal inventory, you considered your positive and negative supervision experiences. If you only knew the negative supervisory experience, imagine how inferior a clinician you would be today. Similarly, if you only knew the positive supervisory experience, imagine what a fantastic clinician you would be today. You were also asked to explore your positive and negative experiences with supervision. Most addiction professionals have experiences with supervision that likely range from harmful to the pinnacle of satisfaction, and everything in between.

Supervision makes a big difference in every aspect of our practice. With good supervision we are able to cope with conflicted agendas, ensure good client welfare, build positive clinical relationships, and embrace cultural diversity. With good supervision, we are able to make sense of our confused roles, gain guidance in using clinical material properly, and ensure that we respect the different ethical tiers. Supervision drives us to build our competency and to make our practices more responsible through continuous learning. Supervision can also help us to prevent Clinician Burnout and to cope with the factors that cause it.

There is still much to be learned about Clinician Burnout, and more studies are needed (Morse et al., 2012; Vilardaga et al., 2011), especially related to addiction professionals. Still, there are many steps you can take to prevent Clinician Burnout. You can learn your optimal stress level and organize your work and world in a way that optimizes it. Write down your major influences that infused you with the passion that drives your work so that you may be reminded if needed. Analyze where you fall on the SDEPS scale, and acknowledge which areas need to be strengthened. Make a great effort to avoid bleeding the personal into the workplace by ensuring you have the support you need outside of the workplace. Finally, do the best you can to set up your supervision to be the supportive and challenging collaboration you need it to be. Let's take a closer look at what makes supervision advantageous and what can make it detrimental, so that you can examine your own supervision against it and judge what you are receiving.

Practical Application

When Supervision Is Not So … Super …

Clinicians today are not all guaranteed ongoing supervision as a part of employment; many have to request it or seek supervision outside of employment. Often employers are not offering regular supervision because unfortunately it is erroneously viewed as an unnecessary expense (Powell & Brodsky, 2004). Yet ongoing supervision not only protects the clients and strengthens the clinician, it also supports best practices for the agency itself and bolsters the professionalism of the field (Powell & Brodsky, 2004). It is unacceptable for agencies not to require, or at the very least offer, regular supervision to all clinical staff.

Good supervision is both challenging and supportive, both educational and collaborative, both enlightening and securing, both informative and inspirational, and, of course, ethical. Table 14.1 gives an outline of the basics. A good supervisor is someone you respect, even when disagreeing with him or her, and someone who learns when to push you and when to pull you back, when to support you

Table 14.1 **Supervision**

Supervision is:	Supervision is not:
Collaborative	Therapy
Educational	Case Management
Informative	Gossip Hour
Challenging	Grievance Forum
Enlightening	
Inspirational	
Securing	
Ethical	

by challenging you to reach further, and when to support you by pulling you back to gain perspective. It is not an easy task, supervision, and most supervisors get little to no training on how to give it properly. Supervision should be something you are generally looking forward to in your week, even with exceptions from time to time, not the hour you dread in your week. If you are dreading it, take that as a clue that your supervision may be less than effective.

Many clinicians do receive regular individual supervision, but the supervision is of poor quality and the clinician does not reap the needed benefits to grow his or her practice to the height of its potential. Clinicians operating without effective, regular supervision are at risk for damaging their clients, themselves, their agency, and the profession of which they are members. The importance of maintaining supervision cannot be understated, and the danger of ignoring it cannot be emphasized enough. Many of us have horrible stories of neglectful or harmful supervision, thus it may appear that statistically you are more likely to have a faulty supervision than a successful one. Poor supervision exists on a wide spectrum, so while the supervision you are experiencing may be faulty, it is not necessarily horrible, yet the supervision you are getting may be far from what you need. What is your supervision like? Here are seven common answers:

1. I do not have supervision. I did have supervision with a licensed person, but once I got my

credential/license, my agency said I did not need it anymore.
2. I do not have individual supervision, but I do have group supervision one to two times a month.
3. I do not have regular supervision unless I am having a crisis. I can get time with a supervisor until the crisis is resolved.
4. I have supervision in which we discuss all of my clinical cases one by one.
5. I have supervision in which we discuss my thoughts and feelings and mental health.
6. I have supervision in which we discuss interagency happenings.
7. I have supervision in which we discuss my supervisor a lot.

Do you see your supervision listed here? If you do, you are not getting all you can from the supervisory experience.

Supervision as credential prep: Many agencies offer supervision as the clinician is pursuing a professional credential or licensure in the helping professions, including addiction counseling, because it is a requirement of the credentialing or licensing process. All fields have a specific requirement for on-the-job supervision, thus if agencies want credentialed and licensed professionals in their agencies, they are willing to provide the supervision. Yet many agencies cease this supervision when the clinician successfully achieves the goal, unveiling the agency's unfortunate priority of satisfying requirements rather than of effective support of the clinician's practice.

Supervision in a group: One way agencies have addressed the expense of weekly supervision is to have group supervision in place of individual supervisory hours once a week for all clinical staff. While group supervision is beneficial on several levels it is not the same as individual supervision. Group supervision involves planning a presentation on a general topic that is believed to relate to the most staff possible. It typically involves a topic that is lectured followed by a discussion. There is no question of the value in this type of supervision, as both the topic and the discussion material are helpful in building an ethical practice. However, this type of supervision should be an addition to individual supervision, not a replacement, as clinicians need their individual time to address their own needs and development.

Supervision as crisis intervention: Many of the clinicians who do access supervision only seek it out when they have a specific question or are caught in a conscious ethical dilemma. But this is the same as praying only when something in your life is drastically wrong, or exercising only 2 weeks before putting on that bathing suit, or quitting smoking after learning you have lung cancer. These are all good ideas, but each misses the maximum benefit of the action. One of the best parts of supervision comes not from asking for direct help on an issue, but from exploring issues that have never been considered. The supervision that is beneficial is that in which direct questions may be posed, but which also leaves time for casual exploration that can lead to new insights and can strengthen your practice in areas you didn't even know needed strengthening.

Supervision as case management: Similarly, supervision is not case management. You do not want to use supervision solely as a place to discuss your cases, which many people do. Case management is a vital aspect of supervision, but it is only one aspect of what supervision should be. You want to go over challenging cases, as well as successful cases, but you also want to discuss theory, principles, new ideas, journal articles, opportunities to grow and strengthen your practice, collaborative relationships with colleagues, professional goals, and other topics. Don't simplify your supervision or allow your supervisor to make that mistake either; you want to stretch it to the corners of all that it can be.

Supervision as therapy: Your supervision may also be lacking if it feels more like therapy than supervision (Powell & Brodsky, 2004). You will have moments when a good therapy session is exactly what you need, when you ask the same questions or pleas to your supervisor as you would to a therapist, but those moments need to be the exception. The rule of your supervision should be quite different from therapy, and your supervisor different from a therapist. You go to therapy to achieve personal goals, to work on the aspects of your personal life that trouble you. You go to supervision to achieve professional goals, to work on the aspects of your clinical practice that either trouble you, or in which you can grow. Since this book shows how often your personal world can seep into your professional world, you will and should discuss personal issues in your supervision, but you want to discuss them in the context of what is occurring on the professional level.

Supervision as occupational venting: Supervision is also not a gossip hour, a place to joke, complain, tattle or whisper about clients, colleagues, or nonprofessional persons. Life can be one big bowl of drama if you allow for that, and really it is dramatic enough without spending an hour focusing on that aspect of your surroundings. It is unethical to gossip about clients or clinicians, but it also makes for pretty lousy supervision. Look at all the gifts you are missing by wasting the hour away. Similarly, supervision is not a grievance forum. It is an appropriate place to bring serious grievances, as your supervisor is the best choice when seeking an audience. However, this should not be the rule in your supervision, meaning if you find that the majority of your hour each week is spent drumming up new grievances to report, you are struggling to use supervision to the best of its benefit. You may also benefit from discussing your tendency to form grievances with your supervisor and analyze why that may be, as it may be an indication of something awry in your practice that needs to be addressed. Remember you want your supervision to be many things, not just one thing. If you are not getting the complex version of supervision you are not getting the best, most useful kind.

Supervision as a role reversal: Poor supervision can result in a confusion of roles. For example, you start interning at a facility that offers detox, inpatient, outpatient, and residential treatment. You love the job and the opportunity to work with some fascinating clinicians. You are assigned to Cathy, who supervises all the interns. At the time of your appointment in the facility, you are the only intern and thus the only clinician that Cathy supervises. Cathy recently had a baby boy and returned from maternity leave about a month before your internship began. In your first supervisory meeting, Cathy asks a few questions about your background and makes several statements indicating she is impressed with your resume. She then spends the rest of the supervisory hour telling you about her own background, with a particular emphasis on her married life and her experiences as a mother to her two children. Because this is the first meeting, you chalk up her candid disclosure to a meet-and-greet session informality and don't expect it to continue. But continue it does, and her self-disclosure grows. She discusses her experiences pumping breast milk, and fighting with her husband, and favoring her baby boy over her young daughter. In short, she gives you way too much information about personal topics that are unrelated to your work at the agency. When you attempt to bring the conversation back to work, she simply tells you that you know what you are doing and will be fine. There is no guidance, no strengthening or stretching of your skill base. She accepts you as is, and is encouraging, but not in the least challenging. She also begins to share interagency gossip with you, prefacing her comments with "I shouldn't be telling you this, but...."

When you finally gain the courage to address these issues with her, suggesting that perhaps you could stick to work-related topics, she is offended and ceases communication with you. When it is time for your scheduled supervision sessions, she begins to have unexpected tasks she must complete, and you sense she is avoiding working with you. You are concerned that she is your boss and in charge of your performance review that will allow you to advance. You are also concerned that you are not learning new skills and are not being challenged in the skills you already possess. You have no one to talk with at the agency because no one else is supervised by her, and the general impression of everyone else is that she is a competent clinician. Plus, you don't feel it is appropriate to gossip to others about your struggles, especially since one of your main complaints is that she gossips to you. What is your next move? What options do you have to address these two concerns?

Your first concern—that she is in charge of your internship—can be addressed by considering who else has a stake in your development. Is there someone at the school you attend that is in charge of internships, one who can aid you in troubleshooting how to handle conflicts at the internship? There should be a formal staff member assigned to this task. If there is not, approach a professor or administrative staff person whom you trust and ask for guidance. You should also consider other staff to approach at the agency. It is not best to approach colleagues, but it is likely that your supervisor reports to someone above her. Perhaps this person is approachable and willing to help you manage the situation. While you don't want to get her into trouble, you do want her unethical behavior addressed.

Your second concern, that you are not growing or being challenged, also must be addressed. What you need is good supervision, and if it is not given to you, you must go and seek it. You may attempt to hire a supervisor you once had at a previous place of employment who has a private practice. You may ask him if you can hire him for regular supervision since you are struggling with what you've been given. If he doesn't agree, you could ask other colleagues for ideas of a therapist in private practice. Once you access good supervision, you can not only receive the supportive collaborative, challenging experience you are seeking, but can also get guidance about addressing the poor supervision you are receiving at the facility. You can also take the following tips to your current supervisor to discuss your supervision needs.

Tips for Good Supervision

Whether your supervision is nonexistent or is lacking collaboration, is not challenging, or is uncomfortable, it is up to you to ensure you are getting what you need. So how on earth do you accomplish that? All agencies should be providing decent, healthy, ongoing supervision, and hopefully that will be your reality. If you do not have supervision, or if the supervision you have is faulty or ineffective, the burden often falls on you to secure adequate supervision on your own. If you do not have supervision that achieves these necessary components, what should you do to ensure you get the important support, where are you supposed to get it? You have five options: (1) approach your current supervisor, discuss what it is you are needing that is not being provided, and make a plan to meet your needs; (2) approach your agency director, discuss what it is you are needing that is not being provided, and make a plan to meet your needs; (3) approach your EAP, or similar personnel, and have the same discussion and planning, asking for help in finding an adequate supervisor with whom to work; (4) engage in a peer assistance program, if offered, and gain the help and support you need; or (5) obtain healthy supervision outside of your agency by hiring an external supervisor. The first three options involve trying to enhance the services you are being offered, and the final two options involve going into the community and creating the support you are not getting on the job.

Enhancing What You Do Have

Approaching Your Supervisor: If you have a decent rapport with your supervisor, or if your supervisor is one who takes constructive criticism well, then approaching your current supervisor could be a fantastic way to reach your supervision needs. Perhaps your supervisor is unaware that your needs are going unmet, or that there is a superior way to give supervision. When you approach him or her, be sure to show your gratitude for what he or she has given you thus far, and explain that you have learned about some specific supervision techniques that you would like to try out. It may be more successful if your approach is less critical of the supervisor, which may make him or her embarrassed or defensive, and more neutral in tone, suggesting that these changes are aspects you would like to try. Bring in material, such as Powell and Brodsky's (2004) book on supervision for your supervisor to read.

Approaching Your Agency Director or EAP: If you try speaking with your supervisor and it fails, or if you feel you cannot approach your supervisor, another option may be to approach your agency director or someone in your employee assistance program, if you have one, or an alternative human services department. You want to use a similar tactic of explaining what you have learned and what you are hoping to obtain in the agency. Produce materials if needed. You may feel more comfortable highlighting what you are currently missing in your current supervision, and this other professional may have good ideas about how to get your needs met that you have not thought of, especially if this professional has had previous experience with your supervisor.

Creating What You Do Not Have

Find the Right Supervisor: Ask your colleagues if they have a supervisor they love, and find out if they do private supervision work, as many do. You can also seek out a therapist in private practice who also offers supervision to clinicians, as many do. This last option is certainly more costly to you, as you may have to pay for these services if your insurance will not, but it is your ethical obligation to make sure you are getting the support and encouragement that you need in order to do your job effectively. Don't mess around with it, you are only hurting yourself … oh yeah, and your clients, agency, and profession, too. If you cannot find a supervisor, there are some clinicians who can be accessed through their websites for consultation, which may get you started on the path. Search the Internet for clinicians in your area with websites, and you may just find someone nearby who can help you. Take the time to research the best match for you. It will be immensely helpful and worth it if you find the right supervisor. Here are four tips to use in creating the best kind of supervision.

Look at His or Her Training: You want to work with someone specifically trained in supervision, not only someone who has good clinical skills. If your place of employment does not offer you a supervisor, or if they offer you an inadequate supervisor, find someone outside of your agency. Don't settle for bad supervision. If you are the supervisor and you feel your skills are inadequate, get trained! Even if your agency will not pay for it, you owe it to yourself and your supervisees to get specific training.

Specifically, you are looking for a supervisor who has clinical expertise, who has worked with actual clients in a clinical setting, and who is respectful of and concerned with both client and supervisee welfare (Bogo et al., 2011a; Powell & Brodsky, 2004). It is essential that your supervisor understands and strives for the ethical pillars of beneficence, autonomy, nonmaleficence, and justice (Powell & Brodsky, 2004). You want a supervisor who has the goal of changing the counselor's behavior by direct and indirect observation and monitoring (Powell & Brodsky, 2004). A good supervisor will have leadership and management abilities in addition to their supervisory ability … and a clear passion for counseling (Powell & Brodsky, 2004). If you are a supervisor, you want to establish the four *As* in your practice. You want to be available, accessible, able, and affable (Powell & Brodsky, 2004).

It is not advised that your supervisor is the same person you consider your "boss" or the person to whom you report. Your supervisor needs to be your ally, and one who can give unconditional support. The supervisory experience will be affected if the clinician is worried that being honest will result in a negative evaluation by superiors.

GARDENERS VERSUS SCULPTORS: What the heck does this mean? In his book on self-forgiveness, Thom Rutledge (1997) introduces the concept of *Sculptors vs. Gardeners*. He uses the term to describe different types of parenting, but the same term can adequately be used to describe different types of supervision. A sculptor supervisor is one who believes his or her role is to sculpt the supervisee into a capable, skilled clinician. A sculptor will manage this by scraping loose clay away until his or her masterpiece is formed in the image he or she defines as desirable. A gardener supervisor is one who believes his or her role is to plant the necessary seeds to allow the supervisee to grow into the image he or she defines as desirable. How the supervisee grows is up to him or her; the supervisor's job is to cultivate a fertile environment for the supervisee so that growth can occur. A sculptor directly molds the supervisee, a gardener indirectly molds the supervisee by tending to the environment around the supervisee. You can take a moment to think about the people who raised you and ask yourself what kind of parenting style they adopted for you. It is too tempting not to think about that for a moment, as it no doubt had tremendous influence on how you got where you are today. Are you done? Okay, now think about the supervisors you have had, those wonderful and terrible, and label each a sculptor or gardener.

You may be able to acknowledge both in your past, and see how both types of supervision are helpful in their own way. Sculptors can be helpful, particularly early in your career, because they put you directly on the path that is helpful to your growth and work to throw out what you do not need so that you can focus on what you do need. They give you all the tools that will allow you to reach your potential. Gardeners can be helpful at any point in your career, because they give you aid in a more indirect way, promoting autonomy by leaving more room for you to roam in your career and figure your own path, choose your own tools, and decide what kind of clinician you wish to be. They cultivate an atmosphere of learning so that

you can reach your potential. Ultimately you want to work with a gardener, because this allows for a more collaborative relationship and works from the start to give you what you need to succeed on your own.

SEEK A CHALLENGE: Supervision is inferior if it is not challenging enough. A good supervisor will nurture the supervisee's professional development, encourage the development of skills and competencies, and promote accountability in services (Powell & Brodsky, 2004). You are looking for someone you respect, even if you do not at first agree. You want someone who will stretch your thinking, produce alternative paradigms of thought, and push you to take risks.

BUT ALLOW FOR FLEXIBILITY: Barriers to good supervision are "workload demands and crisis-oriented attitude" (Bogo et al., 2011a). Often meetings will be cancelled or postponed due to some other pressing task or clinical crisis. Supervision itself can become so crisis-focused, a clinician may never gain the other benefits of supervision beyond putting out clinical fires. Great supervision is more than just addressing what is in your lap; it is also about moving beyond the daily grind and looking at the bigger picture. Sometimes you will come with a list and never get beyond the first few items because what seemed like an easy question morphs into an engrossing discussion. Unless there is a time-sensitive topic that needs to be addressed that day, allow for this flexibility. As stated, some of the best lessons come from these unexpected explorations.

Peer Assistance Program: A peer assistance program (PAP), or impaired professionals program, identifies addiction clinicians at risk of impaired counseling, or those already engaged in poor practices, and provides them with the resources they need to return to providing healthy, effective services (Gallagher, 2010). The benefit of a PAP is that it does not require the clinician to discuss with a superior his or her problem, which can be scary and embarrassing. Instead, a PAP can provide the needed support without fear of repercussion. This may entice clinicians to get help sooner, which better maintains the safety that competent practices require, and, if the clinician is in recovery, may prevent clinician relapse (Gallagher, 2010). If the clinician does not have a safe place to go, everyone (client, clinician, community) is impacted. While not widespread, peer assistance programs are increasing (Gallagher, 2010).

Supervision should be a blend of support and challenge. The support part consists of active listening, asking pointed questions, asking open-ended questions, making observations, bringing in vignettes and role plays, eyewitness/process recordings/audio taping/videotaping, and case consultation. The challenge part consists of bringing up ideas to stretch your skill base and prevent you from ceasing to grow. If your supervision is lacking any of these things, then you are not getting the support you could and should be getting. If you are using supervision to go over active cases on your caseload, that's great, but it is only one function of supervision. If your supervisor is bringing in questions that make you think about hypothetical clinical situations, that's super, but also only one function. And if your supervisor is reviewing your work solely on what observations you bring to supervision, without directly observing your work through eyewitness, process recordings, or audio/videotaping then your growth potential will be stunted. Supervision is more than a quick "how ya doing," it is an active part of building your competency. Furthermore, if you have poor supervision, your risk of Clinician Burnout increases. You need the support at the workplace; your supervisor should be the one helping you ward off burnout. If he or she is not routinely discussing burnout with you, and especially if he or she is contributing to the workplace stress you are experiencing, you may be more likely to experience burnout first hand.

Because low salaries, poor employee benefits, lack of career paths, insufficient mentorship programs, inadequate staff supervision, personnel shortages, and large caseloads contribute to staff turnover and job discontent, the need for healthy, effective, attentive supervision cannot be understated, as it can be instrumental in the satisfaction and retention of staff (Bogo et al., 2011a; Powell & Brodsky, 2004; Whitter et al., 2006), which protects client care and the profession at large. Because supervision is a necessary component of all that we do in our clinical and ethical practices, we could discuss it in every chapter of this book. It can help us develop all four keys, adhere to all 10 principles, and avoid all four common pitfalls. It can aid us in acknowledging our strengths and limitations, and help us to avoid conflicted agendas and explore the ethics around self-disclosure. It can help us respect the tiers of ethics and aid us in addressing of confusion of roles, and staying within our scope of practice. It can aid us in our need for continuous learning, and will help prevent Clinician Burnout. Looking ahead, supervision can also help us make the rules by which we stand and can aid us in catching corners we are cutting, helping us understand issues with gift giving. Supervision can aid us in establishing the rules of our practice and help us to practice the code of ethics in all our affairs. It is no wonder that to help us with all of this it needs to be healthy.

If we accept the premise of the third Key, to seek continuous learning, we will have to adopt our practice to allow for ongoing growth. This growth will aid us in developing responsible and competent practices, because when we are continuously learning, we are continuously strengthening our competency and practicing our professional responsibility. The more responsible and competent we are, the less our chances of sliding into Clinician Burnout. It starts with a pledge to never stop learning and striving to self-improve, and obtaining the necessary support to grow. If you can keep that goal alive, there is no stopping the heights your practice can surpass. It's pretty exciting to consider.

PROTECTING
THE COMMUNITY

Ethics That Protect the Community

Thus far we have examined how to protect our clients, clinical information, and ourselves. There is one more group that needs our protection. Throughout this book we have commented on the profession as a whole, and your responsibility to do your part in ensuring its thriving future. What we are talking about is protecting the community. Your community can be made up of the group, the agency, the profession, the neighborhood, or any other group that involves more than the individual. It is up to each of us to actively work on protecting the community because we are the source of its survival. Don't rely on other people to do the work and take care of things. Think about all the different communities in which you are a member. Now imagine how each community would thrive if all its members took an active role in ensuring its health and survival.

Whether we are picking up trash we see in the neighborhood park or writing a letter to our delegates to increase our professional rights, the onus is on each of us to focus on the bigger picture.

Consider the familiar four pillars of ethics and how they apply to the community. Beneficence dictates that we will do everything in our power to promote goodness in our communities. Our actions are aimed at benefiting our profession, the addicted community, and our individual communities. We have a specific principle in our Code of Ethics that directly mandates us to improve the society around us in some way. Autonomy is another key element of protecting the community. We need to see the community the same way we see the clients. With the clients, we give them control over their own life, helping them develop independence. In the same way, we need to see the community as an entity that needs to be responsible for its own identity. We work to give it a voice, whether it is the community of professionals, the community of addicted persons, or the geographical community in which we live or work.

Nonmaleficence guides us to prevent harm to our communities, to ensure that our actions not only promote goodness, but also ensure no harm. As we have already learned, there are situations that promote goodness but that also harm. We must do everything in our power not to harm our professional community, our clinical community, and the community at large. Justice is an obvious choice to help guide our protection of the community. The notion of justice demands that we give the same treatment across the clinical population. To do this, we must focus on the community, not only the individual client. What we give to one, we want to offer to the others we treat.

The Code of Ethics in your state has several principles that address the protection of the community. All codes have a principle related to relationships with colleagues and other professionals, sometimes referred to as interprofessional relationships. All codes have a principle related to workplace standards, although it may be titled differently, and may

be split into several principles. Finally, all codes have a principle about societal obligations, directives to professionals to better the society at large. Together these principles guide us into protecting the community.

To effectively achieve these principles in our ethical practice, we need to develop the fourth key, Make the Rule, for our practice. This key actually serves to protect all the entities in our practice, our clients, their clinical information, ourselves, and our community. The key asks us to set a standard of our care that is clear and consistent. Although rules can sometimes be broken, it must be the exception to our regular procedure. If we do not adhere to this key, or if we fail to build it into our practice, we are at risk of cutting corners. This pitfall can cause us to get lost, to become unhinged from our profession, even if in small transgressions. Cutting small corners can lead to large holes in our professionalism. Therefore, avoiding this pitfall is an important line of defense against an ethical dilemma. If we fail to avoid it, coping effectively with the dilemma will be paramount to the future of our practices. Let's take a look at how to do that, but first, get out your pencils because here come the questions.

Part Four Questions

1. What circumstances have caused you to bend the rules in your practice? Would you do this again, and why or why not? If you are new to the profession, can you think of an ethical rule you can imagine breaking? What are the circumstances and why is it okay to break the rule?

2. Consider all of the volunteer work you have completed in your career, including anything current, that served to improve the profession in some way. Make a list of your activities, large or small, and your feelings attached to each. Did you enjoy it, and why or why not? Which were your favorite? Your least favorite?

3. How would you describe your flexible nature in most situations (personally and professionally)?

   a. Very rigid (Hospital Corners)

   b. Some rigidity, some flexibility (Soggy Wood)

   c. Very flexible (Loosey-Goosey)

Why do you think you operate this way; is it your innate style or have you been influenced to develop it that way?

4. What is one thing you can do to strengthen the profession? Write down a plan that specifies how you can make that happen. Commit to it.

Key: Make the Rule

I hesitate to say the familiar "If you take away one thing from this book, let it be this ..." because I don't want your brain to say, "Fantastic! Let's drop everything else from the memory banks and just retain this one note," as I would hope most of the material in this book bears some importance to your practice. So do me a favor and retain all of it, but take out a highlighter in your brain and swipe a stripe of brilliant color on this one, so it stays in an extra special place always at the ready.

Make the Rule is about establishing a standard of behavior, a set of actions or rules of conduct that are maintained most of the time. Once the standard is established and maintained then exceptions can be made as a given situation calls for it. But you must make the rule before you break the rule. Let's use a parenting example. If you have a young child, you must establish a bedtime routine for that child, as children rarely come to that naturally. You will receive resistance, but it is your job to make sure that bedtime is the same healthy time each night so that the child's rhythms can be established. Once this occurs, if there is the occasional late night—a house guest, a party, a long movie, whatever activity that might delay bedtime—it is possible to break the routine without much of a negative consequence the next day. The routine snaps back, and the child usually can adjust well. However, if a bedtime is never established, occasional exceptions can't be made because every night is an exception. This means the child has no routine or nighttime rhythm, which will cause later problems. Similarly, as clinicians we must establish our standard of practice *before* we can be allowed to make exceptions. There will always be exceptions, but there must be a routine against which an exception can be made.

Unfortunately, our profession has been swamped with exceptions to the rules so that now the rule has been lost, or was never established in the first place. Addiction professionals often refuse to make an ethical decision based on their need to accept all individuals and their presenting problems (Taleff, 2010). The problem with this thinking is that if all opinions are acceptable, or moral, then any ethical choice is equal to another and unethical behavior can be preferred over a more ethical option. We tend to respond to ethical questions with "it depends" without critically weighing our choices, to the degree that "it depends" becomes our standard (Taleff, 2010). We want to lead with the rule, not the exception, otherwise the exception *becomes* the rule.

For example, we discussed the problem if a client in your residential program relapses while in the program. Most residential programs need to have an established protocol for relapses, as relapses are frequent enough to demand a predetermined rule. Establishing a rule in this case is complex because you need to consider what is best both for the individual client and for the climate of the house. An individual may warrant a second chance, but what message does it send to the other residents in the program? If you adopt the "it depends" credo, the number of relapses will likely increase and the program will fail. If all clients are treated with their own set of rules, then the clients will behave with no regard to general rules and the system will collapse. Instead, a protocol must be created that dictates to the staff and residents what exactly will happen should a resident relapse. Once this is established and maintained successfully, then if a truly special situation arises and the staff wish to bend the rules and give a particular client a second chance they may do so without sacrificing the integrity of the rule, as long as the exceptions are infrequent, and can be unanimously agreed on as exceptions. For example, treatment teams may make special accommodations for a terminally ill patient, knowing that this is an unusual circumstance that humanely asks for a little rule breaking.

Clients certainly benefit from clear rule setting, as they know what is expected of them, what behavior is allowed, and what will not be tolerated. This structure, so often neglected in their personal lives due to the chaos of the addicted lifestyle, is a vital component of a good recovery program. It may feel harsh to set rules, especially as clients feel they are unfair and pull at your heart strings when pleading their case. You will have to weigh promoting autonomy with nonmaleficence. At times, standing your ground is a healthy and beneficial treatment, even if the client does not see it. Just as a teacher demands more of a student knowing it will help the student realize his or her potential, so, too, will

clinicians find themselves in the position of challenging clients, at times with a bit of resistance from the clients even if you know they need to address whatever behavior is being discussed.

For example, you might see that a client's friend, who is actively using and dealing drugs, is making it impossible for a client to continue his or her recovery efforts, and you may challenge the client to change the nature of the relationship to a safer one for the client. You can't make someone change, but you can demonstrate the benefits of that change more easily if you have a rule already established. Clients may resist dropping their friend, feeling that their friend is supportive or that they need the friend or that it will be worse for them if they say good-bye, but you have the wisdom and objective perspective to know your clients are likely to have a better chance at success without this peer influence.

Clients can also benefit from consistency in what they experience around them. For example, reconsider the case of Ronald, our clinician from Part One who used different language for different ethnic groups. We discussed that some clients may not want to be addressed in the familiar language that is different than how Ronald addresses others. In the same way, clients may observe Ronald's behavior with envy, or may be offended by it, or angry, embarrassed, or humiliated. Thus, by treating clients differently, Ronald may have the opposite effect of what he intended. He meant to be welcoming and friendly to one client, but he may have been offensive and hurtful to other clients.

Clients are not the sole beneficiaries of rule setting; the clinician, the agency, and the profession are all bolstered by established rules. Clinicians benefit in numerous circumstances where it is helpful to fall back on an established rule, rather than to establish a rule in the moment with the client. If you have a client who recently relapsed sitting in your office in obvious remorse, begging for a second chance you cannot give, it is far easier to explain the rules of the program to the client rather than explaining your opinion on the matter. It takes the responsibility away from the clinician, which allows that clinician to maintain rapport with the client and help him or her find alternative solutions. It is one example where it is helpful to attend to the agency level of ethics rather than to the personal.

In addition, the agency and profession can benefit from clear rules and boundaries. The agency can benefit from streamlining the standard of care among the clinicians. It promotes a professional consistency that may aid in treatment effectiveness measures, and is likely to give a more even orientation experience across employees. The profession can be bolstered by an increase in ethical clinicians and ethically sturdy agencies and programs. The more consistent the rules across clinicians and programs, the stronger the profession, particularly when you consider how the profession is viewed by other professionals and groups.

If it can be established that there is a strong code of conduct across the profession, it is hopeful that the profession will be more highly regarded and respected as a contributing member of the helping professions, which strengthens the future of the profession. If the exception is the rule, the profession is left with a collection of clinicians and programs that have no standard of care, that are so flexible they are groundless, and the entire profession is weakened. It may sound melodramatic to state that having no established policy on accepting gifts from clients will weaken the entire profession, but any profession is created by the actions of its members, and it is quickly affected by even small missteps. It does not take many clinicians or programs to hurt the profession, but it does require every clinician and program to participate in making the profession solid.

At a recent conference of addiction professionals, a lauded expert in the field was giving the keynote address. When discussing general ethics this revered speaker told the group that although ethics was important we should not lose sight of the importance of being human. His example was seeing a client on the side of the road in a snowstorm. He stated that although ethics would teach you not to stop and drive him to the agency, that your humanity should trump your ethics. This is not a false statement, but it is faulty. It is sensible that you want to avoid being so ethically rigid that you neglect your empathy for human life. However, we do not want our empathy controlling our ethics either, and it can be detrimental to suggest it. What should be taught instead is that there are times when human empathy outweighs ethical principles, but that these should be the clear exception to the rule.

Consider the snowstorm example. In some parts of the country, a snowstorm would be a rare event, so this would be a good example of human empathy outweighing ethical mandates. But if you live in the northern half of the country, a bad snowstorm will probably not be an exception. In those states, agencies should be writing policies about what clinicians should do in the inevitable event of snowstorms. Then clinicians will not have to agonize between doing what they feel is the right thing on a human level and what they know to be right on an ethical level. An example policy would allow for the clinician to pick up the client in the event of inclement weather and transport the client to the agency. An alternative policy might allow for the clinician to wait with the client in the clinician's car while the agency van comes to the location to pick up the client. Whatever policy variation is created, it will protect the client, clinician, and agency. Natural disasters, such as hurricanes, tornadoes, earthquakes, or tsunamis, may be better examples of acceptable times situations when human empathy should exceed ethical principles. It is vital that we all make this clear, particularly if we are training others.

Examining the questions at the introduction to Part Four, the first, *Can you think of an ethical rule you can imagine breaking? What are the circumstances and why is it okay to break the rule?* asks you to explore your own limits and allowances to the ethical code. What you write is not necessarily acceptable to another, or to your agency or your profession within an ethical practice, but it is vital that you are aware of what exceptions you would make, real or imagined. It should be asked of your clients: What set of circumstances would render a relapse acceptable to you? Some gawk and say, "Well none, of course. There is nothing that makes for an acceptable relapse. Is this a trick question?" But other clients have found this an easy question, quickly revealing a situation. These answers should be acknowledged and the team should analyze how this relapse would go, and what to do to avoid it in case their imagined situation ever becomes a reality. Clinicians may be able to prepare true stories of clients who went through those exact situations and found the strength to get through them without using, or those who did use and felt terrible about it. It is not enough to shrug off this question without an answer. Many addicts have an answer if they are honest, and the therapy is in talking it out and planning around it, rather than avoiding the possibility.

Similarly, you want to think this question through seriously. You don't want to answer "Oh I have no exceptions, I follow the ethical rules to the letter in all situations" because you don't; no one does. Instead of denying the possibility, it is better to plan for the possibility and see how you could work around it. At the very least, whatever you answer will make great conversation in your next supervision session. You may not change your mind about whatever your exception may be, but you will be a better clinician if you talk it out with a trusted advisor rather than to stuff it away. Often situations that appear unsolvable without breaking an ethical rule can be solved by a supervisor or a trusted advisor. If you talk through it you may get a solution you never thought possible *before* you need it.

The second question, *Consider all of the volunteer work you have completed in your career, including anything current, that served to improve the profession in some way. Make a list of your activities, large or small, and your feelings attached to each. Did you enjoy it, why or why not? Which were your favorite? Your least favorite?* obviously wants to explore your volunteer history, because that will be an important requirement in the Code of Ethics you sign. Our profession values altruistic activity that benefits the organization, its members, and those it serves. We will discuss how to obtain these experiences,

navigating through your choices and finding the right fit for your time and interest. A great place to start is with your own history. Think about what has worked and what has not worked in your volunteering history. Analyze why things went well, if they did, and why they were unsuccessful, if they were. This analysis will allow you to steer clear of potential failures and navigate toward potential successes. If you haven't volunteered, consider where you would like to work or not work and why. It is just a guess at this point but you will need to volunteer in your future so it is good to begin thinking about your options now. Begin.

The third question, *How would you describe your flexible nature in most situations?* asks you to contemplate your typical degree of flexibility both at home and at work. While we all employ a variety of reactions in different situations, we tend to lean in one direction in most scenarios. So in which direction do you lean? "Hospital Corners" describes someone who is least flexible, who develops a style and technique and then sticks with it, applying it to his or her work without exception. Someone with this label typically uses the same treatment methods with the majority of clients, regardless of the individual characteristics of each client case. "Loosey-Goosey" depicts someone who is very flexible, who embraces different ideas and ulterior methods of operation, often changing styles and techniques as new ideas are obtained. "Soggy Wood" denotes someone who is in the middle, with some flexibility and rigidity. Someone with this label employs a solid foundation in his or her work, setting a strong standard of practice, but allows a certain pliability, so that it can be modified as needed. There are benefits to all three styles that will be discussed.

First, you must identify yourself honestly. Then explore why you believe you have adopted the style you have identified. Have you also operated in this fashion, indicating it is part of your personality style? Or have you developed your style because of an external influence or set of influences? If that is the case, identify your influences so that you can understand how you developed into the clinician you are today. For example, Nora may intuitively be Soggy Wood, but perhaps she worked for 15 years under a supervisor who required her to be Loosey-Goosey, so that now she has adopted that way as her own. Alternatively, Jayson may have switched to a Hospital Corners style after his own son fatally overdosed. Some utilize different styles in their personal and professional lives. Once you identify how you are similar or different, ask yourself why. This self-awareness will identify for you how you typically address your work tasks, which will be analyzed later in this section.

The fourth question, *What is one thing you can do to strengthen the profession? Write down a plan that specifies how you can make that happen. Commit to it.* asks you to think about your contribution to the profession. In what ways do you want to leave this profession better than when you entered it? We all want to be competent, to help people, to work well with others, and to make a difference. Take it further than those truthful, yet typical answers. You are unique, so what will your handprint be? Once you decide what you want it to be, consider how you can make it happen. It is likely to be a large, long-term goal, unless you have already set up the goal at another point in your career. Looking at your long-term goal, how can it be broken into smaller, more manageable goals? What can you do now that will ensure your future success? Think this through and make a realistic plan. Commit to it. Try to avoid setting a grand scheme to which you are unlikely to comply, or making a sweeping promise without considering the reality of your time and availability. The profession is counting on you to make a difference. Whatever you commit to doing, thank you for setting the goal.

Consider how you answered all the questions in this book collectively. Do you find that you tend to be generally consistent in your thoughts and behavior, or do you show more of an erratic pattern? When describing your performance do you find yourself saying, "Here is how I am in most circumstances, although there are many exceptions" or "It really depends on the situation. I modify my behavior based on the circumstances"? Although it may seem that being a flexible chameleon is the preferred way to be, it also shows that you are at risk of being without standards, that you may show no pattern of principles that acts as a yardstick or benchmark to guide you. Remember, exceptions in your practice will always be evident, but for them to be exceptions, you must show a standard of conduct on which you and other people may rely. Establishing this standard of conduct is among your first tasks in developing an ethical practice.

To establish this standard you turn to the Code of Ethics, which provides you with a map of guidelines that serves as the backbone of your practice. You want to make your rules of conduct before you are swayed to break any of those rules. Some rules should never be broken in any circumstance. Much of professional behavior can afford exceptions when warranted, yet the standard of even the smallest, most innocuous-seeming behavior must be established. Even if you make a grievous ethical error in your career, and you face the consequences of your actions, it is far better to have that error be a clear exception in your record than part of a regular pattern.

Specifically, the Code of Ethics in each state includes a section on workplace standards, which examines the needed ethical standards in the structure at your place of business; a section on professional rapport, which examines the ethical way to treat colleagues and other professional relationships; and a section on societal obligations, which examines the ethical mandate of giving your services to the larger community in order the strengthen the profession as a whole. If we ignore this Key, if we don't make the rule but instead promote the exception, we run the risk of falling into the ethical pitfall of cutting corners. Cutting corners in our practice can often feel like the wise choice, but in most cases will tarnish your ethical practice. It is far better to decide on a standard practice, knowing that a special circumstance may require an altered response, than to have no standard and create a different response each time a situation occurs.

Principle: Workplace Standards

An essential aspect of protecting the community is the standards you employ at the workplace itself. We have discussed the standards in client welfare and the relationship between clinician and client, in the use of clinical material in all aspects of our work, and in the development of a responsible practice and a competent clinician. Now we turn to the standards of your workspace and the professional relationships within. If you are in private practice, you will want to pay close attention to this section, as you must set up these standards on your own. Similarly, this section may be particularly helpful if you are an agency director, or a professional responsible for the design and implementation of programs.

Although there is not a wealth of published literature that focuses on setting up the workplace in an ethical manner, it is an important part of developing your ethical practice. Perhaps we tend not to talk about workplace standards as much as some of the other principles, but the workplace is really the culmination of everything that we do, and therefore deserves a place of prominence in our ethical practice. While much of our great work occurs behind closed doors in client sessions, our ability to reflect our ethical standards in our work can be seen with the observable eye. How you set up your workplace has a great bearing on your ethical practice. There are standards of the clinical setting, the policies and procedures you design, the treatment programs you offer, the personnel you employ, and the advocacy you practice.

The Clinical Setting

The physical space is important, as clinicians must provide an appropriate setting in which clients receive services. You must offer an office setting that is clean, quiet, safe, and conducive to confidential conversations. We discussed creating a confidential space in Part Two. Go back and review it, or read it for the first time if you skipped it (cheaters!). There are many factors in creating a space that ensures the confidentiality of your clients while maintaining a safe place to work (Pope & Vasquez, 2007).

In most cases, this is an easy item with which to comply as the majority of our work is in agency settings that have been developed with the protection of all entities in mind. However, some of us work

187

in private practice, or in myriad settings that may not be ethical. I am reminded of a friend who arrived at her first therapy session with a counselor, and was shocked to be led through his house to his basement, where they sat on fold-out chairs in full view of the laundry in progress. He may have been a great clinician, but she never returned due to the discomfort of his "office" space.

When creating a space, you have to ensure that you are not disclosing more than is appropriate, and that your decor doesn't make your clients feel uncomfortable (Powell & Brodsky, 2004). For example, a clinician puts up a framed photo of Jesus. When a client comments that the portrait makes her uncomfortable, the clinician says, "Nah, Jesus is welcome in my office." If this was an office where counseling does not take place, if it is an office that is only used by the clinician to conduct paperwork or other administrative duties, then the clinician can decorate the office how he or she sees fit. But if the office is to be used for counseling or supervisory sessions, then the office space does not belong to the clinician alone. It is shared space that must be decorated in a manner than will appeal to the majority.

You also must ensure that your therapy room is comfortable, appropriate, and safe. The seating should be arranged so that everyone in the room, clinician and client, has a clear, unobstructed path to the door, should they feel the need to leave. You never want to put yourself between a client and an escape path if he or she is agitated. You can become physically injured if a client is desperate to leave and senses you are in the way. Similarly, your space should evoke a safety in verbal sharing, so that your client is encouraged to open up to you. All of these things are helpful in setting up a clinical space that is held to a high workplace standard.

This may be particularly difficult for those counselors who work in the field without a stable office space, such as case managers or any clinician who works outside of an office. You must ensure an adequate space to conduct your sessions. Sitting in a coffee shop with a teenage client may seem like a good way to relax the young client in a hip environment, but the fact that everyone can overhear the session deems it unsafe.

Some clinicians operate sessions in their car while transporting a client. If no one else is in the vehicle, confidentiality is not a concern; however there is no way out of the car if the client wishes to leave, and you are therefore holding the client hostage while your vehicle is in motion. A good office will always allow a decent, barrier-free departure route should the client feel the need to use it. You may not have a great deal of choice in where you meet your client—at times you have to make the best of what you have to work with—but be mindful of making the very best.

Policies and Procedures

Remuneration: It is true, we are an underpaid, overworked bunch if ever there was one, so this is a touchy subject for many. It would be lovely if the Code of Ethics could put something in here about getting paid more for the exact same work we do, but alas, that is not the purpose of this principle. Instead, this principle is about ensuring that clinicians are asking for appropriate compensation as delineated by professional standards. Securing appropriate compensation protects the client, in that they are not overcharged for your services; protects the clinician, in that you are not underpaid for your services; and protects the profession, in that there is a defined standard that is valid and reliable across clinicians.

Clients must be made aware of all financial policies, including those arrangements made with counselors completing private work for the agency. These financial policies should be presented at the beginning of treatment, typically as part of the overwhelming orientation packet we give clients before treatment begins. You must produce the financial policies then, yet you should reproduce the document a few weeks into treatment, depending on what level of treatment the client is receiving.

If you are a detox counselor or brief inpatient rehab counselor, you are not likely to have another chance at paperwork, given that you see clients for a mere smattering of days. For anyone who sees clients for 3 weeks or more, it is a good idea to reproduce the financial policies, and all other important paperwork for that matter. The reason, which you have likely guessed, is because a client is usually quite cloudy at the start of treatment, most often withdrawing from at least one drug, and may be in a medication fog to help their bodies adjust to withdrawal from their drugs of abuse. Plus have you *seen* how much paperwork we throw at our clients? It would be difficult to remember any individual sheet in there, so we can't expect them to, particularly given their mental state when they meet us. Take a few minutes after a couple of weeks have passed and some brain healing has occurred and go over the documents again, to ensure the clients are aware of important policies, such as this one.

Notifying clients of financial policies is particularly important if you are in private practice for addiction counseling. It is important that clients understand how you are compensated, and what part of that compensation is their responsibility to pay. This should be in writing, called a *fee schedule*, and should not change, unless you have a small increase to all your charges in accordance with yearly inflation.

The importance of having your fee schedule in writing is to protect both you and your clients by setting a standard policy. A set fee schedule in writing also protects the profession and shows the professionalism of the clinician, which is always a goal. It is inappropriate for you to change your fee from client to client. There are some allowed exceptions, but you must establish a standard for the majority of your patients first. There are three exceptions to the standard fee. First, if you offer a sliding scale to your clients based on their ability to pay. The sliding scale is a great idea, but often difficult to carry out, as it becomes difficult to define and ascertain a person's ability to pay. If you leave it solely up to the client to determine, the majority of clients will probably lowball you, aiming for the bottom of your scale. Who wouldn't? If it is up to you, perhaps you would highball it, aiming for the top of your scale. With each sliding scale client, you may have a bit of a dance until you can both agree on a number. If you enjoy this, and are good at doing this, go right ahead. If you are uncomfortable doing this, you may want to stick to a middle-ground fee for all. It is up to you, but remember that the sliding scale, while giving more than one payment amount, is fixed in itself. Don't say you have a sliding scale to offer and then change the parameters of the scale you are offering. Pick one scale range and advertise that on your fee schedule, create the standard.

The second exception is if you offer pro bono work, which you do not need to advertise. For yourself, however, you may want to reserve one or two spots on your caseload for clients who have no insurance and no ability to pay, but desperately need your services. It is your business, and you are entitled to make that choice; you just need to be very clear in your documentation that this is a pro bono client, and notify your accountant or whomever prepares your taxes that this category exists. It can be extremely rewarding to offer pro bono for special cases. You shouldn't offer too many of these or you won't make any money and your expertise will be exploited. But it feels great to be able to say to someone, "Don't worry about paying for now, just show up for our next appointment."

The final exception to your standard of pricing is if you offer discounts to specific groups. No, I do not mean family members because you shouldn't be treating family members! If you are doubtful, go look up the principle of Client Relationships in the first section. But come right back to here. Okay, welcome back, believe me now? Be very careful about who you agree to see at your agency or in private practice. Friends of family members, or friends of friends, may be too close for comfort. The discounts to which I refer are groups of people linked by a common factor, such as veterans, or specifically veterans who have served in the recent war zones. I know colleagues who offered a discount to anyone living in New Orleans at the time of Katrina, or to those directly affected in the attacks of 9/11. It is wonderful to be able to offer discounted help to people; just document your decision and rationalize it on paper.

While setting your fee is either within your control (private practice) or given to you (agency), there are several restrictions we need to highlight.

Referrals: The clinician should not receive or give a commission based on making referrals, what is commonly referred to as a *finder's fee*. Making referrals is an integral part of our core duties as addictions counselors, so we do not get to charge an additional fee for this action, or split the fee with the clinician to whom we are referring. This is mentioned specifically because there are other businesses, such as real estate, where a finder's fee is permitted, but in our field we should not be accepting specialized fees for any action or service that is a part of what we normally do as counselors.

Gifts and gratuity: Clinicians should not accept a fee, gift, or gratuity from a client who is entitled to those services through the agency or program. In other words, you can't pay a counselor for running your group, or tip them when you have a particularly helpful session, nor should you give them a gift when the client graduates the program. Oh, I know, this gets some of you all worked up. Don't worry, we will talk about gift giving in just a moment. An exception to this rule is if an agency agrees to compensate a clinician for private work they give a client, but this arrangement must be made clear to the client. For example, an agency may compensate clinicians if they use their own vehicle to drive clients to court dates. There is likely to be a fixed fee based on the current mess of gas prices, and a rate of salary paid for travel time and court time, in addition to their regular salary. This is a written policy that applies to all clinician staff should they choose to accept the work.

Etiquette: What rules you develop for both the clients and the staff to follow in the workplace must be clear and specified in writing (Pope & Vasquez, 2007). With clients, for example, you need to clearly spell out the expectations for their behavior, delineating what is unacceptable at the workplace. Practically speaking, will you agree to be paged by your clients in the middle of the night; will you navigate the 12 steps with your clients that attend self-help; will you attend scary situations with your clients as a good support? Or are these examples of duties that are outside the parameters of addiction counseling? Would it be better to leave these roles for recovery coaches, who can help them establish helpful connections in their own communities (White, 2006)? Since 50% of discharged clients relapse, typically in the first 30 days, recovery is not really stable until 4 years, thus peer-based recovery service can give support outside of what a clinician can give (White, 2006). Because we like to be helpful and support those in need around us, it can be easy to confuse what we can do to help with what we are supposed to be doing to help. Here are some ways clinicians can confuse these roles. You also need to include a grievance policy that describes what to do, and designating with whom to report a problem should one be experienced or observed. For example, what is the appropriate etiquette when clients need you between session times? How will you handle both anticipated and unexpected clinician absences (Pope & Vasquez, 2007)? These and other etiquette concerns must be covered in your policy and procedures documents.

Recovery/relapse policy: Although the available research regarding the relapse of addiction counselors in recovery and the prevalence and contributing factors remain unknown (Doukas & Cullen, 2010), it is important to acknowledge that relapse does occur and a policy that addresses the potential is helpful for both agency and clinician. The topic of clinician relapse may be avoided because it can be embarrassing for both staff and agency (Doukas & Cullen, 2010); however, adopting a policy now that dictates the protocol can make it easier to discuss. You want to establish a policy that fairly addresses all of your employees, not only those who have identified as recovering.

Ethical compliance: The ethics committees of organizations are there for an important purpose that is vital to the life of the organization. To have a working profession, we must have a Code of Ethics, but we also must have a set of procedures to ensure adherence to the code. This is the purpose of the ethics committee, which strives to protect the client, the clinician, and the profession. It is equally interested in protecting the right of the person allegedly wronged in a claim as well as the clinician allegedly committing the wrong in the claim. For any claim to be appropriately investigated, full cooperation from all involved parties is required. A good ethics committee will be thorough and exhaustive in its search for the truth, and it serves both their investigation of the specific claim and the general profession at large. If we do not help, we may feel we are attempting to protect a colleague and friend, but in fact we are hurting the profession and are in danger of hurting ourselves because we broke our ethical code.

If an ethics committee comes knocking, you are required by your code to comply with their demands. If an ethical committee is communicating with you, there is a very specific, very *serious* reason for it, and neglecting to cooperate will not only hurt you, it will hurt the committee's ability to follow their procedures that ensure a fair process for all ethical cases. Although you typically cannot divulge confidential information about your clients, the ethics committee, when investigating a claim involving your clinical performance or the clinical treatment of a client, is entitled to know the particulars of the ethical claim. Members of an ethics committee are bound to serious confidentiality laws of their own, and the information pertaining to both a client and a clinician are kept strictly private in all ethics cases.

For example, Pete is asked by the ethics committee to divulge information regarding the conduct of his colleague Audrey. Pete loves working with Audrey and thinks she is a stellar clinician. He believes she has been falsely accused, and thinks he knows which of their colleagues has fabricated the complaint. He also knows what Audrey stands to lose if she is fired or loses her license. Pete feels it is acceptable in this situation to lie and states he does not have information on Audrey, even though he does have information the committee wants for the case. After several months of an investigation, the ethics committee is ready to drop the case for lack of evidence, when Audrey suddenly approaches them and confesses, stating the guilt over her actions was eating at her and she could no longer stand by and watch her conduct go unpunished. Although Audrey is sanctioned, the ethics committee also goes after Pete, whose lies were revealed with her confession. In fact, he receives harsher sanctions than did Audrey. Don't lie, as you will likely be in a load of trouble if discovered, and you will have to live with your unethical choices.

Personnel

An important part of workplace standards is creating a healthy group of personnel to support each other, the clients they serve, and the profession at large. While your agency or place of business is likely to have several different types of personnel, depending on the size and type of facility, the following personnel are required: (a) clinicians, (b) supervisors, and (c) supportive personnel and services, that is, EAP resources or peer assistance programs. If you set up these staff supports, the profession will be more likely to benefit.

Advocacy

Finally, whether you are in private practice or an agency setting, there should be an emphasis placed on advocacy. What are you doing to further the future of the profession? Don't worry, we will address this adequately when discussing societal obligations.

Feeling Crispy?

You have always considered yourself a hard worker. Although it seems nothing has come easy to you, you have fought hard to reach the healthy goals that were first set for you, and then those you set for yourself as an adult. Some people would say you beat the odds when looking at the lack of accomplishment in your family of origin. Although you would agree that none in your family achieved an impressive status in business or family, and that many family members are poorly educated, financially bankrupt, and in some cases, heavy in a life of crime, you also know you received significant life education from your family that was of great value to you. You felt love and acceptance, and were given encouragement to develop an inner drive to grow. Some may judge your background harshly, but you believe it helped you to develop into the person you have become. Part of the pride you hold in association with your career is the knowledge that you persevered against great odds, and weathered significant challenges in order to achieve your current employment.

You have established yourself as a hard worker and a team player. You started as an intern at an outpatient facility, and have worked your way through the system until you achieved the position of senior counselor. You have your sights set on becoming a supervisor, and are close to achieving that goal. You have worked through the ranks quickly because there is no task you will drop, no opportunity you will decline. This makes you ambitious, but it also makes you exhausted and overworked, with no one to blame but yourself. At first your superiors advise you to slow down and refrain from overloading your schedule. When that has no effect, they continue to ask you for more involvement figuring you will speak up when you have enough on your plate. But you never speak up; you simply do more. When you begin to feel symptoms of burnout, you ignore them and explain them away based on whatever current project you have cooking.

Soon your burnout symptoms worsen to include headaches, and you begin struggling to remember mundane details, especially when put on the spot. The little sleep you do get is plagued with dreams that you are late or unprepared for some function. When in supervision, you are asked what you are doing to prevent Clinician Burnout and you list some activities that you are not actually doing, but things you know will keep your supervisor at bay. On one particular day, the stress bubbles over and you yell at a colleague. Your colleague, who knows you well, yells back at you, questioning your ability to do your job. You reply that you have pressures he knows nothing about, and that you have dealt with much worse in your life. After a few minutes of silence, in which you both calm down, your friend gently suggests to you that your pride is clouding your need for help. That asking for help and doing less does not dishonor your family and your goals for making a better life for yourself. You realize that in order to be proud of yourself, you need to care for yourself. And that is the beginning.

My Hero

Here is another example highlighting how we want personnel to work together. A supervisee named Alan comes to you at your appointed hour of supervision. He talks to you about his list of clients and as usual you are impressed with his ability to show compassion and creativity in his approach to treating them. But when he begins to speak of his new client, you feel a tug of something faintly wrong. He uses a slightly stronger tone when describing her history and takes a longer amount of supervision than he customarily does with new clients.

As your supervision sessions continue over the next several weeks, it becomes more apparent to you that something else is at play here. Alan becomes notably more emotional when talking about this client than his others. He seems to take on her issues as if they are his own, and he appears firm in his belief that he can "rescue" her from her problems. You begin to suspect that there is some countertransference occurring in this relationship. To help Alan see this countertransference, you decide to probe him for information that may explain the link he feels to this client.

Over the next few sessions, you learn a lot about your supervisee and begin to see a pattern that links him to this client. It appears clear to you that this client reminds him of one of his family members who died a drug-related (and preventable) death early in Alan's life. Alan was too young to help this family member, but you suspect that the experience has driven him to take on this career. You see this as a potential ongoing barrier to his treating clients, and decide to talk with him about your impressions. At first Alan adamantly denies any connection between this client and his family member, but as you point out the details within the connection, his defenses begin to break down. Before you know it, Alan is crying and admitting to the pain surrounding his family member's death. This leads to emotions surrounding other family members and their failure to help the family member in trouble. You have now opened his Pandora's Box, and because you do not have enough time in your supervision hour to adequately discuss all of these surfacing issues for Alan, you suggest that he meets you in your private practice hours outside of the agency. Alan seems grateful at the offer and immediately sets up a weekly appointment with you.

Is there a breach of ethics here? Where? How should the situation have been handled differently?

What is the difference between a client and a supervisee? What should the supervisor do now? Think it over, jot down some responses, I'll wait. Okay, what did you come up with? There is a breach of ethics here, which occurred when you offered to see the client in your private practice. Until then, you traveled a thin line between supervision and therapy, yet could adequately show that your exploration of his transference was necessary to understanding and preventing barriers in his clinical work. But once Alan showed the emotional depth of this personal issue, it became more of a therapeutic concern than a supervisory one. You will not be able to get Alan to a place of providing good clinical care to this client without addressing these emotional issues from his past, and that is a task better suited for therapy. You can continue to work with him on how to work with this client, or, if he is unable to, how to refer the client to another practitioner. You will also clearly need to ensure that he has a therapist and is willing to work on these issues that are clearly vital to his ongoing personal and professional health. If he does not have one, you must help him find a clinician, or direct him to the EAP if you have one, and check back to make sure his needs are met.

It is important to note that the better your workplace is designed to reflect the ethical practice within, the better your ability to protect the community. Building a healthy set of workplace standards is crucial to protecting the community, as is nourishing professional relationships.

Principle: Professional Rapport

17
Chapter

This principle highlights the other important type of relationship in a clinician's practice: those involving other clinicians. High-quality relationships are filled with respect, courtesy, and fairness, and have been linked to lowering Clinician Burnout risk (Fernet, Gagné, & Austin, 2010). This can be wonderfully easy with some colleagues and terribly difficult with others. You do not need to agree with all of your colleagues' opinions or actions, but you do need to respect your fellow clinicians as members of your field or profession. There may be exceptions during your career, but you need to make this the rule of your professional conduct. Remember that your actions, including how you treat your colleagues, are reflected back on the profession as a whole.

Who are the colleagues and professionals who make up our community? You have the community within your agency, which is made up of all staff, both administrative and clinical. You may have students, interns, volunteers, and paraprofessionals that share your workplace, in addition to the variety of different staff. You will have supervisors, directors, and other executives to whom you must answer. Perhaps your agency is part of a broader company, with its own level of colleagues. For example, you may work in a residential setting, in which the house that is your workplace is part of a larger system of connected houses. All of these potential personnel coexist and must be included in your thoughts on professional rapport, even if they are members of a different profession, or if they are not part of a profession. Your ethical responsibility is to all in your workplace.

In addition, you will also have relationships with the clinicians in various helping professions that work in your geographical community, professionals who may work with you on specific cases and with whom you refer cases reciprocally. There are also members of different professions with whom you will collaborate during your work, such as the legal system (judges, attorneys, probation officers, police officers), the social service system (caseworkers, investigators, group home staff), the health care system (doctors, nurses, therapists, technicians), the managed care system (caseworkers, adjusters, attorneys, investigators), and the vocational system (employers, supervisors, teachers). These providers will be involved with the transfer of care, referring in or out, and the ongoing coordination of care. Finally, you will also collaborate with a client's support system (family, friends, sponsors, teachers).

Whew! There is a whole lot of communicating and collaborating in our work, hence the importance of maintaining ethics that protect the community. For each of these entities with which we work, we must satisfy our ethical pillars and ensure appropriate relationships. Specifically, we must work to establish a bond, and to develop healthy boundaries. We must avoid harmful dual relationships and refrain from poaching clients or exploiting members of the community. We want to be consistent in these actions in order to develop a professional rapport that is built on integrity.

Bond

An important part of a professional identity is your professional demeanor (Corey, Corey, & Callanan, 2007; Pope & Vasquez, 2007). How you interact with others in the community reflects your professional values. Are you kind and helpful, warm and fun, serious and considerate, reliable and honorable? Certainly we all have unique personalities and there will be ample opportunities to let them shine, but it is important that you develop a standard demeanor that is consistent in your work. Imagine someone you work with who has these qualities. Is he or she easy to work with? Do you look forward to interacting with him or her? Do you trust that you will have a positive collaboration with him or her? This is what you are striving for in your interprofessional relationships. Similarly, imagine someone who does not possess these qualities. Is he or she easy to work with? Do you look forward to interacting with him or her? Do you trust that you will have a positive collaboration with him or her? This is what you want to avoid to the best of your ability. You won't always succeed, there will be moments when your demeanor is less than stellar, but remember we are establishing a rule to your practice.

If you recall the examples of Leroy and Declan from Part Three, you will see in both cases the power of bonding with your co-workers. Leroy and Declan may have differed in their degree of integrating their personal life with their professional setting, but they both were successful at bonding with the people they worked with at their respective agencies. What we do is tough work, draining and challenging, and it eases the difficulty to have meaningful relationships with other professionals. It may help prevent Clinician Burnout, because support has been shown to be a significant factor (Leykin, Cucciare, & Weingardt, 2011; Lim, Kim, Kim, Yang, & Lee, 2010).

Respect: Addiction clinicians must respect each other, even if we are not always afforded the same respect as other disciplines. You want to treat people as you want to be treated. This is something that we learn in other places—kindergarten, for example—and would seem an obvious custom, yet there are barriers that may cause us to forget the simple maxim.

It may be difficult to treat supervisors and other advisors with respect, even though it is ethical to do so (Powell & Brodsky, 2004). Those who have power over us, in that they are evaluating our work and have the ability to sanction, demote, suspend, or fire us, should be worthy of our respect by position alone. But some inappropriately exercise this power, as we learned in the last section. How do you show respect for a supervisor with whom you disagree, or whose guidance you question? Perhaps it is someone who you believe to be acting unethically, or someone you think has inferior standards or is confusing his or her roles. How can these people be respected?

These situations present challenges to our professional rapport building, but we must persevere. Establishing respect may be easier with people similarly minded to us or with whom we are in accordance, but it is no less important to establish with people with whom we struggle. If you can acknowledge that you are on a professional journey, that you have strengths and differences in both your personal and professional worlds, that you are continually learning and growing into an improved model of yourself, then you have what you need to give respect to your community regardless of an individual's behavior. Why? Because if you can see that you are on a journey of growth, then you can acknowledge that on a given point of that journey you were not as developed as you are now, you were an inferior copy, missing some essential lesson, experience, or time to practice that made you into the superior version you are today. And a few years into the future, you will be an even greater version than who you are today.

That is the growth we expect in our profession, thus the same principle is true of the other people with whom we work. The people you encounter at the workplace are on their own journey, some in the beginning, some at the end, and some at all points in between. Wherever they are, they are hopefully growing. You may not be likely to see the growth unless you have known them professionally for a considerable time and have been in the position to observe their growth. Therefore, you may need a bit of professional faith to believe that the people around you are on growth journeys. If you can believe this, you can acknowledge that the behavior they exhibit today may not be the most superior behavior possible, but it may be appropriate to where they are on their journey. You will still be frustrated or worried by their behavior, but if you can see that they are on a learning trajectory, it is easier to respect the individual regardless of their behavior. You may still want to take steps to protect yourself, the clients, and the profession against their behavior, but you can do so while respecting the individual.

If you are in a position of power, or higher on an established hierarchy, it is imperative that you afford decent respect to those professionals in positions below yours. Undermining staff, adopting a condescending attitude, and applying inappropriate pressure are all examples of poor rapport building

and unethical treatment of your colleagues, staff, or students. Whether you are in a position of power, such as a senior counselor, or a position directly responsible for the growth of the individual, such as a supervisor, you must ensure that you treat each individual with courtesy.

Recovery status: As we have mentioned, many clinicians treating addiction were also once clients themselves struggling with their own addictions. It is not that there are more addicts in our field than in other fields, as addicts are, sadly, everywhere, but unlike other helping professions, the recovery status of clinicians is openly discussed. It may be the only profession where the researchers feel a need to self-disclose in their journal articles (Doukas & Cullen, 2010). Clinicians share their status with other clinicians, which can form the idea that being in recovery is related to being a member of the field. Clinicians may then reveal their recovery status to clients, which can instill in them the idea that a good clinician is also in recovery. This is not a true fact, as we have discussed, but it is often the general belief. Purposely or without intention or realization, we can discriminate against clinicians who are and are not in recovery.

On the one hand, our field seems to accept and even encourage a counselor's recovery status as something to spout to others, almost as if it is a membership requirement to a special club of skilled clinicians. So what of the clinicians who are not in recovery? Are they denied entrance into the club? Are they seen as less qualified members of our field? Are they believed to be less skilled than other clinicians in recovery? You may think, "Gosh, of course not." But have you asked the clinicians who are not in recovery to describe their experiences?

Clinicians who are not in recovery may be uncomfortable and there is no platform to safely discuss their concerns. Contrastingly, if you are a counselor in recovery, you are encouraged to be open about yourself simply by hearing others in your field constantly disclosing their status. Like the example at one state's annual conference, where a clinician exclaimed, "Oooo, I love coming to this conference. There is nothing like sitting in a room with a bunch of people in recovery trying to help others." This is a good description of a self-help meeting, but should not be the description of a conference for addiction counselors.

On the other side of things, clinicians in recovery may experience stigma and discrimination (Doukas & Cullen, 2010, 2011). For example, we can do this in a simple way, in our employee paperwork. Many places of employment will stipulate that if you are in recovery, you must spend a certain amount of time, typically a minimum of 2 years, in recovery before you can work there, and if you relapse there is often a set of procedures with which you must comply that could involve either suspension or termination. This makes sense if you consider that you don't want an addict actively using while being employed at your company. Yet what about those who are not in recovery, who may also use alcohol and other drugs either infrequently or with some regularity? Is it acceptable for a clinician who is not in recovery to go on a social bender Sunday night, showing up late and hung over at work the following day? There is likely no suspension or termination for these employees, no discussion of what treatment the clinician needs (unless this is a repeat offense, in which case I would hope there would be some discussion about what help the clinician may need).

The only way to prevent discrimination is to adopt a policy that can be applied universally to all employees, as it is unethical to highlight one group and create a policy just for them. Adopt a policy that states that all staff, regardless of recovery status, must show no patterns of substance abuse or dependence for a minimum of 2 years prior to hire. No staff may attend work in an impaired state due to substance abuse, and if any staff member is found in that state, the following procedure will take place...and then name your procedure if a clinician is in trouble. This is the way to treat all of your staff as the equal members they are.

Cooperation: It is the reality of your job that you must work together with various staff. You have a choice in how cooperative you will be when working with others. You can be difficult, act as a barrier to other's accomplishments; you can try to push people aside, take credit for their work; you can be argumentative and contrary, or uncooperative in other ways. In your career, you are likely to meet uncooperative co-workers and may be intimately aware of how frustrating and harmful they can be. You don't want to be described this way; it is harmful to your co-workers, to you, and to the profession. Instead, you want to adopt a collegial attitude and cooperate with everyone involved in clinical cases and other professionals at your place of business. For example, you must cooperate with the Ethics Committee should they come inquiring about you or what you have observed.

Boundaries and Dual Relationships

We discussed boundaries between counselor and client in Part One. Similarly, setting boundaries with colleagues is a vital but often challenging aspect of a professional practice, as it requires both the boundary setter and the boundary receiver to agree, acknowledge, and maintain the boundary. This process can be exhausting, as some professionals, like clients, will continue to challenge the boundary setter.

Boundaries must be fair, clear, and reasonable. Fair boundaries take into account the needs of both (or more) parties that are affected by the boundary and strive to fulfill the desires of all. If all desires cannot be filled, a fair boundary will explain why and will attempt to give the best balance between involved parties. Admitting new clients from the waiting list in order, and not allowing potential clients to skip over others on the waiting list, is a good example of a fair boundary. Accepting gifts from some clients but not others is an example of an unfair boundary. Clear boundaries are described well, orally and in writing, without confusing rules or variables. "The alcoholism and drug abuse counselor should not engage in any type of sexual activity with a client" is a good example of a clear boundary. Reasonable boundaries are sensible and realistic given the type of relationship involved. Dual relationships often occur between two professionals, including supervisees, trainees, interns, and students. The same principles that guide the counseling relationship guide the supervisory relationship (Reamer, 2012).

Poaching: You must respect the rights of other clinicians to have access to the work that is ethically theirs. It is not ethically cool to manipulate your way into stealing clients or opportunities that belong to other clinicians. For example, if you work at both an agency and your own private practice, it is unethical to tell your agency clients that their needs would be better served by your private practice. For another example, Carla is both an individual and group counselor. In staff meeting, she listens to Fatima discuss the case of her client, Seb. Carla thinks she can do a better job of meeting Seb's clinical needs. Seb is in her group, so Carla already has a rapport with him, thus in the next group session she approaches him and suggests that they work together individually, outlining the treatment goals she would recommend. This is called poaching, and it is unethical.

You are also not allowed to duplicate services without notifying both the client and the other professional of your plan. Whichever professional engaged in therapy with a client first has right of therapy, and he or she will have to agree to terminate with the client in order for you to see the client professionally. When you can clearly articulate why your services are different, and therefore not a duplication of the services of the other professional, and the client and both clinicians agree to the treatment plan, you can proceed without ethical violation.

For example, Constance likes both Ted and Raul as clinicians. She wants to see both, figuring the more counseling the better the outcome for her. She interviews them both at the same time and finds that while they have some similarity in their approaches, they have significant differences that interest her and make her feel the duplication of services won't be too bad. For some time, she doesn't tell the clinicians of the existence of the other, but in the fourth session with Ted, she accidentally mentions Raul. Ted catches the comment, and probes for its meaning. When he discovers that Raul is also on the case, and saw Constance for the first session 3 days before his first session, he tells Constance that she should sign a release for him to speak with Raul. He speaks with Raul, and they agree that one therapist is best. Ted tells Constance that she has to choose a therapist, and that if she cannot choose between them she should stick with Raul, as the case was his first. Constance pleads with him, giving him evidence to support her desire to keep herself on both caseloads. But Ted is not to be swayed, stating that the only action he feels comfortable with is to bow out now. This is a good example of how a clinician's personal feelings can dictate what action he or she takes. Other clinicians may have been willing to work with the client, but Ted suspects he will never feel good about it, and the best course is to exit.

Exploitation: This puts a complex mandate into a simple sentence: You can't exploit relationships with any other professionals, including those at a higher level, an equal level, or a lower level than you, such as supervisees, students, research participants, or volunteers. This is a particular risk with those under your level of employment, namely supervisees, employees, students, research participants, or volunteers, but it can occur with anyone. You surely would not want to be exploited; therefore if you are treating everyone like you would want to be treated you will avoid mistreating all of your colleagues. It is not ethical to be disrespectful or unreasonably demanding to colleagues, especially interns, volunteers, supervisees, or students.

For example, Joseph works with five interns and loves helping them along their career. But he also finds it helpful to distribute some of his workload onto the interns. They get experience and he gets the work done; everyone wins. Most of his interns don't mind the work, as it gives them good experience. However, on one occasion the clinical director takes notice of the work they are doing, and comes to congratulate Joseph. Joseph shakes the director's hand in front of his interns and graciously accepts the congratulations, making no mention of the interns standing there, who did most of the work that pleased the director. The interns feel exploited and jaded about the profession, the opposite of how we want the future of our profession to feel. We must be good to each other and take care of those working for us.

Evaluating Others

You must prevent the counseling practice of unqualified or unauthorized persons. What? How are you supposed to do that; you're not the police! I realize this may sound like an inappropriate or impossible request from your Code, but we do not have elected or hired personnel whose purpose is to scan the field and root out the unqualified or unauthorized. The profession has no way of knowing impersonators unless they are reported. It is up to every member of the profession to do their part to pay attention to people who may not belong. There are two ways you can do this, depending on what role you have in the agency.

If you are a supervisor or a director, you have more power to say who works for you, and to complete a thorough check of employees' qualifications. It is your ethical obligation to thoroughly investigate all incoming employees. Do not accept an application as fact without discussing each element of the application with the applicant and checking every reference and resource that is provided (and you should be requiring a minimum of three). If the applicant is claiming to be credentialed or licensed, check with the credentialing board to be sure he or she is credentialed in good standing. And do not hire the applicant if he or she is not! If you are a staff member without authority, you don't have access to employee records, but you do have access to your ears and eyes. If someone is claiming to have

experience you know does not exist, do not ignore that information. Your silence hurts the profession.

The second way to prevent the practice of unauthorized persons is to be mindful of a person's qualifications before you set them to task. If you are a supervisor or director, you need to be sure an employee is ready (i.e., trained, oriented) before throwing them into a task, and you need to make sure that task is within the guidelines of the scope of practice. "Of course!" you may exclaim, but this error occurs in our field every day. Supervisors and directors often use their observations of an employee's performance as the basis of choosing him or her for a task, rather than examining his or her qualifications to ensure he or she is best trained for the task. Frankly, many supervisors and directors choose whomever is available to complete a task, and do not take into account whether he or she is professionally appropriate on paper or by observation. How many of you, for example, have been thrown into a role without consideration of your background or training, and without orientation for the job?

This is also important for those of us who are not supervisors or directors, but who have the authority to ask someone to help in a task. If you are asking clinicians to fill in for you, or work with you on a task, you must know their qualifications to ensure that you are not suggesting that they work outside of their Scope of Practice, which may be different than yours. Consider the example of clinician Amir, who asked a colleague, Penny, to run his group for which she was inadequately competent? We may deduce that it was Penny's ethical responsibility to tell Amir she was not competent to take his place. Here, let's examine this scenario to determine if others had an obligation.

The problem with this scenario is that Amir doesn't know whether Penny is qualified to run the group. He knows she is a good clinician, based on his observations, but that is not enough information, ethically speaking. What is her background in trauma? If she doesn't have one, and only has an addictions credential, then this group is outside of her Scope of Practice, even if she would do a good job with the group. Ethically, he can't use her. In fact, if he has specialized qualifications, he may not be able to use anyone else in the agency to cover for him. This is an important aspect to factor in when designing a group. You must ensure there is someone else, even if he or she is at the supervisor or director level, who can cover your group when you are absent. Or the group must be cancelled for the time you are away, which most agencies cannot afford to do. If there is no one capable of doing this, the group is not a good fit with the agency, or vice versa.

It may seem too stringent to suggest that you ensure the appropriate background for every clinician that could work with you, but it is an important aspect of protecting our profession. Consider how much training you endured to obtain the qualifications you have. You wouldn't want to hear that other clinicians with fewer qualifications were allowed to do the same job. Remember that it may seem like no big deal to pass someone like Penny into the job for a mere 5 days, but there are many people like Amir and Penny out there, and if everyone is making these small allowances, it quickly affects all of us as a group. Little choices have a big, often invisible, impact.

This principle demands that you will report violations to the appropriate authorities when you encounter the violation. Many are uncomfortable with this idea, feeling it is uncool to snitch on colleagues or others both above and below one's staff positioning. But what good is it to do nothing? Not only are you hurting the profession by staying mute, you are potentially hurting any clients affected by the ethical infraction, and you are hurting the unethical clinician by not getting him or her the help he or she needs to return to an ethical path. Selfishly, it might feel like you are better served by keeping quiet, but in the long run you may feel worse for not doing your part in protecting all parties, including the profession.

As an ethical member of this profession, you want to always keep your ears and eyes open to the professional climate around you. Pay attention to the people you work with, not in a stalker way, but in an interested-for-the-profession way, meaning that you should listen to conversations you have with colleagues and clients, and attend to observations you make about the people around you. If you see behavior that is questionable or suspicious, there are several things you can do. First, keep an eye on what you observe; gathering all possible details to report. Hear me: You are not in a position of authority; you are not a police officer or a private eye. You do not want to make it your life's mission to try to catch people making ethical errors. You won't make any friends that way, and you will likely lose your job. You are not the ethics police, and in some situations you could put yourself in danger. Your job is to report concerning behavior you witness, or that which is reported to you, to a supervisor or an ethics board, who will then conduct a thorough investigation.

Second, in all cases, you want to go to the people who committed the questionable ethical behavior and ask them about it *when it is safe and appropriate to do so.* It will not be in all cases, to be sure, but if you have a good rapport with the alleged ethics violators, and certainly if you have any authority over their position, you want to talk to these people first. They may not be aware they have committed a violation, because by now I hope I have proved to you, reader, that we all commit ethics violations, often without being aware. They may have an alternative explanation for what you observed, especially given that many ethical situations are not black or white, and are subject to interpretation. The clinicians may have background information that you did not observe that can help to justify their actions. Finally, they may be willing to address whatever the infraction was on their own, rather than you reporting them. It is better for the clinicians to approach their supervisor and ask for help in the area of the infraction than it is for you to report them, assuming they tell the complete truth to the supervisor and that the supervisor is willing and able to correct the behavior with the clinicians so that it is not repeated.

To ensure they do, you may want to either go with them or speak with a supervisor yourself, telling the clinicians that you will do so, depending on the situation and your rapport with the clinicians.

If you cannot go to the clinician, or if you do and no changes occur, especially if you observe the ethically shoddy behavior again, what do you do? The next person in the chain of command is a supervisor, if you have not yet approached one. The design of a supervisor is to be the person that you can approach with clinical issues, including those you observe. This requires that you have a good supervisor, which is a major assumption, as many of us do not. You may choose not to approach supervisors if (a) you do not have a trusting, supportive relationship with them, (b) you do not trust that they will be able to keep your words confidential, (c) you do not trust that they will behave rationally and professionally in this case, or (d) they are involved in the faulty behavior you witnessed.

In these cases, you will want to go to another supervisor on staff, or a clinical director. Be careful here, though; only go to a clinical director if you feel you truly cannot approach a supervisor, and be prepared to explain why you approached the director instead. You don't want to overstep agency rank unless you feel you must. Many clinicians approach a clinical director simply because they have a better rapport with him or her, and enjoy consulting with him or her more than with the supervisor, but it is most likely in violation of the agency procedure to do so. Some agencies have an open culture, where speaking with other ranks is not discouraged. If you work in one of these places, you have the benefit of speaking with whomever you feel most comfortable. If, however, you work in a place that takes its staff hierarchy seriously, you want to make sure you follow the grievance procedure it has set in place, unless you feel unsafe doing so.

In addition to your agency personnel, there are other noted professionals with whom you may wish to speak. If you have a personal therapist, or a trusted professional friend outside of your agency, or a mentor from your past experiences, you may want to talk through the ethical dilemma with them. You may also opt to consult with an ethics consultant before speaking with anyone connected to the case. Just be sure to omit or change any identifying characteristics when speaking about the case. In fact, read Part Two before attempting to present a case to anyone, as there are many common pitfalls committed by the most well-intentioned clinicians that should be avoided.

Ultimately, the decision of what to do will be yours. Supervisors or directors can advise you on what the agency wishes and what they believe is appropriate to that specific setting. A therapist, colleague, or mentor can advise you on what is best for you knowing you as they do, and can give you a bit more of an objective take on your situation. But ultimately you must live with the decisions you make. Thus, even if an agency tells you that you are not required to make a formal accusation with an ethics board, you may feel you need to follow through with it.

In addition to the alleged violator, the supervisor, director, therapist, colleague, and mentor, you also have an ethics board/committee in your corner. The accessibility and proficiency of the ethics board, unfortunately, varies by state. Some states have an ethics board/committee on paper, but for all important purposes, it is inactive. Other states have active boards, but they are poor in their execution of investigating claims. Still other states offer strong ethics boards with a clear set of procedures that dictate how claims are investigated and how individuals are sanctioned if necessary. Most states do not give clear, accessible information for their members about the ethics board, even if they have a decent working board. If you live in a state that does not give information easily, or certainly if the board is inactive or subpar, I urge you to make a formal complaint with your membership or credentialing agency. As noted in the introduction, our profession is in peril if we do not streamline both our ethical code and our complaint procedures across state lines. The only way we can do this is if we use our collective voice to tell the people in charge that we want the change. Our collective voice comes from all the individual voices that make up our national profession … that means yours!

An ethics board/committee should have a written guide on policy and procedures that is part of the bylaws of the organization. This set of procedures should be clearly and exhaustively written, edited, and published for all members to read if they so desire, and revisited at regular intervals. The procedures of the ethics board exist to protect both the clinician who is making the accusation, and the clinician who is accused, as well as any clientele involved and the larger profession. That is a tall order! Thus, the procedures need to be written with all of those entities in mind. The procedures need to clearly state that a clinician is not deemed guilty until a thorough investigation can take place, especially considering that false accusations are a strong possibility, either through misunderstanding or an ulterior motive. The procedures should clearly state how the board handles each complaint that comes to them, which should be identical regardless of the complaint or who made it, and how often the board/committee meets. The board should outline the different types of sanctions, of which there are many, ranked by severity. Sanctions can range from a warning to a loss of credential or license or a report to police or other agencies with higher authority. Sanctions must be clearly set with timelines, follow-up procedures, and consequences of failure to meet sanctions included in the report to the clinician.

There also must be a written standardized appeal process in place. Clinicians must be granted an appeals process that they may choose to accept or waive. Within this appeals process, it is imperative that those who hear the appeal are not the same people involved in creating the sanction, meaning the executive board of the state organization must identify appropriate members outside of the ethics board/committee who can hear the appeal fairly. As you can see, it is a complex process that needs to be thoroughly defined in order for it to be a successful process.

You must be mindful of what you are putting out there and ensure it is of the utmost professional and ethical quality. This is *especially* true if you are teaching ethics. If you are in the audience, and a trainer makes an unethical remark or shows unethical behavior, it is your duty to report this, at least in the evaluation form that the trainers can read. Let's look at a vignette to see how this principle comes to light in the clinical setting.

VIGNETTE: OBSERVING AN AMBUSH

Bert is a counselor at an inpatient program. A male client, Hal, enters the program and is assigned to him. Bert is warned by staff that "this one is going to be tough—a real attitude he's got." From the start of Hal's treatment, Bert starts to notice that the staff is quick to complain about his behavior and seems to be more passionate about correcting his rule breaking than they are with other clients. When a conflict arises between Hal and another client, the staff is quick to blame Hal and take the word of the other client as truth. They do not seem to see potential in him, only flaws. The longer Hal stays, the harder it seems they are trying to get him out. Bert has noted that all the involved staff are White and Hal is African American. Hal is loud, argumentative, a clear instigator at times, and stubborn as hell, but does this mean he should be treated that way? He also shows kindness, the will to get well, humor, and hope. When Bert is on a 3-day vacation, he returns to find Hal

(continued)

has been discharged for rule breaking. He suspects unethical behavior on the part of his colleagues. What should he do?

Wait, this vignette is hard! Ugh, okay, what do we do here? Let's make it easier on Bert and imagine that there is some supervisor, clinical director, or other authoritative person who was not involved in discharging the client, and to whom it is appropriate for him to turn. That would be lovely, as he can bring up his concerns to that official and leave it to him or her to assess the appropriate action. Case solved, next!

But wait, what if he doesn't have such a handy official waiting to hear his plea and take the mess off his hands? What if superior figures in his agency were involved with discharging the client, then what does he do? He could do nothing, but this would not make him a very responsible clinician. He has an obligation to report the unethical behavior of his colleagues if he observes it, so he can't really get away with just letting it pass. The bravest action he could take would be to approach staff members involved and discuss with them why they chose to discharge the client and gently wonder with them whether there was any unintentional discrimination at play. That works when you have a good enough rapport with your colleagues to explore these issues, especially colleagues who are comfortable exploring their own clinical decisions with a critical eye (that should be you now, reader!). If you have that kind of work environment, do a little dance around the room right now because that is phenomenal, and probably rare. You should also never ever leave your job! But let's say poor Bert is not blessed with such a collaborative and nondefensive environment; what should he do?

The first thing Bert can do is ask himself if there is anything he can do for the client. If there is a chance of revoking the discharge and keeping Hal on as a client, then Bert will want to try to do that. The best way to do that is to go to the highest person in charge and make his grievance. However, if Bert doesn't believe he can help the client, he can still do his part in helping the agency and the staff within. He can go to the same authority figure to make his grievance, and suggest they use the experience as a learning tool to prevent it from happening again. If Bert is correct that discrimination was at play, the staff are in danger of repeating the unethical behavior unless they receive training and supervision to prevent it. If the agency is unwilling to even entertain his grievance, or if they decide to do nothing about the case, Bert can go to his ethics board and run the issue by them. They supposedly are trained to investigate claims, and should tell Bert if he has something reportable or not. Bert definitely does not want to make any decision alone. He should confidently discuss the case with his trusted advisors and his therapist, if he has one. He can also check with an external supervisor, a mentor, teacher, colleague, friend, or family. They all have different gifts, and talking out his thoughts, feelings, and plan of action before making a move may be helpful. It can help immensely to gain a healthy perspective.

VIGNETTE: FUDGING
THE NUMBERS

Lorraine is a program director who has just hired Toby, a clinician who has been working in the field for 15 years. Toby has all the qualifications she is seeking, including stellar references and the required training hours and employment history. Just after his hire, Lorraine is filing away his employee paperwork, when something on the paper catches her eye. She looks closer and notices that some ink has been rubbed out and replaced. It looks like one answer was exchanged for another answer. Suspicious, she calls the previous supervisor on record in his application and inquires about the number of hours he completed under her care. The supervisor checks her records and gives Lorraine a smaller number of hours than those reported on Toby's application. It appears that Toby has falsified the number of previous hours required in order to get the job. What should Lorraine do? Think about it and jot down an answer; I'll wait.

Lorraine suspects that Toby has falsified his information, so a good place to start is with Toby. She needs to confront him with what she has learned and ask him to account for the change in hours. Yes, she can approach her boss or the ethics board of the organization of which Toby is a member. Those would be appropriate; it would not be unethical to approach either. However, the best idea may be to approach Toby first. There are several reasons why this is her best course of action. First, Toby deserves a chance to speak about what occurred before anyone else is brought into the conversation. Lorraine, as his supervisor, should give him the right to do so. Second, it is always best in any grievance procedure to go to the source first. In addition to the respect it affords the subject, it is also smart for you because it will give you more information that you will use if and when you have to bring in another party (e.g., director or ethics board). Those entities will likely ask you about Toby's response to the accusation, so it is best to get Toby's response first. Third, Toby may give Lorraine a reasonable explanation that closes the case before she needs to bring in other people, making it the most efficient choice.

There may be cases where it is unsafe or inappropriate to approach the subject, especially alone. Lorraine may opt to bring in another supervisor or director, and they may approach Toby together. She will want to avoid making Toby feel "ganged up" on, but it is smart to have another set of ears listening to the conversation. It avoids the he-said, she-said condition that comes from one-on-one conversations and protects all participants. She will want both responses verifiable either through another set of ears, an audiotape, or in writing that both parties sign. It will protect both Lorraine and Toby.

So Lorraine approaches Toby with the supervisor, and he gives an excuse, but Lorraine feels it does not merit his actions and tells him so. He quietly agrees, but then begs her not to report his actions to the credentialing board. Surely you are

(continued)

smart enough to guess what the recommended response is, but let's consider why. In this example, Lorraine does not know Toby well as he was just hired, so it may be easier to report him to the board, as she is ethically required to do. But what if we make this scenario more complicated, and say that Toby is someone Lorraine has worked with for 20 years, that he was one of the first people she ever supervised and she has watched him grow from a talented intern to a skilled clinician. Learning of his unethical behavior is likely to have an additional impact on Lorraine, as she may feel a sense of betrayal because of the time, work, and emotional support she has given him over the years. The close bond she feels with Toby could easily lead her to agonize over what to do. On the one hand, she has someone she knows well, someone she knows is a good clinician, one that effectively treats hundreds of clients a year, and one that she feels confident will continue to grow. This is not someone who she wants to get in trouble, and this is definitely someone she feels should not lose their license or credential, especially by her hand. On the other hand, he clearly committed an unethical act, and she is not in the business of condoning unethical behavior from anyone. Lorraine believes in her ethical code, and expects others—especially those she has mentored—to abide by its guidelines.

Let's discuss one more reason why Lorraine should make the report, one that hopefully you, reader, will identify as the most important. While she can certainly agonize when looking at Toby individually, what happens if she looks beyond Toby and thinks of the profession as a whole? Her actions affect everyone, the profession itself, so if she does not act and report Toby, it becomes a hit to the profession. Sure, her actions may seem small in the large scheme of things, but if everyone felt that way, what kind of profession would we have? Where would our ethics stand; who would uphold our Code of Ethics? No, our profession cannot afford to have members looking only at individuals, rather than the bigger picture. Making this report may hurt Toby, which may in turn cause Lorraine pain, but it is critical to remember that by making this report she will also be protecting the profession.

VIGNETTE: CHATTY CATHY

Elias does not yet have a release to speak to the agency that referred a client, but his most trusted colleague, Maria, works at that agency, and knows the case well. When out for dinner, she says to him:

> Oh yes, by the way, that certain person that was referred to your agency today...you know the one I mean? Well, I want you to know that she is very slick, and will tell you that she is only using alcohol, but really she is using all sorts of drugs. I know drug tests are not routine in your program, but if you order a drug test, you will see what I'm talking about. Oh man, the stories I could tell you about the things she made up. This one time she said she had

dated the high school prom king, but I came to find out she didn't date anyone until college. So, what do you have planned for her?

What are the ethical problems with this, and how should Elias answer her question? How many ethical problems did you find? First, Elias does not have a release to speak with this agency, so he cannot even acknowledge that he knows the client, let alone discuss her past or current treatment. As we discussed earlier, even though he may suspect that this person has relevant information that will be helpful to his treatment planning, he cannot listen to what she has to say without a signed release from the client. Second, what is she doing discussing a case during dinner? That is not an appropriate setting to be discussing confidential work information under any circumstance. Work-related issues need to be discussed at work. If he is one of the many clinicians who is social with colleagues either within his agency or within his field, Elias must work harder to separate his social life from his work life. He can't blur the two by discussing personal issues at work and work issues on personal time.

Third, the information that Maria is divulging sounds more like gossip than true clinical concern. It may be appropriate to mention that the client had lied in the past about drug use, but it is the language Maria is using, calling the client "slick" instead of reporting that the client lied in the past. The part about lying concerning her dating life is more gossip that has no place in a referral discussion, unless you are using it as an example of her general tendency to lie. Again, if that is the case her language should show her comments as clinical nuggets, not gossip. A good rule of thumb is to consider whether people who are overhearing your conversation would be able to detect whether you were talking about business or pleasure. If they can't tell the difference, then you are blurring the two. Someone overhearing you should be able to hear from your tone and language that you are talking about business … you hope someone is not overhearing you, as that would be a major breach of confidentiality!

Finally, it is not appropriate for the referral agency employees to ask what Elias has planned for the person. Their job is to give him pertinent information about her treatment at their facility, and then perhaps wish a merry good luck or convey a similar sentiment. But good consent-to-release forms for a referral are written in one direction, meaning that you can obtain information from the referral but not give information to the referral. They are usually written in a bidirectional format for identifying information, meaning that you can call the referral and state that you know the client and give enough identifying information for the referral agency to find the record and release it to you. But aside from identifying information, all clinical information, including treatment planning, should not be discussed with the referral, simply because it does not matter to the referral source what future treatment the client will undergo, other than a general treatment plan, as on referral the case has been closed at their facility. Anyone asking about it is

(continued)

likely curious for personal reasons. Some programs and clinicians make follow-up calls postreferral to ensure that the client was successfully linked. However, in those cases the client would have signed a consent form describing this plan.

The answer as to what Elias can say to Maria can vary depending on how simple or complex he wishes his response to be. A simple response would be to say, "I'd love to talk about the case but not here and not without a release. Let me get a consent and I'll call you from the office tomorrow." He would want to give this statement the moment she brings up the case, cutting her off before she can divulge too much information. A complex response would be to say the same statement above, and then comment on all the ethical concerns he has about the way she brought up and discussed the topic. In other words, the complex route allows Elias to use the example as a teaching point for his colleague in the hopes that she will see the error in her ways and correct her confidentiality before she speaks to anyone else. Which type of response is recommended will depend on your relationship and your colleague's ability to take criticism. No one likes a backseat driver, and unsolicited supervision is not often welcome either. It is your duty to report unethical behavior, so if you can try to find a nonpreachy way of suggesting that her behavior is unethical, you can protect two principles at once. Well done, you.

VIGNETTE: CLAIMING CLIENTS

Trudy wants to work with Nasir in her private practice. He was referred to her by a colleague from an agency at which she was employed in the past. Nasir is a client at that agency now, attending groups and meeting with an individual counselor there. Trudy is both an addictions counselor and a licensed social worker, and her colleague refers Nasir to her practice to address his mood and anxiety disorders. Trudy understands that Nasir will get his addiction treatment at the agency and she will focus on his other mental health concerns. Nasir agrees to see both clinicians.

In her intake assessment, Trudy can see that Nasir's mood and anxiety disorders are tightly wrapped around his addiction (can you think of a case where this would not be true? Neither can I), and knows it won't be possible to truly separate out his mental diagnoses from his addiction diagnosis. But she wants to work the case, and thus recommends he see her for individual therapy for both addiction and mental health concerns. She does not ask if Nasir has cleared this idea with his individual counselor at the agency, nor has she spoken directly to that clinician. In fact, she has no knowledge of the background of that clinician, and just assumes that person is not a licensed mental health counselor, and therefore is unable to treat the mood and anxiety disorders.

When she sends in her insurance claim to Nasir's insurance company, it is denied on the grounds that he is already receiving individual therapy at the agency. Trudy anticipated this, and already worked out with Nasir that his family would pay a private fee out of pocket to avoid having to claim the therapy with his insurance. This way he can receive both services without a problem. Problem solved, right? Why not?

There are a few big mistakes you may have spotted. First, this whole idea is unethical if his clinician at the agency is not included. Clinicians often make the mistake of thinking that if they speak with someone at the agency it is the same as speaking with the appointed clinician, but it is only ethical if you speak with the treating clinician. In this case, Trudy has only spoken with her colleague, and we don't know her colleague's position; she could be an administrator. We do know she is not the individual clinician assigned to Nasir, who is the person Trudy needs to reach. No matter what other action she takes, if she does not speak with this clinician she has violated this principle. Speaking with Nasir is not enough of a consent, as he may be likely to agree to what is advised to him by the professionals who are paid to give him expert treatment.

There are a few other problems to mention in case a similar scenario occurs in your career, reader. Trudy has red flags come up in her very first session with Nasir, which she ignores for personal gain rather than for the welfare of the client. One red flag is her knowledge that she will not be able to separate Nasir's addiction from his other mental health diagnoses, which means she will have to treat both. This fact negates the whole point of having Nasir employ two separate clinicians, and indicates that Trudy is aware that services will be duplicated and that she will slipping out of the defined scope of practice for her. She is credentialed to treat him, but her requested scope on this case is limited to the mood and anxiety disorders. Knowing she will be unable to uphold this boundary, she should either take on the case in its entirety, or submit the case back to the agency. Because the agency had him first, the ethical action is to give him back to the agency and find a clinician there who can treat all of Nasir's needs. They may refer him to her practice, if they determine that his needs will be better met in her practice than in their agency.

Her other red flag occurred when she realized this predicament, but decided to treat him anyway because she wanted the case. The vignette does not specify why she wanted the case, either for clinical interest, financial benefit, or for another reason. But it is clear that her reasons for accepting the case are personal and not based on Nasir's needs. This violates the principles of client welfare, the counseling relationship, and responsibility. The more ethical choice is to examine the best treatment options for Nasir, even if that means Trudy loses the case. Aside from being ethical for this case, it is also the wise choice for future referrals from this agency. If she errs on this case, the agency may be disinclined to work with her in the future.

Finally, the response to the insurance company is troubling. Insurance companies should not be dictating how we perform our work, and in today's clinical climate they are involved more than most of us would like. However, the concept of avoiding duplicating services is sound, even if we may support it for different

(continued)

reasons. Insurance companies don't want to duplicate services simply because they do not what to shell out money for two people when they can satisfy the need with one person. We don't want to duplicate services because it can be confusing to the client and unfair to the treating clinicians. It is not that it *never* works—I'm sure we could drum up examples together of cases where clients benefited from a duplication of services—it is simply that it should be the exception not the rule. If Trudy asks Nasir to pay out of pocket on top of what insurance will pay for the same services at the agency, Trudy is also making an ethical error unless she can argue *with* the agency clinician that her services are beyond what Nasir will receive at the agency.

We spend so much time ensuring that we do right by our clients, we risk falling behind on tending to our relationships with each other. But we need each other. We cannot be good clinicians without each other and our profession will disintegrate if we fail each other. Whether it is Ted protecting Raul's work with Constance, or Joseph respecting his interns, or Pete honestly reporting his colleague, or Trudy communicating with Nasir's treatment team, we must take care of each other. If we don't, we fail to satisfy the mandates of several tiers of ethics. Healthy interprofessional relationships can also help guide us in our societal obligations by strengthening our network connections and bolstering our involvement in the community.

Principle: Societal Obligations

18

Chapter

Woodrow Wilson said: "We are not here merely to make a living. We are here to enrich the world." This is both a heartwarming and humbling principle, and is the cornerstone of all that is good in what we do. We have discussed that adhering to the profession as a primary concern is ethically responsible. In the same way, looking outside of our work with individual clients in our specific place of business to the greater community is an ethical focus. Focusing on a larger scope brings a different type of work, and a different mode of change, both of which are needed and beneficial. In the same way that only treating the client in front of you does not necessarily guarantee appropriate treatment of the profession, treating the individual does not necessarily guarantee appropriate treatment of the addiction community at large. If we all worked a portion of our time in community organizing, it is unimaginable the heights to which we could grow the community and the profession. This is particularly true of public policy and political legislation, which stand still without a large vocal majority making waves for officials to hear. The greatest advantage we have is not only our ears to listen to the plight of those we aim to help, but also our voices, which can shout and be heard,

bringing sound to the voiceless, ensuring that those disadvantaged by addiction will also be heard. You can be warmed when you think of helping an individual; you can be overwhelmed with tingling when you think of helping society.

It brings to mind the words of President Obama, who spoke these words about community service when running for the seat in 2008,

These days, it's easy for us to get caught thinking that there are two different stories at work in our lives. There is the story of our day-to-day cares and responsibilities—the classes you have to take or the bills you have to pay; the bustle and busyness of what happens in your own life. And then there is the story of what's happening in the wider world—a story seen in headlines and websites and televised images; a story experienced only through the price you pay at the pump or the extra screening you pass through at the airport. This is the divide that separates you from the ability to shape your own destiny. So I am asking you—on this 4th of July—to reject that divide, to step into the strong currents of history, and to shape your country's future. Because your own story and the American story are not separate, they are shared. And they will both be enriched if together, we answer a new call to service to meet the challenges of our new century.

http:/www.rockymountainnews.com/news/
2008/jul/02/text-obamas-speech/

211

In the same way President Obama illustrates the disconnect between our daily lives and the world around us, so too can we become bogged down in the daily grind of our jobs and neglect the larger community. But if we don't take care of it, who will? By signing your Code of Ethics every 2 years, you are committing to follow through with all principles, not most, because one is too tiring or overwhelming. You took an oath when you signed that Code, swearing that you would do your part. What have you done lately? Some of you do quite a lot, some not so much. But perhaps all you need is a little guidance. Two common problems with completing societal obligations are: (1) no time, and (2) no idea what to do; both reasonable concerns. Time availability seems hard to solve, as most of us are overtaxed with work and personal activities and commitments, and the idea of finding an additional chunk of time to devote to the same general group that we already serve is undesirable. The second problem is also understandable, and there are few websites or documents that give ideas about societal obligations in our field, how to create new ideas, or the process of accessing volunteer work.

If clinicians are likely to be overwhelmed because the idea of volunteering seems too complicated, and too much of a commitment, let us simplify the choices. The issues of time and what to do to volunteer can be addressed in a three-part system: (1) choose a time level; (2) choose an access point; and (3) choose a work type. If you can follow these steps, an appropriate volunteer job for you should become easier to find.

Choose a Time Level

A friend recently described how she comes to the amount of money she gives to her church every year. She comes by the tithe with a mathematical equation; 10% of her annual gross income goes to the church. She takes the annual number and then breaks it down into an even monthly pledge, then slightly alters the months of December, April, and August due to an increase need for funds elsewhere during those months (Christmas season, tax season, and summer vacation). She decreases her church pledge in those months and spreads the difference over the other months of the year, slightly increasing each evenly. For those mathematically inclined, perhaps you can use this percentage plan to decipher how much volunteer time you can donate.

For example, Steve works a 40-hour workweek, which becomes a 45-hour week if you include commuting time. He is in recovery, and spends 5 hours a week attending self-help meetings. He receives poor supervision at his place of business, and therefore pays for his own supervision once a month for an hour. Steve is married with three children, all school age. He and his wife try to have a date night every week, let's say 4 hours for that. Because Steve leaves early for work and misses morning prep with the kids, he is in charge of bedtime most nights, so let's give him 2 hours a night to bathe and bed the kids. Eating meals will give him 14 hours a week. Steve is an 8 hours of sleep kinda guy, so we will give him 56 hours of sleep a week. Although he usually doesn't exercise, he wants to and won't commit to volunteer work that would take away exercise time, you know … once he gets around to exercising! Let's give him 7 hours of exercise a week. Weekends perhaps he attends a religious service, 3 hours for that, and house projects at 8 hours a week, another two social nights at 3 hours each. Using a 30-day month, there are 720 total hours and Steve uses up 649, leaving 71 available hours. Poor Steve needs some of those hours to himself, and certainly no one can realistically schedule every hour of the month as it leaves no flexibility for the unknown, unexpected, spontaneous activities. We certainly hope Steve has some of that in his monthly life, don't we? But let us allow a reasonable 10 hours a month for volunteer work, leaving 61 flexible hours. Now these 10 hours a month can be used all at once, say if he takes a weekend a month to do some work, or they can be spread out over the month, as in 2 hours a week plus 2 hours added in somewhere. Or he can save the 10 hours from each month and put them together at a time he devotes to volunteer work, such as 120 hours all at once over the summer, or 60 hours twice a year. This would work well for clinicians who have particularly busy times of year in work or personal life, but have other times that are lighter. Therefore, when considering time, you need to figure out the hours you can commit and then decide the format (weekly, monthly, twice a year, once a year).

Choose an Access Level

Once you have an idea of how much time you can commit and the desired format, the question then becomes one of access. This will require a bit of research on your part. Consider the communities in which you live and work (if different), and the available options for volunteer work. For example, if you live in a small, rural area you will have different access than if you live in a metropolis. If you live in your state's capital city, then you will have even more options in the legislative/political arena. Are there local advocacy groups in your area, or is there an opportunity to start one? Don't worry if there seems to be nothing suitable in your area. With the gifts of technology, there are loads of options via telephone, email, and the Internet. Start in your community and then fan out through your county, then state, then nation, and find the groups that exist. For example, every state has a membership board for addictions professionals. Active states have local representatives and some even have regional meetings. This is the ideal place to start because these meetings and/or leaders should have information about the opportunities in your area and what the specific organization needs. It is also a good place to meet comrades who can help you realize an idea you may be working on that is needed in your community. If your region has no group, or your state organization does not provide it, look into starting one up. Call around to agencies in your area, and ask clinicians if they would come to a start-up meeting. Good use of your volunteer work time! Some states have Political Action Committees (PACs), which are always looking for good volunteer help.

Choose a Work Type

Once you have outlined your time, and have listed the various (or one) access points for your volunteer work, you need to consider what type of work you are interested in. Do you like organizing people, or talking on the phone, or writing letters, or doing craft work? Do you have any particular skills, like a talent in computers or knowledge of legal jargon? What volunteer experience have you already had, and what was your reaction? Are there activities you tried that you didn't like, and if so is there a way to improve the experience or should it simply be avoided? For example, if you have a job cold calling agencies to ask for their support and dislike the work, you have to explore whether you simply don't like calling agencies in any volunteer circumstance, or if you wouldn't mind calling them if it was to notify them of an upcoming rally, rather than ask for financial support.

Go back to your answers in the second question at the start of this chapter. Are there activities that you have tried that were successful, and if so what were they and why were they successful? Gather this information and think about what specific activities you are interested in trying. The nice thing about volunteer work is that if you don't like the activity you do not need to continue to suffer, as many do when employed. You do, however, need to respect the commitment you have made and work to find a replacement if you decide you no longer want to volunteer, or give an appropriate amount of notification time to enable the group to find your replacement. It is never kind or professional to suddenly drop a commitment without warning, as often there is no one else to fill your job without seriously taxing the other workers. You wouldn't want someone to force you to commit more volunteer time to get the job completed, so don't force someone else to pick up the slack you create with an abrupt departure, unless it is unavoidable.

Now, armed with your amount of time, your access point, and your work type, let's apply it directly to the ethical principle. There are three types of societal work by which we must abide: (1) advocacy for public policy, (2) participation in community affairs, and (3) adopting a professional stance. Notice whether your code gives you an either/or choice here, or if your code expects you to perform all three types of work. Let's examine each more closely.

Advocate: The stigma surrounding addiction continues, in several different ways. The general public reportedly sees drug addiction as the lowest priority for health care and highest danger to the public (Doukas & Cullen, 2011). Insurance policies and financial aid are denied, such as the 1996 welfare reform that imposed a lifetime ban on welfare benefits for those convicted of possessing or selling drugs (Whitter et al., 2006). In one study, psychiatrists were more likely to rate alcohol patients as less difficult and less in need of treatment (Doukas & Cullen, 2011). Stigma prevents people from accessing treatment they need, which makes treating them more costly, and stigma deters professionals from the profession (Whitter et al., 2006). No current studies examine the stigma between co-workers (Doukas & Cullen, 2011), thus future research needs to examine exactly what current trends of stigma exist, if any, with counselors in recovery.

Widespread stigma creates a need for advocacy. Advocacy is seeped in history, beginning with the first settlement house in the late 1880s (Nassar-McMillan & Niles, 2011). Advocating for the profession is a challenging role (Nassar-McMillan & Niles, 2011), especially when working in large agencies and other institutions. Advocating is a vital aspect of a clinician's ethical practice, but one must be mindful of the different ethical tiers when choosing for whom one is advocating. For example, Doukas and Cullen (2011) advocate for the clinician in recovery, by suggesting the clinician's perspective. However, other perspectives, such as that of the profession, are not included. When presenting a view, it is responsible to consider multiple perspectives when advocating the perspective you are focusing on.

Advocating for changes in public policy and legislation requires you to get familiar with the legislative happenings in your area and state. Some states make this easy by discussing these issues on websites, in newsletters, and in membership meetings. Other states are less organized and you may need to do a bit of sleuthing to learn what is happening in your neck of the woods. Every state has some public policy work that is related to our profession, some more than others, but every state has a need for help in this area. The legislative arena is both frustrating and fascinating, but one thing is certain: It simply cannot achieve its goals without the help of you, yes you. One organization has an individual who is knee deep in public policy and the legislature. He happens to have the helpful combination of loving the work and being particularly good at it, which is a match made in heaven for the state organization. But people refer to him as the *legislative guy* as if the organization only has and needs one. We all need to be the legislative guy in order for public policy to push through the myriad hoops set before it. It takes a mountain of people to make change happen at this level, so don't leave the work for a select few. Get in there and get dirty. There are tons of tasks, large and small, that are needed, which require a wide range of hours and pose a wide range of challenges. You don't have to give up your life to it; even writing a few letters or making a few phone calls helps. Every bit helps.

Participate: Civic and professional participation in community affairs often makes people wary as it is easy to get hooked in and bogged down by time commitments to get this work done. If you have a hard time saying no to people when they ask for your help, this will be particularly challenging. The best way to go about this is to first reason out your available time commitment and set that boundary up front when strategizing your participation with the community organizer in charge. Let them know in advance that you have a set limit in your time availability, which will help them plan and make it easier for you to pull back later if the boundary becomes strained. Where to find community affairs is usually not too difficult. Look for the flyers or emails that come your way; check out the local newspaper of the bulletin board at the local coffee shop. Ask around; ask your colleagues and superiors at work, as they often hear of organizing efforts, particularly if they have been following their own ethical practice and dabbling in community organizing themselves. If you are interested in developing something that is nonexistent in your area, then good for you! That is loads more work, but imagine the satisfaction you will get from it when you are successful. In this case, you will want to be the one advertising to gain help from others, so use the suggestions described above and start a movement.

Professional stance: Adopting a professional stance that promotes well-being is another way of saying "practice the principles in all your affairs." It means that you need to have the dignity and well-being of others at the core of your professional life, which must be observable to others. It is not enough to advise that other people maintain their ethical practice, especially if you are in a supervisory role; you also must do the same. Practice what you preach; design a professional life that is focused on this one grounding principle. Don't hide behind your desk and eek out your professional world through silent administrative tasks, important as they may be. Take a stance, be vocal, have a presence, do your part in moving our field along.

For example, Colin tells his membership organization that he is interested in helping advocate for counselor licensure. He is a vocal supporter at the annual conference, and helps direct other members who want to know how to support the cause. But when he goes to cast his vote on election day, he votes against the profession. This is an incongruent professional stance. Clinicians who go rogue in their professional stance and act either personally or professionally against their societal obligation are violating their ethical practice.

Okay, so you understand the three components and you are ready to develop your professional stance, jump into community participation, and add your voice into advocacy efforts. Your enthusiasm is here, now what? How do you grow from a believer into a do-er? Luckily, there are numerous options for you to try.

Ideas for Volunteer Work

Here is a nice idea: My runner friend commits to two marathons a year: One he runs, and for the other he volunteers his time handing out water to the runners. He says, "I figure I wouldn't be able to run my marathon without the help of those volunteers, so I try to give back by helping out the runners in my volunteer marathon. I'm going for good karma." You, reader, could adopt the same idea to your societal obligation. You could register for one conference to satisfy your training requirements, and you could offer to volunteer at another conference in the year and get in all of your volunteer hours in one event. Or there may be an opportunity with some conferences to attend part of the conference and volunteer for another part of the conference. Committee leaders are always looking for good workers to pull off a big conference. Seven other ideas include:

1. Call or write letters to your local representatives (e.g., lobbying for a certain bill).
2. Start a resource blog that allows your target audience (e.g., clients, clinicians) to access helpful services or resources.
3. Help your local membership organization or agency build its website (if you are skilled to do so).
4. Input data for an organization, or help in the office with administrative tasks (filing, copying, answering phones).
5. Create flyers for upcoming events.
6. Join a board of directors.
7. Join an existing committee.

You will notice that one activity is not listed here, notably giving a financial donation. Although it is truly a wonderful thing to donate money to an organization if you have the means to do so, and you should feel most encouraged to donate if you do, it does not replace time spent volunteering. Certain types of advocacy, such as PACs or anything to do with lobbying, really do take loads of money, and your money will be well spent in fighting for the profession, its members, and the clients we serve. Donate to your local or national PAC! Just don't use writing that check as your yearly societal obligation requirement. Roll up your sleeves and get active somewhere, and you will lend your hand in enriching the world. You just want to be sure that as you are donating your time, and creating new ways to strengthen the profession, you don't wander away from your foothold on the fellow clinicians and structures around you.

Otherwise you know what you are doing? Yep, you guessed it, you are cutting corners. If you give a check instead of actively volunteering you are cutting corners on your societal obligations. And if you volunteer too much, you run the risk of cutting corners on your day job. Hmm, all this talk of corner cutting makes me think we should start discussing our final pitfall: cutting corners. Nice segue! Let's discuss.

Pitfall: Cutting Corners

$$19$$
Chapter

The first pitfall explored the problem of conflicted agendas. The second pitfall described the ethical danger of confusing our various roles. The third pitfall investigated the complicated hazard of Clinician Burnout. Now we are going to study our final pitfall, cutting corners. When we fail to navigate through the sea of choices, when we deliberately ignore the best ethical choice, or when we fail to respect the ethical tiers, we cut corners in our practice. We make small concessions, seemingly innocuous acts of discretion that can quickly push us into ethical violations. This common dilemma weakens the profession in addition to compromising our integrity and the welfare of the client. Common examples of cutting corners can be found in your administrative and clinical work, your interprofessional conduct, your supervisory experiences, and your attention to the profession.

Administrative Corner Cutting

We discussed the deluge of paperwork with which we clinicians are swamped on a daily basis. Balancing all that work with the clinical pressures we face in the wee time we have to accomplish it all is beautifully fertile ground to entice us into cutting some corners. In your administrative world, cutting corners could be writing the same progress note for all of your group members, or writing your notes during group, or writing the absolute bare minimum that is required, leaving out significant clinical information in the process. Perhaps you fill in several answers on the intake form, having a fair idea of how the client will answer, questions you either failed to ask or ran out of time before asking.

This may seem innocuous but it is not a far leap for clinicians who omit or falsify information on consent-to-release documents, a serious and punishable offense. Cutting corners would even entail neglecting to file your paperwork properly in the chart, which means the next team of clinicians or administrative staff working on that chart will have an incomplete or disorganized mess to sort out. What other examples of administrative corner cutting can you think of?

Clinical Corner Cutting

We have discussed several examples of clinical corner cutting throughout this book. The clinical error

217

of telling callers on the phone that you cannot convey information about clients, but are happy to listen to anything they have to say? Because you would only make this statement for people who are your clients, you are indirectly verifying that the caller is speaking about one of your clients, which violates their right to privacy. The clinician is cutting corners by trying to get information they do not have a consent to get, in a way that appears innocent and ethical, but is neither.

At another moment, when we were discussing the agency tier of ethics, there was an example of an agency policy for assigning clients to clinician caseloads. One agency had a policy of assigning each new case in order, so that clinicians get new cases evenly. If clinicians deviate from this system, it is an example of cutting corners. For example, if a clinician prefers cocaine users and tries to jump them to the caseload, or if a clinician prefers a specific gender, insurance, veteran status, psychiatric diagnosis, or any other characteristic, this is a violation. Although this action may serve the clinician's job satisfaction, it cuts a corner that the agency set.

Clinical corner cutting would also be shortening a session because you are hungry or tired or want to do something else, regardless of what the client needs. Another example is pushing clients into graduation either because their insurance will no longer pay, there is a great need for the bed the client is using, or because you have grown tired of working with him or her. What other clinical examples can you name?

In your clinical world, a good example of cutting corners is referral-nepotism. Referral-nepotism is when you have a relationship with someone in a referral agency and call your friend to ask if your client can be admitted. You are told that there is a waiting list, but "For you, I'll bump the client up to the first position." Sounds good, if it were not for the equally deserving clients you have just bumped down the line. This is soggy networking, unfair, unethical, and definitely corner cutting. To be fair, your asking is not as faulty as the organization accepting your referral. Some may argue that there

is nothing wrong with attempting nepotism, that it is up to the agency to maintain ethical boundaries, and if they do not and it benefits a client then this is acceptable and the clinician is not culpable. This is an understandable argument, but if we were always to leave our ethical standards to others, how could we stand on our own ethical ground? It is the same as feeling that breaking the rules is acceptable as long as you don't get caught. Isn't breaking the rules still wrong even if you are not caught? You must maintain ethical standards whether people are aware of your actions or not, whether they maintain their own ethical standards or not. Remember, at the end of the day you will know whether you acted ethically or not, and you will not build integrity if you cannot stand by your own decisions.

For example, Pete is an addiction counselor at a residential setting. He became a counselor after his younger brother was paralyzed when his car was hit by a drunk driver and developed an opiate addiction. Pete is a good counselor, and he is driven to give addicts the help that his brother never received. In this way, his brother's situation positively influences Pete to help many people. Yet there is one type of client that Pete finds a challenge to help—can you guess who that might be? Yes, those clients who drank and drove a car during their active addiction, clients similar to the person who hit Pete's brother. Pete has a difficult time mustering the empathy needed to effectively treat this subpopulation, because his anger with what happened to his brother is difficult to put aside.

To manage this, Peter applies to be senior counselor and succeeds. One of the roles as senior counselor is to assign new cases to all clinicians. He reads the initial paperwork on each case and if the incoming client has any driving-related issues, Peter assigns the client to another clinician. Peter does not discuss his feelings or coping strategies in supervision. In this way, his brother's situation drives Pete into an ethical dilemma because he is blurring his personal and professional agendas. Pete can't avoid working with clients who have driven while intoxicated if he is to remain a counselor, but if he can see this limitation and ethical risk he can address both in supervision to ensure he maintains the best practice.

Interprofessional Corner Cutting

Just as we can cut corners with clients, so, too, can we cut them with each other. We cut corners when there is a specific action we are supposed to take with each other, but for time, efficiency, or personal gain we can manipulate our environment to serve us. For example, if two colleagues are assigned in staff meetings to be a part of one of the new staff committees, but one refrains from meeting until the very end, making it impossible to complete her committee tasks without asking for help from her colleague, this is corner cutting. This cutting of corners is not a good way to build your integrity, objectivity, or standards in your responsible practice.

In another example, Youssef and Daniel work at the same agency, in the same position as substance abuse counselors. Daniel, a licensed social worker, also has a private practice office in the community. Youssef approaches Daniel at work one day and asks if he has any openings in his private practice. At first Daniel thinks Youssef is asking for himself, which he feels would be inappropriate, but Youssef says that he has a friend who is looking for a good therapist, and that he would like to give him Daniel's number. Daniel agrees and begins seeing this person in his practice. Daniel feels this was a marginal call in terms of a dual relationship, but decides it is acceptable … until Youssef begins to ask him about the case while they are at work. His questions are subtle, seemingly innocuous, such as, "How's it going with my friend? Interesting case, isn't it?"

But the questions make Daniel feel uncomfortable. He tells Youssef he doesn't want to discuss the case, that it is unethical for him to ask Daniel about it, and Youssef says, "Sure, sure, of course." But he continues to ask questions sporadically. Unfortunately, Daniel now feels trapped. He is not comfortable, and wishes to terminate the client relationship so that he can work again with Youssef

without awkwardness. But he feels he cannot terminate with the client, who has built a rapport with Daniel, is working on treatment goals, and is not at fault in the situation at all. He can't let it affect the client, which means the only answer is to continue addressing it directly with Youssef, a task Daniel dreads. Daniel decides the dread is too agonizing and develops a strategy that will allow him to avoid Youssef. He asks his supervisor to transfer Youssef to another building so that he does not have to approach him and resolve the issue interpersonally.

In another example, do you recall the vignette with Carter and his staff that included clinicians with private practices? Carter was conflicted between wanting to support his staff in their endeavors and wanting to protect the clients that he worried would feel pressured to seek private therapy with the staff. His administrative director believed it was not a good idea because the agency would be competing with its own employees for the same clients. She believed this was fertile ground for interprofessional corner cutting, that clinicians would bend the rules to serve themselves and disadvantage other competing colleagues. Furthermore, she believed that these clinicians would be competing with the agency itself for clients, and would steal business away from the agency.

Carter is unconcerned with the latter point, as he believes that the more services for clients the better, and that the majority of services are not duplicated. Clients looking for group and a team approach will not be looking for therapy in the private practice sector. He believes clients in private practice are typically of two types: Those who have completed a formal program like his that are looking for ongoing individual counseling and those who prefer individual counseling to a formal program (in other words, clients who would not be using his program in the first place). He also believes it is helpful to have private practice clinicians he knows well and who know his program well. It would be beneficial for the agency to be able to care for clients by getting them the clinicians that will work best with them, and to establish positive referral relationships with these clinicians in order to receive referrals back to the agency as needed. This symbiotic referral relationship benefits the client, the clinicians, and the agency. Everybody wins. Carter is wary of the competition between clinicians vying to fill private practice openings with warm bodies, and will need to find a way to address it in the future.

Supervisory Corner Cutting

Corner cutting is also evident in supervision. Supervisees who only report positive conduct without addressing known ethical or clinical challenges are an example. Supervisees who do not complete required paperwork, or who do not attend meetings as scheduled, are cutting corners, trying to get by without fulfilling all of their duties related to supervision.

Processing recordings in one week, when they are supposed to be a random sample of your work over time and not in one clump, is another example of supervisory corner cutting. Similarly, omitting important concerns from the supervision discussion, whether the supervisor or supervisee is instigating the omission, is corner cutting. Pretending to be busy and unable to meet when you know the supervision discussion is going to address some recent questionable behavior is another example.

Supervisors are also at risk of cutting corners. Supervisors may skim evaluations instead of thoroughly reading and preparing them, or may neglect evaluations altogether. Supervisors may fail to establish appropriate observation of their supervisees' clinical and ethical conduct, instead relying only on what is reported by the supervisee. Supervisors may also cut corners by failing to keep abreast of professional knowledge and research.

Profession Corner Cutting

In the same way that we cut corners in our administrative, clinical, and supervisory practices, so, too, can we cut corners in the general profession. Any time we make an ethical decision without considering the impact on the profession, we are cutting corners.

Corner cutting occurs for many reasons. There are times when clinicians deliberately cut corners because it feels like the best decision when given two lousy choices of action. In these cases, cutting corners may be the best option to support nonmaleficence. It may be harmful to the profession to cut the corner, but the alternative may be far worse. For example, you are the counselor working with several clients through a drug court program. You attend weekly meetings with the judge and other members of the treatment team. One of the drug court clients is doing really well and is motivated and inspired to live a drug-free life. You have seen a lot of clients go through your program, and this one seems like he is really going to make it. He follows every aspect of the program, is sociable with other clients, is helpful with staff, and is insightful about his illness. He follows suggestions even when he dislikes them and talks about his feelings, both negative and positive.

Part of the drug court mandates that he attend every session at the clinic with absolutely no exceptions. One day, he misses a group and a med check. He shows up an hour later, apparently lucid and looking normally dressed, showered, and groomed. Nothing in his physical appearance or verbal behavior would indicate suspicion of use. He explains why he couldn't be there and his excuse seems reasonable. You know if you write him an unexcused absence, he will go to jail. He is terrified of going to jail. You decide to help him instead of hurt him, and write the absence as excused, stating that the client called to say he could not be there but would come into the clinic later that day (as he did). What are the ethical concerns here? Who is the counselor hurting by not telling the truth?

You may squirm as you read this because this is one way ethics can get really disheartening and can lead a clinician into despair. It is easy to sympathize with this clinician, as many of you have been in similar situations with a client who is really taking to the program well and encounters some small problem that puts them at odds with the rules. You then must decide whether to back your client, who you believe is really doing well and deserves what the program can provide, or whether to uphold your ethics and stand by the standard that has been set regardless of who the client is to you. Ethics is not black and white, and this is surely a gray area. On the one hand is the argument to keep the client in the program, as you do not want to see the chances for this client dashed on a technicality. It is noble, the desire to do everything in your power to protect the client. But the thing that keeps gnawing is that the client knew of the consequences if he did not show up for his scheduled appointments, and yet he did not come. He may have had a great excuse, but it is the judge who should hear that excuse and rule, not you. It is the reality of entering into a program such as drug court that there may be such instances, but your clients know this going into the program. At the very least, you should not be the only one making this decision. Make it a team decision, or a court decision if appropriate, so the best action can be taken and so you are not in the position of violating any ethics. The last point to remember is that while you may be protecting this one great client, how are you protecting the program and the profession by lying for this client? What would happen to the profession if everyone lied on behalf of their clients? Just sayin'.

For another example, Neil is Siobhan's counselor at an outpatient facility. The facility has a strict policy that the agency transportation is limited to clients in the daily group program only. Clients coming for individual counseling or one to two groups a week are not permitted to use the agency transportation system. Neil agrees with this policy, and understands it is in place so that the transportation system does not get flooded with transport requests. While in daily groups, Siobhan uses the agency transportation as designed. However, when it comes time for her to graduate out of the daily groups, Neil knows that she will not be able to come to individual counseling and the twice weekly groups if she is no longer transported. Siobhan does

not have her own transportation or funds for public transportation. She is not eligible for any government assistance in the area of transportation, thus she is at the mercy of the agency. Neil decides to go to the executives of the agency to ask for special consideration of her transportation needs. He advocates for her because without their help she would not be able to access needed treatment at their or any other facility. For Siobhan, Neil is willing to make an exception to the rule, and sides with the welfare of his client over the policy of the agency.

For another example, Robby is elated when he lands a job with a local radio station, his dream job and original goal before his addiction led him in a different direction for several decades. His counselor, Rubén, sees this as a vital step in Robby's recovery, and a step that he was worried would not be achieved by Robby. The only snag is that the job conflicts with one of the days of Robby's treatment, and the agency has a strict policy against modifying the set treatment schedule. Rubén, however, feels this is a special case that should be granted consideration. He doesn't want Robby to have to choose between treatment and this job, and feels they can find a way to schedule both.

You will notice that in the last two examples the decision by the agency is not mentioned or discussed. The reason for this is that it doesn't matter, from an ethical standpoint. This is about putting the client first when there is a professional conflict, and both Neil and Rubén have given us examples of putting their clients first. The reality is that counselors win some battles and lose some. Perhaps Neil won his transportation case, but Rubén lost his scheduling plea, or vice versa. We do not always get what we ask for, but the ethical achievement lies in the attempt. In other cases, you may battle with the client and side with the agency, all in the name of client welfare.

Thus, going back to my earlier question: Where do you cut corners in your administrative or clinical practice? If you still maintain that you don't, you are not stretching your brain far enough. We all cut corners at some point or another, and usually are not caught at it. But if you signed your Code of Ethics, which you must in order to practice, then you agreed to maintain the highest standards in all your affairs. You made the commitment, it is your professional responsibility, so what areas can you strengthen in your practice? What corners need sharpening?

Sigh. Are you with me? Alright, fine, I can tell I have lost you to a sea of thoughts about gift giving. I was going to give you another example, but I can sense you aren't paying close attention. You're no good to me now until we can address the gift issue, so let's get to it.

Practical Application

'Tis The Season of Gift Giving …

… or is it? The question of whether to accept gifts from clients is another complicated dilemma that challenges the minds of many a clinician (Reamer, 2001, 2012). What is your policy about gift giving? What, if any, is your agency's policy about gift giving? Here are 11 common answers I hear:

1. I accept gifts from my clients. I do not want to hurt them by saying no.
2. I accept gifts only when they are graduating from the agency. It is their way of thanking me for helping them and I think showing gratitude is a positive behavior we should support.
3. I accept a gift only if it is something that the whole agency can enjoy (e.g., food, flowers).
4. I accept a gift only if it is food.
5. I accept gifts only if they are handmade. How am I supposed to turn down a gift that they made? As long as they did not spend money on it, it is okay.
6. Certain cultures communicate thanks through food sharing and it would be rude of me not to accept. Since I strive to be "culturally competent" I do not want to offend anyone's culture, therefore I accept gifts when clients are from certain cultures.

7. I only accept gifts from clients in private, never in front of other clients or staff.
8. I only accept gifts from clients of the same sex. I do not want other clients to get the wrong idea.
9. I assess the individual offering the gift. I accept gifts from some clients because it is an important part of their therapy, and I decline gifts from others because it would not be helpful therapeutically.
10. I accept cards from clients because they are not really gifts.
11. I never accept gifts from any client. I tell them "I'm not allowed to" and leave it at that.

So which is the correct plan of action? Well, the first thing as always is to go to the Code of Ethics. When you do that you will notice that gift giving is not necessarily specified, depending on your home state. Some are quite clear in discouraging the acceptance of any type of gift. Typically, however, personal nonfinancial gifts are not clearly discussed. This is because gift giving was thought to be a personal choice, dependent on your personal tier of ethics, or an agency choice, dependent on the agency's tier of ethics and rules of conduct. Unfortunately, this only makes it possible to have 10 different responses to the same question, and it would be helpful to the profession and all of us in it if we could clarify a plan of appropriate action on the licensure tier.

If you are following a good ethical regime, your first three questions should be: (1) What is the client's intention in giving me this gift to the best of your knowledge? (2) What is the potential effect on the client, the clinician, and the therapeutic relationship if I accept his or her gift? and (3) What is the potential effect, if any, on the other clients, the agency, and the profession if I accept this gift? All of these questions are important to consider, and usually difficult, if not impossible, to answer with certainty.

The first asks you to consider his or her motivation for giving you the gift. Is your client able to separate the boundaries necessary in a clinical relationship? In other words, what is the difference for them between giving a gift to a friend, a significant other, or a clinician? Is there a difference for you? I would hope there is a difference between giving and receiving gifts to and from your loved ones and from your clients, which is another way of saying: Please tell me you don't have the same feelings, and certainly not the same relationship, with clients as you do your family and close friends. If you do, then you will need to spend some extra special time pouring over the previous sections, and may want to bring this up in your next supervision session.

Assuming you can make the distinction between those two types of relationships, how do you know your client can? How can you assume that they understand the boundary between clients and clinicians? How can you assume that their motives of gift giving are appropriate? Actually, how can you be sure that their motives are whatever they say their motives are? The answer is, you can't. You cannot be inside anybody's head but your own, which means you cannot be certain of the client's intention in giving a gift. There may be an ulterior motive (Reamer, 2001). You may think it is a simple gift of thanks, but to them it may mean much more, and they may not tell you, so you may be communicating back a message to them you do not intend to give.

The second question asks you to consider what the client's response will be if you accept the gift. Will he or she be confused about your relationship? Will he or she think that there is a special bond that was not there before? The problem with gift giving and receiving is that it is important to know a client's motivations, and to plan for his or her reactions, before accepting any single gift. And how can you know these things? Again, a client may tell you that he or she only wants to thank you, but perhaps there is a hidden meaning, one that even he or she doesn't understand.

The third question asks you to think of the larger picture, who else may be affected by your gift giving and receiving. We tend to get absorbed with the small world tightly wound around us, understandably, and we often fail to see past our own involvement. Yet there are many who are affected by the decisions we make: clients as a whole, colleagues, the agency, our bosses, and those who work for us. The profession as a whole is affected by the individual actions we take. Our family is affected by the actions we take at work, yet we often exclude them from our consideration. Let's look at an example of how gift giving can play out and then analyze our choices of action. This isn't a vignette, this is a full story, so get cozy, grab a cup of something warm, and read on.

At several points in my career I was an outpatient counselor at a facility that had a weekly group for graduates of the regular day program. I had a client, Larry, who was very grateful to the agency, and to me in particular for helping him get into recovery. He had been a client for a year and a half and was clean and sober for the same amount of time. Larry really wanted to give me a gift showing his gratitude, and asked several times if he could. The agency I worked for did not have a gift policy, but I was personally uncomfortable with accepting gifts. I felt that if I helped a friend outside of my employment I would be okay accepting a gift, but that accepting a gift in addition to getting paid for my job seemed inappropriate. I like my job, but it is a job! I wouldn't be sitting in my office for 8 hours a day helping these clients for free; even if I wanted to, it surely wouldn't pay my mortgage. I am compensated for helping people; an additional gift that took time or money from my client makes me feel uncomfortable.

Perhaps you cringe at the idea that clients feel that they are in recovery because of you or the agency, as if we did all the work. You know, reader, that no matter how much work we pour into our clients, it is up to them to obtain and maintain recovery. Some clients understand this, and just want to thank anyone who helped them along the way. But other clients say, "You saved my life, if it weren't for you I would be dead." This just isn't true. We may have helped, but the client saved his or her own life. You don't want your clients thinking they need someone else to save their lives, because they may need some life saving in the future, and you want them to understand that they can save their own lives without having to rely on another person, because they can!

So I told Larry that I did not accept gifts, but Larry was persistent. I then approached my employers and begged them to adopt a gift policy for the agency, something I could use with my clients so that I didn't have to argue my personal feelings on the subject. They agreed and adopted the popular policy of accepting gifts only if they could be shared with the whole agency, such as food or flowers. I still didn't like this policy, feeling a no-gift policy would be an easier boundary for clients and clinicians, but at least it was something. So Larry baked for every group, and was slightly mollified, although he would still have loved to do something for me personally.

Fast forward many months to another client, Grace. Grace had been in the same program for 3 years and had decided to cease her after-group attendance. As was the custom at the agency, we were having a bit of a graduation party during group, which consisted of food, an AA coin donated by the agency for all graduates, and a chance for every group member to say something to the departing member. We did this for Grace, and it was as lovely as these ceremonies always are. At the end, Grace presented me with a wrapped gift. Shocked, I held the gift at arms length and said, "Grace, you know I can't accept a gift from you. You know we have a policy...." But she cut in and said, "No, no, I checked with staff here and they told me it was okay, that this was within the policy." All of my red flags were flying in my face, but I took the gift and opened it, thinking perhaps it was a big box of chocolate. Instead my eyes widened as I gazed down on a "smart" electronic device, such as a smart phone or a tablet. So, because I was really wanting that device, I accepted it and went home.... *No!* What kind of a clinician do you take me for! I may have *wanted* to do that, but I knew I couldn't. I passed it back

to her, saying something like, "Thank you so much Grace, but you know I can't accept this." To which, she burst into tears and fled the building. You know that feeling of dread that rises from your feet to your head, making every body part hot and tingly as it migrates? That was me, holding this gift, knowing that Grace had no future appointments at the agency. I was stuck.

So I did what I had been taught: The next day I flew to my supervisor's office and cried *"Help!"* Luckily, I had a great supervisor at the time, who listened to the story and said, "Hmm. There must be a very important reason for her to give you this gift. I wonder what the gift means to her." This had not occurred to me, as I was too focused on my own panic that I had made a grave ethical error. But my supervisor reminded me that this was not all about me (shocker) and that there was a client involved here, who was trying to tell me something, I just wasn't sure what. So my supervisor suggested I call the client and ask her to come in for one last appointment. My supervisor told me to leave the gift on my desk, not to mention it, and to see what she said. I thought there would be no way she would return to the agency, but she did. She eyed the gift as she crossed the room but did not say a word. We began by talking about her impressions of her last group, discussing what each group member had said and her feelings attached to the event. Just when I figured I was going to have to bring up the gift, she brought it up.

"My friends told me you would never accept that gift," she said, a bit shyly. I responded, "I'm glad you brought that up because I wanted to talk about it with you. It's true, I can't accept your truly generous gift, but I wanted to talk about why you gave it to me. I've been thinking that a gift can mean lots of things. What does the gift mean to you?" She said, "Well, that's just the thing. I know the agency policy, but I wasn't giving you this gift because you are my counselor and treated me here. I'm giving it to you personally." Well, wait, I thought to myself, that's worse! But I could sense we were getting somewhere, so I asked, "Can you tell me more about what you mean?" And she said, "I was giving the gift to you because I like you, love you, I mean because I'm attracted to you." And there it was. Now the situation had changed from my discomfort with accepting a thank-you gift to her revelation of her feelings for me, a different clinical issue to be sure, and an important one to address.

If you are squirming in your seat while reading this, thinking how uncomfortable it is to have a client attracted to you, and wondering how on earth you address something like this, then I'm glad you picked up this book. I understand it can feel awkward knowing that a client has feelings for you, but before you get too twitchy, let's see this issue for what it is. The truth is that the majority of the time the clients are not in love with you, even though they feel they are, and are not attracted to the real you, beyond perhaps a physical attraction. What they are attracted to is what you present them in therapy. You listen, always put them first, ask supportive questions, refrain from judging their thoughts and behavior, infuse humor into every session if possible, encourage them in all of their goals, and always have a smile for them regardless of your personal mood that day. What is *not* to love, right? I would fall in love with me, too. But this is not the complete you. Your clients know the parts of you that you allow them to see, but typically, if you are a good ethical clinician with strong boundaries, this is a small portion of who you really are. They don't see your stormy moods, your irrational moments, your selfishness, your manipulations, your, shall we say, less than desirable side. You are not these challenging traits all the time (I hope!), but every person has a combination of sour and sweet, yet your clients never see the sour. They also don't see all the sweet, they only see what is appropriate in the work setting. Therefore, your clients do not really love *you*. Are you feeling a little more at ease? You should, because this is a very important point.

The second issue here is that the fact that your clients are attracted to you is actually a clinical victory in many cases. Often, the kind of people your clients have been attracted to in the past have been poor choices for one reason or another. When drug use is involved, clients typically narrow their social pool over time to include only those interested in using. These fellow addicts, while certainly good people, are addicted themselves and not likely to be good relationship material while in the grip of their addiction. In addition, have you noticed the odd phenomenon that you attract people who confirm how you feel about yourself? Many people in the throes of addiction have chronically low self-esteem, and therefore can attract people to them who will only validate their feelings of low worth. Perhaps they have suffered an abusive relationship, or a neglectful relationship, or a combination. The fact that they are attracted to the traits you bring to therapy is actually a sign of their growth and their healthy feelings about themselves. If they can view kindness and support as attractive, they may be more likely to seek out similar relationships in their personal life.

The third issue is that it shows a great emotional maturity in them, which is also a victory. Typically, clients are one big emotional mess when they enter recovery, and it can take a significant amount of time for each client to learn how to appropriately express their feelings, and to validate that they feel emotions in the first place. Substance abuse robs you of your emotions, covering over those that do not feel comfortable, allowing you to avoid and suppress that which you don't want to feel. When you stop using drugs, most people experience an emotion overload they are not accustomed to experiencing, and it takes awhile to sort out all of the emotions, make sense of them, and then learn how to express them in a healthy way. The fact that your client can come to you shows the emotional growth they have achieved. They are able to say this out loud, which is also a sign of therapeutic success. They are saying what they feel, and subsequently revealing what they feel they need, directly to the object. This direct honesty takes courage, and a sense of confidence they likely did not have at the beginning of treatment.

Finally, your client could be using transference, displacing feelings they have for another onto you. There are many reasons why clients use transference, and it is not always comfortable for the clinician, but if addressed correctly, it can be a therapeutic turning point for the client. Often clients have to work through issues with you, which is safer than working through issues with the true object of their feelings. If they practice through you, they can either resolve whatever issues they are having and move forward, or they can be ready to address the issues with the true object. Either way, the client has a positive outcome. Working through transference is an important clinical tool, so if you suspect that is where the client's attraction is originating, it is important not to ignore it.

So what do you, as the clinician, do in this situation? Clinicians don't always react well in these situations, usually because the discomfort quickly flickers into fear, and no one makes the best choices when driven by fear, unless you are in physical danger, in which case fear can be entirely motivating. But these situations are not about physical danger, they are about emotional discomfort, and that kind of fear can make anyone act poorly. Some clinicians brusquely state, "It's not appropriate for you to be attracted to me," and walk away, leaving the client hurt and rejected. Other clinicians brush off the client comments, stating, "I can't be involved with clients," and walk away, leaving the client hurt and rejected. Some clinicians scream and run down the hall, leaving the client hurt and rejected. It is important to remember that although you may be uncomfortable, this is a good time to focus on the client and how you can help them work through the issue. If you do not, you are missing a grand therapeutic opportunity.

Specifically, you explain how great it is that she felt able to express herself to you, that it takes great courage and that you think she is very brave. You explain that it shows great emotional maturity, and here I would put in a joke, if your rapport is able to withstand it, such as "Which is saying a lot considering when I met you, you couldn't put two emotions together properly!" You also explain that you see great progress in what she finds attractive. Here again is a great place to put in some humor if your rapport will entertain it, such as "I mean, let's consider what you used to go for: dishonest, manipulative, obnoxious drug users!" Please understand that you are using this in humor; this is never appropriate to say in a serious manner, as I hope you understand name calling is not a favorable technique in any therapy. Because I had known Grace for three years, I was able to put in all sorts of playful jibes, which made her laugh and put her at ease, which I wanted, but only use humor if it is already part of your style and if you think the therapeutic relationship can sustain it. Otherwise, you run the risk of the client feeling you are making fun of his or her feelings, which is an error from which you may never recover; the damage may be too great to undo. If you suspect transference, this is when you would explore that with her, asking if there are other people for whom she feels similar emotions, or, if after working with the client for awhile you have an idea who the primary object is, you can explore her feelings for that person.

Whether you explore transference, your next move is to gently say,

> *I can't be in a relationship with you, but I am really glad you brought this up. I'm happy to know how you feel and I think it shows how far you've come in your treatment, given all of the reasons I just mentioned. I think you should feel really good about this conversation, and I hope that you do. As for the gift, I still can't accept it, but I understand it and I thank you for making the effort to bring me some happiness. I hope you can either return it, or find someone else in your community who would really enjoy it. I think it would be awesome to give it to someone who would not otherwise be able to have such a kingly prize. That always feels good.*

Ask if the client has questions, repeat any statements that bear repeating, but do not divert too far from the script you have been given. You may need to gently repeat what you have said in some areas, and the repetition is superior to giving additional reasons. Keep it simple. I have used this script in several situations, and know of other clinicians who have as well, and it has rarely proven to be ineffective or a negative experience. Typically, as with Grace, it was therapeutic, positive, and made both the clinician and client feel good on exiting.

But before you go applauding me and feeling like this gift issue is sewn up into a positive clinical tool, let me spin it by revealing that this story is actually not about Grace, at least not completely. Can you guess who this story is really about? Let's go back to that night of Grace's graduation group. There I am, sitting with Grace and the rest of the group members. We have a nice closing for Grace, and then she hands me the gift, which I take into my hands and open. The moment I do that, before we even see what is inside, I have already hurt someone in the group. Who, you ask? Well, Larry of course, who is sitting in the group with us. After I have turned down his gifts for nearly 2 years, he just watched me take a gift from Grace the first time she offered it to me. I did not say no, or I did try to say no, but only after I had accepted it. After I took the package, I looked up to see Larry's fallen facial expression, and I felt badly. I could explain to Larry that I made an error, and I advise that you do in your own situation, but I knew that it would never completely repair the rejected feeling he experienced.

I bring up this story because it illustrates several important points in this book. First, we all make mistakes, even those clinicians with the best intentions. Second, this story is a good example of the clashing of different ethical tiers. If you recall, the agency had no policy regarding ethical gift etiquette, and therefore no known ethical policy regarding gifts. If I had accepted gifts from clients, I would have been acting ethically on the federal, state, licensure, and agency tiers. Some of you out there are unconcerned personally about accepting gifts; therefore your personal tier would have also been satisfied, and there would have been no ethical violation at any level. My personal tier was telling me not to accept gifts, so there was a clash between my personal and agency tiers. My personal tier was uncomfortable with accepting any gifts, the

agency tier was unconcerned with accepting gifts, and only created a policy when I begged, and chose the easiest policy they could. My actions, however, could have gone with either tier. I could have concluded, "Well, I'm uncomfortable on my personal tier, but since it is acceptable on the agency tier, I will accept the gift." I also could have concluded, "It is acceptable on the agency tier, but I am still uncomfortable on my personal tier, so I am not going to accept the gift."

It is helpful to ask your agency to adopt a rule that supports your ethical practice. It is far easier and more comfortable for a clinician to say to a client, "I would love to accept your gift but this agency has a strict policy against accepting gifts," which essentially makes the agency "the bad guy" and allows you to maintain a supportive relationship with your client without having to say "I am not comfortable accepting a gift from you," which can lead to a client feeling rejected.

This story also illustrates those three initial questions we must ask: (a) What is his or her intention in giving me this gift? (b) What is the effect on the client, the clinician, and the therapeutic relationship if I accept his or her gift? and (c) What is the effect, if any, on the other clients, the agency, and the profession if I accept this gift? In this story, Grace had an entirely different intention in giving the gift than I thought, using the gift as a token of love rather than a token of thanks. If I had accepted the gift, I may have just told myself I was allowing her to thank me. But imagine what message I would have inadvertently given if I had accepted the gift. She would have left feeling like I accepted her feelings for me, and there is no telling what positive or negative responses within her would have come from that. Finally, there was a great effect on the other clients with my accepting the gift, at least there was one who was greatly affected, poor Larry. There is also an effect on the profession because I was not consistent in my rule, saying no to Larry but yes to Grace. When we make such loose decisions without a standard, we affect the profession, which relies on consistency and reliability across clinicians.

Let us go back to the initial 11 response options listed earlier: Which do you think is ethically correct? Have you guessed? If you guessed none of them, you would be correct! Really none of these answers takes the clients' needs and the professional boundaries into account effectively. Let us look at them:

1. *I accept gifts from my clients. I do not want to hurt them by saying no.* This answer is really more about the clinician not wanting to confront the client, and feeling awkward in giving the gift back. True, if you simply say no and hand the gift back to the client, you are at risk of hurting their feelings. But you can explain why you can't accept the gift in a way that minimizes that hurt. This is a brilliant example of using the backward honor code motto, by putting the client over both the clinician and the profession. Individual clients may be happy to accept this, but you will not ultimately feel good about it, and the profession will suffer.

2. *I accept gifts only when they are graduating from the agency.* This is a common response, and a seemingly appropriate one. It is good for the clients to express gratitude, but there are ways they can do this that do not blur the boundaries between the client and clinician. Tell them if they want to thank you for helping them they should tell others about this agency, or let clinicians know good areas to put up clinic advertisements. I once had a client who made a billboard advertising the agency that he pasted on his car window, so that everywhere he drove he was advertising. Tell them a good way to express gratitude is to (safely) help someone else in recovery. I often tell clients the best way they can express gratitude is to stay sober and keep working on their recovery. It sounds hokey to some, but really it gets at what you want to express. Despite what they might think, we are not in the business of saving lives—we do not have that kind of power. Clients succeed because they fight for themselves. We help guide them and support them, but we cannot do the work for them. And we don't want them thinking that they could not have done it without us; they can and need to continue the fight without us.

3. *I accept a gift only if it is something that the whole agency can enjoy (e.g., food, flowers).* This is a common agency policy. The problem, as my example shows, is that some clients can use this as a way to give you a personal gift. But more importantly, it gives the impression that giving a gift is an acceptable form of saying thank you. Really you want to reserve gift giving for friends, family, and loved ones—clients and clinicians should not fall into any of these categories. Therefore, showing thanks in the ways listed above are better than baking brownies for the whole agency. This depends on your agency. Some clinicians have no problem setting the boundary of accepting gifts for the whole agency. This is fine, but can you be sure the clients are able to understand and maintain the same boundaries?

4. *I accept a gift only if it is food.* Haven't you heard that the way to enter the heart is through the stomach? Food items seem innocent enough, but food can be prepared with a lot more love than you realize. Depending on the client, cooking can be a personal and intimate gift. Be careful about assuming it is no big deal. It is a gift like any other.

5. *I accept gifts only if they are handmade.* Actually, a gift is a gift is a gift, meaning that there should not be distinctions between types of gifts. First of all, you may be able to understand the distinction, but can you be sure your clients do? Second, a handmade gift often has more love poured into it, takes more time, and is more personal, and it can often cost money to buy the craft supplies. Also don't forget that if one client tries to give you a purchased gift and you decline, then accept a handmade gift from another client, will that first client understand the distinction? Will they feel you are playing favorites?

6. *I accept gifts when clients are from certain cultures.* This is the most common response at trainings, and perhaps the most damaging because it separates out your clients into groups that have different rules. Working as a group, this special attention can be harmful, as my mistake with Grace hurt Larry deeply. Again, at first glance it seems appropriate, but being culturally competent does not mean you have different rules for different cultures! Being culturally competent means you take into consideration the cultural influences of each of your clients, and discuss those influences with the client. It is a way of understanding, not excusing, client behaviors. If you are worried about being rude to a client given his or her cultural expectations, sit them down and explain that while you understand how his or her culture values food gifts, you need to adhere to the rules and traditions of the agency's culture, which doesn't allow for food gifts.

    While clients come into treatment with all sorts of different cultures and backgrounds, the agency has its own culture and your client is a member of that culture. Most importantly, *listen* to what the client tells you about his or her culture, and what the gift would mean. By listening, you are allowing the client to express the thanks and meaning the food would have expressed, thereby allowing better communication for that client while maintaining the boundary.

7. *I only accept gifts from clients in private, never in front of other clients or staff.* Where you open the gift is not as important as whether you accept the gift. The gift is still a gift whether opened in private or in public. In fact, it can be safer to open gifts while other people are present, not necessarily in your conversation, but in the room. This can help prevent the boundaries from becoming blurred into a personal and not a professional thank you. You may need to discuss the gift and why you cannot accept it in your private office, which may be a more appropriate setting.

8. *I only accept gifts from clients of the same sex.* Ah, this is clearly probably from a heterosexual clinician, but there are all sorts of intimacy you should be thinking about, not just one form. Obviously your clients could be homosexual or bisexual and thinking of you in a sexual way, and be giving the gift as a token of those feelings. But also gifts can be intimate without being about sex. Clients of any gender can become connected or attached to clinicians of any gender in more of an emotional than a sexual way. These connections can be just as dangerous as sexual ones if left unaddressed, and by accepting a gift you can inadvertently be encouraging these connections.

9. *I assess the individual offering the gift. I accept gifts from some clients because it is an important part of their therapy, and I decline gifts from others because it would not be helpful therapeutically.* Usually treating clients individually is a good plan, but here is one area where it is not recommended. You should have a blanket policy about gift giving that is appropriate for most, if not all, of your clients. Clients observe much of what happens in the agency and they often talk to each other. Consider the above example of declining a gift from one client and accepting one from another. You may have clinical reasons for doing this, but the declined client would not know what those reasons were. What they see is you playing favorites, or that there is something wrong with them that would make you decline their gift. Be very careful here. You can actually do a lot of damage without intending to by treating clients differently. Even if you didn't think that two particular clients talk to each other, I would still strongly advise you not to treat clients differently in this way. Remember, your definition of therapeutic and the client's definition of therapeutic may not match, and your assumptions about who needs help and who does not need help could be wrong.

10. *I accept cards from clients since they are not really gifts.* Many clinicians accept cards feeling that it is a good way to support client expression

and is not considered a gift. If clients send you cards, you can't send them back. But cards can also be dangerous. Think of what some clients write in a card. Taken out of context, those cards may suggest relationships that never existed. Sadly, I know several clients who were legally reprimanded—in some cases with serious consequences—largely due to cards found in the clinician's possession. If you receive cards from clients, share them with your supervisor immediately, then place them in the client chart for filing. Do not keep them in your personal or professional belongings.

11. *I never accept gifts from any client. I tell them "I'm not allowed to" and leave it at that.* This may sound like the answer, as not accepting gifts from clients is typically a good idea. But simply stating, "I'm not allowed to," is a good way of closing the issue for you, but not as good for the client. You want to explain why you can't accept this specific gift, but you want to explore what the gift means to the client, give them a chance to express in words what the gift was meant to express. This is therapeutically important for them as we have mentioned. You also want to suggest ways they can express gratitude as we have mentioned. Use the gift as a great therapeutic opening instead of immediately closing it. Then you will be both ethically and clinically astute.

In summary, think about the following things when creating your personal gift policy:

- Remember that a gift can bear a lot more meaning than is obvious to you. Accepting a gift can bear a lot more meaning than you intend.
- Have a policy that is applicable to all clients.
- Encourage (beg if you need to) your agency to develop a gift policy so that you have the support of the agency behind you. Some clients may fight you on your personal gift policy and it can be helpful to explain that in addition to your feelings the agency has rules about gifts. This also helps if you are explaining your agency as a culture in the cultural example above.

- Explain your gift policy up front to clients in group or individual settings so there is no confusion. If your agency has a gift policy, make sure it is part of the intake paperwork so that clients can understand that policy from the beginning of treatment.
- Always think of how to use these circumstances in a way that clinically benefits the client as discussed. There is often great clinical opportunity here.
- Do not underestimate the importance of expressing gratitude, which is often what is intended by the client. It is healthy to be able to thank those who have given help, and often this is a challenge for our clients. You want to create an atmosphere where the client can thank you. If you give them the gift of listening, they can give you the gift of verbal thanks, and that is the best, most meaningful and ethical gift exchange we can give.

Thus far we have only discussed gift giving in one direction, but what about the flip side of clinicians giving gifts to clients, particularly at graduations? What do you do in these situations? Do you always give gifts to departing clients, do you never, do you sometimes, and if so what are your rules? Are there other situations where you give gifts to clients? Birthdays, condolences, weddings, babies, anything else? Here is the skinny: Giving gifts to clients is even more ethically sticky than accepting gifts from clients, which is sticky enough. Giving a gift sends a message, and the message you intend to send may be entirely different that the message that is received.

Tread very carefully here. The most ethical action is to refrain from giving any client a gift, unless it is part of the agency policy to give all clients a gift at the same occasion, such as a graduation. These gifts are best if they are clearly from the agency, for example, a mug or pen with the agency name on it, or a recovery gift, such as a slogan coin (e.g., "One Day at a Time"). Remember there are many ways to give and receive the holiday spirit. Emphasize togetherness, family, support, love for others, and gratitude—all things that can be expressed without gifts.

In ethics training, the question: "Is it ethical to accept gifts from clients?" is one of the most popular. When the question is returned to the group, there are a few yes or no responses, but the vast majority is a resounding "it depends." It sure seems like a nice client-centered response, supportive of meeting the client where they are at, and being flexible to the individual needs of the client before you, all satisfying, healthy, and appropriate responses that we are taught in counseling classes. But ethically speaking, this response loses value. Your primary answer to a question of ethical behavior should never be "it depends." You should always have a standard of action, even if you expect there will be exceptions to the rule. In the gift example, a more appropriate response would be, "as a general rule I do not accept gifts from clients, although there may be exceptions."

Well! That's a lot to think about. At the very least, the question of gift giving highlights how easy it can be to cut corners if we do not make the rule. If our goal is to protect the community by establishing ethical workplace standards, including a solid professional rapport and inclusion of societal obligations, the act of cutting corners makes the goal unattainable. In fact, if you look at all of the entities we are charged with protecting, cutting corners would affect our ability to safeguard each of them. We all cut corners in our practice, at times deliberately and at times unknowingly; just as there are times when the profession can weather a little corner cutting and there are other times where the snipping significantly changes our shape. Be mindful of your ethical scissors. If you keep your eye on the bigger picture, rather than what is right in front of you, there is a much better chance that you will act in the best interest of the profession and build a practice any clinician can admire.

Conclusion

Addictions counseling is still a new field, one that borrows from other disciplines. We need literature on models of treatment (Whitter et al., 2006). Addiction treatment needs to adapt to the changing conditions in the field (Powell & Brodsky, 2004), and ethics need to adapt simultaneously. Ethics are not timeless. True, addiction ethics ask some ancient questions that helping professions have asked in the past, but with a progressive understanding of the issues (Geppert & Roberts, 2008). Our understanding of the principles of both addiction and recovery are changing, growing as new scientific paradigms emerge, and the ethics surrounding the profession must keep up (Geppert & Roberts, 2008).

This book was an attempt to keep up, although there were considerable limitations. One of the most obvious obstacles to the research for this book was the lack of published material specific to our field. This has improved considerably in the past several decades, but we continue to borrow heavily from other helping professions. Perhaps they are happy to share, but we may lose a bit in the translation and do not authentically represent our unique profession. We need gobs of research, conducted by our people for our profession, on every topic discussed in this book, and any that did not make it in. Right about now I am realizing how helpful it is to have multiple authors on books this large. It takes quite an effort to compile all of the information necessary to adequately discuss ethical principals of addiction treatment, and working solo may be another limitation. This book is one contribution, but the profession will benefit from additional concentration in addiction ethics. I'm talking to you, reader! What can you contribute to the growth of our profession? Go study an aspect of ethics you find interesting, set up a study and write about it.

In summary, all addiction professionals "need to uphold standards of practice that reflect professional integrity and pride" (Powell & Brodsky, 2004, p. 273). To build such an ethical practice, a perspective away from the ethical dilemma is helpful, and you must be critical of yourself (Taleff, 2010). In order to come to the truth, or the best possible action, deliberation and discussion is required. "If there is to be confrontation (and often there is in addiction ethics), it is orderly with an added element of a willingness to learn … with a goal of understanding" (Taleff, 2010, p. 10). If there is question regarding ethical behavior, counselors should err on the conservative side (St. Germaine, 1996).

One extremely helpful tool to use for ethical decision making is an ethical checklist (Pope & Vasquez, 2010; Taleff, 2010). To avoid ethical blunders, Reamer (2001, 2012) recommends identifying all possible actions; reflecting on whom the decision affects; searching all input from codes, pillars, laws, and advisors; and using the gathered information to weigh the pros and cons of each possible action. From this, one must design a plan and document it; then develop a strategy to carry out the plan, documenting as you go; and finally carry out the plan, monitoring it for needed adjustments.

Because there is such a variety of information informing your ethical practice, it is helpful to develop a checklist to aid you in your decision process (Taleff, 2010). All you need is to go get your banjo picks. Huh? Do not worry, you don't have to be musical. BANJO PICKS consist of:

Benificence	Pitfalls
Autonomy	Intuition
Nonmalficence	Code of Ethics
Justice	Keys
Opinion	Supervision

The components that you used to build your ethical practice are the same ones you are going to use when you find yourself in an ethical dilemma. Convenient, isn't it? So there you are, in the midst of an ethical dilemma and trying not to panic, a sea of ethical considerations dancing in your head. The first thing you want to do is sit down. You need your brain to be as functional as possible. The second thing you do is breathe. Seriously. Just take a moment. Then bring out your BANJO PICKS.

First, consider what is the best move you can make to promote goodness in your practice (*Beneficence*). Then consider what move will heighten independence and freedom for the people involved (*Autonomy*). Your next step is to consider the action least likely to cause harm for all involved (*nonmaleficence*). Then what is the action that is most fair and consistent across a group (*Justice*)? Compile all of this information and form your initial opinion about what action is the best to take (*Opinion*). You may need to mull it over for a bit before coming to your opinion.

Now take that opinion and lay it against the following (the order does not matter as long as you end with supervision). What pitfalls, if any, are potential risks in the given scenario (*Pitfalls*)? Once identified, what can you do to ensure you don't slip? What is your gut saying? You may not be able to explain it, but in which direction your intuition leans is a part of your checklist. Looking at your Code of Ethics; what principles are at play in this scenario (*Code of Ethics*)? Are there any principles you are at risk of violating with a given action you could take? What keys are involved in the ethical dilemma (*Keys*)? Finally, and importantly, gather your BANJO PICKS and take it all to your supervisor, and all those who advise you professionally (*Supervision*). Discuss your opinion, how you came to it, weighing all the other components of your checklist. Consider the advice you receive from your advisors, let it marinate as long as you can, and then take action.

If you are lucky, you will have lots of time to ponder your options and gather your BANJO PICKS.

Often, however, we are not given much time to make a decision. Ethical dilemmas can creep up and then ... bam! The pressure mounts all around you because you need to make a decision that will affect others and you can't dawdle, playing with the "what ifs." So. Your first defense is to build a practice where the chances of you falling into an ethical dilemma are few and far between. Can you see now that building a sound ethical practice benefits you as much as it does those you serve and the surrounding profession? While a healthy ethical practice ensures that your clients will receive good treatment, enhances positive relationships in your professional life, and helps to solidify the validity of our hopeful profession, it also benefits you by decreasing the amount of time you spend struggling in an ethical dilemma. If you have already found yourself agonizing in such a scenario, you know how difficult it is and how wonderful it is to avoid going there. You have a lot of power in preventing your own professional unhappiness from an ethical perspective. This is your first defense.

Your second line of defense is to use your BANJO PICKS and make the healthiest, swiftest decision that benefits the most entities possible. Remember that the goal is not to not make mistakes, because we all make them, or to always know exactly what to do, because none of us achieves that all of the time. The goal is to recognize when you are unsure or in trouble, and take the necessary steps to make the best ethical decisions you can. This may seem like a daunting process, but you now have everything you need to intuitively do this in your practice.

You know that to protect the client, you must ensure his or her happiness and satisfaction, actively seek an understanding of the impact of his or her culture, and work tirelessly to build a positive bond with each client. The key to achieving this is to accept your personal and professional strengths and limitations, and to avoid or cope with conflicts between your various agendas and those of others around you. You know that to protect the clinical information, you must pledge to the proper use of written and spoken material. The key to achieving this is to respect the tiers of ethics, and to avoid or cope with the confusion that can come with having so many different roles in our work. You know that to protect the clinician, you must build a practice that has objectivity, integrity, and standards, while achieving accomplishment and proficiency. The key to achieving this is to seek continuous learning, and to avoid or cope with Clinician Burnout. Finally, you know that to protect the community, you must focus on growing an office of the utmost standards that treats other colleagues and the greater society with attention and care. The key to achieving this is to make the rule before you break the rule, and to avoid or cope with cutting corners in your daily practice. These sections are not mutually exclusive. Ethical principles are related to each other, as are keys and pitfalls, and each of the dilemmas fits with all the keys. It's one happy family.

We aim to be the book that keeps on giving, so we are going to throw in an extra key to use just because you've been such a good reader. Congratulations! You win ... a fun game. Here it is, take out those pencils or hold your arms high one more time: (a) Do you know all of the principles in the Code of Ethics? (b) Do you have a copy of the Code of Ethics in your offices? (c) Do you pull out the Code of Ethics when you are facing an ethical dilemma? Can you guess the results? They are not so good. Even the most seasoned clinicians and elected officials, such as the agency directors and organization presidents in the room, regularly fail to answer all three questions. It is humorous that sometimes the same folks who complain about the 2-year ethics requirement are among those who cannot name all the principles. What does that tell you? It says that some of us are skimming through the Code and signing it every 2 years to recredential. And because most ethics trainings discuss ethical vignettes, but not the full Code, the only place clinicians are getting the Code is at the time of credentialing or recredentialing, which is not very often. Why then should anyone be surprised that the specifics of this document are not well known?

We call it the backbone of our profession, and yet many don't know it. We call it the foundation, and yet states cannot agree on what should be included in it. It should give us all a bit of pause. Each state wrote its Code of Ethics with purpose, each word specifically chosen, and yet we largely believe it to be obvious enough that we do not need to know every bit of it. When a missed principle is pointed out, usually people nod and roll their eyes as if to say, "Well, yes, of course that is included. I *knew* that one." This again speaks to the idea that ethics are assumed, not actually taught. We should all just inherently know what is in the Code and automatically abide by it, at least in most of our daily practices. Yet research into state codes shows how much variability there is between codes. One simply cannot abide by a code one does not know, and one must know all of it, otherwise you cannot be a fully ethical clinician. Many of us have been to ethics trainings where the trainer stated a certain behavior was ethical when the Code clearly states it is not. At the least it is embarrassing, but consider how many clinicians left that training armed with false information that would guarantee them to commit ethical violations. So this leads us to our last key.

Learn the Code. Love the Code. Live the Code

There is learning the Code, and the next step is loving the Code. What does this mean? It means you must sleep with the Code under your pillow, take it with you everywhere, buy it things from time to time, and treat it like the queen it is. No, that's just weird. What is meant here is to respect the Code. Most of us had nothing to do with writing the Code, yet we need to respect and abide by it. You may have written it differently, but you were not given the chance, so we need to respect that our individual states are requiring us to use it. As stated in the introduction, it would be beneficial if states came together and produced a national framework to decrease the degree of variability between states and thus strengthen our profession as a whole. But until that future day, we must individually strive to create the most inclusive Code of Ethics possible. Loving the Code also infers that you believe in the basic ideas set forth in the document. The state codes do vary, and if you don't approve of the Code of your state, you can go to your state organization, get involved, and recommend changes or additions. If you do not believe in the principles, you may want to rethink your career path. If you stay in the profession, you need to respect this Code, as the framework and backbone.

Once you learn the Code, and decide to love the Code, then you must live the Code. This means you must practice the Code in all your affairs. You must not only "talk the talk"; you must "walk the walk." You must live an ethical life professionally, and do your best to live one personally. It is not a requirement to be perfect in all your affairs, professional and personal, but striving toward perfection is the goal. When ethical complaints are investigated, it is often the case that clinicians are able to name and understand the principle they have violated, but could not alter their behavior prior to violation. In most cases one could see the clinician starting to veer away from the ethical practice he or she had established some time before the violation occurred. At times, respected elders and leaders in our profession tout ethics in one breath, then turn around and commit ethical violations with the next breath. There are volumes of sad tales of supervisors committing egregious violations while teaching supervisees how to be ethical clinicians. Many fail to place the Code of Ethics in its proper position in the throne of our clinical kingdom. It is the backbone of our profession, and should therefore be the foundation of our individual clinical practices, the script that informs our actions and the beacon that can guide us home. Learn the Code. Love the Code. Live the Code.

As we know, our field needs a bit of work, particularly if we want to strive to be the profession we are so close to being. There are many needed changes, some larger than others, such as streamlining our name and credentialing process, or adopting one true national voice. Those will take a whole lot of time and a major communal effort by many people. But we can also strengthen our profession by smaller changes, by individually developing and maintaining our ethical practices. With all the possible avenues to take it can be overwhelming, and clinicians often lean toward focusing only on one entity, typically their needs or the needs of the client, and the situation in front of them, which leads to making different rules for each client.

The best way to reduce confusion and tackle all the choices is to make a standard course of action that protects client welfare in most situations, with rare exceptions. Uncommon exceptions suggest a regular practice that is steeped in ethical principles, one that has effectively established the four basic keys to an ethical practice, and one that has successfully prevented a significant slide into the land of ethical pitfalls. Such a practice would be one that ensured fair treatment across groups, that promoted the independence and freedom of all its members and those served by the members, that strived for worthy and beneficial treatment interventions that aggressively avoided harming anyone involved. Neat, huh?

Well, we've come to the end of our ethical journey together and perhaps you are dizzy with principles, keys, and pitfalls (oh my!) dancing about your brain. Don't worry, that's normal. But I also hope you have even the smallest kernel of excitement or inspiration somewhere inside you, a tiny voice saying, let's get building! Don't lose that kernel; you want to nurture it and attend to it and give it room to grow. Come back and read certain passages if you need to be reminded or reinspired. We will always be here waiting to pat you on the back or kick you in the butt all in the name of creating an ethical profession. Thanks for spending some time here. Come again. And never forget the level of practice we all must pin up as our goal. We must work toward it, our professional eye permanently fixed there. Can you see it? Good, don't lose your focus, even as you … close … this … book.

Ethics Exam

1. You and your client have been working on establishing sober social support in the client's recovery program, and the client discovers a beneficial group that meets in the mornings, but it conflicts with the programs the agency has set in motion. You approach the agency for a special compensation but they say no. Who do you support, the agency or the client? Why?

   a. I support the client and try to convince the agency to allow an exception.
   b. I support the agency and tell the client to choose between treatment and meetings.
   c. I have another idea:

   _____

   _____

2. Anastasia is a capable counselor with 15 years of her own recovery from alcohol and cocaine. She runs groups for people in early recovery at a local outpatient facility. She shows great empathy for the clients she works with, and is thorough in assessing all of the needs in each individual on her caseload. Her group topics are diverse, and she demands participation from all of her clients. During a group check-in one day, a client states he does not plan on attending AA/NA meetings as part of his recovery plan. Anastasia encourages him to attend, but he stands firm in his disinterest in participating. Anastasia continues to press the point that he *must* attend AA/NA as part of his recovery plan (this is not the policy of the agency or program), because it is vital to his success. The client grows upset, and Anastasia tries to gently explain, "It's just that I know the AA program works. I've seen it. I've lived it." Are Anastasia's comments unethical?

Identify the principle and write in your reasoning.

   a. No, her comments are ethical.
   b. Yes, her comments are unethical.
   c. I have another idea:

   _____

   _____

3. Bob and Marcia are on call for all walk-in intakes that come in to the outpatient program. Two arrive at the same time, and the receptionist asks Marcia which intake she wants. Bob walks up just as Marcia is deciding which case to take on, so she asks him, "Which case do you want Bob, the sleeping heroin addict or the wired cocaine addict?" Bob responds, "I'm kinda feeling low energy myself, sleepy from my lunch break, so I'll take the cocaine patient. Might help wake me up." Are Bob's comments unethical? Identify the principle and write in your reasoning.

   a. No, Bob's comments are not unethical.
   b. Yes, Bob's comments are unethical.
   c. I have another idea:

   _____

   _____

4. Simone works in an addiction facility as an outreach worker. Her position involves driving into the community and meeting for individual counseling with clients who do not have transportation to reach the facility, and with clients who have dropped out of treatment in an attempt to entice them into returning. Simone is told to bring the client records with her and

keep them locked in her trunk, and that she must put the agency billboard in the window of her car so that it is clear she is there on official business. Simone feels that both these demands violate the confidentiality principle of the code of ethics. Do you agree? Identify the principle and explain your reasoning.

a. The issue of client records is unethical, but the billboard is ethical.

b. The issue of client records is ethical, but the billboard is unethical.

c. Both issues are unethical.

d. Both issues are ethical.

e. I have another idea:

_____

_____

5. After sitting through an intake with you, Honey flat out refuses to attend your treatment facility. What is the *most* ethical response to give her?

a. "Thank you for meeting with me. If you change your mind, our door is always open to you."

b. "I understand you don't want to be treated here. Let me give you a referral to another agency."

c. "You really need daily treatment. What can I do to convince you to come here for groups?"

d. I have another idea:

_____

_____

6. The agency where you work refers to your private practice the father of a client who is refusing to attend family treatment at the agency. Is this an ethical action?

a. No, this is a conflict of interest and you can't treat the father.

b. Yes, this is ethical.

c. I have another idea:

_____

_____

7. Holly sweeps into the staff break room and slumps into a chair next to her colleagues. "Oh man, I just had the toughest session with June. Have you guys met her yet? She is *so* borderline. I was talking to her and she kept bringing up how her parents treat her and how the world is going to abandon her because no one cares about her." Her colleagues nod their heads in sympathy. John sighs, "Did you hear about the new supervisor? Started last week. Can you say bipolar?" They all groan, and roll their eyes. Are their comments unethical? Write in your reasoning.

a. Holly's comment is unethical, but John's comment is ethical.

b. Holly's comment is ethical, but John's comment is unethical.

c. Both comments are unethical.

d. Neither comment is ethical.

e. I have another idea:

_____

_____

8. Matteo is a counselor at an outpatient facility. He has worked with Virginia for several years and has always got along well with her. She is a bit slippery with her client boundaries but he has not seen any clinical behavior that warranted speaking to any superior. Once, a year ago, it looked like she was favoring one client and when questioned, Virginia admitted that she had felt an attraction for the client but said that she would never act on it. Last week, Matteo presented a policy change to the staff, something he had worked on for many months and of which he was very proud. The staff was very supportive and everyone voted to pass the new policy into effect … everyone, that is, except Virginia. Because the agency had a unanimous requirement,

his new policy was rejected based on her vote. Infuriated, Matteo stormed into his office, called the director, and revealed Virginia's poor boundaries with clients, noting his concern that she crossed an ethical line with a particular patient last year. The director stated that she doubted Virginia would ever act unethically, and needed evidence to support his claim. Feeling unsupported, he then called his state membership organization and reported Virginia to the ethics committee, who agreed to temporarily suspend her credential while they investigated his claim. Are Matteo's actions ethical? Why or why not?

All those who think it is an ethical move, raise your hand. Just kidding, I can't see you. But if you fell for it and just raised your hand, you're wrong! Thank you for playing. The problem here is Matteo's motive. If he was concerned about her boundaries with that client last year, he should have reported that behavior last year. Ask yourself whether he would have reported her if she did not vote against his proposal; if your answer is no, then you know this is not a fair complaint. It is not professional to use ethical complaints as attacks against people with whom you have a personal grievance. It is unfortunate that Virginia voted against him after all his hard work, but that is her prerogative. Of course, he may complain to her, or even to his supervisor, about the vote. But that is a clinical, not an ethical, issue, and bringing in a separate ethical claim is not just. The vignette clearly states that her behavior was not concerning enough to bring to the supervisor. If that changes, and her boundaries continue to slide, it would be appropriate to approach Virginia or a supervisor. Matteo needs to make sure he is making a complaint for the right reasons.

9. Caroline is a new clinician, excited to be a part of this great profession and eager to get started helping people. At work, she adopts a beneficial attitude of hope, encouragement, empathy, and stability to her clients. At home, she has a healthy social life, and therefore doesn't worry about Clinician Burnout. Every weekend she parties with her friends, has as much fun as possible, and then writes out the details on her Facebook page. For example, just last night she wrote, "Got so wasted! Listening to sad addict stories all day just make me want to cut loose. Yeah!" What is the problem with Caroline's behavior?

a. There is no problem. She is successfully separating work and home.

b. There is no problem. She should be able to do what she wants outside of work.

c. There is a problem. She should not be drinking or partying if she is an addictions counselor.

d. There is a problem. She is exhibiting a conflict in her professional stance.

e. I have another idea:

———————————————————————

———————————————————————

10. You tell your client Morgan that you are going to use some of your session material in a mini-training you are giving. She says "that sounds like fun." Then you go to the big National Conference, where you are a keynote speaker, and begin telling your client's complete story, including what actions your colleagues took with the client and your opinions about their work. Many colleagues are in the audience with shocked expressions on their faces. You get lots of applause for your talk and drive home, enjoying the feeling of being a competent clinician. Who have you failed to protect? Why?

a. The client

b. The clinical material

c. The colleagues

d. The community

e. All of the above

References

Baer, R. A. (2010). *Assessing mindfulness and acceptance processes in clients: Illuminating the theory and practice of change*. Oakland, CA: New Harbinger.

Barsky, A. E. (2010). *Ethics and values in social work: An integrated approach for a comprehensive curriculum*. New York, NY: Oxford University Press.

Bass, L. J., DeMers, S. T., Ogloff, J. R. P., Peterson, C., Pettifor, J. L., Reaves, R. P., ... Tipton, R. M. (1996). *Professional conduct and discipline in psychology*. Washington, DC: American Psychological Association.

Beam, A. (2001). *Gracefully insane: The rise and fall of America's premier mental hospital*. New York, NY: Public Affairs.

Belitz, J. (2008). Ethical aspects of the treatment of substance abuse in children and adolescents. In C. Geppert & L. Roberts (Eds.), *The book of ethics: Expert guidance for professionals who treat addiction* (pp. 115–128). Center City, MN: Hazelden.

Bissell, L. C., & Royce, J. E. (1987, 1994). *Ethics for addiction professionals*. Center City, MN: Hazelden.

Bogo, M., Paterson, J., Tufford, L., & King, R. (2011a). Interprofessional clinical supervision in mental health and addiction: Toward identifying common elements. *Clinical Supervisor*, 30(1), 124–140.

Bogo, M., Paterson, J., Tufford, L., & King, R. (2011b). Supporting front-line practitioners' professional development and job satisfaction in mental health and addiction. *Journal of Interpersonal Care*, 25(3), 209–214.

Brown, J. (1992). *The definition of a profession: The authority of metaphor in the history of intelligence testing, 1890–1930*. Princeton, NJ: Princeton University Press.

Carise, D., Love, M., Zur, J., McLellan, A. T., & Kemp, J. (2009). Results of a state-wide evaluation of "paperwork burden" in addiction treatment. *Journal of Substance Abuse Treatment*, 37(1), 101–109.

Castillo, D. T., & Waldorf, V. A. (2008). Ethical issues in the treatment of women with substance abuse. In C. Geppert & L. Roberts (Eds.), *The book of ethics: Expert guidance for professionals who treat addiction* (pp. 101–114). Center City, MN: Hazelden.

Cline, C. A., & Minkoff, K. (2008). Ethical issues in the treatment of persons with co-occurring disorders. In C. Geppert & L. Roberts (Eds.), *The book of ethics: Expert guidance for professionals who treat addiction* (pp. 55–66). Center City, MN: Hazelden.

Corey, G., Corey, M. S., & Callanan, P. (2007). *Issues and ethics in the helping professions*. Belmont, CA: Brooks/Cole.

Doukas, N., & Cullen, J. (2010). Recovered addicts working in the addiction field: Pitfalls to substance abuse relapse. *Drugs: Education, prevention and policy*, 17(3), 216–231.

Doukas, N., & Cullen, J. (2011). Addiction counselors in recovery: Perceived barriers in the workplace. *Journal of Addiction Research & Therapy*, 2(3), 1–7.

Feller, C. P., & Cottone, R. R. (2012). The importance of empathy in the therapeutic alliance. *Journal of Humanistic Counseling, Education and Development*, 42(1), 53–61.

Fernet, C., Gagné, M., & Austin, S. (2010). When does quality of relationships with coworkers predict burnout over time: The moderating role of work motivation. *Journal of Organizational Behavior*, 31(8), 1163–1180.

Finley, J. R., & Lenz, B. S. (2005). *The addiction counselor's documentation sourcebook: The complete paperwork resource for treating clients with addictions*. Hoboken, NJ: Wiley.

Flexner, A. (1915). Is social work a profession? In National Conference of Charities and Corrections, *Proceedings of the National Conference of Charities and Corrections at the forty-second annual session held in Baltimore, Maryland, May 12–19, 1915*. Chicago, IL: Hildmann; reprinted in *Research on Social Work Practice*, 11(2), March 2001, 151–165.

Frey, J. (2003). *A million little pieces*. New York, NY: Anchor Books.

Gallagher, J. R. (2010). Licensed chemical dependency counselors views of professional and ethical standards: A focus group analysis. *Alcoholism Treatment Quarterly*, 28, 184–197.

Geppert, C. M. A., & Roberts, L. W. (2008). Ethical foundations of substance abuse treatment. In C. Geppert & L. Roberts (Eds.), *The book of ethics: Expert guidance for professionals who treat addiction* (pp. 1–28). Center City, MN: Hazelden.

Grob, G. (1994). *The mad among us: A history of the care of America's mentally ill*. New York, NY: The Free Press.

Hayes, S. C., Bissett, R., Roget, N., Padilla, M., Kohlenberg, B. S., Fisher, G., … Niccolls, R. (2004). The impact of acceptance and commitment training and multicultural training on the stigmatizing attitudes and professional burnout of substance abuse counselors. *Behavior Therapy, 35*(4), 821–835.

Hohman, M. (2012). *Motivational interviewing in social work practice*. New York, NY: Guilford Press.

Hollander, J. K., Bauer, S., Herlihy, B., & McCollum, V. (2006). Beliefs of board certified substance abuse counselors regarding multiple relationships. *Journal of Mental Health Counseling, 28*(1), 84–94.

Jackson, J. A. (2010). *Professions and professionalization: Volume 3, sociological studies*. Cambridge, England: Cambridge University Press.

Jacobs, E. E., Masson, R. L., & Harvill, R. L. (2009). *Group counseling: Strategies and skills*. Belmont, CA: Thompson/Brooks Cole.

Jaffe, C., Bush, K. R., Straits-Troster, K., Meredith, C., Romwall, L., Rosenbaum, G., … Saxon, A. J. (2005). A comparison of methamphetamine-dependent inpatients with and without childhood attention deficit hyperactivity disorder symptomatology. *Journal of Addictive Diseases, 24*(3), 133–152.

Katzman, J. G., & Geppert, C. M. A. (2008). Ethical dilemmas in treating chronic pain in the context of addiction. In C. Geppert & L. Roberts (Eds.), *The book of ethics: Expert guidance for professionals who treat addiction* (pp. 129–144). Center City, MN: Hazelden.

Knudsen, H. K., Ducharme, L. J., & Roman, P. M. (2008). Clinical supervision, emotional exhaustion, and turnover intention: A study of substance abuse treatment counselors in NIDA's clinical trials network. *Journal of Substance Abuse Treatment, 35*(4), 387–395.

Larson, M. S. (1978). *The rise of professionalism: A sociological analysis*. Berkeley, CA: University of California Press.

Lee, J., Lim, N., Yang, E., & Lee, S. M. (2011). Antecedents and consequences of three dimensions of burnout in psychotherapists: A meta-analysis. *Professional Psychology: Research and Practice, 42*(3), 252–258.

Leykin, Y., Cucciare, M. A., & Weingardt, K. R. (2011). Differential effects of online training on job-related burnout among substance abuse counselors. *Journal of Substance Use, 16*(2), 1–9.

Lim, N., Kim, E. K., Kim, H., Yang, E., & Lee, S. M. (2010). Individual and work-related factors influencing burnout of mental health professionals: A meta-analysis. *Journal of Employment Counseling, 47*, 86–96.

Manuel, J., & Forcehimes, A. A. (2008). The therapeutic relationship in substance abuse treatment. In C. Geppert & L. Roberts (Eds.), *The book of ethics: Expert guidance for professionals who treat addiction* (pp. 29–40). Center City, MN: Hazelden.

Martin, D. J., Garske, J. P., & Davis, M. K. (2000). Relation of the therapeutic alliance with outcome and other variables: A meta-analytic review. *Journal of Consulting and Clinical Psychology, 68*(3), 438–450.

McGovern, M. P., Fox, T. S., Xie, H., & Drake, R. E. (2004). A survey of clinical practices and readiness to adopt evidence-based practices: Dissemination research in an addiction treatment system. *Journal of Substance Abuse Treatment, 26*(4), 305–312.

McLellan, A. T., Carise, D., & Kleber, H. (2003). Can the national addictions treatment infrastructure support the public's demand for quality care? *Journal of Substance Abuse Treatment, 25*(2), 117–121.

Miller, W. R. (2008). The ethics of harm reduction. In C. Geppert & L. Roberts (Eds.), *The book of ethics: Expert guidance for professionals who treat addiction* (pp. 41–54). Center City, MN: Hazelden.

Miller, W. & Rollnick, S. (2002). *Motivational interviewing: Preparing people for change*. New York: Guilford Press.

Morse, G., Salyers, M. P., Rollins, A. L., Monroe-De Vita, M., & Pfahler, C. (2012). Burnout in mental health services: A review of the problem and its remediation. *Administration and Policy in Mental Health, 39*, 341–352.

Mottley, M. M. (2012). *Ethics & professional development for addiction counselors: Principles, guidelines & issues for training, licensing, certification and recertification*. Life Management Publishing.

Nassar-McMillan, S. C., & Niles, S. G. (2011). *Developing your identity as a professional counselor: Standards, settings, and specialties*. Belmont, CA: Brooks/Cole.

National Association for Addiction Professionals (NAADAC). (2011). *NAADAC Code of Ethics*. Alexandria, VA: Author.

Pope, K., & Vasquez, M. (2007, 2010). *Ethics in psychotherapy and counseling: A practical guide*. San Francisco, CA: Wiley.

Powell, D. J., & Brodsky, A. (2004). *Clinical supervision in alcohol and drug abuse counseling: Principles, models, methods*. San Francisco, CA: Jossey-Bass.

Racker, H. (2002). *Transference and countertransference* (5th ed.). London, England: Hogarth Press.

Reamer, F. G. (2001). *Tangled relationships: Managing boundary issues in the human services.* New York, NY: Columbia University Press.

Reamer, F. G. (2006a). *Ethical standards in social work: A review of the NASW code of ethics.* Baltimore, MD: NASW Press.

Reamer, F. G. (2006b). *Social work values and ethics* (3rd ed.). New York, NY: Columbia University Press.

Reamer, F. G. (2012). *Boundary issues and dual relationships in the human services.* New York, NY: Columbia University Press.

Rogers, C. R. (1957). The necessary and sufficient conditions of therapeutic personality change. *Journal of Consulting Psychology, 21,* 95–103.

Rutledge, T. (1997). *The self-forgiveness handbook: A practical and empowering guide.* New York, NY: New Harbinger.

Safran, J. D., & Muran, J. C. (2000). *Negotiating the therapeutic alliance: A relational treatment guide.* New York, NY: Guilford Press.

Scott, C. G. (2000). Ethical issues in addiction counseling. *Rehabilitation Counseling Bulletin, 43*(4), 209–214.

St. Germaine, J. (1996). Dual relationships and certified alcohol and drug counselors: A national study of ethical beliefs and behaviors. *Alcoholism Treatment Quarterly, 14*(2), 29–44.

Substance Abuse and Mental Health Services Administration (SAMHSA). (2005). *A national review of state alcohol and drug treatment programs and certification standards for counselors and prevention professionals.* Rockville, MD: DHHS.

Taleff, M. J. (2010). *Advanced ethics for addiction professionals.* New York, NY: Springer.

Tanner-Smith, E. E., Wilson, S. J., & Lispey, M. W. (2013). The comparative effectiveness of outpatient treatment for adolescent substance abuse: A meta-analysis. *Journal of Substance Abuse Treatment, 44*(2), 145–158.

Torrey, E. F., & Miller, J. (2001). *The invisible plague: The rise of mental illness from 1750 to the present.* New Brunswick, NJ: Rutgers University Press.

Trimpey, J. (1996). *Rational recovery: The new cure for substance addiction.* New York, NY: Simon & Schuster.

Venner, K. L., & Bogenschutz, M. P. (2008). Cultural and spiritual dimensions of addiction treatment. In C. Geppert & L. Roberts (Eds.), *The book of ethics: Expert guidance for professionals who treat addiction* (pp. 67–86). Center City, MN: Hazelden.

Vilardaga, R., Luoma, J. B., Hayes, S. C., Pistorello, J., Levin, M. E., Hildebrandt, M. J., … Bond, F. (2011). Burnout among the addiction counseling workforce: The differential roles of mindfulness and values-based processes and work-site factors. *Journal of Substance Abuse Treatment, 40,* 323–335.

Volkow, N. D. (2009). *Principles of drug addiction treatment: A research-based guide* (2nd ed.). National Institute of Health (NIH) Publication No. 09-4180. Darby, PA: Diane.

Washington, D. B., & Demask, M. (2008). *Legal and ethical issues: For addiction professionals.* Center City, MN: Hazelden.

Whitaker, R. (2002). *Mad in America: Bad science, bad medicine, and the enduring mistreatment of the mentally ill.* New York, NY: Perseus Books.

White, W. L. (2006). *Sponsor, recovery coach, addiction counselor: The importance of role clarity and role integrity.* Philadelphia, PA: Philadelphia Department of Behavioral Health and Mental Retardation Services.

White, W. L., & Kleber, H. D. (2008). Preventing harm in the name of help: A guide for addiction professionals. *Counselor, 9*(6), 10–17.

Whitley, C. E. M. (2010). Social work clinical supervision in the addictions: Importance of understanding professional cultures. *Journal of Social Work Practice in the Addictions, 10,* 343–362.

Whitter, M., Bell, E. L., Gaumond, P., Gwaltney, M., Magana, C. A., & Moreaux, M. (2006). Strengthening professional identity: Challenges of the addiction treatment workforce. Retrieved from http://partnersforrecovery.samhsa.gov/docs/Strengthening_Professional_Identity.pdf

Winters, K. C., Botzet, A. M., & Fahnhorst, T. (2011). Advances in adolescent substance abuse treatment. *Current Psychiatry Reports, 13*(5), 416–421.

Wolff, M. C., & Hayes, J. A. (2009). Therapist variables: Predictors of process in the treatment of alcohol and other drug problems. *Alcoholism Treatment Quarterly, 27,* 51–65.

Yalom, I. D., & Leszcz, M. (2005). *The theory and practice of group psychotherapy.* Cambridge, MA: Basic Books.

Jennifer D. Berton, PhD, LCSW, CADC-II, is the founder and principal trainer of Clinical Trainings Institute, which provides national trainings on topics related to substance abuse and mental health. Her trainings on ethics have been the most popular. She is in private practice in West Hartford, Connecticut, where she provides counseling for adolescents, adults, and families. Dr. Berton also consults with and supervises professionals across the country. Previously the Ethics Chair on the Board of the California Association of Alcoholism and Drug Abuse Counselors, she currently maintains a blog on ethics, clinicalethicsblog.com, and provides consultation to ethics boards. Her articles on ethics have appeared in *Counselor* magazine and membership newsletters. Additional information can be found at clinicaltrainings.com or jenniferberton.com

Ethics for
Addiction
Professionals

Author Index

Subject Index